English Garden Eccentrics

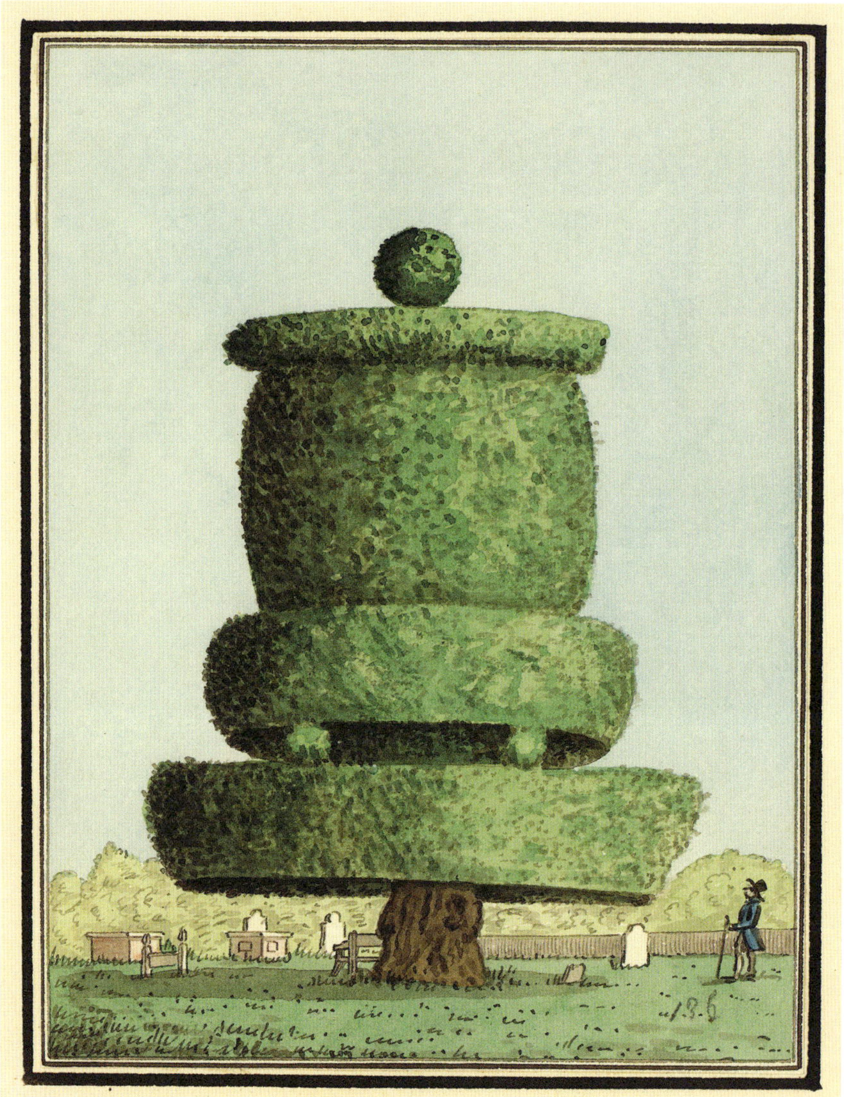

Todd Longstaffe-Gowan

English Garden Eccentrics

Three hundred years of extraordinary groves, burrowings, mountains and menageries

Paul Mellon Centre
for Studies in British Art

DISTRIBUTED BY YALE UNIVERSITY PRESS
NEW HAVEN AND LONDON

First published in 2022
by the Paul Mellon Centre for Studies in British Art
16 Bedford Square, London, WC1B 3JA
paul-mellon-centre.ac.uk

Copyright © 2022 by Todd Longstaffe-Gowan

All rights reserved. This book may not be reproduced or transmitted in any form or by any means, electronic or mechanical, including photocopy, recording or any other information storage and retrieval system, without prior permission in writing from the publisher.

ISBN 978-1-913107-26-0 HB
Library of Congress Control Number: 2021944801

British Library Cataloguing-in-Publication Data
A catalogue record for this book is available from the British Library

Designed by Robert Dalrymple
Set in Mark van Bronkhorst's Celestia Antiqua type
Origination by D L Imaging
Printed by C & C Offset Printing Co., Ltd

Endpapers: Fynedon Gothic, c.1790. Hamilton Weston Wallpapers.
Frontispiece: John Oldfield, *The Harlington Yew, Harlington, c.1820.*
Corporation of the City of London.

[CONTENTS]

Acknowledgements vii

Introduction 1

1 The 'Enston-Rock': 'A Mad Gim-cracke Sure' 13

2 Lady Broughton's 'Miniature Copy of the Swiss Glaciers' 27

3 Friar Park: 'Alpinism at Home' 41

4 Sir Charles Isham's Gardens at Lamport Hall: 'A Disconcerting Eruption' 53

5 Topiary on a Gargantuan Scale: The Clipped 'Yew-trees' at Four Ancient London Churchyards 69

6 Lord Petersham's Gardens at Elvaston Castle: 'A Modern Palagonia' 83

7 The Countess of Dudley's 'Stop and Buy' Topiaries 99

8 Lady Reade and her 'Gaudy Natives of the Tropics' 111

9 Lady Dorothy Nevill and her Ephemeral 'Exotic Groves' 127

10 Brookes's Vivarium: 'A Curious Assemblage of Life and Death' 143

11 Russell Collett and Sir Robert Heron: Gardens and Goldfish 161

12 Charles Waterton: 'Unwearied Outdoor Observer' 175

13 Antediluvian Antiquities at Banwell Caves and Pleasure Gardens 195

14 Hawkstone: 'A Kind of Turbulent Pleasure between Fright and Admiration' 209

15 The Burrowing Duke at Harcourt House 227

16 Denbies: 'A Persuasive Penitentiary' 241

17 'Do You Know Thomas Bland?' 255

18 Stukeley's Travelling Gardens 271

19 West Wycombe Park: 'Pretty, but very Whimsical' 287

20 Dr Phené's 'Senseless and Bewildering Accumulation of Incongruous Things' 305

21 Bedford's Modern Garden of Eden 319

Coda: The Present Status of the Gardens 335

Notes 339

Select Bibliography 370

Index 380

For Tim

– who, like Squire Waterton, is a keen ornithologist and observer of nature,
and is possessed of an irrepressible sense of fun.

[ACKNOWLEDGEMENTS]

I AM GRATEFUL TO THE FOLLOWING INDIVIDUALS WHO HAVE IN SOME way contributed to my book: William Ashworth, Alex Bagnall, Bruce Bailey, Roger Bowdler, Claire Brainerd, Lauren Butler, Christopher Catling, Sydney Chapman, Cristina D'Alessandro, Stephen Daniels, Sir Edward Dashwood, David Dawson, Graham Deacon, Edward Diestelkamp, Brian Dix, Sarah Flynn, Kirsty Garrod, Sean Gillen, Blanche Girouard, John Goodall, Vicki Grimmitt, Sophia Hall, Annemarie Hawes, Mark Herrod, Richard Hewlings, Kate Holliday, Peter Howell, Wendy Jewitt, Cindie Johnston, Christopher Joll, Sylvia Kelly, James and Clare Kirkman, Amanda Kistrup Vallys, Hayley Kruger, David Lambert, Lucy Lambton, Karen Lawson, Neil Lyon, Vicki Manners, Christina McCulloch, Sue Palmer, William Parente, Daniel Partridge, Caroline Robinson, John Martin Robinson, Ruth Scurr, Jane Shaw, John and Dianne Smith, Paul Stamper, Liz Taylor, Craig Tollan, Edward Town, Dave Walker, Stephen Wass, Roger Watts, Gareth Williams, Sally Williams, Dustin Frazier Wood, Jan Woudstra and Samantha Wyndham.

The Marc Fitch Fund has generously contributed toward the procurement of images.

The staff at the Paul Mellon Centre have been – as always – exceptionally helpful throughout: Mark Hallett and Martin Postle encouraged me to pursue my then nascent idea of English garden eccentrics; Tom Powell co-ordinated the submission, preparation and delivery of my manuscript; and my editor Emily Lees has been remarkably supportive at every stage. Nancy Marten has been a genial and punctilious copy editor, whose interventions have been felicitous and helpful. Robert Dalrymple has expertly and imaginatively combined my text and images to create an exceptionally beautiful book.

Chloe Chard has been my constant muse. We have discussed every aspect of this book, and she has enriched immeasurably the whole through her insightful comments and criticisms. Her great enthusiasm for this project has, moreover, boosted my own.

I owe the greatest debt of gratitude to Tim Knox, who suggested I write the book, and who has for over three decades encouraged me in my multifarious pursuits and enhanced and nurtured my fascination with and appreciation of eccentricity.

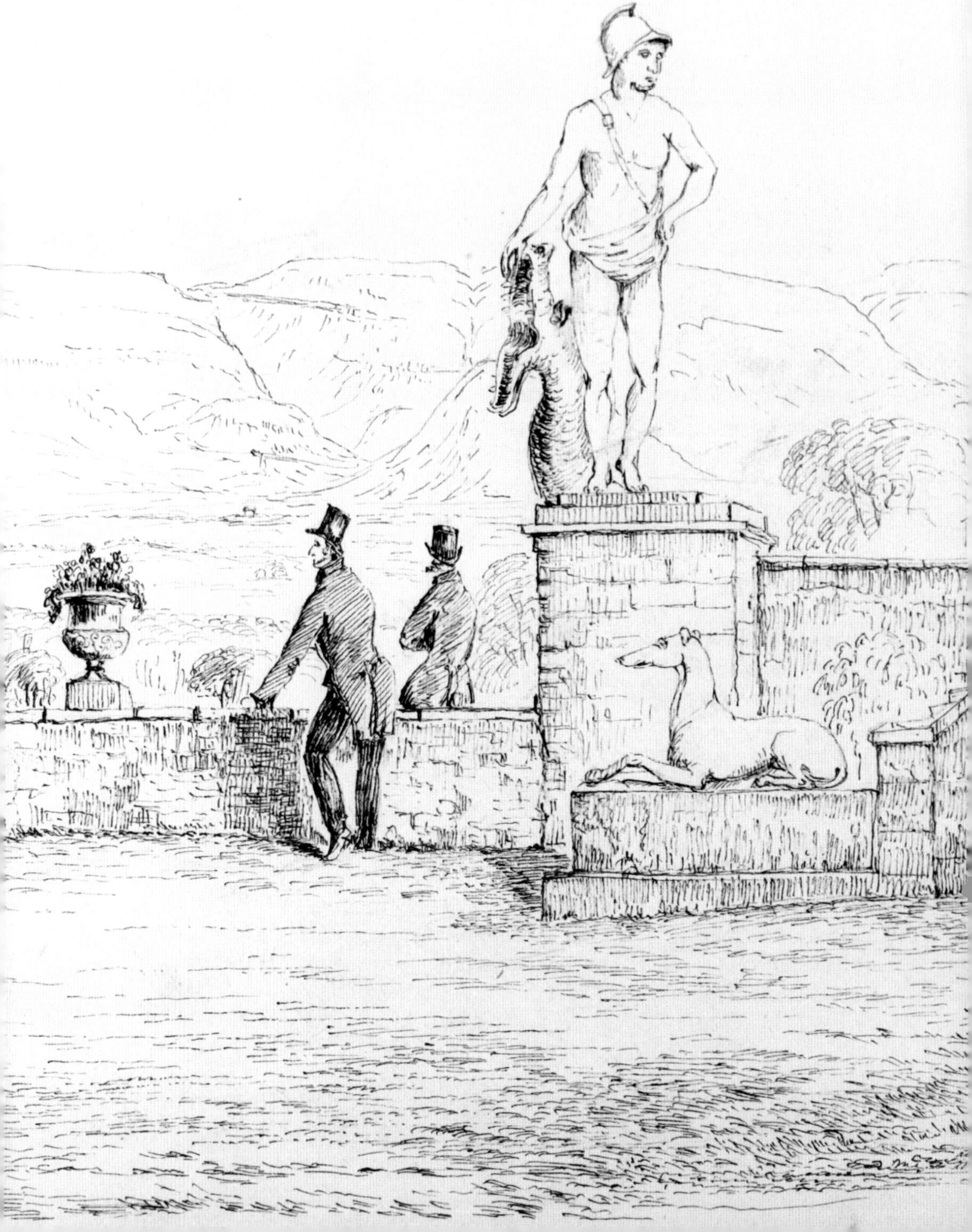

[ENGLISH GARDEN ECCENTRICS]

Introduction

> *In this age, the mere example of non-conformity, the mere refusal to bend the knee to custom, is itself a service. Precisely because the tyranny of opinion is such as to make eccentricity a reproach, it is desirable, in order to break through that tyranny, that people should be eccentric. Eccentricity has always abounded when and where strength of character has abounded; and the amount of eccentricity in a society has generally been proportional to the amount of genius, mental vigour, and moral courage which it contained. That so few now dare to be eccentric, marks the chief danger of the time.*
>
> JOHN STUART MILL
> 'Of Individuality, as One of the Elements of Well-Being'
> *On Liberty* (1859)

MY INTRODUCTION TO ECCENTRIC BIOGRAPHY BEGAN WITH EDITH Sitwell's *English Eccentrics* (1933), and her essay on 'Ancients and Ornamental Hermits' in particular. The book appealed to me because I had long found myself inexorably drawn towards eccentric personalities or individuals who undermined classificatory boundaries: people who did not belong to the present, who seemed out of joint with their time – some of whom were trapped in the past and others who were ahead of their time. The allure of eccentric biography was further enhanced by my love of gardening, as I became aware that many of the gardeners or garden-makers I most admired were perceived as in some way dangerously excessive – that gardening had induced in them a playful incipient lunacy [fig. 2].

Eccentric biography has its origins in the nineteenth century, at a time when, some time after the initial formation of a concept of eccentricity, there developed a fascination with varieties of physical and behavioural abnormality that occupied a 'contested space at the juncture of madness and sanity, functioning as a foil against which both madness and "normality" could be defined'.[1] Most studies of eccentricity – such as Kirby's *Wonderful and Eccentric Museum; Or, Magazine of Remarkable Characters* (1820), John Timbs's *English Eccentrics and Eccentricities* (1866) and Sitwell's *English Eccentrics* itself – consist of biographies of strikingly unusual individuals. It is possible to dip into my book for narratives of this kind, since it is structured as a series of individual essays; but my project differs from such works in so far as I am preoccupied less with examining what makes individuals eccentric than with how they have used landscape to map out their own personal biographies – how landscapes have shaped their personae – and what it is about the activity of gardening that allows them to do this. My eccentrics are defined by what they have built.

Another way of putting this is to say that I am concerned with gardens that function as a form of autobiography. Of course, any garden can produce some impression of its maker, however faint, but eccentric gardens do so in an especially ebullient and insistent manner. Paul de Man defines autobiography in literature as 'not a genre or a mode, but a figure of reading or understanding that occurs, to some degree, in all texts'; such a definition, transferred to constructed landscapes, encapsulates the sense of an encounter with a distinct personality that in some gardens is scarcely present and in some is very strong. Eccentric gardens obviously belong in the second category: their autobiographical effect is especially powerful because the conventions that mask individual quirks and obsessions operate less strictly and consistently in them. In this sense, they register an engaging willingness to accept the risks of such an effect; to quote de Man again, 'autobiography always looks slightly disreputable and self-indulgent in a way that may be symptomatic of its incompatibility with the monumental dignity of aesthetic values.'[2]

As all the people I examine have approached gardening as a dynamic process, their gardens lack finitude; each one is a work in progress, and the product of sustained, sometimes obsessive and frequently piecemeal activity. They have been built with or animated by a range of diverse materials, from bones to fossils, mummies to marsupials, minerals to fragments of the Rock of Gibraltar and the Matterhorn. Many eccentric gardeners, in other words, are also collectors who continue to add new elements to their gardens over many years. Though plants, too, are important constituents, they are seldom the defining characteristic: they are more often deployed for scenographic effect than for horticultural interest. Plants, however, bring a particular quality to these assemblages of objects and beings; since they are constantly growing and changing (or, in sadder cases, failing to flourish), they enhance the dynamic quality of the gardens. A drama unfolds in which the gardener is at grips with nature – a nature that is often amenable to control, but might just possibly prove recalcitrant.

The close relation between collecting and eccentric garden-making is hardly surprising, since an ambivalence about the relation between the public and the intimate is characteristic of both activities. On the one hand, eccentric gardens, like many collections, function as a form of public display: most of the gardeners considered here welcomed or positively encouraged visitors. On the other hand, eccentric garden-makers, like collectors, also sought to forge a highly personal relation to the elements that they assembled. Perhaps the most poignant example of a gardener caught between public and private domains is that of Dr Phené, who in 1907 held a 'Fête in the Ancient Greek Style' to acquaint visitors with the complex iconography of the statues and other objects in his house and gardens in Chelsea, but whose property was described by the *Evening News*, at a grand sale in 1912 after his death, as 'only a mad lumber-room after all' [fig. 1].[3]

In as much as this book is about specific individuals and their gardening efforts, I have focused on the achievements of my selection of eccentrics during the course of their own lifetimes. I am not here concerned with the material afterlife of their gardens and how they have come down to us today. I concur with Sir Charles Isham of Lamport Hall, who in 1899, when contemplating the

R. A. Inglis, Dr Phené in his garden of Cheyne House, Upper Cheyne Row, Chelsea, c.1907, photograph. Royal Borough of Kensington & Chelsea.

2
G. S. Garrett, 'View of the Rockery, with its constructor, Sir Charles Isham, Bart.', photograph, *Strand Magazine*, 19, no. 110 (February 1900). Private collection.

fate of his very singular gardens after his death, remarked: 'so soon as the soul leaves the visible constructor, so soon will the soul depart from that structure.'[4] After the originator of an intensely personal and idiosyncratic living work of art ceases to play a role in its development, it invariably loses something of its animated soul and immediacy; it is transmuted from a lively autobiographical narrative to a poignantly bereft historical layer in the landscape.

Although my study is confined to English garden patrons and builders, it is not a meditation on Englishness. I explore personal idiosyncrasy, but never aim to use it as a starting point for an analysis of the place of eccentricity within the English national character. My reason for choosing England and English gardeners as the focus of my field of study is that the English have a long-standing and profound infatuation with making and tending gardens, and garden visiting. Gardening has long been a national obsession. As for the period that I consider here, this is partially determined by a need to find a convenient cut-off point and partially defined by the history of eccentricity. Oddity of behaviour, Sophie Aymes-Stokes and Laurent Mellet argue in their introduction to *In and Out: Eccentricity in Britain* (2012), begins to be perceived as a recognisable category around the early eighteenth century; around this time (although they themselves do not say this explicitly), it becomes possible to chart the formation of a concept of eccentricity that embraces forms of behaviour that are defined as strange and, intriguingly, both engaging and disturbing. I myself find it plausible that this concept might have been formed slightly earlier: I locate an early seventeenth-century gardener, Thomas Bushell, within the same tradition, since he creates a garden that is acclaimed (and seen as baffling as well as pleasurable) not only for its beauty and curiosity but also for its determined oddity.[5] I did not, however, wish to encroach too far into the twentieth century, since I see eccentricity after the 1920s or so as becoming increasingly fragmented into diverse forms, many of which are self-consciously and assiduously cultivated. As a result, it becomes vulnerable to a suspicion of affectation, and loses a quality common to all the gardeners considered here: a sense that they are acting in 'good faith'. However theatrical their creations might seem, they convince the viewer or visitor (or reader of contemporary descriptions) that they are spontaneously pursuing personal preoccupations.

In the context of much of the period with which I am concerned, the slippery nature of eccentricity – its resistance to easy definition – is increased by an overlap between the eccentric and a concept that, paradoxically, is central to the aesthetics of the time: the picturesque. Malcolm Andrews, in his essay 'Dickens, Turner and the Picturesque', argues that this concept, in the course of the nineteenth century, 'is increasingly a synonym for singularity, and distinctiveness of character, put under pressure from the homogenizing forces of modernity'. Andrews quotes William Hazlitt's essay 'On the Picturesque and Ideal' (1822): 'The picturesque is that which stands out, and catches the attention by some striking peculiarity: the *ideal* is that which answers to the preconceived imagination and appetite in the mind for love and beauty.'[6]

The picturesque, however, simply through the survival of the word, continues to pay a certain deference to the conventions of pictorial composition. While eccentric gardens often incorporate qualities that are associated with the picturesque – as Dr Johnson implies when he describes the Grotto at Hawkstone as 'not hewn into regularity, but such as imitate the sports of nature by asperities and protuberances' – they take the quality of surprise, noted by Hazlitt as crucial to the picturesque, to an extreme: an eccentric garden, unlike a merely picturesque one, produces a feeling that no one else would have thought of doing precisely *that* to the terrain.[7] To cite just one example: Lady Broughton's decision to build a replica of the Mer de Glace, with white marble to represent snow, in the vicinity of Chester, and to set it next to a colourful flower garden, was, as Henry Winthrop Sargent observed, 'an extraordinary caprice'.[8]

Eccentricity is to me a state apart – as already noted, an interstitial category, somewhere between madness and dull normality. It flourishes if and where it can make a space aloof from everyday reality. As few spaces offer as many possibilities for self-expression as gardens, the individuals included within this book have pursued the activity of gardening to create their own distinctive spheres, not so much to escape from the world of mundane experience, but to make sense of it and to enrich it – to engage with it on their own terms. While a number of figures who might be described as 'society women' are considered here – Lady Dudley and Lady Dorothy Nevill, for example – none of them approaches their garden as a mere prestigious backdrop; it becomes, rather, a space in which to pursue their own interests and obsessions.

The themes that I explore within this book include the building of miniature mountains and risings, the shaping and moving of topiaries, the collecting and display of birds and animals, the excavation of caves and other burrowings, the assemblage of architectural fragments, the erection of garden buildings and the evocation of the Garden of Eden [fig. 3].

Whereas we may now perceive the people examined within this book as being eccentric, they were not necessarily defined as such within their own lifetimes. The well-born bird- and animal-loving Lady Reade (d.1811) was, it must be conceded, described by her contemporaries as defiantly individualistic, devoid of feminine reserve and delicacy, and grotesque in appearance when 'in the midst of her living animals'.[9] The pleasure-ground proprietor Jonathan Tyers (d.1767), on the other hand, who showed no outward signs of personal eccentricity, created one of the gloomiest and most perverse anti-pleasure gardens in Georgian England, and the fervidly pious Miss Jane Hill (d.1794) remains such a shadowy and enigmatic figure that we are unlikely ever to know the full extent of her role in the building and the mythology of the strikingly Romantic gardens at Hawkstone in Shropshire [fig. 4].

All the gardens analysed here, however, were understood in relation to the biographies of the garden-makers. As already argued, these gardens produced an autobiographical effect; they served to construct a persona for the gardener, and the two were seen as continuous – both garden and gardener attracted gossip and fascinated commentary. Jane Hill was unusual in that she was to a large extent sidelined in perceptions of Hawkstone, but

3
Joseph Hardman, statues carved by Thomas Bland at Yew Tree Farm, Reagill, c.1950, photograph. Bridgeman Images.

4
Laing (Swiss photographer), 'Hawkstone: Grotto Rocks looking S.W.', c.1865, albumen silver print. Artokoloro/Alamy Stock Photo.

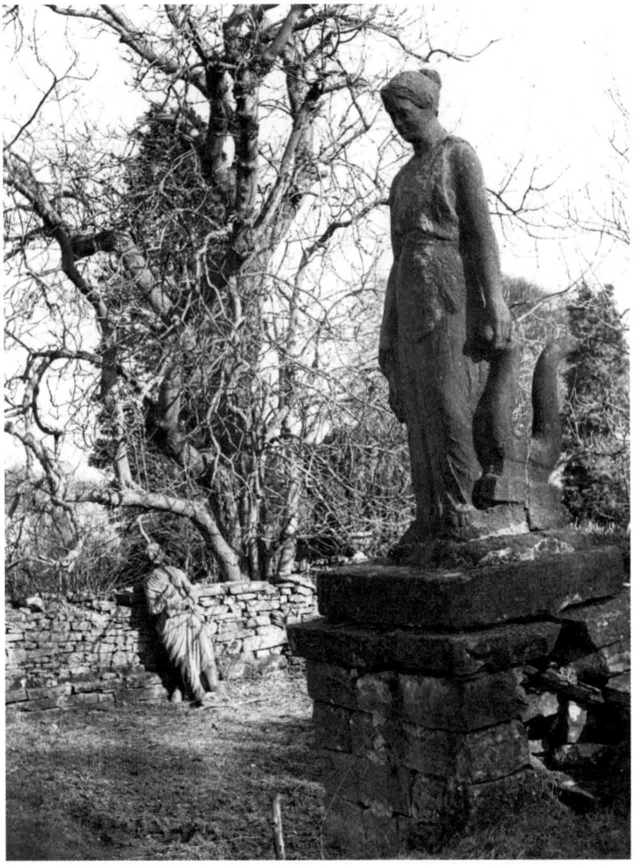

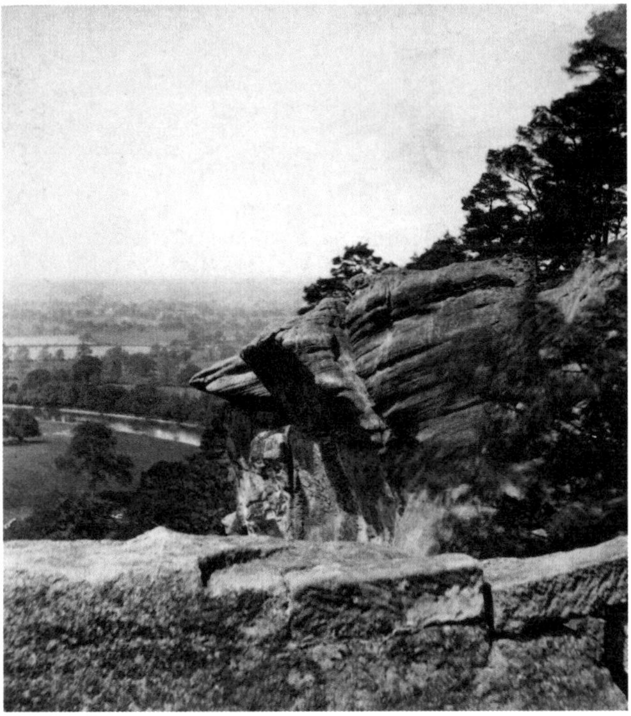

5
Anon., Mabel Baltrop sitting beneath the Yggdrasil tree in her
Garden of Eden in Bedford, c.1930, photograph. Panacea Charitable Trust, Bedford.
Copyright and image supplied courtesy of The Panacea Charitable Trust.

the garden was not seen as devoid of individual motivating force: she was simply displaced by her father and brother. This elision between garden and gardener worked both ways: knowledge of the life of the garden-maker played a part in shaping the reception of the garden. I have therefore included brief biographical details of the gardeners – details that contributed to the contemporary awareness that a singular and striking intervention in the landscape or townscape was underway.

It is worth noting at this point that my book is concerned with contemporary accounts of the gardens and gardeners not simply as evidence of what the gardens looked like, and of how the gardeners approached their horticultural enterprises, but also for their role in determining the identity of the instances of eccentric gardening that I set out to analyse. Gardens are not simply pieces of terrain that assume a particular visual form; they are also cultural formations determined by their reception. In defining what elements are at work in them, it is relevant to my project that one garden is seen as aberrant and another is accepted and applauded – seen as exceptionally impressive rather than exceptionally odd. While I set out to chart forms of eccentricity that can now be seen as such, from a historical distance, in relation to the conventions of the time, I also consider the reactions of critics who had internalised these conventions but were not wholly guided by them in developing strategies by which to assess unconventional gardens. The book concludes with a garden that is hardly subjected to aesthetic scrutiny at all, but is nonetheless recognised as playing a central part in a religious movement: the garden of the Panaceans in Bedford [fig. 5].

Where the comments of contemporaries demonstrate an attraction towards gardens that would seem not altogether aligned with the expectations of their time (the eighteenth-century expectation of simplicity and restraint, for example, as violated by the perceived excesses of Lady Reade), these comments often implicitly register a pleasure in the quality that has been defined by the psychoanalyst Donald Winnicott, in *Playing and Reality*, as one of 'creativity', a term that he defines while 'not letting the word get lost in the successful or acclaimed creation but keeping it to the meaning that refers to a colouring of the whole attitude to external reality':

> *It is creative apperception more than anything else that makes the individual feel that life is worth living. Contrasted with this is a relationship to external reality which is one of compliance, the world and its details being recognized but only as something to be fitted in with or demanding adaptation. Compliance carries with it a sense of futility for the individual and is associated with the idea that nothing matters and that life is not worth living.*[10]

6
Thomas Bland, *Crossfell Range of Mountains (from Reagill)*, n.d., pen and ink.
Kendal Local Studies Library, Cumbria.

One way of defining eccentric gardeners is to see them as people who robustly resisted 'compliance', and attracted attention from those who at some level recognised the appeal of this approach to life – and to gardens. There are various different forms of eccentricity, which I set out to define more closely by the end of this book, but an attribute that eccentric gardeners have in common is a determination to be 'creative' rather than 'compliant'.

Although the garden-makers mentioned above – Reade, Tyers and Hill – were sufficiently rich to allow their eccentricity to flourish on a prodigious scale, and to protect them from outside intervention in their highly unusual enterprises, others with less lavish resources engaged in similarly unconventional projects, which gained a degree of recognition from their contemporaries. The 'worthy yeoman' Thomas Bland (d.1865), who had modest means, used his 'unusual gifts and vigorous originality' to create a 'garden truly grand' of great local acclaim, and the engagingly absurd, ingenious and superstitious antiquary William Stukeley (d.1765) constructed eye-catching confections using 'mechanical artificialls', 'old reliques', antiquities and utensils [fig. 6].[11] There must have been many eccentric gardeners of far humbler origins and more restricted circumstances; the range of my analysis is, like that of other cultural historians, limited by the disappearance of so much of the evidence of their enterprises.

A central aim of this book is quite simply to give pleasure and encouragement to fellow gardeners, and to inspire those who feel a spirit of freedom welling up inside them to dare to be eccentric – to pluck up the moral courage and indulge with impunity. In a culture in which garden centres, popular journalism and purveyors of 'makeovers' often encourage a dull compliance with conventional strategies of garden-making, the stories of eccentric gardeners reveal how readily an engagement with gardens – places that are exciting in their innate unpredictability – allows scope for a more vital and experimental approach. As Edith Sitwell remarked: 'I am not eccentric. It's just that I am more alive than most people. I am an unpopular electric eel set in a pond of catfish.'[12]

To the most Illustrious Lady, the Lady CHARLOTTE Countess of Lichfield Viscountess Quarrendon & Baroness of Spelsbury &c. This 12. Table Shewing the interior Prospect of ENSTON Waterworks, with the greatest devotion is humbly Consecrated by R.P. LLD

[ONE]

The 'Enston-Rock': 'A Mad Gim-cracke Sure'

IN JUNE 1663 THE CELEBRATED DANISH POLYMATH OLE BORCH PAID a visit to a desolate and melancholy estate just north of the village of Enstone, near Woodstock in Oxfordshire.[1] The 'Professor Extraordinary' of philosophy, poetry, chemistry and botany was on a protracted leave of absence from the University of Copenhagen, and roughly a year into his six-year tour of Britain and the Continent – an ambitious and carefully planned peregrination that was to take him not only to the great centres for the study of anatomy, chemistry and alchemy, but to gardens as varied and distinguished as the Fontana Miranda at Cleves, Hampton Court Palace, the Oxford Physic Garden, Wilton, the Luxembourg Palace and the chateaux of Fontainebleau, Vaux-le-Vicomte, Versailles and St-Germain-en-Laye [fig. 7].

The fact that the 'Grotto' at Enstone figures in the professor's tour, and is described in his encylopaedic *Itinerarium*, is an indication of the former celebrity of this then ruined garden. Focusing on the artificial embellishments of the place – the waterworks and another ingenious contrivance for the enjoyment of guests – he mentions them only as vanished glories. The one feature that survives the 'devastation' is the hermit:

> We travelled by horse 11 miles from the city, where we examined the Inston Grotto, where there was an old man of 105 years. There are also two Egyptian mummies there, but now that Cromwell has driven all things to devastation, both are nearly ruined. In the hollow of the grotto, small mushrooms were growing out of a millstone of solid rock. The hydraulic works there are now broken. In a nearby patch of woods there is a table, at which people used to recline, and some in a certain hollow of earth under the table would suddenly burst into song to the delight of the guests.[2]

7
Olavus Borrichius [Ole Borch], Ole Borch botanising with a group of students, 1673, pen and ink. Royal Library, Copenhagen, NKS 375 quarto.

Only twenty-seven years earlier, King Charles I and Queen Henrietta Maria had visited the same place to witness at first hand, in a newly 'ornated' condition, the striking rock formation that had been uncovered as a result of Thomas Bushell's improvement there. This was not, in fact, the king's first visit: he had come to see the 'natural curiosity' in September 1635, at which time he gave directions to the Earl of Danby 'to preserve that rarity of nature at Enstone, which was first discovered by Thomas Bushell, and brought to maturity through his industrious charge': 'His Majesty, having viewed the place of that natural curiosity, not only thinks fit that the rock ought to be preserved, but ornated with groves, walks, fish ponds, gardens and waterworks, and to that end he has taken that said rock into his protection, and given direction to Bushell for perfecting so good a work.'[3]

The king not only endorsed Bushell's efforts, but encouraged others in authority to assist him in improving the setting of his natural 'maister-peece', and the queen was so 'Gratiously Pleased to Honour the said Rock, not only with Her Royall *Presence*; but commanded the same to be called after her owne *Princely name*, HENRIETTA'.[4]

The antiquary John Aubrey credits Thomas Bushell (*c.*1600–1674) with a 'good witt and a working and contemplative head', and one whose 'genius lay most towards naturall philosophy'; William Blundell observed a few years later that he had a 'vast wit for inventions' [fig. 8].[5] Bushell was born into a family of minor gentry from Cleeve Prior, near Evesham, in Worcestershire. At fifteen years of age he entered the service of Sir Francis Bacon – later Lord Chancellor – to whom he was an amanuensis and laboratory assistant, and with whom he shared a fascination for mining, scientific mysteries and the occult. Following Bacon's death and a period of 'pensive retirements', Bushell embarked on the eremitical sojourn to the 'desolated isle called the Calf of Man'.[6] Here, 'in obedience to my late dead lord's [Bacon's] philosophical advice', he resolved to 'make a perfect experiment upon myself, for the obtaining of a long and healthy life, most necessary for such a repentance as my former debauchedness required'.[7] In 1626 the self-styled 'superlative prodigall' emerged from his 'cave of a hollow rock' to marry an heiress.[8] The couple promptly removed from London to Enstone, where Bushell embarked on what was to prove to be among his most imaginative and successful endeavours: here he 'discovered and perfected natures ingenious designes upon my rock at Enston in Oxford-shire, by making it such an artificiall delightfull Grotto'.[9]

Aubrey visited the 'marvellous grotto' in August 1643[10] and records how Bushell had the good fortune to find a remarkable plot of land 'lyeing on the hanging of a hill facing the south':

8

Anon., 'Thomas Bushell', c.1628, woodcut, frontispiece to Bushell's *The First Part of Youths Errors* (1628). Album/Alamy Stock Photo.

at the foot whereof runnes a fine cleare stream which petrifies, and where is a pleasant Solitude, he spake to his servant, Jack Sydenham, to gett a Labourer to cleare some Boscage which grew on the side of the Hill, and also to dig a Cavity in the hill, to sitt and read, or contemplate. The Workman had not worked an hower before he discovers not only a Rock, but a rock of unusuall figure with Pendants like Icecles as at Wokey Hole, Somerset, which was the occasion of making that delicate Grotto and those fine Walkes.[11]

The earliest account of Bushell's 'strange and admirable Rocke' is supplied by a Lieutenant Hammond of Norwich in 'A Relation of a Short Survey of the Western Counties made by a Lieutenant of the Military Company in Norwich in 1635'.[12] Hammond praises the 'naturalnesse thereof, and the Art and Industry that the ingenious Owner hath added thereunto' which rendered it 'vnparralell'd'. He then provides a detailed explanation of Bushell's ingenious waterworks, including a 'Silver Ball' that 'riseth or falleth' on a jet of water, 'playing, tossing and keeping continually at the top of the sayd ascending Streame', and a 'hedge of water' like a 'plash'd Fence', where 'some-times faire Ladies [who] cannot fence the crossing' are caught 'flashing and dashing their smooth, soft and tender thighs and knees, by a sudden inclosing them in it'.[13]

At this juncture we must supplement Hammond's account with Bushell's own later recollection of Enstone as it was during its heyday. He recounts how he had 'beautyfied' the 'desolate Cell of Natures rarities at the head of a Spring near my own House' with 'artificial Thunder and Lightning, Rain, Hail-showers, Drums beating, Organs playing, Birds singing, Waters murmuring, the Dead arising, Lights moving, Rainbows reflecting with the beams of the Sun, and watry showers springing from the same Fountain'.[14] Aubrey, too, offers an additional insight from 1643, describing the presence of a 'very little pond' by the Grotto, in which there stood a 'Neptune, neatly cutt in wood, holding his Trident in his hand, and ayming with it at a Duck which perpetually turned round with him, and a Spaniel swimming after her'.[15] The antiquary in fact made a drawing of the statue, which he described as 'about three quarters of a yard high ... and looks very pretty' [fig. 9].[16] The diminutive god bears more than a passing resemblance to Bernini's *Neptune and Triton* (1622–3), formerly at the Villa Negroni-Montalto in Rome, and now in the Victoria and Albert Museum.

Hammond continues to describe how the 'very rare and admirable' rock itself is set within a 'fayre Chamber' in a building 'all of Freestone, the top whereof is flatt with Battlements about, and couer'd with Lead, and a neat Garden adioyning to itt'. The ceiling of the banqueting room on the first floor

9
John Aubrey, fountain at Enstone, 1643, pen and ink.
Bodleian Libraries, University of Oxford, MS Aubrey 17, fol. 18r.
Aubrey's sketch depicts the 'Neptune, neatly cutt in wood' that surmounted Bushell's fountain.

was 'curiously and artificially painted to the Life' depicting 'the woman of Samaria drawing water for our Sauiour: Hagar and her son, Ishmael and the Angell directing her and Susanna with the 3. Elders'.[17] Hammond likened the 'naturall Rocke' in this chamber to the 'Head of a Beare':

> *on the top thereof, the water rises and spouts forth, falling in the Rocke, you cannot discerne whither: from about the middle of this Chamber, they make a Canopy of Raine, which poures downe all ouer the lowest Roome, where the Ball playes, the plasht Fence and Rocke stands, as fast as any showre, yet iust vnder the Canopy, a man (in the Showers full Carreere) may stand dry, which with the reflection of the Sunne at high Noone, makes appeare to our fancies Rainbowes and flashings like Lightning.*[18]

From this rock there also bristled a veritable menagerie of artificial curiosities: 'many strange formes of Beasts, Fishes and Fowles doth appeare; and with the pretty murmuring of the Springs; the gentle running, falling and playing of the waters; the beating of a Drum; the chirping of a Nightingale, and other strange, rare and audible sounds and noyses doth highly worke vpon any Mans Fancy.'[19]

The building was in the Gothic revival style – possibly among the earliest in England[20] – and possessed two additional rooms: Bushell's study was 'hung with blacke Cloth, representing a melancholly retyr'd life like a Hermits', and his bed chamber had hangings bearing images of the 'History of our Sauiours Natiuity and Passion, most curiously wrought … and at the head his Picture artificially drawne'.[21]

The garden that lay beyond the 'faire Rocke' was set out with three 'neat, curious, long Walkes 30. paces [long] descending, and ascending againe, one aboue the other on the brow of the Hill', six sets of freestone steps leading to 'pleasant fruitfull Plumtrees, and other Fruit Trees; On the other side are pleasant delightfull Gardens of Flowers.' Beyond the rock, at the bottom of the hill, near the house, there were 'curious Pooles and rare Waters', as well as an arbour which ran 'the whole length of the foresayd Garden'.[22] Aubrey notes in 1643:

> *A decade ago, when Mr Bushell was designing his gardens, he decided that he was advanced enough in years to mean he could not plant his hedges in the usual way and wait for them to grow, or he would hardly live to enjoy them. He sent his workmen all over the country, searching for white-thorn, plum trees and so on that had already reached fifteen or twenty feet. He transplanted them in the month of October, before All Saints Day, and they did very well. I have never seen better hedges.*[23]

The *tout-ensemble* was, Lieutenant Hammond concluded, a 'most pleasant, sweet and delightsome Place'.[24] Yet it seemed to him that 'a Gentleman should be so strangely conceited and humour'd' to spend so much money as he has on a plot of land he did not own. Why form a 'Paradise' and then lose it? It was a 'mad gim-cracke sure, yet hereditary to these Hermiticall and Proiecticall Vndertakers'.[25]

Bushell's own account of his 'maister-peece'[26] contained in his *Severall Speeches and Songs, at the presentment of Mr Bvshells Rock to the Qveens Most Excellent Majesty* (1636) suggests that he may also have had a commercial motive for creating his 'Paradise', and that he probably considered his money well spent. He devised a 'Presentment', or flamboyant theatrical entertainment in five acts, in which he pressed his waterworks into service in order to ingratiate himself with the king and queen, and to promote his own political and economic ambitions: the performance opened with a speech of welcome by a fictive hermit, who expressed a hope that the king would preserve the rock from those threatening to destroy it.[27] (Aubrey avers that Bushell 'had so delicate a way of making his Projects alluring and feazible, profitable'.)[28] Bushell was at the time negotiating access to 'Mineral Treasures' in Wales, and hoped that the monarch, who in 1635 had conceived him 'capable … to do him some more acceptable service in Mineral discoveries (for the Honour of the Nation)', might look favourably upon his proposition.[29]

The 'Presentment' appears to have succeeded in its aim: Bushell was appointed warden and master-worker of the Royal Mint at Aberystwyth in 1637, using silver from the Welsh mines of which he was lessee; and throughout the Civil War he 'placed himself and his silver at the king's service' [fig. 10].[30] He did so, however, at great personal cost: he borrowed vast sums of money which he could never hope to repay. As Aubrey recounts: 'His tongue was a Charme, and drewe in so many to be bound for him, and to be ingaged in his Designes, that he ruined a number.'[31] As a consequence of his self-professed 'licentious prodigality', the last years of his long life were sad and lonely, and he spent most of his time on the run from creditors.

And what of the fate of the 'Enston-Rock'? Bushell appears to have resided at Enstone as long as possible, as Aubrey recounts that during the Civil War he 'swathed his grotto in soft black woollen cloth', and his bed in black curtains that hung from 'four ropes wrapped around with more of the black cloth, instead of bedposts'; in 1643 Queen Henrietta Maria presented him with an Egyptian mummy which he placed 'in the grotto that bears the Queen's name, but I fear that is too damp a place and the mummy will grow mouldy. Something so old and rare should not be ruined' [fig. 11].[32]

There can be little doubt that Bushell's rock was a significant milestone in English garden design: Roy Strong has suggested in *The Renaissance Garden in England* (1979) that it is an example of 'the very real interconnection that existed between the development of garden delights and scientific advance in seventeenth-century England'.[33] He also posits that the development of Bushell's estate may have been influenced by the *New Atlantis* (1627) – Bacon's fictional island in which the inhabitants have 'great and spacious houses, where we imitate and demonstrate meteors; as snow, hail, rain, some artificial rains of bodies, and not of water, thunders, lightnings'.[34]

10

Anon., 'The Impressa of Mr. Bushels Golden Medal', woodcut, in Thomas Bushell, *An Extract by Mr. Bushell of his late Abridgment of the Lord Chancellor Bacons Philosophical Theory in Mineral Prosecutions* (1660). © The Trustees of the British Museum.

J. Berjeau affirmed in *The Bookworm* (1869) that Bushell's 'many failures ... [and] his imprisonment for debt ... leave no doubt that he was the canal through which ran the fortune of Lord Bacon, to be sunk in unprofitable mining schemes.'

11

Anon., Egyptian sarcophagus, seventeenth century, copperplate engraving. Science Photo Library.

Although Bushell's hydraulic machinery was at the time reasonably novel in England, it had earlier and more grandiose Italian antecedents: the sphere supported on a column of water was derived from a prototype at the Villa Aldobrandini, and the organs and birdsong were well-known conceits at the Villa d'Este. Many of the other ingenious devices and *giochi d'acqua* were presumably based on Bushell's first-hand observations of Salomon de Caus's waterworks in the gardens at Somerset House and Greenwich Palace, or Isaac de Caus's grottos at Whitehall and Wilton, and illustrated in contemporary publications such as Salomon de Caus's *Les Raisons des forces mouvantes* (1615).[35] The hydraulic confection most similar to Bushell's 'mad gim-cracke' was de Caus's Parnassus fountain designed for Anne of Denmark at Somerset House [fig. 12]. This 'Rocke' was described in 1613 by J. W. Neurnayr, a member of the Duke of Saxony's entourage, as a 'mountain or rock ... made of sea-stones, all sorts of mussels, snails and other curious plants put together: all kinds of herbs and flowers grow out of the rock which are a great pleasure to behold ... It is thus a beautiful work and far surpasses the Mount Parnassus in the Pratolino near Florence.'[36]

The publication of two engraved views of the 'Enston Waterworks' in Robert Plot's *Natural History of Oxford-shire* (1677) affirms their importance [figs 13 and 14]. The professor of chemistry and first Keeper of the Ashmolean Museum recounts how Bushell's *'structure*, with all the ingenious Contrivances about it, continued in a flourishing condition for some few years, till the unhappy *Wars*

12

Salomon de Caus, *The Parnassus at Somerset House*, copperplate engraving, in *Les Raisons de forces mouvantes* (1615). Linda Hall Library, Kansas City, Mo. Courtesy of the Linda Hall Library of Science, Engineering and Technology.

coming on, it became wholly neglected, and so sensibly decayed ... (being next door to ruine)'. The plates, however, illustrate the waterworks in excellent form, and are dedicated to the fourteen-year-old Edward Henry, Earl of Lichfield, and his even younger bride, Lady Charlotte Fitzroy[37] – the former is credited with 'all imaginable respect' for erecting 'in part' and restoring the whole of Bushell's work.[38] Lichfield 'not only repaired the broken Cisterns and Pipes, but made a fair addition to it, in the small Island situate in the passage of the Rivulet, just before the building set over the Rock; which though the last in erection, is yet the first thing that presents it self in the exterior Prospect of the whole work'.[39] The young earl was possibly encouraged in his refurbishment by his uncle, the libertine poet John Wilmot, 2nd Earl of Rochester. Aubrey credits Rochester for repairing the statue of Neptune.[40]

Aubrey records, rather coyly, that Bushell 'had done something (I have forgotten what) that made him obnoxious to the parliament or Oliver Cromwell, about 1650; would have been hanged if taken'. He therefore went into hiding 'in his house in Lambeth marsh where the pointed pyramid is':

> In the garret there, is a long gallery ... At the end where his couch was[,] an old Gothic niche (like a monument) [was] painted [with] a skeleton incumbent on a mat. At the other end, where was his pallet-bed, was an emaciated dead man stretched out. Here he had several mortifying and divine mottoes (he imitated his lord [Bacon] as much as he could) and out of his windows a very pleasant prospect.

Bushell was now about seventy, 'still a handsome proper gentleman', with a 'perfect healthy constitution: fresh, ruddy face and hawk nose', though oppressed by 'money troubles'. The 'painted skeleton' and the 'emaciated dead man' inhabiting his lodgings were presumably memento mori.[41]

Egyptian mummies, too, had the potential to function as memento mori and induce reflections of a serious nature. In *Worldly Policy and Moral Prudence: The Vanity and Folly of the one, the Solidity and Usefulnesse of the other* (1654), a moral discourse by Bushell's contemporary, the clergyman Charles Herle, the author addressed aspects of personal integrity, and in so doing introduced as devil's advocate a speaker who rejects the strictures of 'Morality', and describes the person who would adopt stern moral rules as a mere 'piece of Egyptian Mummy':

> What would you have me do? (saies another) be unbowel'd alive, and imbalm'd like a dead Corps with stiffning cold gumms and spices of Morality instead of blood and spirits? as if I were to converse but a while with mournings and

TAB. XI.
chap. 9.
§ 52.
ad pag. 343.
To the right Honorable
Edward Henry Earle of
Lichfield Viscount QUARRENDON
and Baron of Spelsbury, &c
This Eleventh Table
Shewing the exterior Prospect of ENSTON
Waterworks, in part erected, all restored
by his LORDP. with all imaginable
respect is justly dedicated.
by R.P. LLD.
M. Bur sculp.

lamentations like a Hearse, would you make me a piece of Egyptian Mummy[,] a Confection, a Statue of moulded Ginger-bread, a Jelly of insipid moronity by your Morality, would you have men turned into monuments, to stone?[42]

Although Aubrey was under the apprehension that Bushell's mummy had 'long before this time' been spoiled by the 'dampness of the place ... with mouldiness',[43] we know from Ole Borch that when the hermit, then an old man, returned to Enstone after the Restoration, he was kept company by an Egyptian mummy (or possibly two?). John Evelyn paints an even more poignant image of Bushell and his ruined paradise, reporting in October 1664 that when he went to see 'the famous wells, natural and artificial grots and fountains, called Bushell's Wells', he found it an 'extraordinary solitude. There he [Bushell] had two mummies; [and] a grot where he lay in a hammock, like an Indian.'[44]

13 & 14
M. Burghers, 'Exterior Prospect of Enston Waterworks' and
'Interior Prospect of Enston Waterworks', copperplate engravings, in Robert Plot,
The Natural History of Oxford-shire (1677). Private collection.

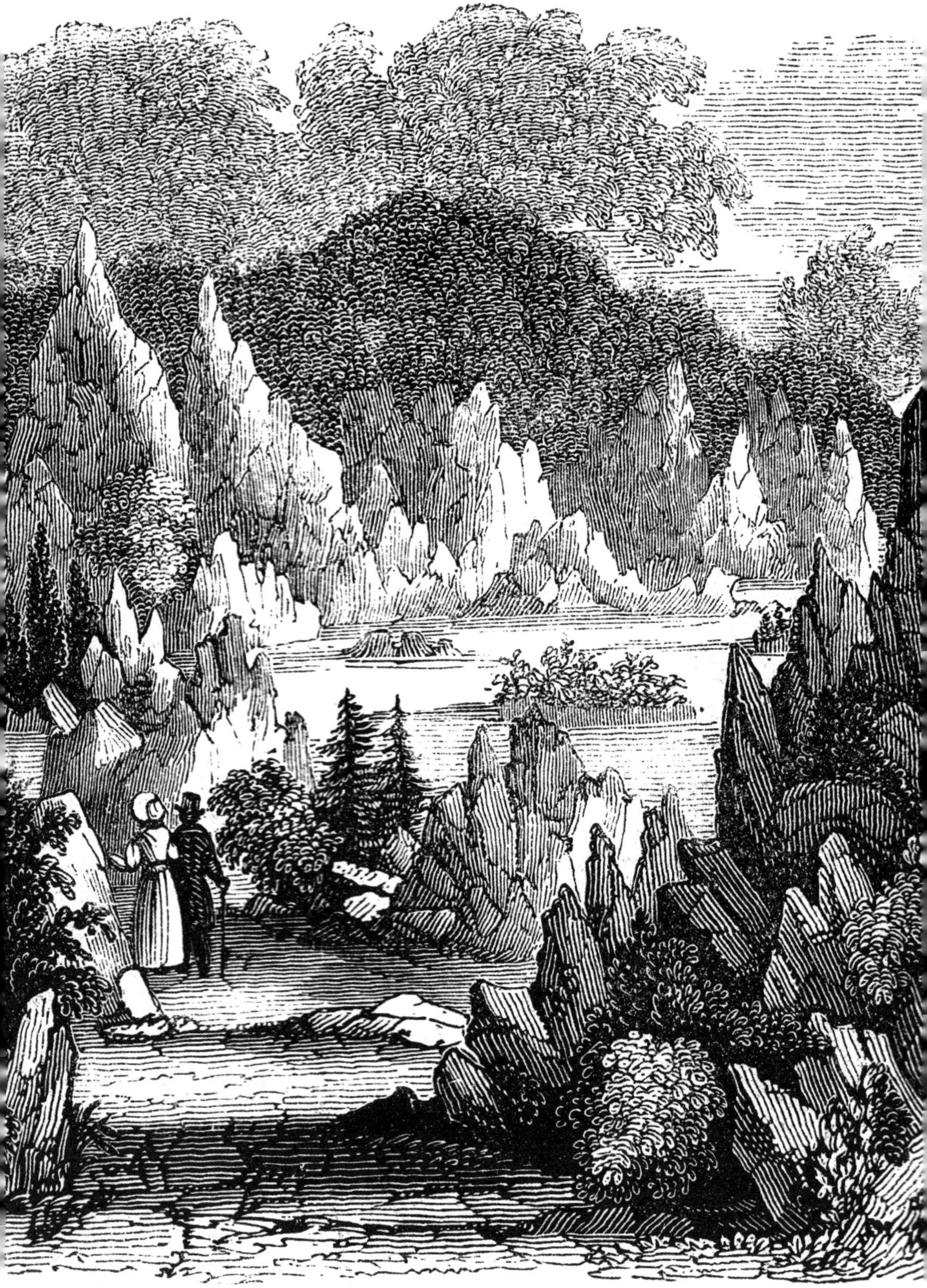

[TWO]

Lady Broughton's 'Miniature Copy of the Swiss Glaciers'

IN THE EARLY 1860S THE CELEBRATED AMERICAN HORTICULTURIST and landscape gardener Henry Winthrop Sargent, who had a 'taste for horticultural oddities and freaks', made a special pilgrimage to Hoole House in Cheshire to catch a glimpse of a garden which he had longed to see for over a quarter of a century.[1] In 'Impressions of English Scenery' (1865) he remarked that he had been 'astonished', and his appetite whetted, by an article in 'the English *Gardeners'* [sic] *Magazine*', published in 1838, in which the landscape gardener and horticultural writer John Claudius Loudon (1783–1843) supplied a 'very elaborate account … of a visit he paid to Hoole House, near Chester, then belonging to Lady Broughton, descriptive of a most extraordinary rock garden'. Sargent was determined to ascertain if the house still existed, 'and if so, Where was it, and did the rock garden still exist …?'[2]

On leaving the gardens at Eaton Hall to set off on his journey, Sargent asked three gardeners and the landlord at his hotel whether they could direct him to Hoole. None had ever heard of it. Finally, an 'old cabman' recollected the whereabouts of Lady Broughton's house in the Liverpool Road. After 'much trouble' Sargent discovered what he believed to be his destination – a garden with 'a short but exceedingly well kept avenue, the verges and sides beautifully cut, and densely planted with large masses of rhododendrons, laurel, yews, deodars, araucarias, all, except the araucarias, being closely clipped'. He observed that 'this formal treatment of the trees augured favorably for the rock garden, but I saw no evidence of it.' After venturing further into the pleasure ground he met an 'old gardener striking some geraniums',[3] who informed him that the garden he was seeking still flourished and was 'kept up just as Lady Broughton had left it … when he had helped build and unbuild it, (as a young man,) as Lady Broughton was continually altering it'. The mansion was, he continued, now occupied by 'a Mrs Hamilton, an old lady of 80, living by herself', and 'no one ever came to the place, and probably no one knew the garden existed.'[4]

Having been granted permission to see the garden, Sargent was led up to the house and through a small postern immediately adjoining the front entrance, whereupon, he exclaimed, 'a perfect scene of enchantment suddenly broke upon me' [figs 15 and 16]:

> Imagine a little semi-circular lawn, of about half an acre, of most exquisite turf, filled with twenty-eight baskets, about six feet in diameter, of the most dazzling and gorgeous flowers. Each basket a complete bouquet in itself, of three different colors, in circles; for instance, the lower circle would be Coleus, the 2d, yellow Calceolaria, the 3d, or upper, White Leaved Geranium. On the top, as a sort of pinnacle, a group of Scarlet Gladiolus ... These 28 baskets seemed a succession of circular terraces, each color was so vivid, so gay, and so continuous.[5]

This 'bright parterre' was laid out upon an emerald lawn that was surrounded by the famous rockwork, which ranged 'from 15 to 30 feet high, built up against the stables and offices, as support, and brought down irregularly to the lawn in front, filled with every variety of fern and rock plant that would stand the summer climate of England; most of the more delicate being removed in winter to green and even orchidaceous houses'. The visitor was overwhelmed:

> I thought nothing could have been gayer than the 28 circular beds, until I looked up and saw a much more gorgeous scene in this semicircle of rock, 30 feet high, crammed to overflowing, with every sort of Palm, Cactus, Cereus, Yucca, Gladioli, Geranium, &c. &c., in full flower, interspersed with Deodars, clipped into pyramids, Irish Yews, Golden Yews, Abies cephalonica, Pinsapo, Normandiana, &c., all clipped into pyramids. The object being not only to keep them in harmony in size, with the rocks and the garden, but in appearance; since the highest pinnacles were intended to represent the Alps, for which purpose white spar was used to represent the glaciers and snow peaks, and small Pinus Cembra (the pine of the Alps) were interspersed along the edges, and near some yawning crevice, over which Alpine rustic bridges were thrown; through the whole of this rich and intricate maze ran a little wild path, bordered with heath and furze, and broom, which crept up the rocky sides of the cliffs, among the wild distorted looking firs, some 8 to 15 feet high, though 30 years old many of them, until they disappeared among the icy summits, apparently, of the Alpine heights.[6]

Sargent concluded his account by affirming that 'the whole thing was an extraordinary caprice, wonderfully carried out, and admirably described and illustrated, if I remember at this distance, by Mr Loudon.'[7]

15 & 16
Anon., 'Flower-garden at Hoole House, from the Drawingroom Window' and
'Conservatory at Hoole House, forming the Front Entrance', engravings,
Gardener's Magazine (1838).

Loudon was certainly impressed by the *tout-ensemble* when he made his first visit to Hoole in July 1831, and had been 'exceedingly desirous of giving some account of it' in the *Gardener's Magazine*. He could not, however, then 'prevail on Her Ladyship to accede to our wishes'. Although Loudon professed that the garden was then 'very perfect', it is likely that the owner was of the opinion that it was still a work in progress.[8] Hoole House had become the home of Lady Broughton – born Elizabeth Egerton in 1771 – from 1814, after she had become estranged from her husband, Sir John Delves Broughton, 7th Baronet [fig. 17]. It was then a 'modern mansion'[9] and Dame Eliza, as people came to title her, had only begun creating her garden in the 1820s.[10]

In 1838 Loudon renewed his application, having seen some 'exquisitely beautiful water-colour drawings (by Mr. Pickering of Chester) of the flower-garden and rock-fence'. This time Lady Broughton 'reluctantly consented', supplying Loudon with original drawings by 'Mr. Harrison of Chester, the late celebrated architect' for the veranda, geranium house, greenhouse and

17
Henry Raeburn, *Dame Eliza Broughton*, c.1794, oil on canvas.
Houston Museum of Fine Art.

conservatory, and permitting him to take a general plan and views of the garden for publication.[11] Loudon was delighted, and told his readers that the flower garden 'has been by far the most celebrated garden of the kind in that part of the country for the last ten years; and, as will shortly appear, it is in design altogether unique'.[12] The resultant article was published in August 1838, and the description was 'rendered more perfect' by 'beautiful wood-cut[s], in the superior style for which this Magazine is famous'.[13]

Loudon admired the distant views to the Welsh mountains, the Peckforton Hills and Beeston Castle, and was flattered to observe that the owner had put in place a recommendation he had made on his last visit:

> In 1831, when we saw the flower-garden, the flower-beds on the lawn, instead of being circular, were in the shape of the letter S; they were all of the same form and dimensions, and in rows, like the circular beds, and also placed at uniform distances; but the effect, though good, was not equal to what it is at present: the perfect unity of the circular beds producing a more complete contrast to the diversity of the rockwork, than the S-shaped beds.[14]

As Loudon's woodcut suggests, the effect of the new circular beds 'from the Drawingroom Window' was striking, and produced the desired effect: 'the smooth flat surface of the lawn, with the uniformity of the circular beds' contrasted strongly with the 'great irregularity of the surrounding rockwork' [figs 18 and 19].[15]

Loudon then proceeded to describe the reformed flower garden and its Alpine setting in greater detail.

> The length of the flower-garden, within the rocky boundary, is 60 yards, and the breadth is 34 yards. The baskets, twenty-seven in number, are in five straight rows, and each basket is a circle of 9 ft. 5 in. in diameter. They are made of wire, worked on an iron rod; the rod placed upon small pegs, to keep the basket to the level of the grass; and they are painted a yellow stone colour, to harmonise with the rocks and the veranda ... [and] they are planted with spring, summer, and autumn flowers mingled together.[16]

The design of the rockwork, we are told, was 'taken from a small model representing the mountain of Savoy, with the valley of Chamouni: it has been the work of many years to complete it, the difficulty being to make it stand against the weather':

> Rain washed away the soil, and frost swelled the stones: several times the main wall failed from the weight put upon it. The walls and the foundations are built

of red sandstone of the country; and the other materials have been collected from various quarters, chiefly from Wales; but it is now so generally covered with creeping and alpine plants, that it all mingles together in one mass.[17]

Although lushly planted, the 'outline' was 'carefully preserved; and the part of the model that represents "la Mer de Glace"' was 'worked with grey limestone, quartz, and spar'.[18]

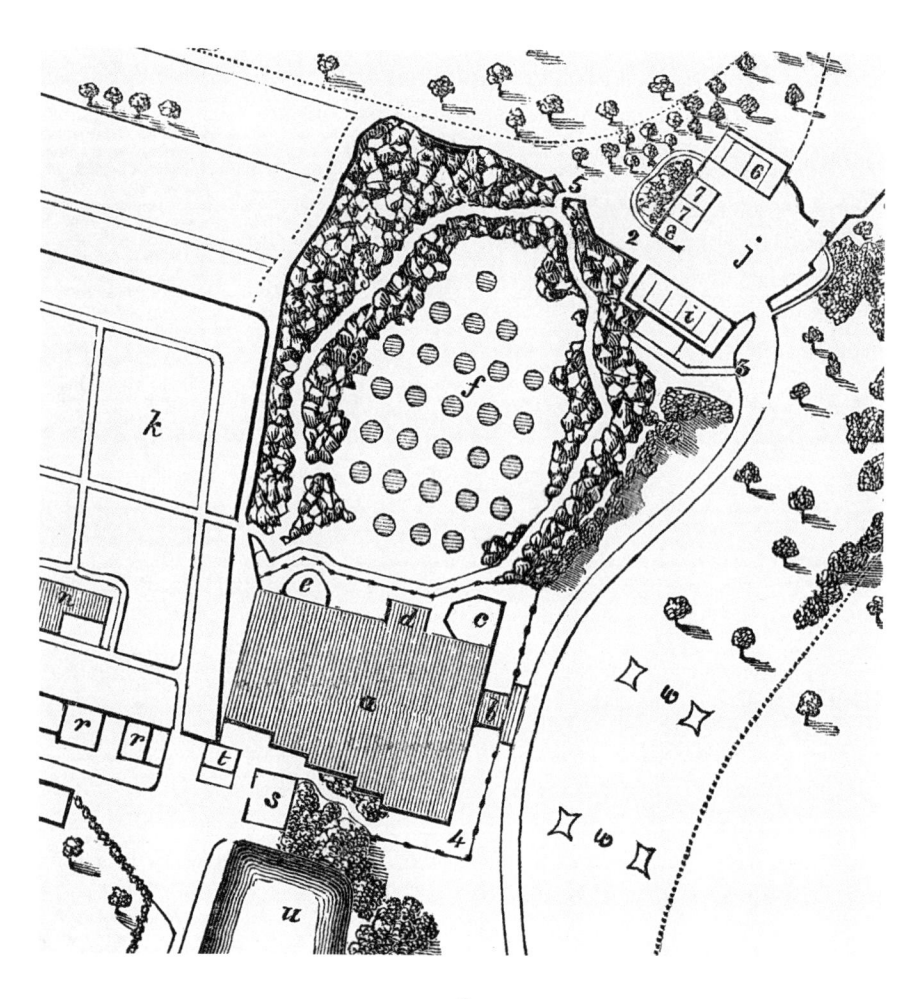

18
Anon., plan of the Flower Garden at Hoole House, engraving, *Gardener's Magazine* (1838).
The letters on the plan refer to the following (partial list):
a. House; b. Conservatory forming main entrance to house; c. Camellia-house,
e. Geranium-house; f. Flower-garden; g. 'rockwork surrounding the flower-garden';
j. Stable-yard; k. Kitchen-garden; w. Flower-baskets on lawn.

19
Anon., 'Rockwork, Lawn, and Camellia-house, at Hoole House from the North-East',
Gardener's Magazine (1838).

Rockwork, Lawn, and Camellia-house, at Hoole House from the North-East.

It has no cells for plants; the spaces are filled up with broken fragments of white marble, to look like snow; and the spar is intended for the glacier. On the small scale of our engravings, and without the aid of colour, it is altogether impossible to give an adequate idea of the singularity and beauty of this rocky boundary; and we may add that it is equally impossible to create anything like it by mere mechanical means.[19]

By setting the garden in contrast to one produced by 'mere mechanical means', Loudon presumably set out to emphasise that a landscape so personal, and so dependent upon a willingness to experiment and take risks, could hardly have been produced through the more conventional method of employing an architect or a landscape gardener to ensure a degree of structural safety and soundness.

Loudon, eager to praise Dame Eliza, then states firmly – and flatteringly: 'There must be the eye of the artist presiding over every step; and that the artist must not only have formed an idea of the previous effect of the whole in his own mind, but must be capable of judging of every part of the work as it advances, with reference to that whole'.[20]

LADY BROUGHTON

In the case of this rockwork, Lady Broughton was her own artist; and the work she has produced evinces the most exquisite taste for this description of scenery. It is true it must have occupied [a] great part of her time for six or eight years past; but the occupation must have been interesting, and the result, as it now stands, must give Her Ladyship the highest satisfaction.[21]

Jane Loudon – who presumably accompanied her husband on his 1838 tour – was equally effusive when she described the Savoyard set piece in the Ladies' Magazine of Gardening (1842) as producing 'a scenic illusion perfectly unique of its kind':

[It]...is perhaps the most remarkable and best executed rock garden in existence. It is formed on a level surface, and consists of an imitation or miniature copy of the Swiss glaciers; with a valley between, into which the mountain scenery projects and retires, forming several beautiful and picturesque openings, which are diversified by scattered fragments of rock of various shapes and sizes, and by mountain trees and shrubs, and other plants.[22]

The 'open part' of the rockwork was planted with a collection of the 'most beautiful Alpine plants, particularly those of low growth; each is placed in a little bed of suitable soil, the surface of which is covered by broken fragments of stone, clean-washed river gravel, the remains of decaying moss, &c. according as the object is to retain moisture around those plants which are liable to be injured by drought.'[23] The heady climax of the scene of 'wild irregularity' was the 'part representing the "Mer-de-Glace," where the imitation of the glaciers is so complete, that a sensation of coolness is felt even in the midst of summer' [fig. 20].[24]

Despite the eccentricity of Dame Eliza's decision to embosom her flower garden in a crystalline landscape, her fascination with the glacier and its setting near Chamonix was not in itself surprising or unusual [fig. 21]. It is possible that she visited the glacier during the short period of peace between Britain and France following the Treaty of Amiens (1802) or after the end of the Napoleonic Wars in 1815, but in any case the pass through the Chamonix valley had become a popular route for northern European travellers since the late eighteenth century. In 1818 her near neighbour, the Liverpool cleric Revd Thomas Raffles, described the valley as containing 'some of the sublimest objects in nature'.[25] Lady Broughton's rockwork could be based on a close reading of Mary Shelley's Frankenstein (1818), which supplies a vivid description of the Mer de Glace which she and Shelley had visited in 1817:

20
Anon., 'Rockwork at Hoole House, from the Centre of the Flower-garden', *Gardener's Magazine* (1838).

21
William Pars, *Mer de Glace, Chamounix*, 1770, pen and grey ink and watercolour.
© The Trustees of the British Museum.

I descended upon the glacier. The surface is very uneven, rising like the waves of a troubled sea, descending low, and interspersed by rifts that sink deep. The field of ice is almost a league in width, but I spent nearly two hours crossing it. The opposite mountain is bare perpendicular rock. From the side where I now stood Montanvert was exactly opposite, at the distance of a league; and above it rose Mont Blanc, in awful majesty. I remained in a recess of rock, gazing at this wonderful and stupendous scene. The sea, or rather the vast river of ice, wound among its dependent mountains, whose aërial summits hung over its recesses. Their icy glittering peaks shone in the sunlight over the clouds. My heart, which was before sorrowful, now swelled with something like joy.[26]

What impressed upon visitors to Hoole during Lady Broughton's lifetime, and Jane Loudon in particular, was that her rockwork was such a daring enterprise carried out in a spirit of extreme experimentation – that it 'required the eye of an artist, combined with great good taste, to arrange these materials so as to produce the desired effect; as a single false step would have made the whole pass from the sublime to the ridiculous'.[27] Lady Broughton had presumably been emboldened by her own gardening experience; she was familiar with the challenge posed by major landscape operations, since she had witnessed as a child the dramatic ten-year transformation of her family's park and gardens at Oulton under the direction of the landscape gardeners William Eames and John Webb.[28]

If Dame Eliza spent almost four decades building and unbuilding her garden, her last will and testament suggests that she also gave due consideration to her own end and the fate of her garden after her death.[29] One of her first wishes was that she should have a 'proper but private' funeral, and should be 'carried to the grave by my Gardener [John Edwards] and his first Laborers'.[30] There were many special bequests, among them the 'wire baskets in the flower garden and on the lawn at my present residence and the ornamental beehives' to the widow of the late Revd Peploe William Hamilton; 'french flower stands and two water colour drawings of [my] garden' to Maria S. Bateman; 'the china that belongs to the flower garden and all the plants in the hothouses and garden upon the condition that most of the plants shall be sold' to Mrs Sibylla Wilbraham; and a 'small book of Swiss and Italian views' to George Egerton Warburton.[31]

Most tantalising of all is Dame Eliza's bequest to her nephew Sir Philip de Malpas Grey-Egerton, 10th Baronet, of a 'rosewood commode containing seven Alpine Models'. Might one of these have been the 'small model representing the mountain of Savoy, with the valley of Chamouni' referred to by Loudon in

1838? Sir Philip was an eminent geologist and palaeontologist whose interest in these subjects had been aroused while studying under Dean William Buckland at Oxford in the 1820s. Immediately following his graduation he embarked with his friend William Willoughby Cole, later 3rd Earl of Enniskillen, on a geological Grand Tour of the Continent, and while travelling in Switzerland they met the Swiss palaeontologist Louis Agassiz, who persuaded them both to focus on collecting fossil fishes.[32]

One does not know whether Dame Eliza's 'Alpine Models' still exist, or what they looked like. They may have been something like the plaster models of megalithic subjects contained in John Britton's Celtic Cabinet (c.1824),[33] or Henry Browne's cork model of Stonehenge (1826) [fig. 22].[34] Models of the glaciers, however, are described, with some fascination, by various writers of the time. The well-known botanist Sir James Edward Smith, in his *Sketch of a Tour on the Continent* (1793), describes one such model 'in miniature' as an adumbration of his experience with these great works of nature on the spot:

> At Servos, a village at the entrance of the valley of Chamouni, I called on Mr. Exchaquet, superintendant of the neighbouring mines, in order to see his model of the Glaciers and valley of Chamouni, and was extremely pleased to have such a comprehensive view in miniature of the noble scenes I was going to admire. This model is carved in wood, and coloured; the ice being well imitated by broken glass. Its scale is about a line to 18 toises; that is, 15552 times less than the vast original![35]

Wordsworth, too, proclaims his acquaintance with Alpine models; in the introduction to his *Guide through the Lakes* (1810), he begins not with an account of lake scenery, not of the actual scenery at all, but with the report of a model – one that sounds rather more ambitious in scale and scope than Smith's:

> At Lucerne, in Switzerland, is shewn a Model of the Alpine country which encompasses the Lake of the four Cantons. The Spectator ascends a little platform, and sees mountains, lakes, glaciers, rivers, woods, waterfalls and vallies … It may be easily conceived that this exhibition affords an exquisite delight to the imagination, tempting in it to wander at will from valley to valley, from mountain to mountain, through the deepest recesses of the Alps. But it supplies also a more substantial pleasure: for the sublime and beautiful region, with all its hidden treasures, and their bearings and relations to each other, is thereby comprehended and understood at once.[36]

Smith and Wordsworth recognise the objects that they are describing as models and miniatures. Lady Broughton's glacier garden is not explicitly

22

Henry Browne, model of Stonehenge displayed in John Britton's Celtic Cabinet, *c.*1824, cork, wood and cloth. Devizes Museum, Wiltshire.

Browne was the first keeper of Stonehenge. He made and sold several miniature copies of the ancient monument, depicting it as it was found in 1824 and how it might originally have looked using William Stukeley's measurements.

classified in this way by her contemporaries, but this reconstruction, too, taking models of glaciers as its inspiration, can be viewed as a larger-scale model. One aspect of the miniature that Susan Stewart has identified in On Longing (1993) is its ability to remove the spectator from a sense of time and duration: 'miniature time transcends the duration of everyday life in such a way as to create an interior temporality of the subject.' Both Smith and Wordsworth, in their use of the terms *comprehensive* and *comprehended*, suggest a suspension of the more hesitant time of enquiry and exploration. Dame Eliza's garden institutes no such radical shrinkage of space – and therefore of time – but she does draw on the ability of the miniature to suspend narrative time. Stewart offers an analysis that is useful in understanding the effect that Eliza is producing:

> *The miniature always tends toward tableau rather than toward narrative, toward silence and spatial boundaries rather than toward expository closure. Whereas speech unfolds in time, the miniature unfolds in space. The observer is offered a transcendent and simultaneous view of the miniature, yet is trapped outside the possibility of a lived reality of the miniature. Hence the nostalgic desire to present the lower classes, peasant life, or the cultural other within a timeless and uncontaminated miniature form.*[37]

This sense of the garden of Hoole House as tableau is grasped by the American landscape gardener Andrew Jackson Downing; writing in A *Treatise on the Theory and Practice of Landscape Gardening* (1841), he praises the 'superb *extravaganza* in rockwork' at Hoole House, where Lady Boughton 'has succeeded in forming, round a natural valley, an imitation of the hills, glaciers, and scenery of a *passage* in Switzerland'.[38] In acclaiming the glacier garden as 'striking and complete', he pays tribute to its role as a successful miniature, setting aside the fragmented nature of day-to-day time, and producing a space more enthrallingly self-contained: 'The whole is done in rockwork, the snow-covered summits being represented in white spar. The appropriate plants, trees, and shrubs on a small scale, are introduced, and the illusion, to a spectator standing in the valley surrounded by these glaciers, is said to be wonderfully striking and complete.'[39]

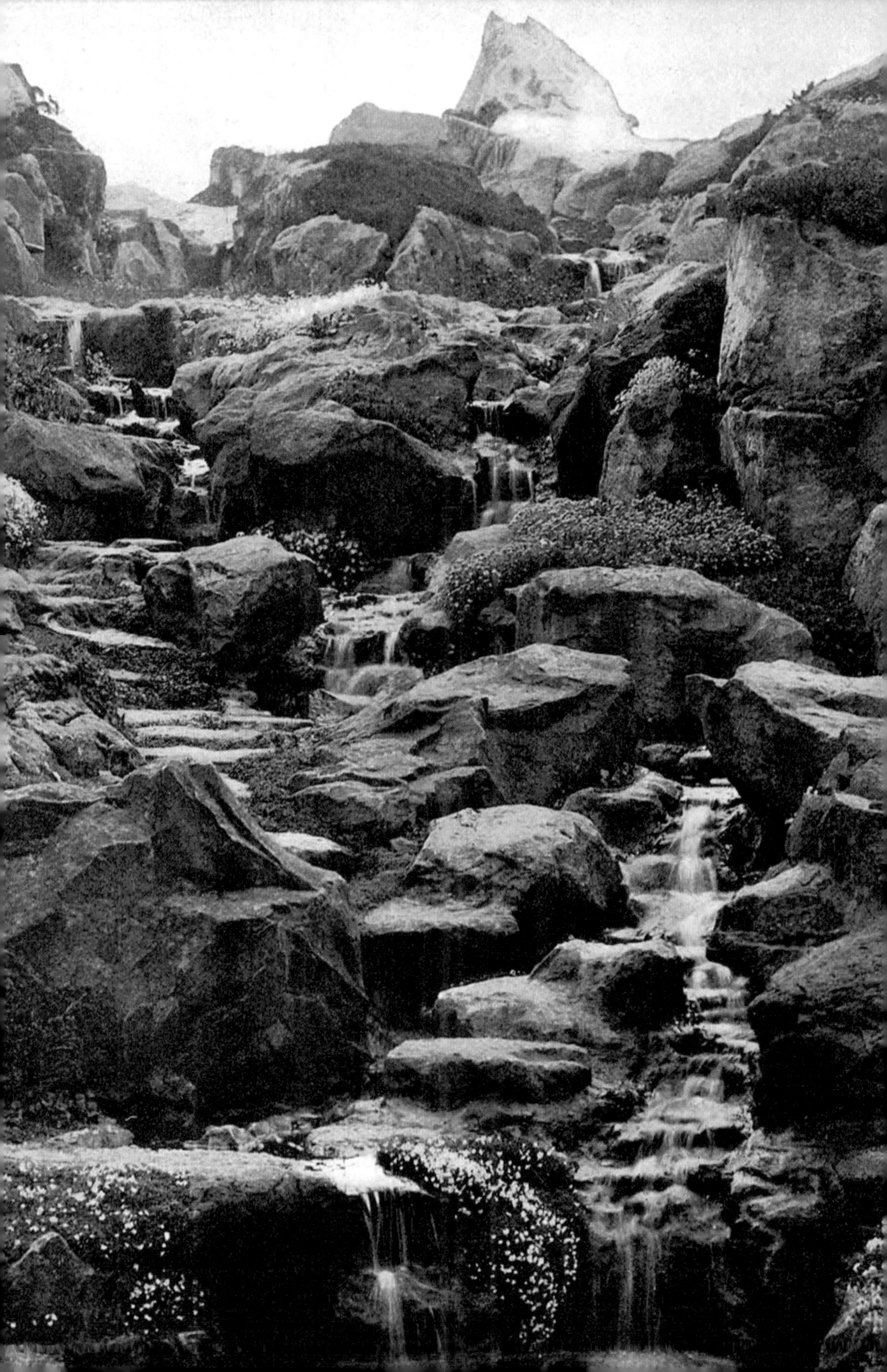

[THREE]

Friar Park: 'Alpinism at Home'

On 14 July 1865, a party of English tourists, including Edward Whymper, Lord Francis Douglas, the Revd Charles Hudson, their French guide Michel Croz and two Zermatt porters, completed their ascent of the Matterhorn. Although successful in their assault of the hitherto unassailable peak, their achievement was overshadowed by the death of four alpinists. Mont Cervin, or the Matterhorn, was the last great Alpine peak to be climbed, and this first ascent was perceived as the end of what the mountaineer Revd W.A.B. Coolidge dubbed the 'golden age of alpinism'.[1]

The Matterhorn tragedy did not, however, dissuade visitors from journeying to the Swiss Alps; in fact, a correspondent to *The Times* observed in September 1865: 'there is no doubt that nothing acted as so strong an inducement for travellers to visit Switzerland this year as the tragic catastrophe of the Matterhorn.'[2] Among these English tourists was a twenty-two-year-old graduate keen to see the world.

Frank Crisp (1843–1919) was born and raised in Bungay in Suffolk. Although his original bent was to become an engineer, he determined upon the law. He was articled at the age of sixteen to a London firm of solicitors, and subsequently graduated with a BA and an LLB at London University. He was admitted as a solicitor in 1869, and as his legal reputation grew, he was brought into partnership in 1871; in 1877 the name of the firm became Ashurst, Morris, Crisp & Co. His interest lay in company law, and he acted for such clients as foreign railway companies and the Imperial Japanese Navy. Known in his youth as 'The Cat' (because he always fell on his feet), he was 'Spyed' in *Vanity Fair* in 1890 [fig. 23], and dubbed 'The Lord High Accoucheur of Joint-stock Companies'.[3] Crisp was legal adviser to the Liberal Party and for this service he received a baronetcy in 1913.

Sir Frank was for many years as renowned for his knowledge of alpine gardening as of the law, and to his last was keenly interested in horticulture, microscopy, natural history and landscape gardening.[4] He became a leading member of the Royal Microscopical Society and the Linnean Society, and acquired a great interest in mediaeval gardens. He began to indulge his interest in garden and architectural design in 1889 with the acquisition of the Friar Park Estate, perched on a hill above Henley-on-Thames in Oxfordshire. Crisp swiftly set about improving the place with the energy and enthusiasm that characterised all his endeavours: he rebuilt the house to his own idiosyncratic design, with the assistance of the architect M. Clarke Edwards, in the 'light ecclesiastical', or French flamboyant and 'highly diversified' Gothic taste [fig. 24].[5] While the exterior bristled with towers and pinnacles, the 'decorative principle of the Friar' pervaded the interiors: according to the 1919 sale catalogue, friars were met with at every point, from light switches to lamp stands.[6]

23
Sir Leslie Ward, 'Mr Frank Crisp', chromolithograph, *Vanity Fair* (31 May 1890).
National Portrait Gallery, London.

24

Anon., 'The House, Friar Park, Henley-on-Thames', 1924, postcard. Private collection. The idiosyncrasies of the mansion and its gardens were described at the time as characteristic of the humour of the proprietor.

The gardens were entirely built from scratch, encompassed dozens of acres, and were laid out over a series of terraces. Crisp collaborated with the landscape designer Henry Milner to create the 'veritable fairyland',[7] and it was his ambition from c.1898 to throw his grounds open to the public – 'from the highest in the land to the poor East-Ender' – on the payment of a small fee, with the whole amount derived from this source devoted to charitable services.[8] Visitors were welcomed every Wednesday from May until October; a guidebook was available from c.1898, and by 1914 visitors could purchase handsomely annotated, fold-up colour plans prepared in the mediaeval style by the calligrapher Alan Tabor. The gardens were immensely popular, drawing visitors from Britain and abroad. Crisp informed the editor of The Times that by August 1913 he had admitted more than 100,000 visitors, and during that fifteen-year period there had only been three cases of 'definite damage'.[9]

Among the gardens included in the visitors' circuit were a maze; a Japanese Garden; a formal 'Dutch flower-garden' ('prim and model-like as possible');[10] an Elizabethan Garden laid out with 'charmingly natural colonies of old-fashioned flowers ... walks of rambling roses, rosemary and lavender to give the effect in

FRIAR PARK

25
Anon., 'Cut Trees, Friar Park, Henley', c.1920, postcard. Private collection.

grey, all shades of crimson and purple from choice groups of Japanese maples';[11] and an old English garden crammed 'full of Conifers and other trees trained in imitative and grotesque shapes and interspersed with curious sun-dials'.[12] Some of the topiaries were in the shape of 'afternoon tea-tables, peacocks, presentation-cups, columns, pyramids, and ovals',[13] and some bore a striking resemblance to the early microscopes in Crisp's collection [fig. 25].[14] The bog garden formed a 'large and conspicuous feature of the gardens',[15] as did the Pinetum and Rhododendron Dell. The flower garden at the east front of the house was laid out in the Dutch taste with geometrical beds, edged with box and the walks laid with 'finely-broken' bricks. Most curious of all was Nebuchadnezzar's 'Garden of all Grasses, dated 570 B.C.'.[16]

As Crisp, like Lady Broughton, had a taste for Alpine gardening, the *pièce de résistance* was the 1.6-hectare/4-acre Alpine Garden, the far end of which was crowned by an 'exact model in miniature of the real Matterhorn'. The mountain was formed of thousands of tons of York gritstone; the peak 'came from the top of the real Matterhorn', and the slopes were mantled with 'snow' produced by pulverised Derbyshire spar [fig. 26].[17] A correspondent for the *Gardeners' Chronicle* remarked in 1899:

A MOUNTAIN YOU CAN STEP OVER:
THE MATTERHORN IN A GARDEN.

26

Anon., 'A Mountain You Can Step Over: The Matterhorn in a Garden', photograph, *The Sketch* (2 September 1908). Private collection.

The correspondent to *The Sketch* remarked that in these Oxfordshire Alps, 'sparkling torrents rush down from the heights … [and] the mountain's peak stands out as boldly as though it were indeed 5000 feet above the snow-field at its base.'

It stretches over a great space of ground, and there are represented in it mountains of greater and lesser height, valleys, mountain-passes ... rustic alpine bridges, overlooking quite formidable precipices; a waterfall, &c. The waterfall commences at the highest point in the rockery, and after winding and twisting in innumerable directions, for a moment conspicuous, then hidden for a time, at last runs into a small pool surrounded by a little greensward at the lowest point.[18]

A contributor to *Country Life* in 1905 was no less enthusiastic in his assessment of this 'portion of the Alps in miniature', declaring that 'only those who have seen the huge natural rocks and boulders, and little crags and pathways winding here and there, can realise the stupendous work involved' [fig. 27].[19]

Visitors not only wandered over alpine landscape: they threaded their way beneath it through an extensive network of caverns and chambers, planned, designed and executed by T. B. Harpham. Day trippers expressed wonder at the grotesque effect produced by colonies of owls and owlets, toads and elves, and at the 'skillfully made ... "illusions"' deployed in the depths[20] – all of which were ingeniously illuminated by electric lights (then a novelty). Most entrancing of all was the 'ice-grotto', enriched with 'counterfeit stalactites that look like icicles' and modelled on the original at the Grindelwald glacier.[21]

The planting of the Alpine scenery, like all of Crisp's creations, was characteristically eclectic, and included species from alpine regions across the globe juxtaposed in a strikingly original fashion:

Everywhere, in happiest combinations of form and colour, is lavished an exuberance of floral life; mountain vegetation has been summoned from every clime to play its part; natives of the Alps consort with those of the Himalaya and of Japan; New Zealand challenges the Arctic, Canada Cathay; the cacti of Mexico spread their thorns near rhododendrons of our Alps, and mountain orchids lift modest spikes beside the schizocodon, the famous soldanella of Nippon.[22]

The 'contriver', Sir Frank, and his 'able assistant, his head gardener, Mr Knowles', were warmly praised by Charles T. Druery writing in the *Gardeners' Magazine* for the 'careful study of geological conditions, and the needs of alpine plants, destined to occupy it'. Part of this credit must also be shared with James Pulham and James Backhouse of York, both of whom had considerable experience in designing and building rockeries.

An immense excavation was necessary to form a veritable valley, whose sides were destined to be walled in and diversified on natural lines ... Over and over again these unwieldy masses had to be shifted and rearranged to satisfy the fastidious

Building Imitation Alps of Rocks and

Every well regulated Alpine garden must have a rocking stone. This shows the carefully balanced imitation at Friar Park

This picture gives a good idea of the great size of the rocks used in making the Alpine garden. A total of 7000 tons was required

27
'Building Imitation Alps of Rocks and Concrete on an English Nobleman's Estate', photograph, *Popular Science Monthly* (August 1918).

taste of the owner ... It was not a mere question of picturesque massing, but also of contriving the myriad congenial nooks, recesses, pockets and tiny platforms, in and on which alpine plants could thrive, and make themselves truly at home.[23]

At the foot of the mountain Crisp formed a 'lake in miniature where trout dispute with tortoises, and aquatic plants in great number display their graces', on the edge of which he built a 'little châlet, a sort of Alpine refuge'. This was, according to the Swiss horticulturist and mountaineer Henry Correvon (1854–1939), 'Sir Frank's favourite view-point for showing off his work; it is the headquarters of the garden, from which have been issued the orders and counter-orders till all has been declared complete.' Here, too, was displayed a 'little bronze model of the Matterhorn which Sir Frank had made for the entertainment of his guests'.[24]

William Robinson pronounced the Alpine Garden 'the best natural stone rock garden I have ever seen', and E. H. Jenkins decreed it 'the noblest example of a rock garden this or any other country has ever seen' [fig. 28].²⁵ Correvon was among the most extravagant in his praise: visiting Crisp's 'rocky flower-gemmed mountain-side' in 1913, he found himself so 'carried in spirit to my native Alps' that he caught himself 'whistling an Alpine song':

> The sight of the Matterhorn under an English sky, ocular assurance that our old lion of Zermatt lifts his sharp-cut outline on the banks of the Thames, cannot fail to interest a Swiss Alpinist. Yet this spectacle, unique though it be in the art of landscape gardening, would not of itself have inspired me confidently to place this rock garden in a class by itself. A copy must always be inferior to an original, and it ill becomes a past president of the Swiss Alpine Club to fall into raptures before an English Matterhorn. It is rather this: throughout the whole design of the Alpine garden at Friar Park there is, from the first, a peculiar and compelling impression of unparalleled extent and grandeur. Some three acres of ground are occupied; more than seven thousand tons of rock are already pressed into service. A portion remains still under construction; its completion will extend the area to four acres, and ten thousand tons of millstone grit will have been conveyed some two hundred miles from Yorkshire.²⁶

The 'Old climber' speculated that it represented an 'immense expenditure of energy, a veritable toil of Titans, for some of the blocks employed (shifted, too, it may be, more than once) weigh as much as twelve and a-half tons':²⁷

> Yet all this gigantic architecture would go for nothing if it were not artistic in the highest sense. Here Sir Frank Crisp, who, with the aid of his head gardener, Mr. F. Knowles, has created this fair prospect, shows a master's skill, for the secret of the success achieved is harmony of line, sense of proportion and contrast, and above all, the art with which a scale has been given to the whole. So harmonious is the picture, so charming are the proportions, that one feels suddenly transported to the secret heart of Alpine nature.²⁸

Correvon records that he once took a group of over 120 Continental visitors around the garden – all of whom uttered 'admiring exclamations':

28
Anon., 'Rocks and Rills', photograph, *Country Life* (5 August 1905).
The rills were designed to provide 'suitable places for the plants which delight in damp soil and cool air'.

29
Anon., 'The Wishing Well Cave, Friar Park', photograph, *Visitor's Guide Book* (1914).
Private collection.
A correspondent to the *Gardeners' Chronicle* remarked in October 1899 that 'the bewilderment and delusion effected by the display of mirrors set at various angles is perfect.'

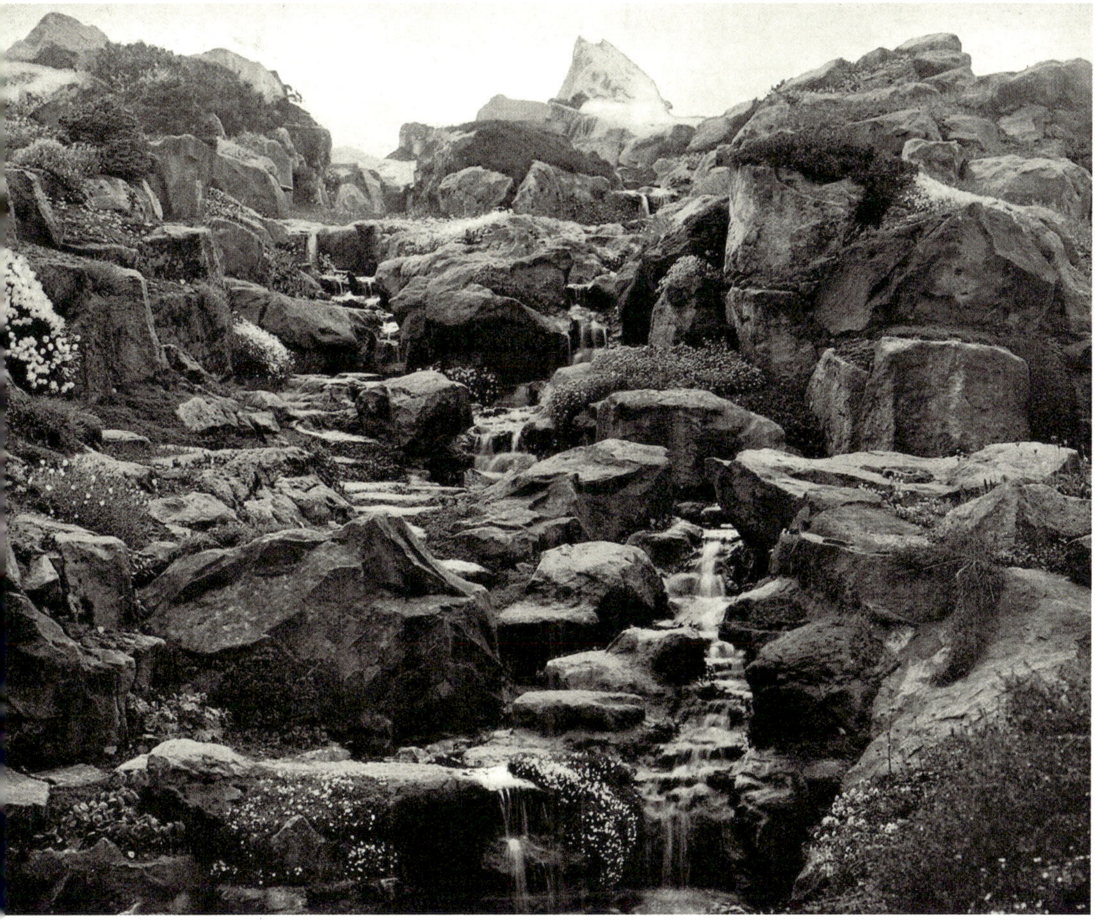

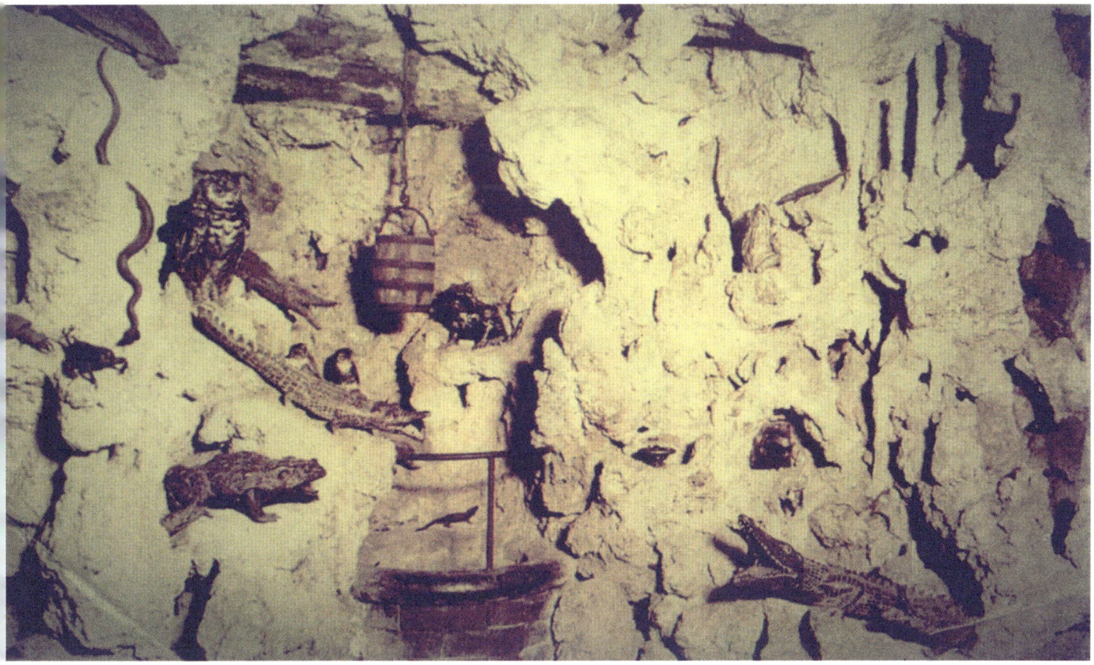

Ladies begged permission to gather edelweiss growing upon the sunny rocks and carry the flowers as precious trophies back to France and Belgium. Among the loudest in his admiration was His Imperial Highness the Archduke Francis Ferdinand, Crown Prince of Austria, when he found upon the slopes a complete collection of flora of the high Tyrolean Alps. He could scarcely trust his eyes, and wondered whether he were the victim of an optical illusion. Nor can the sense of illusion be questioned; indeed, therein lies the true value of the landscape. Every detail proclaims the creative will, not of an architect, but of an artist who has willed to reproduce at home Alpine nature as she is.[29]

The Swiss mountaineer's effusive rhetoric is reminiscent of John and Jane Loudon's praise for Dame Eliza's alpine rockwork at Hoole – which both he and Crisp must have known.

Many of the most revelatory accounts of the gardens come from visitors – most of whom were bemused, astonished or bewildered, and all of whom praised Crisp's generosity for allowing them to inspect the gardens. Many passed comment as well on the 'many and strange … proverbs, legends, illusions, etc. to be met with in this wonderful garden'.[30]

Not everyone was enraptured with Sir Frank's rockwork: Lady Ottoline Morrell, who was entertained by Sir Frank at Friar Park around 1902, records with restrained irony how her host 'worked hard, and earned and ate much, and diverted his mind from company promoting by erecting sham Swiss mountains and passes decorated by China chamois, which had to be spied through Zeiss glasses, and elaborate caves and underground lakes, lit up with electricity, and festooned with artificial grapes, spiders and other monsters' [fig. 29].[31] Montague Free – the head gardener at the Brooklyn Botanical Garden – thought it 'one of the largest and most pretentious rock gardens in existence'.[32] Charles Thonger writing in 1907 regretted 'that the owner of that most precious heritage, an old-fashioned English garden, should be so misled as to convert a sunken court into an Alpine peepshow, which might serve as a sixpenny attraction at Earl's Court':

Until the advent of this pernicious stone work, nothing could have been more beautiful than this sunken lawn with its weathered sun dial, and terraced borders of herbaceous flowers, completely encircling it like the holiday throng at a Grecian amphitheatre … the place is surrounded by an absurd range of beetling crags and frowning cliffs; the ground is strewn with tufa boulders. Small paths and rocky steps suggest a maze, and horresco referens, this 'garden' is approached by rockwork tunnels, in which there is sufficient light to reveal rows of artificial stalactites![33]

A contributor to *Country Life* in 1929 was equally disapproving, advising readers that 'any inclination to create miniature Matterhorns crowned with chamois, Edelweiss and the rest should be sternly suppressed.'[34]

Crisp's model Matterhorn was not in fact the first 'scale Matterhorn' to be raised in south-east England: in mid-March 1889 an 'awe-inspiring model of the towering Matterhorn' had been erected for the Ice Carnival held in the Great Hall at the Royal Albert Hall. A correspondent from the *St James's Gazette* reported at the time that the ephemeral peak, which completed the 'wintry effect' of a huge panorama of the Alps, 'invites the inquiring to mount and obtain a bird's-eye view of the whole scene'.[35]

The Henley Matterhorn was, however, a much more complex, living and lasting miniaturised facsimile of the 'old lion of Zermatt'. Its popular success may be in a large measure due to its optical effects and illusionistic devices that Crisp and his co-conspirators deployed with great mastery – from the presence of distorting mirrors in the subterranean chambers beneath the Matterhorn to the bold, triangular peak of the mountain itself.

The pleasure of illusion depends not only upon its power to convince but also upon the awareness that it *is* in fact an illusion. Were it to delude the viewer entirely, there would be no sense of the ingenuity and play of wit involved – and no reminder of the intriguingly labile character of human perception in general. Correvon, who was so 'suddenly transported to the secret heart of Alpine nature', was aware of this; he recognised that Crisp's compelling impression of unparalleled extent and grandeur was, despite its immense solidity, an effect of visual trickery. Looking up to the peak from Sir Frank's favourite viewpoint he contemplated the picture before him:

> *From this châlet many and many a visitor must have carried away an impression that I have often felt – of a peaceful, fairly-ordered prospect, in which one finds a balanced harmony of Alpine life and Alpine vegetation. Butterflies are foraging, the stream goes murmuring by or breaks in waterfalls; the flowers sing eternal praises to their Maker. But lo! Abruptly comes a bird, perchance a simple sparrow; he perches on the Matterhorn, and with the ruin of the scale every illusion tumbles down, for the charm is broken.*[36]

Having heard of his fame, many visitors come
To judge for themselves of his wonderful home.
Just now there are two, He's too kind to complain
Yet he doubtless alone would prefer to remain.
The one is all active, the other looks on
Whilst owner is wishing them both to be gone.
If Longnose don't mind with his lumbering ladder,
He'll soon come to grief. Now what could be sadder?

[FOUR]

Sir Charles Isham's Gardens at Lamport Hall: 'A Disconcerting Eruption'

IN THE LATE 1890S SIR CHARLES ISHAM GLOOMILY PREDICTED THAT the 'enchanted bit of ground' that he had so lovingly created and ceaselessly cultivated and improved for over half a century would, on his departure from his family's Northamptonshire estate, be obliterated: 'Its doom is sealed the day I leave Lamport. No one has ever touched it but [my]self and no one has or ever will have knowledge to maintain it in anything like its present condition.'[1] It would, he concluded, 'be the wisest thing to remove it altogether'.[2]

Sir Charles Edmund Isham, 10th Baronet (1819–1903), was an inspired rural improver and gardener [fig. 30]. Educated at Rugby School and at Brasenose College, Oxford, he succeeded to the baronetcy in 1846. The following year he married Emily Vaughan (d.1898), daughter of Sir John Vaughan, Justice of the Court of Common Pleas. From 1847, Isham dedicated himself almost entirely to improving his family estate – rebuilding cottages in the village in a decorative style and recasting the pleasure grounds around the Hall. Unlike most members of his social class, Sir Charles rigidly refrained from alcohol and smoking, and opposed all blood sports; and from the 1850s his approach to gardening, and indeed to daily life, was immeasurably enriched by his lively and pioneering enthusiasm for homeopathy, 'Modern Spiritualism' or 'Psychic Science', and mesmerism.[3] To these beliefs, which were not in themselves unusual at the time, may also be added his endorsement of vegetarianism – his views on which he set to verse in a familiar and humorous style in 'The Food that We Live On: Instructive, Astounding, Terrible, True' (c.1877).[4]

Lamport Hall had been in the Isham family since the close of the sixteenth century. When Sir Charles succeeded to the family estate, the house had two principal fronts, one facing the village, in the style that prevailed during the reign of Queen Elizabeth I, and the other towards the road, which had been

30
Hudson & Kearns, Sir Charles Isham at Lamport Hall, c.1900, photograph.
Lamport Hall, Northamptonshire. Reproduced with permission of
the Trustees of Lamport Hall.

31
Anon., 'Seven Box Bowers on the Lawn', c.1895, photograph.
Lamport Hall, Northamptonshire. Reproduced with permission of
the Trustees of Lamport Hall.

recast in the mid-seventeenth century by John Webb. The grounds were 'beautifully diversified in the surface' but generally undistinguished.[5]

The 10th Baronet immediately set about to make some unusual and lasting contributions to the grounds – among them the Box Bowers and the Eagle Walk. It is believed that the bases for what became known as the 'bowers' were originally planted in the 1750s as formal box hedges that subsequently took on a life of their own. It was reported in the *Gardeners' Chronicle* in 1897 that 'they have since thriven in such an extraordinary manner that, by degrees, the central trees have been removed, the Box has filled the space, and it has grown to a height of 20 or more feet. The branches have also extended laterally to a great distance, and the lower ones falling upon the ground, have become layered naturally.'[6] Sir Charles took the imaginative decision to carve entrances into the various groups to form bowers – or 'inner rooms' – and marked this achievement in verse in the 1880s: 'Seven box bowers on the lawn, more than 12 decades old; / With loving hands and anxious care, fresh beauties still unfold' [fig. 31].[7]

No less singular was the Eagle Walk – a broad path flanked with 72 Irish yews planted between 1847 and 1849 [fig. 32]. The baronet clipped and shaped the trees himself, and 'there were not two of them of the same appearance.' In 1897 the sentinels were described as supplying 'a certain weirdness' to the 'somewhat novel picture' of the avenue.[8] Near the extremity of this long walk

32
Anon., Eagle Walk, Lamport Hall, *c.*1900, photograph. Lamport Hall, Northamptonshire. Reproduced with permission of the Trustees of Lamport Hall.

were three enormous cages, reputed in 1869 to have been occupied by a pair of eagles and a horned owl.[9] One of these birds must have been 'Old Jamrach, the great eagle owl'.[10] A garden visitor recollects seeing in 1881, among the caged birds, an empty cage bearing the label: 'One stormy night I broke my head so consequently I am dead. For xxx years you've seen me here, so do not laugh, but shed a tear and call to mind that noted fowl Old Jamrach, the grand old Lamport owl.'[11]

The squire's favourite feature of the garden was his rockery, which lay concealed on the north side of high 'Picturesque Walls' of rough stone clothed with an abundance of flowering plants, set immediately adjacent to the garden front of the house [fig. 33].[12] In 1872 the eminent garden journalist Robert Fish was awestruck by the assemblage:

I had frequently heard, through friends, of the riches of this rockery in plants, &c., and my imagination had revelled in a scene of romantic wildness, where the narrowing overhanging defile, or chasmy dingle, had afforded an opportunity for the artist's skill in evoking ideas of the times when the old giants piled hill upon mountain, or just pitched from their large fists huge masses of stone from some far-off elevation, to enable us to note and compare the wondrous prowess of the past with the comparative weakness of the present. Such are some of the positions

33
G. S. Garrett, 'Lamport Hall – showing back of rockery …', photograph, *Strand Magazine*, 19, no. 110 (February 1900). Private collection.

for a good artificial rockery. Judge, then, my surprise on obtaining the first view of the rockery from the conservatory, and in such nearness to an elegant mansion! Of all positions this, at first sight, seemed to be the strangest. Some would at once determine, without seeing it, that it would be as much out of place in its position as a rough basket formed of tree-roots immediately in front of a Grecian temple.[13]

He was furthermore astonished that notwithstanding the proximity of the rockery to the house, 'no such violent contrast is exhibited':

Except from the conservatory and a bedroom window or two, from no part of the house or grounds do you see much of the rockery until you get inside it. The greatest height in points, and sweeping and swelling curves, is on top of a straight wall on the lawn side, that wall running in a line with the end of the conservatory. That wall was screened with evergreens; but there being a want of neatness about them they were removed, and white-variegated Ivy plants are now growing against it, and will soon cover it. Studs and wire are also placed on the wall, so as to train a few Roses, Clematis, &c., thinly, to give a light, airy appearance to the Ivy.[14]

Once inside, Fish forgot entirely about its position, and focused instead on the rockery's 'deep recesses, bold protrusions, mounds as if fallen from ruins, depressions as of the remains of partly filled moats, and all grouped and studded with next-to-endless varieties of rock and alpine plants'.[15]

Another correspondent writing in the *Gardeners' Chronicle* in 1897 was intrigued to find that there had been 'no attempt to make it resemble a ruin by using columns or such objects; but its shadowy caves, its studied finish, its ruggedness, its extremes, are striking'. He continued:

The Lamport rockery is not remarkable for an extensive variety of alpine plants. The intention has been to clothe it suitably, that the effect of the whole may be pleasing and picturesque, and that every plant when viewed individually should appear to be in just its right position. It is more correct to say that the plants have been selected to clothe the rockery, than the latter was constructed for the growth of a collection of plants.[16]

Though the rockery was less richly and exotically planted than other contemporary examples, there was great novelty in the manner in which the baronet cultivated his charges:

It may be said here that every stone of which the structure is composed has been placed in position by the owner himself, or by his direction, and in his presence. He has done the planting, and no other person has anything to do with it unless by his instruction ... No plant that grows quickly is a favourite for this structure. Everything is in miniature, and if the plants are not so naturally, then their cultivation is directed to that end. It is full of plant curiosities. A stunted individual that refuses to make free growth is just the kind of plant that is sought. Dwarf Conifers form one of its features, and Sir Charles has been at some trouble to procure them. Some of them are known to be upwards of seventy years old, and have not made more than three feet natural growth.[17]

These plants were not only of great age – they were also partly cloaked with ivy 'just as much over its host as it is allowed to do' [fig. 34].[18] According to the correspondent, the strangest looking object among the conifers was a 'diminutive fir, probably seventy years old':

It has five straggling roots, the ends of which only have penetrated between the stones, whilst a few inches of each, and the base of the plants are suspended and disclosed. Evidently when the plant had become established, the stones have been picked away from the roots so far as it was safe to do this. Thus to a large extent, the root system as well as the part that is usually above ground, may be seen.[19]

Among the plants emerging from the alpine setting were 'Utah Agave', Japanese maples, variegated box and variegated bramble – the latter hanging over the rocks and caves. There were also a variety of groundcovers, including common tansy, house leeks, meadow rue and 'a species of hardy Euphorbia'.[20]

Sir Charles was not bothered that many of his plants did not flower – indeed, he formed the rockery against a north-facing wall with a view to suppressing flowering: 'Species that do not flower on the rockery usually present a good appearance for the greater part of the year, but flowering species are apt to look "weedy directly they have bloomed".' The exception to this rule was in spring, when 'almost the whole face of the rockery is clothed with Aubretia deltoides, and it is a sight not to be forgotten.'[21]

Two other features of the rockery captivated the reporter: the Crystal Cave formed of quartz and other uncommon materials, and 'the pretty miniature

34
E. W. Smith, 'View of the Rockery in Sir Charles Isham's Garden', c.1895, photograph. Lamport Hall, Northamptonshire. Reproduced with permission of the Trustees of Lamport Hall.

Mrs Newsham – an admirer of Charles Isham's gardens – exclaimed, 'Sir Charles Isham is an artist who has not *painted* a glimpse of a most beautiful world, but with true artistic patience has *built* it for us; using Nature's own resources to adorn his beautiful ideal world.'

35
G. S. Garrett, 'Gnomes, with Inscription', photograph, Strand Magazine, 19, no. 110 (February 1900). Private collection.

Having heard of his fame, many visitors come
To judge for themselves of his wonderful home.
Just now there are two, He's too kind to complain
Yet he doubtless alone would prefer to remain.
The one is all active, the other looks on
Whilst owner is wishing them both to be gone.
If Longnose don't mind with his lumbering ladder,
He'll soon come to grief. Now what could be sadder?

36
G. S. Garrett, 'On Strike', photograph, *Strand Magazine*, 19, no. 110 (February 1900). Private collection.

Garrett found it 'extremely difficult' to photograph the figures, which were only 6–7 cm/2–3 inches in height.

37
G. S. Garrett, 'The Little Lady from Brussels', c.1897–8, photograph. Lamport Hall, Northamptonshire. Reproduced with permission of the Trustees of Lamport Hall.

Herbert Pratt remarked in the *Strand Magazine* that she was 'a giantess amongst the pigmies'. After her arrival in the garden she was 'presented with a gorgeous hat and a diamond ring by two interested visitors'.

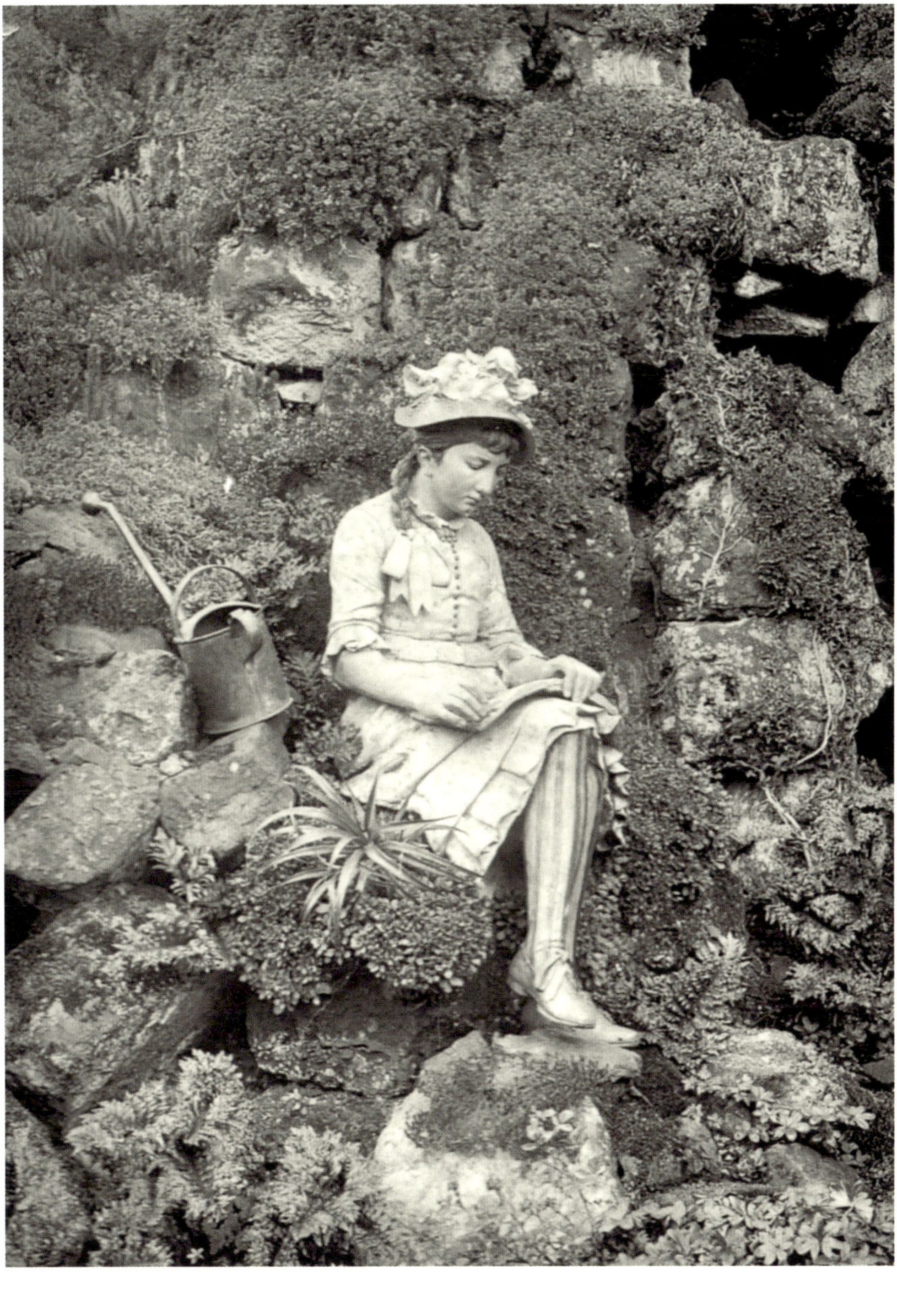

figures or models a few inches high, that represent gnomes or fairy miners at work in the caves and crevices' [fig. 35]. Some of these figures, he observes, 'have caught the trade union spirit and are "on strike"', and were posed loitering by a placard hoisted at the entrance to a crevice, bearing the old rhyme: 'Eight hours Sleep / Eight hours Play / Eight hours Work /Eight shillings pay' [fig. 36].[22] The figures 'certainly increase the weirdness novelty of the scene; whilst the positions some of them have been placed in at Lamport are suggestive of reality. One of these is lying at full length upon a rock gazing over the ledge; at others, apparently walking beneath.'[23]

The correspondent was also startled by the presence – amidst the gnomes – of yet another whimsical conceit: a life-size figure, in painted terracotta, of a 'Paradoxical Lady ... natural to a point of alarming', sitting upon a rock reading a book, which is held in her hands [fig. 37]. The baronet reports:

> ... She graced the Brussels Exhibition ...
> There was a time she sad, but proud,
> Was gazed on by the London crowd.
> Next, rescued from a bankrupt stock,
> She found her home beneath this rock.
> She in winter hibernates,
> But in the season reinstates.[24]

Published accounts abound of Sir Charles's bizarre 'mountain scenery in miniature', and its '"forest-trees" of Chinese minuteness – vegetable dwarfs – grown between big boulders, which afford shelter to pigmy figures of weird and strange appearance'.[25] Viewers – some of whom likened themselves to 'Gulliver amongst the Lilliputians' – generally expressed bewilderment at the quaintness and originality of the 'Fairy Wildernesses', and the lifelike effect of its inhabitants [fig. 38].[26] They also invariably commented on the great labour and thought expended on the structure.[27]

The baronet's own accounts of his rockery provide us with insights into the artist and the constructor. It should, he affirms, 'exhibit a combination of opposite extremes, the utmost wildness of construction, with the highest cultivation. It should be trained that the crevices remain open to produce an effect of light and shade.'[28]

In 'Notes on Gnomes and Remarks on Rock Gardens: The Lamport Rockery' (1888 edn) [fig. 39] he provides an overview of his composition:

> [It] may be described as a carefully constructed combination of caves, crevices and inequalities carpeted and incrusted not so much with botanical treasures as with

a limited selection of more or less common close growing vegetation calculated to adapt themselves to required purposes. A Rock Garden based on these principles, provided it be thoroughly maintained, will be not only attractive throughout all seasons, but, quite unlike the ordinary garden, will be continually improving.

Therefore, whenever inquiries are made as to when the Lamport Rockery is in its beauty? 'Now' would be no inapt reply, and should any person at first sight exclaim from the depth of the soul, 'I never before saw anything like this!' there might be added the following rejoinder. 'There is probably no other piece of ground of such limited dimensions any where to be found which has received so much minute and constant culture over a period of forty years.'[29]

He reports that although the rockery was begun in 1847, it 'has been under almost daily improvements up to the present time, 1888':

Most of these to a casual observer might appear trifling or even contemptible, but it is these which to an observant eye, as in a highly finished painting produces a lasting impression not obtainable in a production of the ordinary type. The

38
Sir Charles Isham, 'Vision of Fairy Blacksmiths at Work', pencil drawing with coloured highlights, in Emily (1899). Lamport Hall, Northamptonshire. Reproduced with permission of the Trustees of Lamport Hall.

This image accompanied an account of fairy blacksmiths witnessed in Anglesey and communicated by Isham, who remarked: 'There are many exquisite china figures of Gnomes on the [Lamport] Rockery, this is added in explanation. I could give several other authentic cases of fairies, even much more remarkable than the following ones.'

> Lamport Rockery impresses visitors with strangely various feelings. One exclaims 'How natural'! Another 'How like a ruin'![,]whilst a third would fain assume the proportions of a fairy to be enabled more thoroughly to enjoy the grove of pigmy spruce firs which fringe the margin of the Lilliputian lake.[30]

In a later edition of his 'Notes' (1894), Isham reveals his inspiration for rockery:

> The idea of introducing life-like diminutive figures into gardens as set off to pygmy trees was first advocated sixty years ago by Mr Loudon when a woodcut in one of his portly volumes gave expression to his idea. The realisation was probably first seen at Lamport where beautifully modelled figures of gnomes three inches high were established twenty years ago, when they were obtainable in the china shops. They represent the Berg-geister, or mountain spirits, of the Germans.[31]

The engraving referred to above is presumably one of the views of Lady Broughton's rockwork at Hoole House reproduced in 1838 in the *Gardener's Magazine* [see figs 19 and 20].

39
Sir Charles Isham, cover of 'Notes on Gnomes and Remarks on Rock Gardens' (1884). Lamport Hall, Northamptonshire. Reproduced with permission of the Trustees of Lamport Hall.
This pamphlet was, like 'The Food that We Live On', designed and printed by the author, every page bearing floral or geometrical designs, and the text written in round hand with bold capitals as easy to read as ordinary type.

40

Miss Dryden, 'Lamport Rockery', c.1897–8 photograph. Lamport Hall,
Northamptonshire. Reproduced with permission of the Trustees of Lamport Hall.

Herbert Pratt remarked that 'these figures ... and their fairy-like proportions, combined
with their surroundings of dwarf trees and miniature caves, compel one to imagine
himself in another world.'

The baronet developed his fascination with gnomes or mountain spirits in the early 1860s; he did not, however, acquire any 'life-like diminutive figures' until 1874. Although gnomes – that is, imaginary beings said to inhabit the bowels of the earth and to be guardians of mines – had appeared in British literature from the early nineteenth century, Sir Charles pioneered the idea of deploying physical models of them in British gardens. He presumably became acquainted with traditional *Gnomen-Figuren* or 'folklore figures' during his travels in Germany in 1847, where they were used by miners as talismans when they descended into the mines.[32] The fairy blacksmiths at Lamport performed a similar function: they served as apotropaic wardens of the Ishams' house and gardens.

There has been much speculation regarding the provenance, and indeed the manufacture and physical composition, of Sir Charles's battalions of miniature miners [fig. 40]. He remarks in 'Vision of Fairy Blacksmiths at

Work' (1889) that his rockery was inhabited by 'exquisite china figures of Gnomes'.[33] He does not say when and where he acquired them. Such matters were, to him, immaterial; his desire to collect and publish testimonials of 'authentic cases of fairies', and particularly those that portrayed them at miniature smithies 'working busily at the bellows and upon two anvils', suggests that he was more absorbed by the 'real' lives and activities of these sentient 'men of dwarfish proportions'. As Sir Charles remarked in 1884, 'had Gnomes been imaginary creations, they would not have been admitted into the Lamport Rockery. Although the nature of Gnomes is at present very obscure, it like all other occult phenomena is receiving attention through the world. Seeing such things is no longer an indication of mental delusion, but rather EXTENSION OF FACULTY.'[34]

He evidently felt the necessity to explain to his garden visitors the tableaux of fairy blacksmiths that they encountered within the rockery. Small placards inscribed with handwritten doggerel verse supplied both descriptions and messages:

> *Under a saxifrage, beautiful home!*
> *There peacefully rests a diminutive gnome.*
> *His food is pure nectar contained in a jug,*
> *Can any kind friend find a suitable mug?*
> *He dwells in this paradise mostly alone,*
> *With occasional calls of a big drumbedrone.*
> *The saxifrage, tufty and perfectly grown,*
> *May compare with a gem in a setting of stone.*[35]

Garden visitors abounded between 1868 and the late 1890s as the Ishams hosted a great number of annual 'grand fêtes' for the benefit of the friends of the Northamptonshire Orphanage for Girls – among the largest of which, in 1869, attracted over 5,000.[36] Sir Charles composed and published verses for these events, including 'Delights of Lamport', 'The Wonders of Lamport and the Orphanage Fete' – all of which extend a genial and hearty welcome to his guests, and celebrate the restorative power of nature.[37]

It is perhaps not surprising that Sir Charles should have emphasised the therapeutic value of his gardens: gardening the rockery was to the baronet not merely what his friend Henry Ormond Nethercote described as a 'never-failing course of amusement', it was an all-consuming passion.[38] By his own admission, he spent as much time as possible in his rockery, titivating and remodelling his abiding obsession. Indeed, so besotted was Sir Charles with it that he extended the Hall eastwards and built his bedroom on the first floor overlooking it, so that he could get a clear view of the rockwork first thing every morning.

The rockery at Lamport Hall, like many great living works of art, was perceived in the eyes of its creator as something so intensely personal and idiosyncratic, and its spirit and animation so wholly reliant on the perpetual stewardship of its originator, that it could not survive him. Sir Charles himself remarked wistfully in 1899: 'so soon as the soul leaves the visible constructor, so soon will the soul depart from that structure.'[39] He was, of course, right: although his 'most artistic, quaint, weird semblance of reality' has in fact come down to us, it is no longer what its maker would have considered a living organism, but a soulless inanimate artefact.[40]

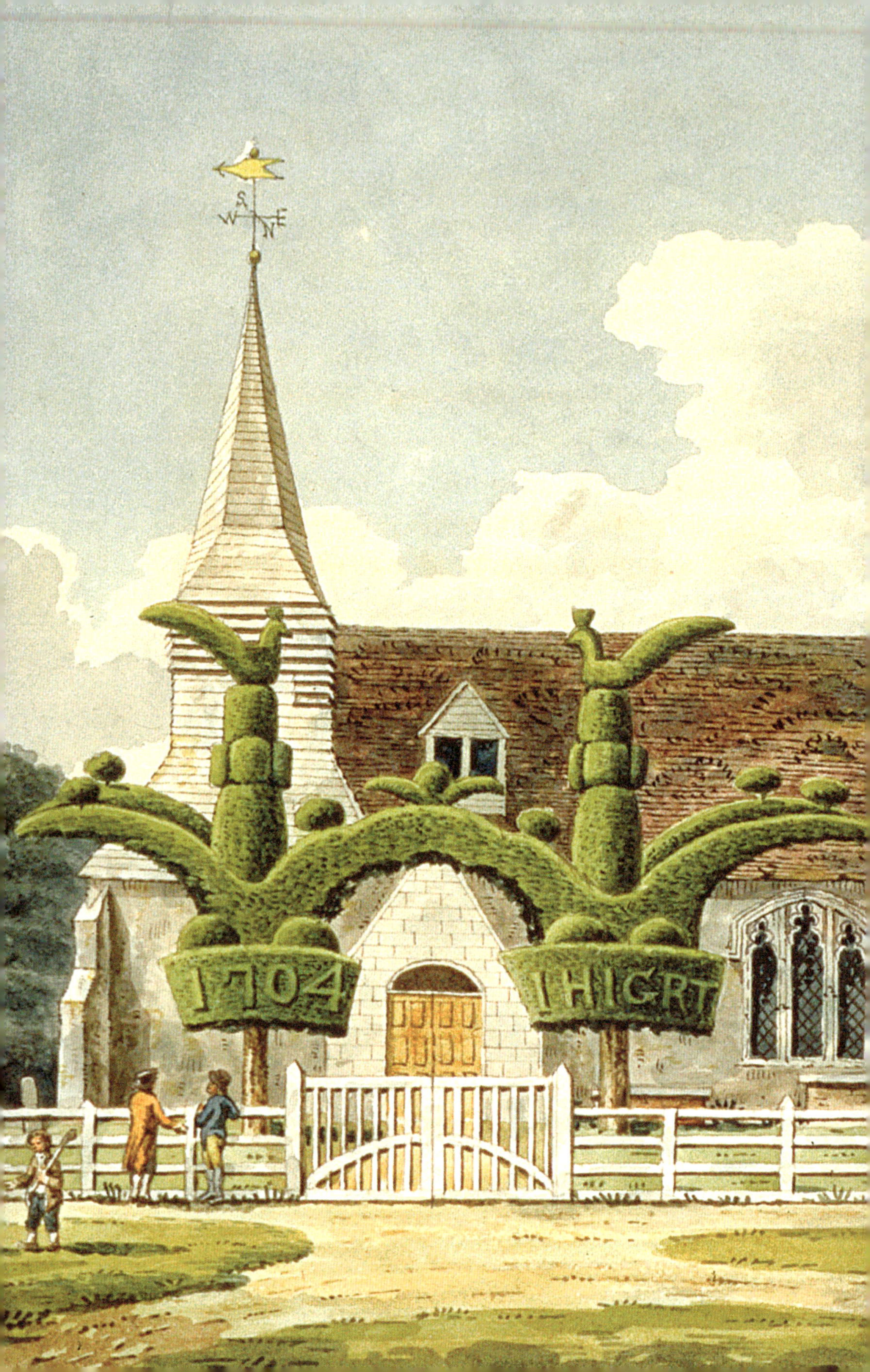
S
W
N
E
1704
I H I G R T

[FIVE]

Topiary on a Gargantuan Scale: The Clipped 'Yew-trees' at Four Ancient London Churchyards

ON A COLD AND BLUSTERY AFTERNOON IN THE EARLY AUTUMN OF 2004 a small celebration took place at St Mary the Virgin, East Bedfont in Middlesex, to commemorate the tercentenary of the Peacocks – two giant churchyard yews cut in topiary to resemble 'the beauteous birds of Juno' [fig. 41].[1] A small throng assembled in the mediaeval church to watch a production of Thomas Hood's *The Two Peacocks of Bedfont* (1822) – the poem that popularised the legend surrounding the origin of the 'two sombre peacocks'. Hood adapted a legend that the topiary giants represent two proud and haughty sisters who declined with disdain an offer of marriage made to one, or perhaps both, by a prominent local man and that he had the yews cut into the shape of two peacocks by way of revenge.[2]

Whatever the truth of this legend, the trees are among the most fantastical vegetable curiosities in London, and it is remarkable that they have survived at East Bedfont, now a suburban London village only a stone's throw from Heathrow Airport. Although giant clipped yew trees are recorded at a handful of suburban mediaeval churchyards, only the Peacocks resemble their former selves – the forms that they assumed when they were first sculpted in the eighteenth century. The ancient yews in the neighbouring parish churchyards of Harlington and Hillingdon are still flourishing, but they have not been shaped since the mid-1820s; and the ancient clipped tree that flourished in the churchyard of St Andrew, Enfield, in North London, was lost sometime in the last century.

Much has been written on the subject of topiary, and in particular on the vicissitudes of this much maligned art.[3] The cutting of trees and shrubs into curious figurative shapes is something of an English obsession. As Joseph Addison remarked in the *Spectator* in 1712, 'British Gardeners ... instead of humouring nature, love to deviate from it as much as possible. Our Trees rise in cones, globes and pyramids. We see the marks of the scissars upon every plant and bush.'[4] Although topiary is said to have very early and exotic origins – certainly as far back as the time of Pliny the Younger – the art was practised in England from at least the early sixteenth century, and accounts abound that describe legions of bizarre evergreen confections.[5] Perhaps the most famous examples are those that once inhabited the Mount Garden at Hampton Court, which were described by Thomas Platter in 1599 as

> *all manner of shapes, men and women, half men and half horse, sirens, serving-maids with baskets, French lilies and delicate crenellations all round made from the dry twigs bound together and the aforesaid evergreen quick-set shrubs, or entirely of rosemary, all true to the life, and so cleverly and amusingly interwoven, mingled and grown together, trimmed and arranged picture-wise that their equal would be difficult to find.*[6]

41
Anon., *St Mary Bedfont, Middlesex*, 1802, watercolour.
Heritage Image Partnership Ltd/Alamy Stock Photo.

Towards the end of the seventeenth century topiary became widely admired and practised, and many London nurserymen's shops were 'plentifully stocked' with evergreens and 'the like Moveable Plants'.[7] *Arte topiaria*, as it was sometimes known, was no longer, however, a royal or aristocratic conceit; it had slid down the social scale to become a popular – indeed, almost vernacular – art form practised by 'cits', tradesmen and antiquarians.[8] It also had many detractors, the most eloquent of whom was Alexander Pope, who remarked in the *Guardian* in 1713 that topiary was 'a politer sort of Ornament in the Villa's and Gardens adjacent to this great City, and in order to distinguish those places from the meer barbarous Countries of gross Nature, the World stands much in need of a Virtuoso Gardiner who has a Turn to Sculpture, and is thereby capable of improving upon the Ancients of his Profession in the Imagery of Ever-greens.' He continued: 'People of the common Level of Understanding are principally delighted with the little Niceties and Fantastical Operations of Art, and constantly think that *finest* is least Natural. A Citizen is no sooner Proprietor of a couple of Yews, but he entertains Thoughts of erecting them into Giants, like those of *Guild-hall*.'[9]

Whereas the use of small-scale yew topiary for the frivolous decoration of modest London gardens was a popular quick, bold, purposeful and inventively whimsical means of enhancing the setting of new domestic premises, the shaping of ancient gargantuan trees – such as the Peacocks at Bedfont – appears to have been a freakish deviation of the conventional practice, fuelled by an antiquarian impulse.[10] The object of this rarefied form of eighteenth-century churchyard art was to remodel ancient trees that grew in the lee of mediaeval churches to resemble relics of antiquity, hauling the past into the present by virtue of their enduring vitality. The attraction of the churchyard yews to the perpetrators of this art was that the origins of the trees, like the churches themselves, were ancient and obscure. Such trees were, in fact, sacred variants of 'Mr [Jacob] Bobard's Yew-men of the Guards to the Physick Garden', Oxford – a pair of 'Gyant' clipped yew sentinels which conferred a semblance of antiquity upon their surroundings [fig. 42].[11] The yews of Bedfont, Harlington, Hillingdon and Enfield were also 'Earth-born Gyants', but they sprang up from the 'London Mould' – they were therefore, unlike the 'Moveable plants' of the nurseryman, firmly rooted to their original settings, and as such they had considerable pedigree and bestowed fame upon their environs.[12]

The Harlington yew was probably the first of the London churchyard giants to be clipped [fig. 44]. When and why this 'Elder Taxas' that stands opposite the south porch of the church of St Peter and St Paul, Harlington (formerly known as Arlington), was first trimmed is a mystery, but by 1729 it

42
Jacob Bobard the elder standing in front of the Danby Gateway leading into the Oxford Physic Garden, engraving, frontispiece to Abel Evans, *Autumnus* (1713). Royal Collection Trust. © Her Majesty Queen Elizabeth II 2021.

Bobard's giant 'Yew-men' were placed on the opposite side of the gateway, greeting visitors as they entered the garden.

Poet IOHN SAXY upon his YEW-TREE Nov.r 1729.

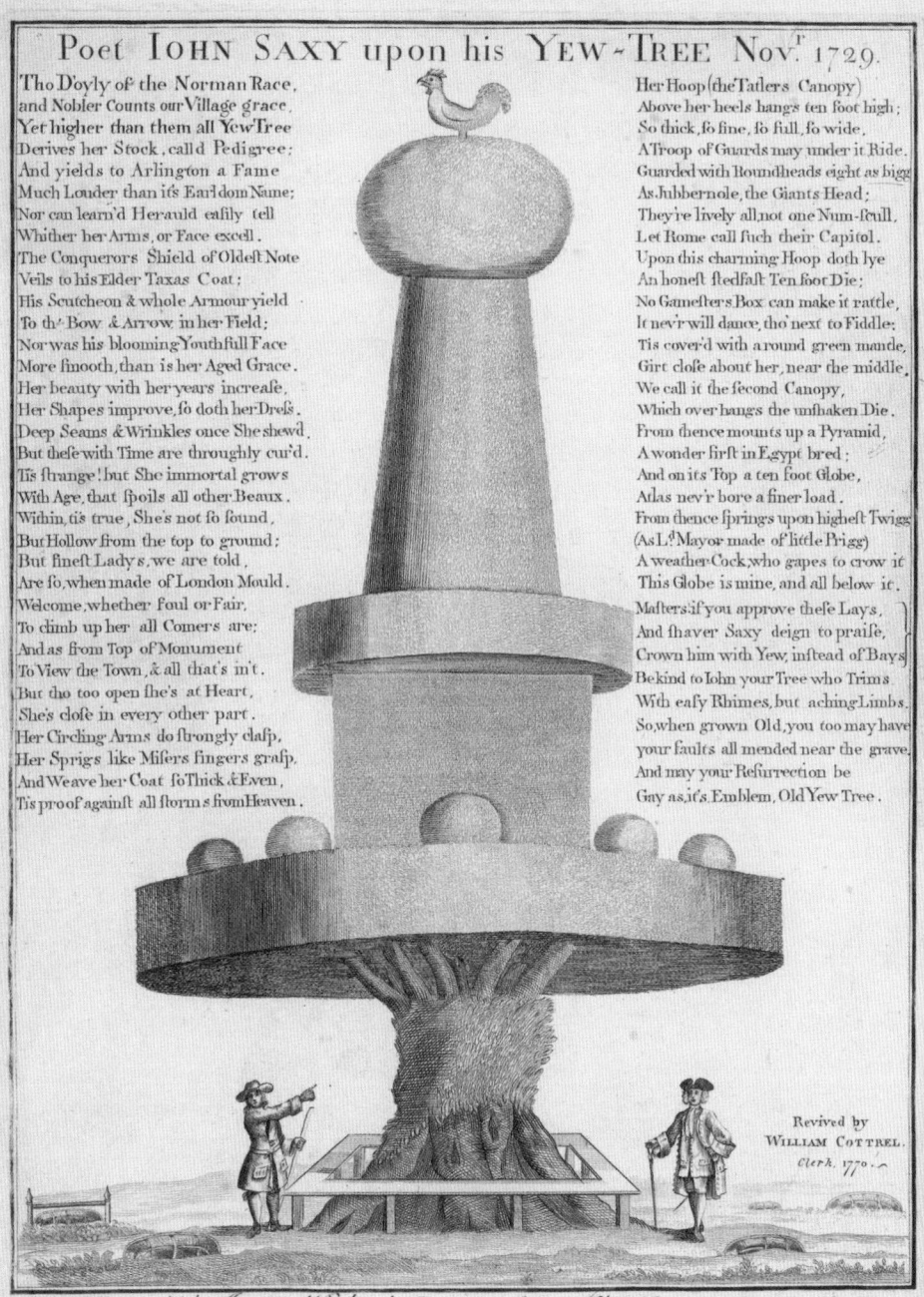

Tho D'oyly of the Norman Race,
and Nobler Counts our Village grace,
Yet higher than them all Yew Tree
Derives her Stock, call'd Pedigree;
And yields to Arlington a Fame
Much Louder than it's Earldom Name;
Nor can learn'd Herauld easily tell
Whither her Arms, or Face excell.
The Conquerors Shield of Oldest Note
Veils to his Elder Taxas Coat;
His Scutcheon & whole Armour yield
To th' Bow & Arrow, in her Field;
Nor was his blooming Youthfull Face
More smooth, than is her Aged Grace.
Her beauty with her years increase,
Her Shapes improve, so doth her Dress.
Deep Seams & Wrinkles once She shew'd,
But these with Time are throughly cur'd.
'Tis strange! but She immortal grows
With Age, that spoils all other Beaux.
Within, 'tis true, She's not so sound,
But Hollow from the top to ground;
But finest Lady's, we are told,
Are so, when made of London Mould.
Welcome, whether foul or Fair,
To climb up her all Comers are;
And as from Top of Monument
To View the Town, & all that's in't.
But tho too open she's at Heart,
She's close in every other part.
Her Circling Arms do strongly clasp,
Her Sprigs like Misers fingers grasp,
And Weave her Coat so Thick & Even,
Tis proof against all storms from Heaven.

Her Hoop (the Taslers Canopy)
Above her heels hangs ten foot high;
So thick, so fine, so full, so wide,
A Troop of Guards may under it Ride,
Guarded with Roundheads eight as bigg
As Jubbernole, the Giants Head;
They're lively all, not one Num-scull.
Let Rome call such their Capitol.
Upon this charming Hoop doth lye
An honest stedfast Ten foot Die:
No Gamesters Box can make it rattle,
It nev'r will dance, tho' next to Fiddle:
'Tis cover'd with a round green mantle,
Girt close about her, near the middle,
We call it the second Canopy,
Which over hangs the unshaken Die.
From thence mounts up a Pyramid,
A wonder first in Egypt bred;
And on its Top a ten foot Globe,
Atlas nev'r bore a finer load.
From thence springs upon highest Twigg
(As L.d Mayor made of little Prigg)
A weather Cock, who gapes to crow it
This Globe is mine, and all below it.
Masters if you approve these Lays,
And shaver Saxy deign to praise,
Crown him with Yew, instead of Bays
Be kind to Iohn your Tree who Trims
With easy Rhimes, but aching Limbs.
So, when grown Old, you too may have
your faults all mended near the grave,
And may your Resurrection be
Gay as, it's Emblem, Old Yew Tree.

Revived by
WILLIAM COTTREL
Clerk 1770.

Engrav'd by James Wigley in Peppings Court Fleet Street, LONDON.

43

James Wigley after an anonymous artist, *Poet John Saxy upon his Yew-Tree Nov.r 1729*, 1770, engraving. © The Trustees of the British Museum.

was of sufficient stature to galvanise the parish clerk and 'Poet John Saxy' to pen his musings upon 'his Yew-Tree'. What prompted 'shaver Saxy' (d.1741), a local gardener, to carve the tree into its distinctive shape, commemorated in a posthumous engraving of 1770, remains unknown [fig. 43]. The playful assemblage of bold geometrical solids crowned by a topiary 'weather-Cock' suggests that the sculptor of this giant vegetable was versed in contemporary monumental sculpture, and possibly had antiquarian interests. Saxy certainly had no hesitation in proclaiming its antiquity; he credited the yew with greater 'Pedigree' than the descendants of the noble Norman founders of the village, and greater distinction than its eponymous overlords – the Earls of Arlington – remarking that it 'yields to Arlington a Fame / Much Louder than its Earldom Name'.[13]

In verses on this yew, the topiarist vaunts the 'Aged Grace' and immortal qualities of his local landmark. He begins by considering the appearance and soundness of the tree:

> *Her beauty with her years increase,*
> *Her Shapes improve, so doth her Dress.*
> *Deep Seams & Wrinkles once She shew'd*
> *But these with Time are throughly cur'd.*
> *Ti's strange! but She immortal grows*
> *With Age, that spoils all other Beaux.*
> *Within, ti's true, She's not so sound,*
> *But Hollow from the top to ground;*
> *But finest Lady's, we are told,*
> *Are so, when made of London Mould.*
> *Welcome, whether foul or Fair,*
> *To climb up her all Comers are;*
> *And as from Top of Monument*
> *To View the Town, & all that's in't.*
> *But tho too open she's at Heart,*
> *She's close in every other part.*
> *Her Circling Arms do strongly clasp,*
> *Her Sprigs like Misers fingers grasp,*
> *And Weave her Coat so Thick & Even,*
> *Tis proof against all storms from Heaven.*

Saxy then describes the forms into which he has clipped the yew, reaching out, as he gathers pace, for comparisons with august monuments of the ancient world:

> Her Hoop (the Tatlers Canopy)
> Above her heels hangs ten foot high;
> So thick, so fine, so full, so wide,
> A Troop of Guards may under it Ride.
> Guarded with Roundheads eight as bigg
> As Jubbernole, the Giants Head;
> They're lively all, not one Num-scull.
> Let Rome call such their Capitol.
> Upon this charming Hoop doth lye
> An honest stedfast Ten foot Die:
> No Gamesters Box can make it rattle,
> It nev'r will dance tho' next to Fiddle:
> Tis cover'd with a round green mantle,
> Girt close about her, near the middle,
> We call it the second Canopy,
> Which over hangs the unshaken Die.
> From thence mounts up a Pyramid.
> A wonder first in Egypt bred;
> And on its Top a ten foot Globe,
> Atlas nev'r bore a finer load.
> From thence springs upon highest Twigg
> (As Ld. Mayor made of little Prigg)
> A weather-Cock, who gapes to crow it
> This Globe is mine, and all below it.

The poem concludes with a plea on behalf of the topiarist himself, and a reminder of his 'aching Limbs':

> Masters, if you approve these Lays,
> And shaver Saxy deign to praise,
> Crown him with Yew, instead of Bays
> Be kind to John your Tree who trims
> With easy Rhimes, but aching Limbs.
> So, when grown Old, you too may have
> your faults all mended near the grave,
> And may your Resurrection be
> Gay as, it's Emblem, Old Yew Tree.

The Peacocks at East Bedfont, already noted as the sole survivors of churchyard topiary, also attracted much attention. They were commonly

44
W. Hampner, *St Peter and St Paul, Harlington*, 1888 (first published 1803), engraving.
Antiqua Print Gallery/Alamy Stock Photo.

45
John Thomas Smith, *Enfield, Middlesex*, 1794, engraving.
Corporation of the City of London.

HILLINGDON.

HARLINGTON.

46
Anon., St John the Baptist, Hillingdon, Middlesex, c.1800, pen and watercolour wash.
Corporation of the City of London.

47
Anon., St Peter and St Paul, Harlington, Middlesex, c.1800, watercolour.
Corporation of the City of London.

thought to have been pruned in 1704, but their probable date has now been established as 1744, the year when the churchwardens John Hatchett and Richard Taylor were appointed.[14] The initials of these two men, 'JH' and 'RT', were reported by the *Gentleman's Magazine* (1825) to have been carved out of the lower canopy of the easternmost of the yew trees (they have now been replaced with the inscription '1990' to mark the date of the latest formative reclipping).[15] It is not known who first clipped the yews, nor why the date '1704' was cut in broad figures on a prominent part of the work (and is still present).[16] No other London churchyard yews could vie with the Peacocks in originality or intricacy of composition. The trees were originally gorged with baron's crowns, from which sprang long arching plumes which joined to form an arch – bearing small globes – that loosely followed the angles of the church's porch gable; at the centre of the plumes sat a pair of large spheres crowned by gadrooned finials surmounted with peacocks. Over the centuries the profiles of the trees have been simplified, but they have retained a semblance of their former selves.

Although roughly contemporary with the Harlington yew, the Peacocks did not, however, achieve a comparable degree of fame until the turn of the nineteenth century – after which the West London churchyard became a draw for antiquarians, amateur artists and poets. Rosa Corder, George Arnold and George Engelheart all drew portraits of the trees, and the first written description is credited to George Coleman the Younger, whose verses incorporate the yew into an account of Harvey, the landlord of the Black Dog Inn at Bedfont, and who 'once scrawled some lines at this Inn, in 1802':[17]

> *Harvey – whose Inn commands a view*
> *Of Bedfont's church and churchyard too,*
> *Where yew-trees, into peacocks shorn,*
> *In vegetable torture mourn:*
> *Is liable no doubt to glooms*
> *From 'Meditations on the Tombs'.*
> *But while he meditates, he cooks,*
> *Thus both to quick and dead he looks;*
> *Turning his mind to nothing, save*
> *Thoughts on man's gravy, and his grave.*
> *Long may he keep from churchyard holes*
> *Our bodies, with his Sauce for Soles!*
> *Long may he hinder death from beckoning*
> *His guests to settle their last reckoning!*[18]

Fourteen years later the topographer J. Norris Brewer reported:

the southern entrance to the church-yard is rendered an object of notice with many travellers, by two aged yews, which would impart solemnity if suffered to retain their natural gloomy umbrage, spreading like a vegetative pall over the ashes of the village-dead. But the ingenuity of some rural designer has displayed itself in torturing these funereal trees into topiary work, forming an arch of entrance, surmounted by shapes intended to represent two peacocks. Careful periodical trimmings prevent nature from obliterating this distortion.[19]

We know considerably less about the lofty clipped yews in the churchyards of St John the Baptist, Hillingdon, and St Andrew's, Enfield [fig. 45]. Views of the former dating from c.1795–1805 show a giant yew clipped in two different forms: one, like the trees at St Mary Bedfont, into a four-tiered cone crowned by a bird – possibly a peacock; the other as a truncated cone surmounted with a disc supporting eight globes [fig. 46]. The tree formerly stood within a small palisade on the south side of the church. The yew (now gone) adjacent to the south chancel window at St Andrew's is depicted in an aquatint by William Ellis of 1793 as being cropped into an inverted cone, after the fashion which we have seen at Harlington and Bedfont. A bench surrounded the trunk of this tree – as with the Harlington yew.[20]

At various points in the first quarter of the nineteenth century the church-yard yews at Harlington, Bedfont, Hillingdon and Enfield ceased to be clipped, and they began to revert to their states of natural 'luxuriancy and diffusion of boughs and branches'.[21] The neglect of the trees coincided with a renewed appreciation of ancient natural growing yew trees – the most celebrated of which was the 'Giant of Lorton' in the eponymous Cumberland village. William Wordsworth praised this 'giant' in his verse 'Yew-Trees' (1815).[22] The poet found in the tree an image that combined the span of years with the idea of heroic survival. It was 'a living thing / Produced too slowly ever to decay; / Of form and aspect too magnificent / To be destroyed'; it was, moreover, a tree whose natural grandeur was not 'uniformed with Phantasy'.[23] This Romantic view of unimproved nature was further bolstered by such authors as J. G. Strutt and John Loudon – the latter of whom, although an admirer of topiary, made much of the natural magnificence of ancient yew trees in his *Arboretum et Fruiticetum Britannicum* (1838).[24]

The pruning of the Harlington tree was temporarily discontinued after Saxy's death in 1741, but was resumed by William Cottrell – a master carpenter – from c.1757 until his own death in 1777.[25] Although the tree was annually cut at the time of Whitsun Fair until about 1825, it soon thereafter began to lose its original shape – first becoming something akin to a giant honey pot mounted on a pair of platters before reverting to its natural form [figs 47 and 48]. The tree was still sufficiently impressive to have caught the eye of the topographer James Thorne, who remarked in his *Handbook to the Environs of London* (1876) that the 'grand old yew' opposite the church porch was 'still sound, and full of verdure'. He continued: 'for the last half century the tree has been allowed to grow at its own free will, and all traces of topiary work have disappeared.'[26]

48
John Oldfield, *The Harlington Yew, Harlington*, c.1820, pencil and watercolour. Corporation of the City of London.

The botanist William Dallimore, who was acquainted with the yew through Loudon's *Arboretum Britannicum*, remarked in 1908 that 'I saw this tree on February 2nd of the present year, and it appears to be in the best of health and shows no sign of its former clipping.' The tree was 'about 50 or 55 feet high, with a girth at 4½ feet above the ground of 21 feet 3 inches, and a diameter across the lower branches of about 60 feet', and the trunk was 'remarkable for its burrs and swollen portions'.[27] The tree remained intact and in good health until a large section of the main trunk collapsed during a gale in 1959, reducing it to a forlorn stump. The yew has since recovered and is flourishing once again.[28]

It is not known precisely when the trimming of the churchyard yews at Hillingdon and Enfield was discontinued, although topographical views suggest that the trees were allowed to grow out from the first quarter of the nineteenth century. The Peacocks, then – in their prim and glossy plumage – are, as already noted, the only trees from the four churchyard sites to have come down to us. They remain objects of pilgrimage for thousands of curious visitors. These trees were regularly clipped from *c.*1744 to 1808, when the practice was discontinued.[29] After being neglected for some years, the yews were recut when the church was restored in 1865, and continued 'to excite the curiosity of visitors as examples of topiary art, though the recognition of their likeness to peacocks calls for some exercise of imagination on the part of the observer. I have heard them described as looking more like a leafy Chinese puzzle than the birds they are supposed to represent.'[30] Indeed, so fanciful was the clipping that in the late nineteenth century the trees were referred to as 'the lions'. In 1908 the 'two curiously clipped trees, about 20 feet high' were described as giving a 'quaint appearance' to the churchyard.[31] Regular clipping was again suspended during the Second World War; although experts called in after the war to explore the possibility of cutting the yews back into their original shape claimed 'this was no longer possible' and critics disparaged the manner in which the trees were formerly 'tortured, clipped and trained', the Peacocks were reshaped in 1990, and remain so to this day.[32]

The pair of verdant birds is, as Bobard's 'Yew-men' used to be, a pair of 'Magnetick Trees', drawing a constant flow of admirers. Their popularity and celebrity might possibly be attributed to their antiquity – to the fact that they have been standing in the same place, in the same immaculately shorn livery, beside the same ancient building for hundreds of years. Saxy, however, who appears to have begun the business of shaving the churchyard yews, places primary emphasis on their vitality. He would have us believe that sculpting artfully an old yew tree gave it new life and new appeal; a handsomely carved tree was, in his view, a joyful emblem of resurrection.

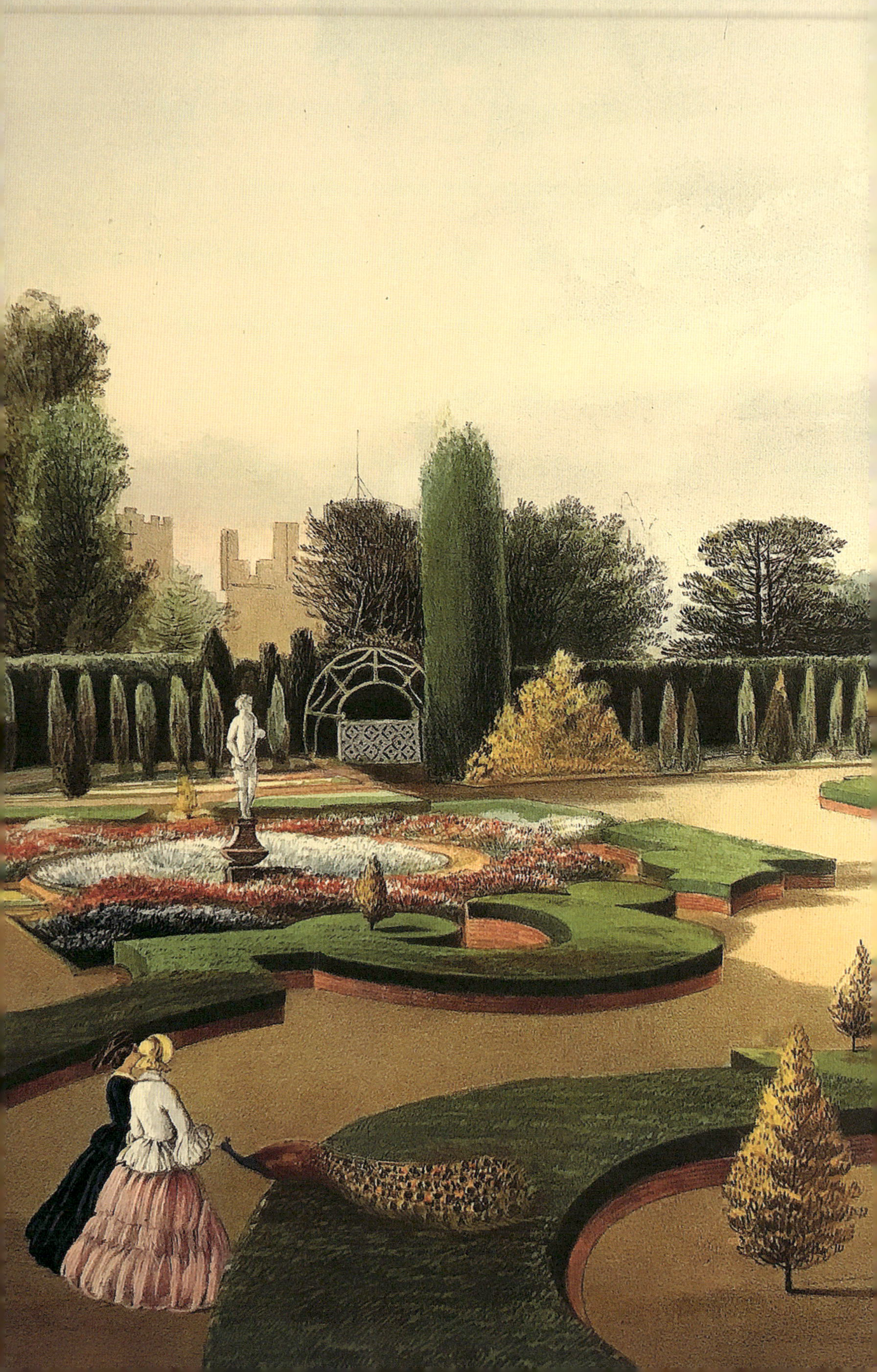

[SIX]

Lord Petersham's Gardens at Elvaston Castle: 'A Modern Palagonia'

WHILE SAXY TRAVELLED AROUND MIDDLESEX IN SEARCH OF ancient churchyard yews to shave, other taxophiles ventured deeper into the English countryside with a view to discovering and acquiring old or established topiaries to populate their gardens. The most acquisitive of all was Major-General Charles Stanhope, 4th Earl of Harrington (1780–1851), who is better known today by his courtesy title, Viscount Petersham. Described by Princess Lieven in 1821 as the 'the maddest of all the mad Englishmen', he was a close companion of the Prince Regent, later George IV, a lord of the bedchamber to George III and George IV, and a 'great dandy, affecting the immaculate dress, exaggerated manners, and eccentricities of behaviour of his kind' [fig. 49].[1] An admirer of the stage, in 1831 he married an actress, 'the elegant, the swan-like, the fascinating Maria Foote', who was henceforth 'lost for ever to her admiring patrons, the public, being removed to a higher, and … to a happier sphere'.[2] More notable for her beauty than her talents, the actress had a great capacity to generate scandal. In 1815 she became the mistress of the rake and liar Colonel William Berkeley, later Earl Fitzhardinge, with whom she had two children. When by 1824 a promise of marriage did not materialise, Foote broke off her relationship only to fall into the arms of another young man of fortune: Joseph 'Pea-Green' Hayne made an offer of marriage, but he too refused to marry her, claiming not to have known that she was under the protection of Berkeley. Foote then sued Hayne for breach of promise and was awarded £3,000 in damages. The case caused a sensation and was taken up by pamphleteers. Having quit the stage to marry Hayne, she returned to the Covent Garden Theatre in 1825 where 'her personal notoriety ensured full houses' [fig. 50].[3]

As the new countess was too infamous to appear in society, her husband, intent on seclusion, retired after their nuptials to Elvaston Castle in Derbyshire,

DUNCOMBE'S MINIATURE CARICATURE MAGAZINE. No.2.
Were mine the land
In all the Strand,
Colonel, I beg your pardon;
I'd Crowns resign
To call but mine,
One Foote of Covent Garden.
Yes, but he has not hurt his Foote
The Colonel has injured his knee
Bills of Costs
Boxiana
Damages 3000!!
J. Jones, f.
Smiles and Tears.
Pub.d by J. Duncombe 19 Lit.e Queen St Jan.y 1825

where, according to W. H. Mallock, the earl, 'animated by a romantic jealousy', refused to let his wife stray beyond the park gates.[4] Here, however, Lord Harrington, who was 'much attached to planting and landscape gardening', embarked on a sustained and ambitious programme of refurbishments that over two decades was to transform his family's arid and rather lacklustre estate into 'one of the most distinct and regal gardens in Britain' – or 'the sublime in gardening'.[5]

Elvaston lies four miles from Derby on the former London Road. As the garden journalist Robert Glendinning observed in 1849:

> those who have travelled that way will be ready to admit that it is anything but a promising country for the effective introduction of ornamental gardening [fig. 51]. There is in this locality none of that bold rugged scenery, with its rocks and

49
Edward Stroehling, *Charles, Viscount Petersham*, 1819, oil on canvas.
Private collection.
Petersham is portrayed in the guise of Henri IV; the bat pendant on his jewelled collar may refer to his nocturnal habits. Petersham seldom ventured out until after six in the evening.

50
Thomas Jones, *Smiles and Tears*, 1825, hand-tinted etching.
© The Trustees of the British Museum.
Maria Foote dances a *pas seul* on stage at Covent Garden.

51
After Benjamin Fawcett and Alexander Francis Lydon,
Elvaston Castle, Derbyshire, c.1880, aquatint.
Antiqua Print Gallery/Alamy Stock Photo.

natural woods, for which Derbyshire is so famous. Flat level pasturage is the chief characteristic of the district ... Travellers in search of the picturesque would find little of interest in this immense agricultural plain.

And yet, he continued, 'in the middle of so uninviting a tract, there ... stands the greatest work of gardening skill, both in extent and design, which perhaps any man ever accomplished in one life-time before; but being kept strictly private, it is scarcely known to exist.'[6]

The metamorphosis of the Elevaston estate began in early 1830 shortly after the 4th Earl succeeded to the title. Among his first steps was the appointment of William Barron, a twenty-five-year-old Scottish gardener who had been a 'sharp lad' at school, studied Greek and French, and 'learned sufficient Hebrew to enable him to read the Bible in the original'.[7] Having developed a taste for gardening, Barron worked his way up through the ranks, gaining admission

52
Anon., William Barron's 'tree-lifting appliance', late nineteenth century, photograph. Royal Botanic Gardens, Kew. © The Board of Trustees of the Royal Botanic Gardens, Kew.
Barron's horse-drawn machine could uproot and move large and ancient trees upwards of 48 km/30 miles.

to the Royal Botanic Gardens, Edinburgh, and latterly working at Sion House in London for the Duke of Northumberland.

Harrington instructed Barron to make him a garden 'second to none', and was prepared to lavish great sums of money to ensure that his head gardener fulfilled this aim – and with great speed.[8] No sooner had Barron taken his post and completed the drainage operations in the park and gardens than he was requested to transplant three large cedars of Lebanon from one part of the gardens to another. Although this initially posed technical difficulties, Barron's ingenuity prevailed and the trees were removed and replanted. The success of this exercise to produce what Loudon described as 'immediate effect' so pleased the earl that it became the driver for most of the gardens' improvements for the ensuing twenty years. Encouraged by his patron, Barron became both a pioneer and an expert in the removal and transplanting of mature trees, scouring the country 'to find fine specimens, and many old Yew trees, some of them hundreds of years old, were brought from distances of nearly 20 miles' [fig. 52].[9] Robert Glendinning reported in the *Gardeners' Chronicle* that 'the size of the subject to be moved or the distance from whence it was to come never deterred nor influenced for a moment the completion of the design. Gigantic trees, which would have made a stout-hearted improver shudder to attack, in order to transpose them even a few yards, considering the risk and magnitude of the undertaking, appear to have been thought lightly of at Elvaston.'[10] The statistics are impressive: by 1850 Barron had transplanted hundreds of enormous trees, among them 'old yews and cedars', some of which included a 'clipped [yew] column, 22 feet round and 28 feet high', a 'clipped [yew] arbour, 19 feet high; several birds and other figures', and eleven yews over 25 feet high 'known to be over 600 years old'. Most of these trees had been transported between 6.4 and 48 km/4 and 34 miles.[11] So it was that the castle's pleasure grounds, which were 'practically non-existent in 1831, were gradually extended and most elaborately laid out, until [by] 1851 they covered about 80 acres'.[12] It was as though the earl were devising every form of horticultural diversion possible to keep his wife from pining for an existence beyond the bounds of her prison paradise.

Whether because of the earl's determination to seclude his wife or simply out of a (possibly shared) wish for privacy, the Harringtons, much to the dismay of the horticulturally curious, did not possess 'the liberality usually displayed by the nobility and gentry of England': the estate remained 'as a sealed book' during the earl's lifetime.[13] As Loudon remarked in 1838, it was 'not a show place: the pleasure-grounds are never allowed to be seen, except by visiters [sic] staying at the castle, or by the personal acquaintances of the Earl and Countess of Harrington.'[14] Indeed, Barron's orders were: 'If the Queen comes ... show her round; but admit no one else.'[15]

The fact that the gardens were inaccessible made them especially attractive to prying eyes, so though the earl was keen to eschew publicity, and to ensure that Elvaston should have 'no public attraction', reports of the estate's Brobdingnagian gardening activities inevitably reached the wider world. In 1842 readers of the *Quarterly Review* were informed that the 'noble but eccentric lord' was the 'Elgin of topiary art, who is buying up all the yew-peacocks in the country to form an avenue in his domain at Elvaston'. Local residents would have been inconvenienced by what Glendinning noted in 1849 as the 'numbers of large plants employed in the formation of this fine garden', including giant yews from Staffordshire, Nottinghamshire and Derbyshire, that 'had to pass in their journey to it through the town of Derby, and so large were they that the windows on both sides of the streets were much broken by them' [fig. 53].[16]

Similar sensational reports doubtless piqued the curiosity of John Loudon, who visited Elvaston in 1839. He was among the first and few garden journalists to record and publish his observations during the earl's lifetime. His opening

53
Anon., 'A Curious Arbour', photograph, *Country Life* (21 January 1899).
Country Life Picture Archive.

It was remarked at the time that 'it seems difficult to believe that the quaint and curious shapes at Elvaston, clipped out of trees of fine and luxuriant growth, are really modern.'

remark in 'Recollections of a Tour' suggests that he was prepared to cast his eyes over something exceptional: 'we had frequently heard this place referred to as a modern Palagonia.'[17] The Sicilian villa of Prince Palagonia, which was reputed to be 'one of the most extraordinary houses on earth',[18] was 'better known by the name of the Palace of Monsters'.[19] It was distinguished by its unusual approach, which one traveller in 1830 referred to as the 'avenue of Pandemonium ... crowded with stone and marble beings, not to found in any books of zoology'.[20]

Describing the scene as it unfolded before him, Loudon continued:

> we knew that it contained an excellent collection of the pine and fir tribe, and also of the Cupréssinæ and Taxàceae ... The situation is flat, or at least without any striking inequalities; but there are some fine old avenues, one of which is nearly a mile and a half in length, but the effect is that of an avenue of ten miles, in consequence of the ground beyond falling below the level of the surface where the avenue commences at the house ... The number of thujas, red cedars, white cedars, Irish yews, hemlock spruces, common yews, variegated common yews, and upright common yews, is quite astonishing. To produce immediate effect, and to serve as background to these comparatively young plants, large spruce firs have been transplanted (many of them of upwards of 50 ft. in height); and these trees being held fast in their situations by guy ropes, like the mast of a ship, scarcely one of them has failed.[21]

As he approached the castle, Loudon became even more engrossed, perceiving what appeared to be an immense forest of yews [fig. 54]:

> but this forest, when examined in detail, is found to consist of a series of ancient flower-gardens, surrounded by and intermixed with yew hedges, and containing yew trees of large size, brought from all parts of the country, many of which have been clipped into curious shapes. Among these, in different positions, are placed numerous plants of Araucària imbricàta, variegated yews, and many of the rarest Coníferæ. There are three extensive gardens of this sort, each occupying several acres. One, though recently planted, has quite an ancient character, with covered walks of arbor vitæ, and flower-beds, &c. This garden is surrounded by a terrace of yew trees, the inward line forming arches, and panel[l]ed with Cydònia japónica, and with araucarias in the open spaces. Another is an Italian garden, richly furnished with vases, statues (many of which are of grotesque forms), richly gilt, basins, fountains and other works of art. A third consists of open lawns, bounded by yews, and by trees of the pine and fir tribe ... Among the other things which struck us as new and extraordinary, were plinths of soil forming pedestals

54
Anon., yew topiary at Elvaston Castle, *c*.1890, hand-tinted postcard.
Private collection.
A contributor to *Country Life* noted in 1899 that the 'strange and unusual gardens ... would never, perhaps, have been created exactly as they are but for the unpicturesque situation they occupy.'

to large yew trees, which were procured when full grown from different parts of the country, wherever they could be found large, or cut into curious shapes; while smaller yew trees were planted at the base of the plinths, and trained over them. The solemn gloom cast over part of the grounds by these yew trees produces an effect never to be forgotten, which harmonises with the fine old ivy-covered church adjoining the castle, which towers proudly above them, and is also in part clothed in ivy.[22]

Loudon concluded that 'on the whole, the grounds at Elvaston Castle abound with objects of great singularity, rarity, and value ... Nine years ago, there was not a single evergreen about the place, with the exception of the very large cedars of Lebanon and a few large Portugal laurels; the whole having been collected, planted and the entire grounds and gardens formed, in less than nine years.'[23]

The gardens were intended to complement the seventeenth-century castle which had been energetically remodelled and Gothicised in 1818 for the 3rd Earl by Robert Walker to the designs of James Wyatt, and latterly improved and recast in the early 1830s by the architect and restorer Lewis Cottingham. Cottingham was a 'designer of the highest quality' with a scholarly interest in mediaeval art and architecture, archaeology and antiquarianism, whose museum of mediaeval antiquities, amassed between 1814 and 1847, was the first major collection of its kind in England.[24] The extent of this architect's creative input at Elvaston remains unclear as all family papers relating to the estate were destroyed in 1964; however, given the extensive landscape improvements he superintended in the late 1820s at the neighbouring Snelston estate, it seems likely that Cottingham had a hand in assisting Lord Harrington.

The most important intersection of the house and the gardens was the 'Hall of the Fair Star' – one of the principal rooms in the castle, which Cottingham had redecorated for the 4th Earl, and which, according to Mark Girouard writing in *Return to Camelot* (1981), became 'a shrine to the two middle-aged but apparently still ardent lovers, and to Lord Harrington's knight-errantry'.[25] Wyatt's earlier fan-vaulted Gothic Hall was re-christened and redecorated in a chivalric taste:

> *Gothic alcoves round the hall were filled with figures in armour and the walls hung with swords and lances. Doors, alcoves and stained-glass windows were decorated with appropriate mottoes: 'Fayre beyond Fayrest', 'Beauty is a Witch', 'Faithful to Honour and Beauty' and relevant if sometimes mysterious symbols abounded: stars by the dozen, flaming hearts, lovers' knots, quivers of arrows, lyres, pomegranates, peacocks and birds of paradise.*[26]

The dedication of the room – and the eponymous garden compartment – presumably alludes to 'that faire Starre' in Edmund Spenser's *Faerie Queene*, in which he refers to Venus as the morning star, queen of love and 'Cyprian goddesse'.[27]

This chivalric theme continued in 'The Garden of the Fair Star' – also known as 'Mon Plaisir' – which lay immediately under the south front of the castle [fig. 55]. A contributor to the *Floricultural Cabinet* (1852) described it as 'enclosed on two sides (right and left) by yew hedges, in the form of walls':

55 overleaf
E. Adveno Brooke, 'Birds Eye View of (Mon Plaisir) in the Garden at Elvaston Castle', chromolithograph, in *The Gardens of England* (1858).
© The Trustees of the British Museum.

E. A. Brooke.

BIRDS EYE VIEW OF (MON PLAISI
THE SEAT OF THE Rt HO

GARDEN AT ELVASTON CASTLE.

56
E. Adveno Brooke, 'The Alhambra Garden ... Elvaston Castle', chromolithograph, in *The Gardens of England* (1858). British Library, London. Trustees of the British Library.

the sides being quite perpendicular, and the tops cut off square as if they were pieces of masonry. The central portion is a covered walk, the direction of which is the outline of a square pincushion having rounded corners, and gently pressed on the four sides. The walk is eight feet wide, and the arch eight feet high. American arbor-vitæ is planted on each side of it, and now completely envelopes the walk, excluding the sun's rays, and rendering it a delightful retreat in hot sunny weather ... At a little distance it presents the appearance of an even light green velvety nap, having various openings and loopholes, which are formed and arranged with architectural exactness ... In the centre [of the garden] stands a remarkable plant of Araucaria imbricata ... [*which*] *has grown twenty inches and a half* [*every year*], *on an average, since it was planted.*[28]

This was not the only garden that bristled with 'works of art ... of the chisel ... and of the shears': the Alhambra Garden [fig. 56] possessed a 'Moorish' kiosk containing a marble effigy of the earl kneeling before his wife (there were no fewer than 'four statuary knights kneeling in worship of the Fair Star at Elvaston'), and the Fountain, Magnolia and the Italian Gardens possessed further wonders.[29] The park, too, abounded with novelties. For instance, the ornamental lake was 'pronounced by all who saw it to be "like a fairyland" and the great Duke of Wellington, when he first saw the lake and rockwork on the islands and mound, exclaimed, "This is the only natural artificial rock-work I have ever seen."'[30]

With the death of the earl in 1851 the gardens were finally opened to the public. It is, however, a grim irony that although they were at the time at their very zenith, they swiftly began to decline. The 5th Earl was forced to reduce significantly the expenditure on the gardens, and Barron, unhappy to watch his legacy unravel, departed to become an eminent nurseryman, tree transplanter and landscape gardener.

Nonetheless, the castle grounds attracted great numbers of visitors, most of whom were entranced by the general effect. Although Barron considered Elvaston a giant pinetum 'artistically treated', it was to become most famous for its avenues: 'complex constructions several rows deep'. In the formal gardens alone there were estimated to be '11 miles of evergreen hedges, shorn as smooth as an Axminster carpet'.[31] It was, nevertheless, the estate's battalions of leviathan, freakish topiaries that captured, most emphatically, the public imagination [figs 57 and 58]. As Thomas Baines observed, rather equivocally, in 1876: 'whatever difference of opinion may exist as to the fashion of training and clipping trees and shrubs into fantastic forms more or less unnatural, there can be none as to the object in view being well carried out here, both in the first conception and down to the present time.'[32]

What is most remarkable about the transmutation of Elvaston is the earl's and his gardener's intense fascination for evergreens, and topiarised yew in particular: 'grotesque Yews ... [shorn] quite smooth, and the forms they represent are thus rendered as perfect as if they were hewn out of stone or marble',[33] and 'clipped yews representing columns, pedestals, minarets, &c., interspersed with marble statuary in subjects too various to particularise'.[34] The men rejected popular taste which decreed that 'yews were merely miserable and solemn trees' to 'reinstate topiary and give prominence to evergreens'.[35] They had, like Saxy almost a century before them, taken 'old, bushy yew that had been growing for centuries' to form 'beautiful, artificially-clipped' topiaries.[36] But whereas Saxy's topiaries were firmly rooted to their ancestral churchyards, Harrington's charges were uprooted and redeployed.

Perhaps not surprisingly, when the garden gates were eventually thrown open, it prompted 'a sudden rush of interest in this ancient horticultural technique'.[37] Few were as spellbound by the gardens as the American nurseryman Robert Buist, who paid a visit during the course of a tour of Britain in 1852. 'So much', he exclaimed, 'was I absorbed with what I could barely realize to be real, that 10½ o'clock of the night found me under the soft silver beams of the moon, still enjoying those magical scenes ... I retired to rest, but found none for my excited imagination.'[38] Thomas Appleby, however, may be credited with the most original response to 'the fresh scenes of beauty' that greeted him at every corner during the course of his visit in 1850: he professed that 'such was the sensations of pleasure the sight gave us, that we actually threw our body down upon the soft lawn in an ecstacy of delight.'[39]

57
Anon., 'From the South Front', photograph, Country Life (21 January 1899).
Country Life Picture Library.

58
Anon., 'Leading to Italian Garden', photograph, Country Life (21 January 1899).
Country Life Picture Library.
After Petersham's death several trees were disposed of: 'a specimen of Picea nobilis going to Osborne for the Prince Consort, while the Crystal Palace grounds were embellished with not a few of the Elvaston trees'.

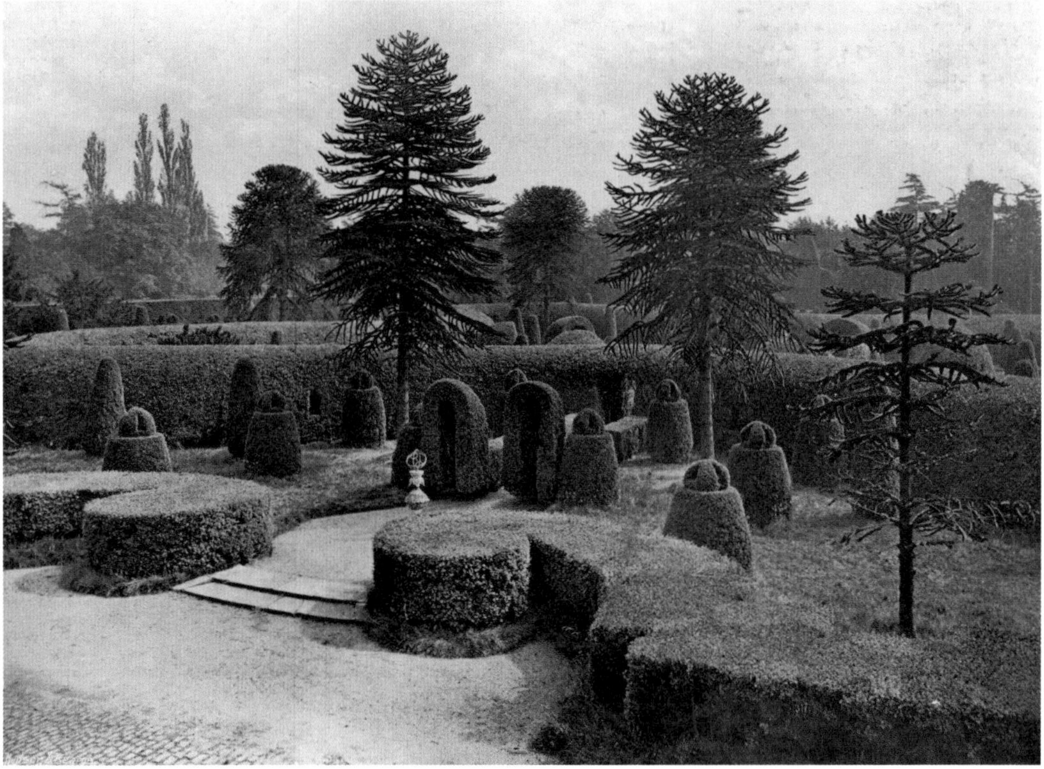

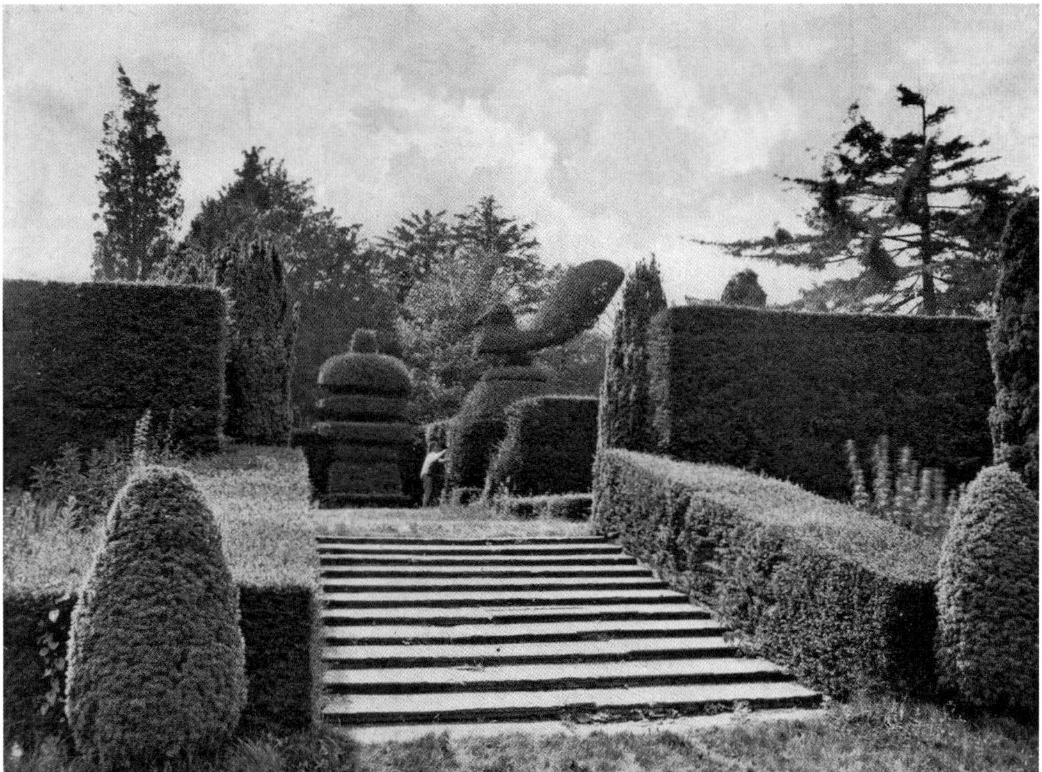

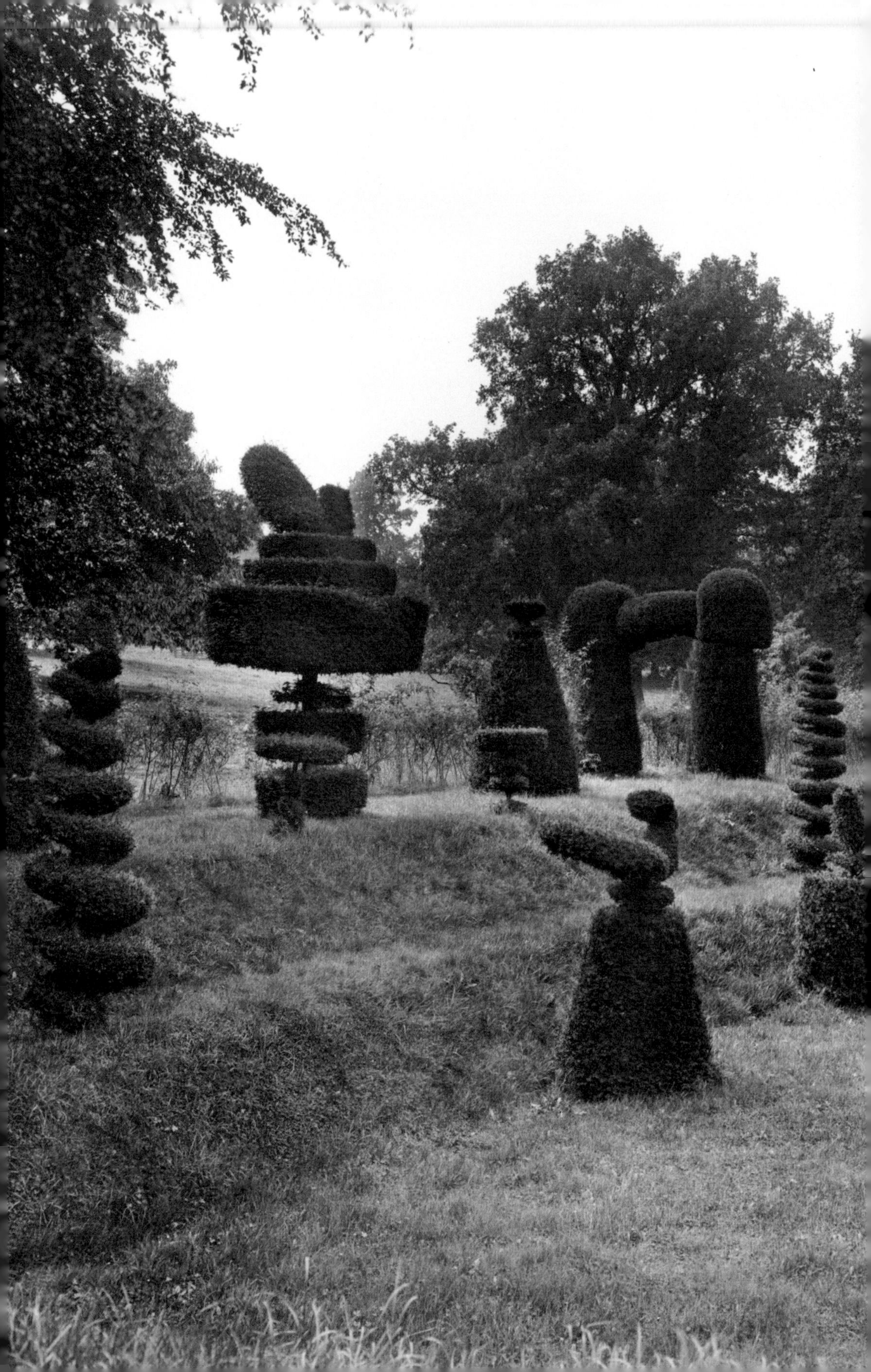

[SEVEN]

The Countess of Dudley's 'Stop and Buy' Topiaries

WE CONCLUDE OUR SURVEY OF YEW LOVERS WITH A POSTSCRIPT ON a minor but enthusiastic acquisitor of topiaries. Rachel Anne Gurney (1867–1920) was credited in her day as 'possessed of uncommon pluck' and among 'the cleverest women in Society'.[1] Born into a family of philanthropic Norfolk bankers, her birth coincided with the demise of her father's family business of Overend, Gurney and Co. – then the largest discount house in the City of London. This 'gigantic failure', which agitated the City and could be felt in the 'remotest corners of the Kingdom',[2] rendered her father penniless and impelled her mother, Alice (née Prinsep), to take to trade and manage a milliner's shop in London's Regent Street to help make ends meet – where Rachel and her sister also later worked as sales assistants.

A writer for the *Sketch* reported in 1903 that Rachel's upbringing was 'all that could possibly be of the best and simplest':[3] as her mother's health prevented her from superintending Rachel's education, she was raised both by her maternal grandparents at Little Holland House, Kensington, and Freshwater on the Isle of Wight, and by her mother's first cousin Adeline, Duchess of Bedford, whose husband, the 10th Duke, supplied his young charge with a good education in Florence where she became proficient in French, Italian and German. She was also a talented vocalist, and through her family connections had a broad acquaintance of artistic and literary friends, including George Frederic Watts, Alfred Lord Tennyson and Julia Margaret Cameron.

In 1891 Rachel married William Humble Ward, 2nd Earl of Dudley (1867–1932), heir to a vast fortune derived from ironworks and collieries, with a reputation for gambling and sexual indiscretions. According to *The Times*, the earl, who had until then lived the life of the ordinary rich young nobleman, 'very soon surprised his friends by the energy with which he began to attach to his public duties ... and began to take part in many movements for solving the social problems of the day'. His metamorphosis was credited to his 'young wife, full of zeal for many ideals of life and conduct', whose influence 'quickly made itself felt' [fig. 59].[4]

Rachel was, according to her sister Laura Troubridge, a 'born dreamer', and the 'romantic and the idealistic in life made an irresistible appeal to her'. Although she enjoyed the social round, this never sufficed for her happiness; she longed to engage in public duty and to use her intellect to transform her idealistic desire for usefulness into practical schemes. From 1902 her 'longing for usefulness' had full scope when her husband was appointed Viceroy of Ireland.[5] Eager to fulfil her own imperial mission as vicereine, and with a special emphasis on female reform, she served as President of the Irish Industries

Richard Bullingham, 'The Countess of Dudley as Queen Esther', 1899, photogravure. National Portrait Gallery, London.
This photo was taken at the Devonshire House Fancy Dress Ball on 2 July 1897.

60
Alexander Francis Lydon, 'Whitley Court', chromolithograph, in Revd F. O. Morris, *A Series of Picturesque Seats of Noblemen and Gentlemen of Great Britain and Ireland* (1866).

Association and established the Irish Central Bureau for the Employment of Women. Her most lasting social contribution was, however, the founding of Lady Dudley's Scheme for the Establishment of District Nurses for the Poor in Ireland in association with Queen Victoria's Jubilee Institute of Nursing, which brought health care to the poorest and most remote parts of the country.[6]

Less well known are Lady Dudley's interests in gardening. When in 1891 she became chatelaine of Witley Court, Worcestershire, the stately classical mansion was then among the most opulent and fashionable in England, and its extensive and high Victorian gardens had been vaunted by a contributor to the *Gardeners' Chronicle* in 1864 as 'first rank' among 'first-class garden establishments' [fig. 60].[7] Their designer, William Andrews Nesfield, suggested as much, describing them as his 'monster work'.[8] Set in hundreds of acres of ancient parkland and located within 14.5 km/9 miles of Worcester, the mansion sat on a gentle eminence surveying 4.5 ha/10 acres of dressed grounds 'redesigned on the le notre principle', which were separated from the deer park by means of a balustraded wall: 'every known contrivance ... [was] employed to render them worthy of their munificent owner' [fig. 61].[9] Here, Nesfield dispensed with the arabesques of box, typical of his earlier Italianate gardens, in favour of much taller clipped evergreens.[10] The flower garden, situated on two sides of the mansion, was according to the *Journal of Horticulture* the 'pride of Witley', and Rachel's predecessor, the dowager countess, had been an 'ardent admirer' of flowers and floral decorations.[11] The chief attraction of the grounds was, however, the colossal fountain group of baroque grandeur depicting Perseus and Andromeda [fig. 62]. Executed in Portland stone by James Forsyth to Nesfield's design, it was trumpeted in the *Illustrated London News* in 1862 as 'probably the largest sculpture in Europe':[12] 140 jets played over the elaborate visual interpretation of the story from Ovid, the most powerful of which pumped water over 30 m/100 feet in the air 'with the roar of an express train'.[13] D. T. Fish, writing in the *Gardeners' Chronicle* in June 1873, was captivated by the allegorical group:

> *what, with the rush of waters, the exquisite beauty, and the infinite variety of form and size of the jets, the coloured spray, driven hither and thither by the breeze, forming dissolving views of shifting rainbows, and the rush, dash, splash and light feathery spray of the many rising and falling streams or jets, one seems riveted to the spot as by the spell of all the water nymphs' enchantments. The flowers even seem to lose their brilliance, the trees and shrubs their freshness, as one watches the cool breath of the water in the soft summer air, and listens to its full-toned refreshing music.*[14]

Sometime around the turn of the twentieth century Lady Dudley created, amidst this princely grandeur, a new and surprisingly modest garden – possibly in collaboration with the estate's head gardener, Arthur Young. 'My Lady's

61
Anon., south front of Witley Court, 1920, photograph. Historic England Archive.
William Robinson remarked in *The English Flower Garden* (1883) that the 'architectural gardening' at Witley Court had been 'pushed so far into the park as to absolutely curtail and injure the prospect'.

62
Anon., Perseus and Andromeda fountain, Witley Court, 1920, photograph. Historic England Archive, Swindon.
The fountain threw a jet over 30 m/100 ft high.

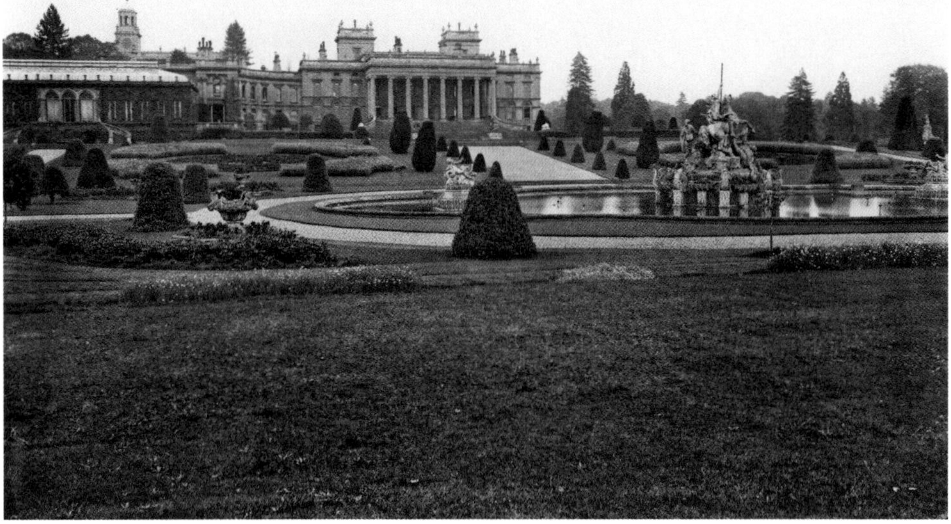

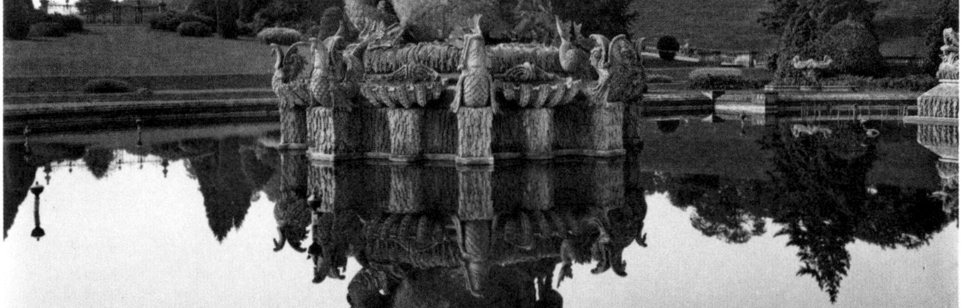

7.

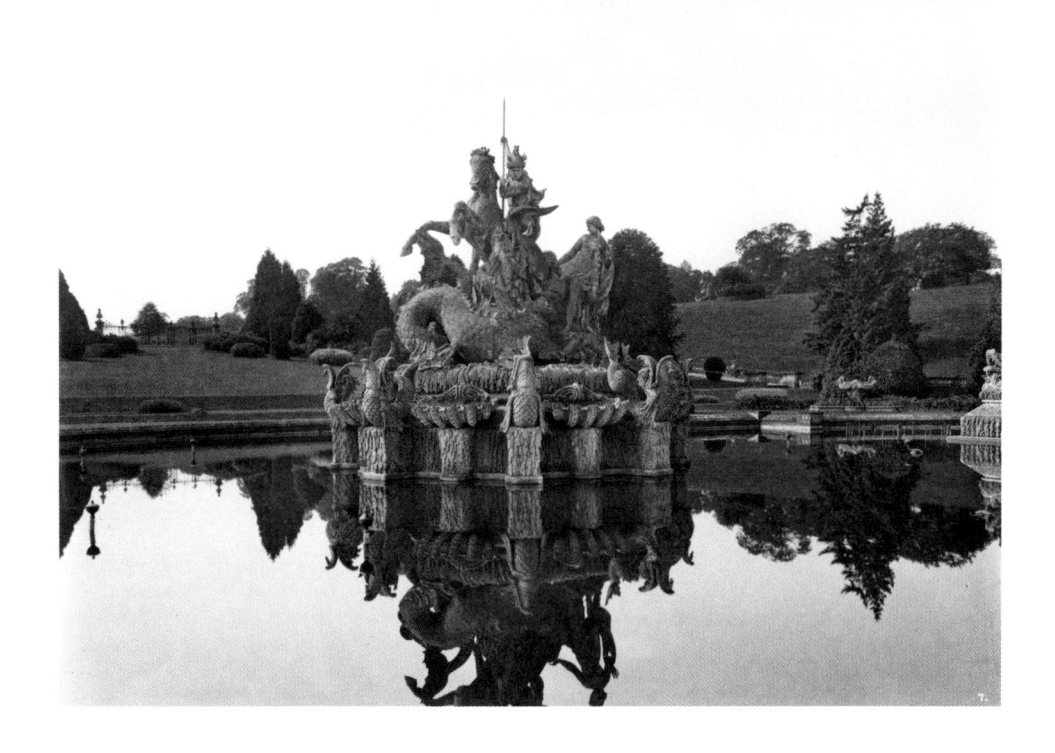

63
Anon., 'My Lady's Garden', Witley Court, 1920, photograph.
Historic England Archive, Swindon.

64
Anon., 'My Lady's Garden', Witley Court, 1920, photograph.
Historic England Archive, Swindon.

Garden', as it was known, was laid out on an 0.4-ha/1-acre slip of ground beyond the stables and south of the walled kitchen garden. Surviving early photographs suggest that it was a motley assemblage. It sat rather uneasily within a forgotten corner of the pleasure ground, comprising a long herbaceous border which ran alongside the outside south wall of the kitchen garden and, on the opposite side of the path, serried ranks of geometric topiaries – verdant spirals, birds on pyramids, arches and round ziggurats surmounted by peacocks – laid out on grassy terraces overlooking a grass tennis court like so many spectators watching a match [figs 63 and 64].

Charles Henry Curtis praised the garden in The Book of Topiary (1904) as an exemplar of the 'modern revival of Topiary' and an establishment 'famous throughout the land';[15] and Leonard Bastin writing in Country Home (1910) admired Lady Dudley's 'excellent instances of modern Topiary' for their simplicity:

> It is quite certain that the modern topiarist's work is more commendable in that there is less tendency to reproduce the fantastic designs of the seventeenth-century gardeners. True enough, we still have plenty of peacocks, swans, sheep and the like, but these forms are recognized as freaks, not as the best interpretations of the art. As time goes on it is exceedingly likely that a somewhat modified form of Topiary will gain increasing favour, giving results which are genuinely attractive.[16]

While most collectors of topiary would have been content to buy their fanciful specimens at the country's leading suppliers, including William Cutbush & Son, Cheal & Sons or Richmond Nurseries,[17] the countess followed the example of Lord Petersham: she acquired her mature clipped specimens from private gardens. She did not, however, scour the countryside far and wide, but stalked her specimens in the gardens of estate tenants and neighbours in the surrounding villages during excursions made outside the park gates in search of topiaries that 'caught her eye'.[18] Indeed, so memorable were her 'stop and buy' expeditions that the locals still recollected them in the late 1980s – some of whose forebears, attentive to Lady Dudley's taste and grateful for her patronage, had cultivated topiaries in the expectation that they might find their way into My Lady's Garden.

Although the name of the garden and its phalanges of bizarre topiaries might suggest that its purpose was rather frivolous and self-indulgent – that it was 'her ladyship's' private demesne, a secluded paradise seeking to reproduce in tangible form the lushly narcissistic *mise-en-scène* set up by the pre-Raphaelite painter John Young-Hunter in his eponymous painting of 1899 depicting a

65
John Young-Hunter, *My Lady's Garden*, 1899, oil on canvas.
Tate Britain, London. Artiz/Alamy Stock Photo.

moment's phantasy in the walled garden of Holland House, Kensington: a richly clad young woman surrounded by three peacocks [fig. 65]. It is also possible, however, that the garden may have acquired its new name – and new meaning – during or after the First World War, in endorsing a sentiment expressed in a selection of wartime garden poems entitled *In My Lady's Garden*. Miss Charton's anthology, published under the pseudonym 'Hackleplume',[19] was, according to its preface, 'originally planted to give pleasure to all who have suffered or are suffering, through the War', and was, according Vivien Newman writing in *Tumult & Tears: The Story of the Great War through the Eyes of its Women Poets* (2016), 'to serve as a living tribute and memorial not only to the dead but also to the wounded. Each combatant nation, corps and Service had its own poetic garden or, occasionally, patch of scrub ground in this horticultural tour de force.'[20] Such a tender sentiment might have appealed to Lady Dudley, who, as one of the first aristocratic English women to offer her services after the declaration of war, travelled to France in August 1914 with the goal of establishing a hospital for the war wounded.[21]

My Lady's Garden was a peculiar and noteworthy anomaly at Witley Court: its frivolous clipped corkscrews and its quaint and homely character contrasted sharply with the stately magnificence of Nesfield's prim and sprawling parterres. Although John Klinkert of Richmond Nurseries remarked in 1920 that 'the topiary garden is obviously a hobby for the well to do,'[22] the art of topiary more often in fact appealed most strongly to amateur gardeners – that is, garden lovers of modest means who, with the help of an occasional gardener, were mainly indebted to their own energy and skill to look after their small gardens.

Shirley Hibberd (1825–1890), editor of the *Gardener's Magazine* and champion of Victorian amateur gardening, had a balanced view on the subject of topiary, remarking in 1879: 'it may be true, as I believe it is, that the natural form of a tree is the most beautiful possible for that particular tree, but it may happen that we do not always want the most beautiful form, but one of our own designing, and expressive of our ingenuity.'[23] He was loathe to 'despise another man's pleasures, or vainly desire to set up a standard of my own in opposition to the delightful variety that is ensured by the free exercise of individual taste and fancy' [fig. 66].

66
Anon., amateur topiary in an English cottage garden,
late nineteenth century, postcard. Private collection.

Let us grant that these things are for children, and what then? They are not thereby abolished. In my opinion they have acquired special importance, for to please children may be a proper employment at times for a philosopher; and if children's pleasures are to be excluded from gardens, then I am prepared to say that gardens are altogether objectionable. That there are men and women with childish tastes must also be admitted, and I propose that we please them as well as the real children.[24]

Lady Dudley would doubtless have agreed with Hibberd when he remarked: 'the man who sneers at me for admiring, as I do, a well-cut peacock, may take my assurance in advance that I will neither kick him nor abuse him; but pity him I must.'[25] Rachel appears to have laid claim to a small part of the Witley gardens with a view to doing with it what she liked – to play outside the domain of the rules set by Nesfield. She, like Hibberd, viewed topiary as a form of play. The psychoanalyst Donald Winnicott considered play the key to emotional and psychological well-being: it was essential not only to children but to adults, and assumed a crucial role in the development of authentic selfhood. In Winnicott's terms (in a passage already quoted in the Introduction), Lady Dudley's attitude towards the world around her was one of 'creativity' as opposed to 'compliance' – that is, she set out to generate imaginative patterns of her own rather than resigning herself to fitting in with the rules of others – possibly least of all with those of her philandering husband from whom she separated in 1912.[26]

Rien ne me fixe.

Je les réunis tous

Je répète tout ce qu'on dit.

des malices.

Je bavarde sans cesse.

Je fais patte de velours.

[EIGHT]

Lady Reade and her 'Gaudy Natives of the Tropics'

One of the most significant improvements that George Spencer, 4th Duke of Marlborough, made to his family's gardens at Blenheim Palace after the Napoleonic Wars and before his death in 1817 was the erection of a magnificent crescent-shaped wood and wirework aviary in the oval flower garden. The new edifice, set up around the Temple of Flora, was described by W. F. Mavor in his *New Description of Blenheim* (1817) as 'from the design of [the architect] Mr Henry Hakewill', of 'considerable elegance and expense', and containing compartments in each wing 'stocked with gold and silver pheasants, some curious doves, and a pair of Curassoa birds'.[1] The aviary had been acquired by the duke in 1812 under the will of his old friend Harriott, Lady Reade, of Shipton under Wychwood [fig. 67].[2]

Much of what we know about Lady Reade and her celebrated aviary derives from a fulsome account from 1812 provided by Revd Dr Thomas Brookes (1732–1814), vicar of Shipton under Wychwood, which was transcribed in the early nineteenth century by the antiquarian and vicar of Eynsham, Revd Thomas Symonds.[3]

Brookes reports that Dame Harriott 'kept up a correspondence with the late Duke of Marlborough', and that when 'this singular woman died at her home in Curson Street, May Fair, London [on] Dec. 23 1811 in her 85th year', she left her aviary 'partly to Queen Charlotte, & part to the Duke of Marlborough & the whole collection was dispersed, & the cages destroyed.'[4] Reflecting on her 'remarkable assemblage of birds', he observed: 'it was magnificent & presented to the eye the wondrous variety of the feathered tribe, in all the pomp of radiant plumage. But it may be long before any person of Fortune is again seized with a similar taste.'[5]

67
After Thomas Sandby, A *View of the Aviary & Parterre in the Royal Gardens at Kew*, c.1763, etching. © The Trustees of the British Museum.
There are no surviving views of Lady Reade's aviary; it must, however, have shared several characteristics with the aviary at Kew.

Harriott, Lady Reade (1727–1811), was the daughter and sole heiress of William Barker of Sonning, and niece of a celebrated beauty, the Right Honourable Susannah, Viscountess Fane (d.1792) – from whom she acquired what is now known as Crewe House in Curzon Street, Mayfair. Of her early life, nothing is known. In 1749 she married Sir John Reade (1721–1773), 5th Baronet, of Shipton Court, Shipton under Wychwood, Oxfordshire [fig. 68]. They had three children, the eldest of whom – their daughter Mary – was, like her mother, a great lover and collector of exotic birds and animals.

Lady Reade and her 'remarkable Aviary' achieved great local celebrity at the turn of the nineteenth century. In 1802 'Athalaricus', a correspondent for the *Gentleman's Magazine*, made a special pilgrimage to Shipton Court, where he professed to having passed 'one of the most agreeable hours I have ever spent':

> I turned out of the road I was going at Burford, and after riding a few miles I became transported from the dreary view of stone fences and a dilapidated forest into a grove adjoining Lady Reade's garden, that seemed as if it were enchanted. The warm light gales that fanned the leaves were scented with the odour of the neighbouring orangerie; and the arms of the majestic elms and umbrageous walnut-trees were adorned with a variety of maccaws, cories, cockatoos, parrots, and paroquets, that perched on and flew among them without restraint, these birds being in hot weather put out in the mornings without any apprehension being entertained of their getting away, long disuse of their wings having deprived them of all propensity to distant volitation; insomuch, that some of the very aged ones will sit all day on one bough, without moving even for food, whilst others flit from branch to branch within the extent of the foliaceous canopy.[6]

Doubtless the contrast between the dreary, ramshackle approach and the garden grove so intensified the pleasure, enchantment and luxuriance of the dowager's aviary garden that to enter the latter was to be transported to a paradisical demesne [figs 69 and 70].

> To see the gorgeous natives of the Torrid Zone preening their radiant plumes, and hearing an English grove re-echo with the fireperous screeches of African and Asiatic birds, are circumstances excitive of sensations novel and surprising beyond description. From this wonderful wood, I was conducted to a range of little

68
J. P. Neale, 'Shipton Court, Oxfordshire', engraving, in J. P. Neale, *Views of the Seats of Noblemen and Gentlemen, in England, Wales, Scotland, and Ireland* (1824). Historic Images/Alamy Photo Stock.

69

Alexandre-Isidore Leroy de Bardes, *Nature morte aux oiseaux exotiques*, c.1803, ink and watercolour. Inv.: INV23691. Photographer: Gérard Blot. Louvre, Paris (Cabinet des Dessins). © 2021. RMN-Grand Palais /Dist. Photo SCALA, Florence.

This watercolour by the French amateur painter le Chevalier de Bardes was one of several he produced to illustrate native and exotic birds displayed in Bullock's Museum in Piccadilly – some of which were also to be found in Lady Harriott's Oxfordshire garden.

70

Alexandre-Isidore Leroy de Bardes, *Réunion d'oiseaux étrangers placés dans différentes caisses*, c.1803, ink and watercolour. Inv.: INV23692-recto. Photographer: Jean-Gilles Berizzi. Louvre, Paris (Cabinet des Dessins). © 2021. RMN-Grand Palais /Dist. Photo SCALA, Florence.

rooms divided by wire network, and fitted with every convenience necessary to the preservation of the large collection of foreign small birds, which are appearing in a state of health, beauty, and docility. Indeed, no expence or trouble is spared. The peculiar diet of each kind of bird is observed as far as can be in this kingdom, the rooms are warmed in frosty nights by stoves, and a careful servant is retained solely for the purpose of attending the aviary. For the curious water-fowls a neat enclosed pond is provided, around which are erected hutches for their places of repose; but the number of these aquatic birds bears not any proportion to the number of land birds; yet, taking it altogether, I believe Lady Reade's aviary is the most valuable and tasteful one in this kingdom.[7]

Athalaricus appears to have seen the dowager's gardens and aviary at the pinnacle of their perfection. The account supplied by Revd Brookes a decade later paints a very different picture. Brookes, who as the vicar of Shipton was long and well acquainted with Lady Reade, provides us with a more insightful and poignant account of the menagerie and its menagerist; he likewise describes the melancholy circumstances that he believed prompted the creation of the 'finest collection of [exotic] Birds in England':[8]

The Mansion House ... in 1812 commanded a delightful tho' not an extensive woodland view. The gardens, useful & ornamental, were of considerable extent. There were forcing houses for pine apples, vines, oranges and lime trees & other exotics & some remarkably large Myrtle Trees, known to be more than a century old. All the outbuildings bore evident marks of decay. But those beautiful lawns where the family & visitors in other Days used to promenade, were at this time & had for 30 or 40 years past, been covered with wooden Frame work, roofed above, the side made of strong wire, in which vast cages, an immense assemblage of Birds, chiefly foreign, were kept. Amongst the specimens then exhibited the most beautiful as to form & the most splendid as to Plumage, were different species of Gold & Silver Pheasant.[9]

He also toured the interior of the house, whereupon seeing a painted portrait of 'the Lady Dowager Harriet Reade, painted by Sir Joshua Reynolds', he compared the 'captivating' likeness of the then youthful sitter with the present appearance of the elderly woman:[10]

The features are fine, the Physiognomy benevolent & it is esteemed one of the happiest efforts of the Great Artist. As the author of this article stood admiring this beautiful work of art, & drew with the mind's eye the present features of this lady at this date between 80 & 90 years of age, he could not trace the slightest resemblance, not a vestige remaining of that Beauty, so eminent in her youthful years.[11]

Brookes declares that 'the History of this Lady affords an eventful illustration of the Folly of making rash vows, & affecting an overstrained delicacy.' The precise nature of Harriott's rash vow is not revealed, but the very use of the term suggests that Brookes saw her as definitively committing herself to lifelong celibacy, rather than simply feeling a disinclination to her husband's embraces and to further childbirth, as a consequence of a distressing double pregnancy:

> *When young, she is presented as having been proud & high-spirited. But her husband, Sir John Reade, hoped that time & Reflection would soften & ameliorate these her only failings. They lived happily till, unfortunately for both, she was delivered of twins (viz Sir John Reade 5th Baronet & Thomas born 8 March 1762 – the latter died). This Sir John, the 5th Baronet, resided chiefly at Oddington, Co Glos. an Estate which he purchased some years since, the Domain of which he greatly improved. His death at the early age of 28, was accelerated if not occasioned by his endeavours to counteract a Propensity he had at one time shown to Corpulency ... From that hour a ridiculous idea of the Indelicacy of having twins filled her mind with such phantasies, that the advice of her dearest Friends was not powerful enough to induce her to reside with her husband, & a separation accordingly took place!*[12]

These events are reported by Brookes as having turned Dame Harriott's mind; he sees her as a woman galvanised to assemble a vast menagerie of birds and animals by personal misfortune and the folly and excess induced by it:

> *The effect of her rash vow upon her future Happiness was strickingly [sic] lamentable, & she that had been the Admiration of the County of the Beauty of her Person, & the Elegance of her manners, retired in Disgust from the polished circle of Society in which she had been reared. And from this period a marked change in her temper, manner & Habits was observed. She becames [sic] attached to Birds & monkies, & from purchasing a few, she went collecting, resolved to possess the finest collection of Birds in England, & being unsparing of money, she realised her intention, & formed a most magnificent Aviary. Having obtained, sometimes as presents, but more frequently purchased specimens of the most beautiful or scarce birds from every quarter of the world, from the largest to the most minute. And to keep alive the gaudy natives of the Tropics she had stoves constructed that kept the air of the Rooms at a proper Degree of Heat. Lady Reade is said frequently to have given 150 guineas for a single bird!*[13]

In passing through the 'apartments where these feathered prisoners were confined', Brookes observed that the 'noise of the different species of Macaws, Cockatoos, Parrots & Parroquets was absolutely deafening. And the air was so foul, notwithstanding every thing that care & Regularity could effect in cleaning their cages, that it was quite noxious. The pale cheeks, & dim eye of the Bird Maid, as the female was called who exhibited the collection to

71
Charles Eisen, *Woman in an Aviary*, c.1750–55, etching.
Mary Evans Picture Library, London.

strangers, sufficiently proved the ill effects of the Effluvia they occasioned' [fig. 71]. The vicar continued:

> Several years since a Fire happened thro' a Defect in one of the Stoves, & a great number of her collection of Birds were burned, & more were suffocated. The latter were embalmed, if the expression is allowable, & having died in the full

72
Louis-Francois Cheron, 'Qui se ressemble s'assemble', hand-tinted engraving, c.1815. Private Collection.

A French satirical print showing a woman of fashion bearing a profusion of birds and animals. Lady Reade took her penchant for 'living attendants' far beyond the bounds of fashion, but this image gives some idea of the perceptions of intriguing excess attached to a woman devoted to living creatures, and revelling in their company.

Brilliancy of feather, they looked almost as well as when living, & formed a study, whence some of our artists are said to borrow specimens to copy in their paintings. These are exhibited on the principal Floor, leading from the Great Stair Case to the Drawing-Room.[14]

We are informed that as Dame Harriott advanced in age, 'this attachment grew stronger, she neglected her person, paid not regard to fashion, intermixed but little with the world, &, by imperceptible degrees, lost every Trait, not only of female Beauty, but feminine reserve & Delicacy; as if she regretted her sex, & wished to conceal it' [fig. 72].[15]

Lady Reade was never a vicious woman. She had not disgraced her character, but her eccentricities in Dress & Manners, being talked of far around, she was followed by crowds, whenever she appeared in public, which irritating & offending the Pride of Wealth & Birth, it helped to put an end to the influence of native Benevolence, & she became an insulated being and Misanthrope.[16]

The dowager's avian zeal appears to have metamorphosed her into a remarkably picturesque character whose infrequent public appearances excited considerable public interest:

When she travelled between London & Shipton, Lady Reade attracted as much attention as Monarchy itself. At the Inns where she stopped the gates were usually closed, to afford her an opportunity of disembling & Landing her cargo of monkies & Birds, & other living attendants, who were stowed in her carriages. As soon as she reached to Magdalen Bridge at Oxford, a crowd was sure to collect, if it were in the Day time who followed or proceeded, accumulating as she advanced, so that by the time she arrived at the Star Inn, it was sometimes difficult to make way & it must be owned that her grotesque appearance in the midst of her living animals, was calculated to excite curiosity in an eminent degree.[17]

Sadly, these very colourful descriptions of Dame Harriott and her curious retinue must suffice: there are no surviving images to attest to this spectacle of gaudy magnificence. Indeed, we know little more of any consequence.[18]

Her daughter, Mary (1749–1818), certainly shared her infatuation with birds and animals. Mary, Lady Impey married the barrister Elijah Impey in January 1768. The youngest son of a prosperous London merchant, Elijah initially pursued a distinguished academic career and then practised at the bar for seventeen years, before being appointed, in 1773, first Chief Justice of the Supreme Court of India at Fort William, Calcutta. Lady Impey joined her husband in Calcutta in 1777, where she became one of the earliest British

73
Johann Zoffany, *Sir Elijah and Lady Impey and their Children*, oil on canvas, c.1783–4.
Museo Nacional Thyssen-Bornemisza, Madrid. Album/Alamy Stock.

patrons of Indian artists [figs 73 and 74]. Her biographer for the *Dictionary of National Biography* remarks:

> Lady Impey channelled her own investigative spirit, perhaps newly discovered through enforced leisure, into natural history, and kept birds and wild animals in the gardens of their mansion. Between 1777 and 1782 she commissioned a series (nearly 200 in all) of large drawings (mostly double folios) of her natural history collection from three Indian artists, Sheikh Zain al-Din (responsible for more than half the drawings), Bhavani Das, and Ram Das.[19]

Lady Impey returned to England in 1784, to live from 1792 at Amesbury on the skirts of Salisbury Plain, and finally from 1794 at Newick Park, near Lewes in Sussex. She does not, however, appear to have kept a menagerie in England.

LEMUR tardigradus.

Although ostensibly misanthropic, Dame Harriott had a close circle of friends who collected birds and animals 'for their pleasure' [fig. 75] – the identities of some of whom may be found in her Last Will and Testament:

> I give to Lady Willes and Mrs Crespigny two parrots each to be chosen by them alternatively Lady Willes to have the first choice I give four Small Birds if I should have so many to Miss Boscawen all the remainder of the small Birds to the Right Honorable Lady Penrhyn I give to the duke of Marlborough (who I hope will do me honor to accept of them) all the Birds of what kindsoever not herein disposed of which shall be in my Aviary and Pens in the Gardens at Shipton at the time of my death together with the nets and appurt[enance]s and also my Mandarin-Ducks of China my american drake and ducks the Indian Widgeon Golden European & S[il]ver pheasants and all my water ffowls and I give to said Lady Penrhyn All the birds called Lowrys [lorys, a species of small parrot] which I may die possessed of and all my [dar]ling-Botany Bay Birds my large blue Mackaw two of my Cockatoos my three beautiful tame macacks [macaques] mongoose small Ring tail monkey [lemur?] and three or four other fforeign quadrupeds if they shall be living and in my possession at my death but in case they shall not be approved of and accepted by her then I direct that my Executors to present them to such person or persons as they will be acceptable to and who may have kept such animals for their pleasure.[20]

Dame Mary Willes (1742–1813) and Mary de Crespigny (née Clarke, 1749–1812) were rich socialites, and Miss Boscawen was a London neighbour and distant relation.[21] The 4th Duke of Marlborough, as we have seen, took receipt of the Shipton aviary and presumably some of its denizens, and the somewhat eccentric Anne Susannah Pennant, Lady Penrhyn (née Warburton, 1745–1818), was the chosen recipient of many of her friend's most resplendent and raucous birds.

74
Sheikh Zain al-Din, *Sulphur Crested Cockatoo on a Custard Apple Branch*, 1777, watercolour. Ashmolean Museum, University of Oxford. Image © Ashmolean Museum, University of Oxford.

It is not known whether Lady Impey supplied her mother, Dame Harriott, with any birds or animals from her Indian menagerie.

75
Sydney Parkinson, *Lemur tardigradus*, 1767, watercolour and bodycolour on vellum. © The Trustees of the British Museum.

In a codicil to her will, Lady Reade bequeathed 'all my Macacks [macaques] and Mongooses and any other of my Little quadruped animals that may be in my possession at the time of my death' to Princess Frederica Charlotte, Duchess of York, at Oatlands in Surrey, as she was 'convinced they will receive the greatest affection and care'.[22] The duchess, wife to Prince Frederick, Duke of York and Albany, a younger son of George III, was 'particularly fond of animals' [fig. 76].[23] Thomas Raikes, writing much later in January 1833, remarks that the 'large menagerie' in the flower garden of this 'très grande dame' was 'filled with eagles, macaws, and various creatures', and 'a little colony of monkeys on the lawn before the windows of her boudoir; a herd of kangaroos, ostriches, &c. in the paddock; but her ruling passion was dogs'.[24] The German-born princess was, of all Lady Reade's friends, perhaps the most similar in her interests and temperament. John Wilson Croker observed in 1818: 'The Duchess's life is an odd one: she seldom has a female companion, she is read to all night and falls asleep towards morning, and rises about 3; feeds her dozens of dogs and her flocks of birds, &c., comes down two minutes before dinner, and so round again.'[25]

Every meaningful item in the dowager's houses and gardens was assigned to a worthy legatee: for instance, she gave her servant Mary Louch a 'little Green talking paroquet' and her 'Little Dog Rosie' (with generous provision for their care), and the Hon. Mrs Dutton of Barrington was left 'all the small Orange Trees which I lately purchased of Mr Shirley Together with the Tubs which contain them and six small stands of Myrtles in pots'.[26] Dame Harriott did not, however, leave any natural curiosities to her daughter, Mary (although she provided generously for her financially), nor to her friend and neighbour Warren Hastings, the former Governor-General of Bengal, who lived at Daylesford House in Gloucestershire, and who had conservatories and a large menagerie.[27]

Whereas both Hastings and Reade were both indulging their interests in natural curiosities, the former statesman is described by his biographer, Sir Charles Lawson, in 1895 as 'an horticulturist and an acclimatisor; and his flower, fruit, and vegetable gardens, his stables, his flocks, his herds, his menagerie, his farm, and his fish-ponds afforded his enquiring and intelligent mind constant delight';[28] Dame Harriott, on the other hand, is portrayed by her unofficial biographer, Brookes, as possessing a disturbing abnormality that sometimes borders on derangement. Her conduct is both extravagant and wild, Brookes implies, since she has allowed her collection of 'monkies & birds' to take the place of the conjugal affection and acceptance of further children that might be expected of a woman; it is as though she enacts an unnerving parody of the kind of behaviour that a more sedate female of her class might display. In disapprovingly charting such a displacement, Brookes inadvertently enlists the modern reader's sympathy on the side of a person who paid such determined attention not just to her own emotional needs but to the welfare and pleasure of her exotic entourage.

76
Peter Edward Stroehling, *Princess Frederica Charlotte, Duchess of York*, 1807, oil on copper. Royal Collection Trust. © Her Majesty Queen Elizabeth II 2021.

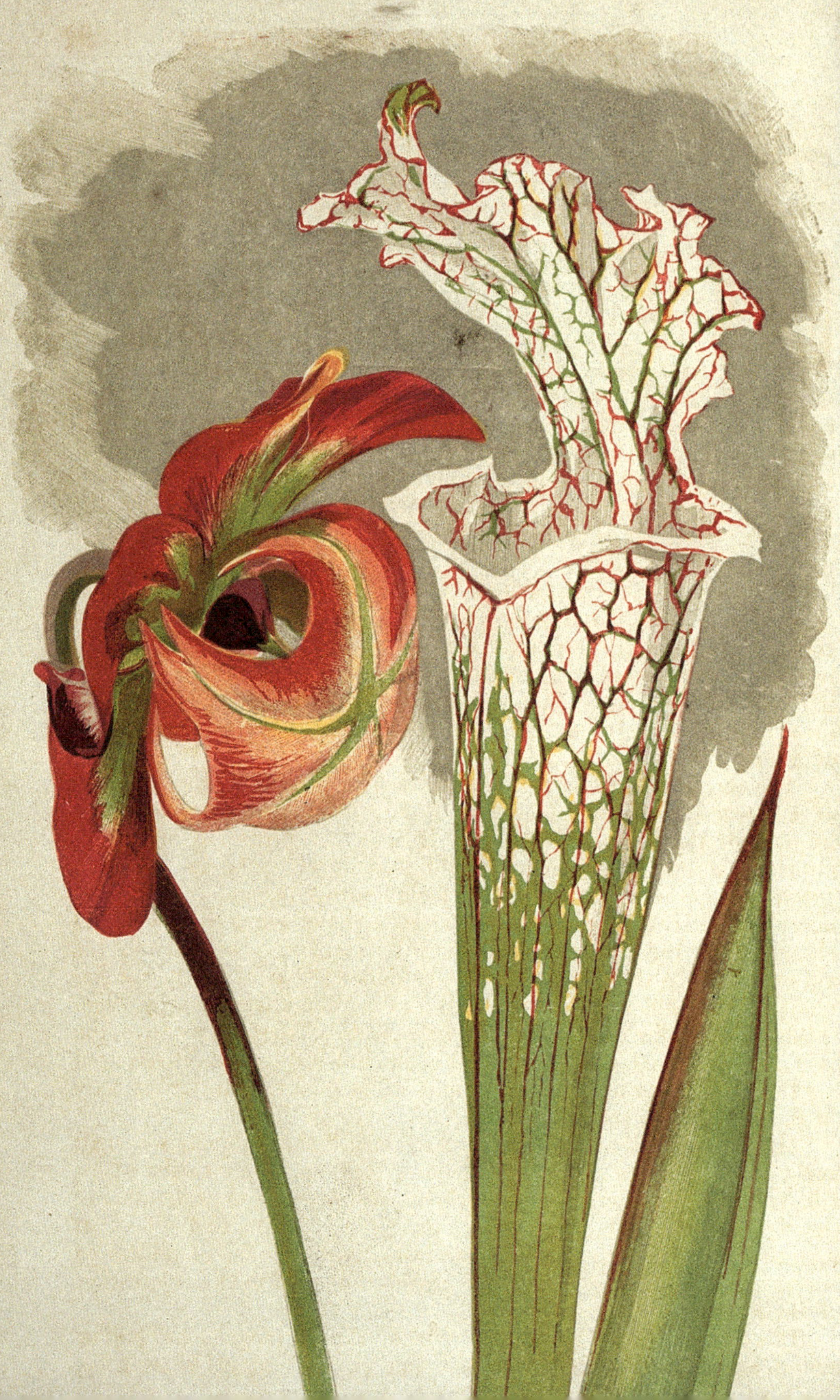

[NINE]

Lady Dorothy Nevill and her Ephemeral 'Exotic Groves'

She was very fond indeed of country life, for a short time, and she was interested in gardens, but she really preferred streets ... she liked bipeds best.[1]

THE POET AND CRITIC EDMUND GOSSE OBSERVED IN HIS POSTHUmous portrait of his friend Lady Dorothy Nevill that she possessed a 'curious static quality, a perennial youthfulness':

> I remember her as always the same, very small and neat, very pretty with her chiselled nose, the fair oval of her features, the slightly ironic, slightly meditative smile, the fascinating colour of the steady eyes, beautifully set in the head, with the eyebrows rather lifted as in a perpetual amusement of curiosity. Her head, slightly sunken into the shoulders, was often poised a little sideways, like a bird's that contemplates a hemp-seed. She had no quick movements, no gestures; she held herself very still ... Her physical strength – and she such a tiny creature – seemed to be wonderful.[2]

He was, like most people who met the 'slight, delicate, almost elfin figure', bewitched by her 'indomitable energy and love of observation', her evanescent charm and petulant wit: she was 'mistress of herself' and her 'strange little activities, her needlework, her paperwork, her collections, were the wonder of everybody, but she did not require approval; she adopted them, in the light of day, for her own amusement' [fig. 77].[3]

Lady Dorothy Fanny Nevill (née Walpole, 1826–1913) was the fifth and youngest child of Horatio Walpole, the bibulous and ill-tempered 3rd Earl of Orford, and his wife, Mary, daughter of William Augustus Fawkener. Dorothy spent her childhood at Wolterton Hall in Norfolk, Puddleton Manor in Dorset, and at the family town house in Berkeley Square. She received no formal education, but was taught to read in Italian, Greek, French and Latin; and from the age of ten Dorothy was initiated into the delights of Continental travel, accompanying her parents on the first of several lengthy tours of the Low Countries, Switzerland, Germany and Italy.

Presented to London society in 1846, her reputation was soon afterwards tarnished by an 'infamous scandal': scurrilous rumours circulated in what her mother, Lady Walpole, referred to as 'one of the *low papers*' of a compromising encounter in a summer house with the feckless libertine (and Benjamin Disraeli's closest aide) George Smythe – an event considered so shameful that Queen Victoria was to banish her from court forever.[4] Her honour was somewhat restored in December 1847 when she married her cousin Reginald Henry Nevill (1807–1878), a grandson of the 1st Earl of Abergavenny with a considerable fortune – and who was twenty years her senior. Whatever the story behind the scandal, she soon found plenty of other outlets for her spirited approach to life.

77
Louisa Lady Waterford, *Lady Dorothy Nevill*, c.1852, pen and ink.
Simon Houfe Collection.

78
Anon., Dangstein House seen from the south-west, 1872, engraving,
Journal of Horticulture (26 December 1872). Private collection.
The pleasure grounds abounded with conifers, including Wellingtonia,
monkey puzzle and a great variety of firs.

Nevill described her life to Gosse in 1901 as 'a treadmill of friendship, perpetually on the go', and she later wrote, 'I am hampered by perpetual outbursts of hospitality in every shape.'[5] She was nonetheless particular as regards her friendships: she disliked people who were 'insipid, conventional, and empty', saying once that 'the first principle of society should be to extinguish the bores.' She was a 'keen conservative' in politics but not a traditionalist one; unlike most members of her social class, she was 'fully alive to the changes that time had brought upon English Society, and determined from the beginning to make the best of the new order of things, and to gather honey from every hive'.[6] Her eager interest in all sides of modern life, and her genuine social gifts, made her ready to know everybody who had made a mark upon the culture of the time, so long as such a figure was personally agreeable – so that her acquaintances, many of whom became friends, included not only the so-called social leaders, but politicians of all parties, financiers, great manufacturers, men and women of letters, artists and men of science.

A contributor to the *Graphic* (1907) remarked that Dorothy was 'a skilful gardener long before gardening became the mode, having been taught in her childhood by the late Lord Zouche at Parham [West Sussex]'.[7] She 'loved everything that had life' – and plants and animals in particular.[8] She did not, however, begin to be recognised for her horticultural skills until 1851 when she and her husband acquired a country estate on the borders of Hampshire.

Dangstein occupied a conspicuous position in the north-west corner of the county of Sussex, 'bounded by the soft rolling undulations of the South Downs' [fig. 78].[9] The principal approach was circuitous and steep, and the gaunt but imposing Greek revival mansion was embosomed in trees. The house had been erected in 1836–7 for a Captain Lyons. Here Mr Nevill indulged his interests in farming, shooting and coach-driving, and Lady Dorothy created her legendary 'exotic groves'.[10]

Dorothy's gardens made their debut in the horticultural press in September 1856 when a contributor to the *Gardeners' Chronicle* noted: 'it is only within the last few years, since it became the property of Mr. and Lady Dorothy Nevill, that Dangstein has been heard of in the gardening world.'

> *Now however without doubt it may safely be said to vie with most of our finest gardens in the richness of its collections of fine exotic plants, the extent of late improvements and garden erections, and in the general order in which the whole place is kept. The grand features of the Dangstein gardens are two splendid houses lately erected, one for the growth of tropical fruits, Palms, and other fine foliaged plants, Orchids, &c.; the other solely for Ferns.*[11]

Others, too, were equally impressed: the Revd Henry Honywood Dombrain praised Lady Dorothy's 'ardent love for and liberal encouragement of all that pertains to a garden' and how she had made Dangstein 'a household word among the lovers of flowers';[12] and the influential gardener and journalist William Robinson commended her 'plant-treasures' and found Dangstein 'one of those places that are perennially interesting – full of life and variety'.[13] Lady Dorothy herself took pride in her perceived role in the 'popularisation of gardening in its best form' and 'artistic horticulture' in particular. She declared that several of her female contemporaries seemed to have developed a 'real aptitude' for gardening and become 'thoroughly practical gardeners'; the cultivation of flowers and the flower garden had, she suggested, become the 'special province of women'. Nevill even credited herself with the introduction of the herbaceous border 'long before it had become generally popular'.[14]

Dombrain observed in the *Journal of Horticulture* in 1865 that Dangstein did not attain its celebrity in the horticultural world on account of its beautiful situation, the picturesque character of the grounds, or its extensiveness. There were 'no grand avenues of trees, no noble specimens of the forest, no umbrageous valleys, or "bushy glens;" the whole place looks new, and the most interesting portion of it is so.'

> *To make what it is has been a work and labour indeed, but it has been one of love; and under the excellent taste and openhanded liberality of its owner, and the scientific management of Mr. Vair, Dangstein has become a famous place – famous for a collection of plants of such rarity and beauty as are seldom to be met with save in public institutions.*[15]

Lady Dorothy's 'fondness for plants and good taste in all that pertains to gardening' was well supported by James Vair (c.1825–1887), her 'intelligent and persevering' Scottish gardener.[16] Vair, who had earlier worked for Sir Walter Scott at Abbotsford, had great enthusiasm, 'excelled in the cultivation of Orchids', and was an 'ardent admirer and cultivator of Filmy Ferns and Sarracenias'.[17] Contemporary descriptions of Dangstein commend the 'excellent order' in which he and his team of thirty-three gardeners maintained the gardens and plants both inside and outside the glasshouses [fig. 79].[18]

Dangstein.—Gardener's Residence and Plant Houses.

79
Anon., The palm house, conservatory and fernery at Dangstein, 1872, engraving, *Journal of Horticulture* (26 December 1872). Private collection.
Two of the greenhouses at Dangstein were entirely devoted to rare plants and orchids which were sent to Lady Dorothy by her friends from every part of the world. Her gardener James Vair was a 'first-class plant grower' and 'excelled in the cultivation of Orchids'.

Dangstein boasted no fewer than seventeen hothouses, including ranges of forcing pits, a peach case, vineries, a tank house (for aquatics), an orchid house, a tropical orchard house (orangery), a palm house, a fernery and a filmy fernery. These contained a staggering array of unusual and exotic plants, and outstanding collections of orchids, ferns, insectivorous (carnivorous) plants, aquatics and tropical trees (including a wide range of citrus fruits).[19] These typically migrated from one greenhouse to another as Nevill's collections expanded, each time gaining greater display space and better growing conditions. For instance, her assortment of insectivorous plants, which was not numerically large but which contained most of the plants that were available at the time, was initially kept in the palm house together with some orchids; it was, however, later transferred to the tank house, and finally, by 1865, to the cool orchid house. Likewise, Nevill's collection of tropical trees, including fruit-bearing and ornamental species, and those that might prove of economic utility, was first kept in the palm house, then known as the 'tropical fruit house'. Later, most of the fruit-bearing trees within this collection were removed to the 'tropical orchard house' or 'orangery'. Lady Dorothy's ferns, of which she possessed 'about 300 different kinds', were also often in locomotion: the bulk of her specimens were kept in the main fernery, but over the years plants found their way into numerous neighbouring houses, and those requiring cooler growing conditions ultimately ended up in the specially built filmy fern house.[20]

No collection was larger, more varied or distinguished than the orchids, which were cultivated in one wing of the palm house and in the East India orchid house [fig. 80]. There were, she remarked, 'orchids without number', and her assemblage of them was the envy of some of the country's most eminent botanists and biologists, including Charles Darwin and Sir Joseph Hooker.[21] Nevill's taste for orchids and insectivorous plants was at the time very unusual; Darwin greatly admired the voracious specimen of the 'almost gigantic' Australian forked sundew (*Drosera binata* var. *dichotoma* 'Giant') that she gave him [fig. 81]. With a diameter of up to 1.25 m/4 ft and leaves 60 cm/24 inches long, the plant was a colossus among fly and crane fly catchers. Darwin remarked in *Insectivorous Plants* (1875) that feeding the specimen 'bits of meat' excited copious secretion from its dark red glands.[22] Nevill, unlike the celebrated naturalist, had no specialised botanical pretensions: her attitude was simply one of informed curiosity. Like Jean des Esseintes in J.-K. Huysmans's decadent novel À Rebours (1884), she was fascinated by plants that were characterised by many as monstrosities of nature and the 'offspring of unnatural adulteries' – 'barbarically-coloured flowers, the plants with barbaric

80
After W. Fitch, *Masdevallia chimæra*, c.1875, coloured lithograph.
Wellcome Collection, London. Wellcome Images.

It was reported in the *Courier* (31 August 1888) that 'Lord Zouche declared that the local archæology and tropical vegetation [in Sussex] under the patronage of Lady Dorothy were both quite as interesting as the monasteries of the Levant.'

81
Ferdinand Bauer, *Drosera binata dichotoma*, coloured print.
Natural History Museum, London. Natural History Museum/Alamy Stock Photo.

Lady Dorothy was particularly absorbed by her insectivorous plants, 'tempting these singular monsters with all kinds of delicacies'. She observed: 'They had I remember curious taste, manifesting a violent repugnance to cheese, and were not all averse to alcohol.'

82
Anon., various carnivorous plants, 1882, woodcut.
Historical image collection by Bildagentur-online/Alamy Stock Photo.

Darwin presented Lady Dorothy with an early and autographed copy of his *Insectivorous Plants* (1875), which she kept among her 'much-cherished presentation volumes'.

83
After H. Briscoe, *Sarracenia drummondii* (now known as *Sarracenia leucophylla*), flower, young leaf and pitcher, *c.*1870, chromolithograph. Wellcome Collection, London. Wellcome Images.

The Revd Honywood Dombrain praised Lady Dorothy for having popularised the cultivation of the richly coloured white-top pitcher plant.

names, the carnivorous plants of the Antilles – morbid horrors of vegetation, chosen, not for their beauty, but for their strangeness' [figs 82 and 83].[23]

Nevill was introduced to Darwin by John Lindley, who suggested that she might be able to send him a few hothouse orchids from her collection. In his first letter to his new correspondent in November 1861 Darwin remarked:

> *I much wish to examine a few more exotic forms, & if you happen to have those which I wish to see, possibly your ladyship would be so generous as to send me two or three flowers ... I chiefly want a member of the great Tribe of Arethuseæ, which includes the Limodoridæ, Vanillidæ &c.*

Mormodes & Cycnoches are especial desiderata ... I also want much Bonatea, Masdevallia & any Bolbophyllum with its lower lip or Labellum irritable.[24]

Lady Dorothy was only too delighted to oblige, and Darwin was for his part grateful that she 'most kindly placed her magnificent collection of Orchids at my disposal'.[25] She confided in her friend Lady Airlie, 'I am so pleased to help in any way the labours of such a man – it is quite an excitement for me in my quiet life, my intercourse with him ... I am sure he will find I am the missing link between man and apes.'[26] Over the succeeding years Nevill would send Darwin numerous orchids as well as specimens of insectivorous plants from her large collection [fig. 84].

Lady Dorothy was attracted to anyone who took an interest in collecting and was herself an inveterate collector. She took pleasure in acquiring and displaying her collections of French porcelain, ephemera, old clothes, portraiture and ironwork, and she formed and kept a museum which contained 'all that is rare, interesting and remarkable in botany':

> *Here are specimens of woods, of Cotton, of tropical fruits, dried and preserved; indeed, everything that can interest and instruct is here to be seen. There is also a very extensive and excellent botanical library. On the table lies the catalogue of the Dangstein collection, most elaborately and beautifully written in various colours by Lady Dorothy herself. Here also lies the book for visitors['] names, clearly indicating that wherever things are worth seeing, no matter how far by railroad, there persons will go.*[27]

Lady Dorothy remarks in her memoirs ('the tangled remnants of my brain') that 'there were a great number of curiosities of different sorts in my garden', among them her 'winged orchestra'.[28] It was, she believed, 'absolutely unique, having never been seen or, rather, heard anywhere else in England':

84
Anon., *Cattleya mossiae*, leaf and flower, 1899, watercolour.
Wellcome Collection, London. Wellcome Images.

The orchid house at Dangstein was over 60 m/200 ft long. A correspondent to the *Journal of Horticulture* remarked in November 1861 that 'the lover of the rare and gorgeous flora of the east will pause to admire how beautiful and curious productions of Nature [that are] here collected together.'

I had sent me from China a number of pigeon-whistles made out of gourds, which were something like small organ pipes, and could be attached with great ease to a pigeon's tail. The effect produced by the flight of these birds with whistles attached was extremely pretty, resembling Æolian harps, the whistles being all of a different note. People used to be astonished at such heavenly music, and their bewilderment and puzzled faces afforded me great amusement.[29]

Dangstein remained a remarkable ensemble until the summer of 1879 when the house and estate were put up for sale. The sale had been precipitated by the death of Lady Dorothy's husband in September 1878, but was already becoming necessary as a result of her immense expenditure on the gardens and other diverse pursuits. She was keen that her plant collections should go to the Royal Botanic Gardens at Kew, but this wish was thwarted by the advent of the Zulu Wars, which diverted funds from the Treasury that might otherwise have been available for the purchase.[30] Dangstein's 'extraordinary collection' of plants, which was, according to a notice in the Pall Mall Gazette, 'with one or two exceptions only (including Kew Gardens), … the largest and most varied in England', was instead sold at auction in June 1879 by J. Stevens:

Amongst these treasures will be found a thousand orchids, more than a thousand stove ferns, and about two hundred of the carnivorous plants, among which are some fine specimens of the rare Darlingtonia Californica. There are also masses of the more rare and beautiful filmy ferns, a large number of terrestrial orchids, camellias of the choicest; in short, as fine a collection as taste, knowledge, and wealth could bring together.[31]

The large tropical and subtropical trees were not included in the sale, and Lady Dorothy kept some of her orange trees for the conservatory of her new house at Stillyans in East Sussex. The remaining specimens were sold to King Leopold II of Belgium 'to fill his large conservatory' at the Royal Castle of Laeken, and to Charles III, Prince of Monaco, to embellish his new public gardens.[32]

Lady Dorothy, who, according to Gosse, was 'totally devoid of sentimentality', expressed no misgivings about giving up her 'exotic groves', remarking to Joseph Hooker: 'I don't regret leaving Dangstein nor the expensive garden which it would have been folly to keep up … I hope to make my new place very nice with hardy plants which after all are more effective than hot-house ones.'[33] She departed from Dangstein for Stillyans (which she rented from the botanist Robert Hogg) in the summer of 1879 with three van-loads of plants, accompanied by Mr Vair. Nevill remarked to her friend the botanist George

Maw that she wanted 'brightness and sweetness' in her new garden; here she kept a large conservatory, and set about creating a 'charming garden for Alpines and herbaceous plants'.[34]

Virginia Woolf paints an irreverent picture of Lady Dorothy in her essays 'The Memoirs of Lady Dorothy Nevill' (1908) and 'Behind Bars' (1919).[35] Despite her perceptible interest in titles and delight in aristocratic manners, Woolf was, according to Alex Zwerdling's essay on her, 'never seriously attracted to this world'.[36] She characterised the stately homes of the English upper classes as 'comfortably padded lunatic asylums', but conceded that Lady Dorothy was 'not an extreme case of aristocracy'. Woolf's tone of condescension allows for an element of sympathy: 'she was confined rather to a bird-cage than to an asylum; through the bars she saw people walking at large, and once or twice she made a surprising little flight into the open air. A gayer, brighter, more vivacious specimen of the caged tribe can seldom have existed' [fig. 85].[37]

Woolf imagined her subject 'hopping from perch to perch, picking at groundsel here, and at hempseed there, indulging in exquisite trills and roulades, and sharpening her beak against a lump of sugar in a large, airy, magnificently equipped bird-cage':

> The cage was full of charming diversions. Now she illuminated leaves which had been macerated to skeletons; now she interested herself in improving the breed of donkeys; next she took up the cause of the silkworms, almost threatened Australia with a plague of them, and 'actually succeeded in obtaining enough silk to make a dress'; again she was the first to discover that wood, gone green with decay, can be made, at some expense, into little boxes; she went into the question of funguses and established the virtues of the neglected English truffle; she imported rare fish; spent a great deal of energy in vainly trying to induce storks and Cornish choughs to breed in Sussex; painted on china; emblazoned heraldic arms, and, attaching whistles to the tails of pigeons, produced wonderful effects 'as of an aerial orchestra' when they flew through the air. To the Duchess of Somerset belongs the credit of investigating the proper way of cooking guinea-pigs; but Lady Dorothy was one of the first to serve up a dish of these little creatures at luncheon in Charles Street.[38]

Nevill was redeemed to some extent, the novelist nonetheless concluded, by her willingness to acknowledge the deficiencies of her class. Woolf quotes a letter that Lady Dorothy wrote to Miss Haldane a year or so before her death:

> I do so agree with you – though I ought not to say so – that the upper class are very – I don't know what to say – but they seem to take no interest in anything – but golfing, etc. It makes me quite sad when I go to any of the museums to see not

85
'K', 'The Lady Dorothy Nevill', chromolithograph, *Vanity Fair*
(6 November 1912). National Portrait Gallery, London.

a soul hardly there, and the few that are there only giggling, etc. One day I was at the Victoria and Albert Museum, just a few sprinkles of legs, for I am sure they looked too frivolous to have bodies, and souls attached to them – but what softened the sight to my eyes were 2 little Jap[ane]s[e] poring over each article with a handbook, so eager to know everything there was to be seen – our bodies of course giggling and looking at nothing. Still worse, not one soul of the higher class visible; in fact I never heard of any one of them knowing of the place ... it is all too painful.[39]

Her son, Ralph Nevill, gave a similar account of her social outlook: she would 'often deplore the indifference shown by the upper class, (a term, it may be added, which she refused to abandon), towards art and learning'.[40]

Woolf affirms that 'no story more aptly illustrates the barrier which we perceive hereafter between Lady Dorothy and the outer world than the story of Charles Darwin and the blankets':

Among her recreations Lady Dorothy made a hobby of growing orchids, and thus got in touch with 'the great naturalist'. Mrs Darwin, inviting her to stay with them, remarked with apparent simplicity that she had heard that people who moved much in London society were fond of being tossed in blankets. 'I'm afraid,' her letter ended, 'we should hardly be able to offer you anything of that sort'. Whether in fact the necessity of tossing Lady Dorothy in a blanket had been seriously debated at Down [House], or whether Mrs Darwin obscurely hinted her sense of some incongruity between her husband and the lady of the orchids, we do not know. But we have a sense of two worlds in collision; and it is not the Darwin world that emerges in fragments.[41]

Ironically, Woolf's avian analogy, and the comparison of Lady Dorothy's comfortable social position to a gilded prison, were the kind of observations that Nevill herself would scarcely have found offensive. Dorothy was a great lover of birds and owned 'all sorts ... in great numbers', but unlike her earlier and equally eccentric rival, Dame Harriott Reade, she appears to have been singularly unsuccessful in her efforts to raise exotic fowl, including parrots, cranes and storks.[42] She conceded wistfully in old age that although she kept an aviary for many years, 'I do not know, however, that aviaries are ever a great success; it is far more pleasant, indeed, to see birds at liberty like my choughs.'[43]

Virginia Woolf's humorous hyperbole, in listing Nevill's multifarious 'diversions', touches on a quality that is also discernible in her approach to gardening, and that marks her out as an eccentric and extraordinary gardener rather than simply a capable and enthusiastic one. Just as she collected an improbable number and range of unusual skills and accomplishments, she also accumulated astounding quantities and varieties of plants, often of a highly specialised nature. Many of the details and descriptions cited so far testify to the numerical dimension of her eccentricity: she had seventeen hothouses, 'about 300 different kinds of ferns', 'orchids without number', a museum that contained 'all that is rare, interesting and remarkable in botany', and, 'in my garden', 'a great number of curiosities of different sorts'. Even the birds were to be found in great numbers. However calmly she relinquished most of her collections on her husband's death, she was not, during his lifetime, a woman to do things by halves – and even this sad event provided her with an occasion for seeking out novelty in the manner that Woolf regards as so bird-like: she turned to alpines and herbaceous plants.

If Lady Dorothy was, as Woolf imagined, an exotic bird and 'the door of the cage was ajar',[44] try as she might to make 'raids' into what Ralph Nevill referred to as 'Upper Bohemia' to engage with 'authors, journalists, actors, actresses, or other agreeable and amusing people' – to make 'a flight beyond the cage' – she was destined to return to her agreeable confinement; she could not escape her class.[45]

Woolf was intrigued by Nevill, seeing in her a woman who was torn between different versions of how to be a thinking, enquiring member of society; she perceived her as someone who aspired to improve herself, but was shaped by invisible barriers. The novelist could not comprehend what stopped her from educating herself, disciplining her mind, fulfilling the potential of her energies and interests, and gaining the authority to correspond with Darwin and other informed botanists and gardeners on their own terms. Although Lady Dorothy did indeed possess a keen intellectual curiosity, her efforts to focus on any particular pursuit were limited by what her son described as a 'curious kind of inconsistency' and her habit of indulging in 'audacious flights of reckless whimsicality'.[46] In refusing to acknowledge established boundaries between 'serious' intellectual enterprise and aristocratic play, she was, like so many eccentrics, content to move between worlds and to belong wholly to none. Rather than opposing a perceived cultural centre, she created 'centres' of her own through her deep immersion in the projects that she was constantly devising – projects imbued with an intensity that allowed them to function especially strikingly as a means of impressing her own personality upon the world.

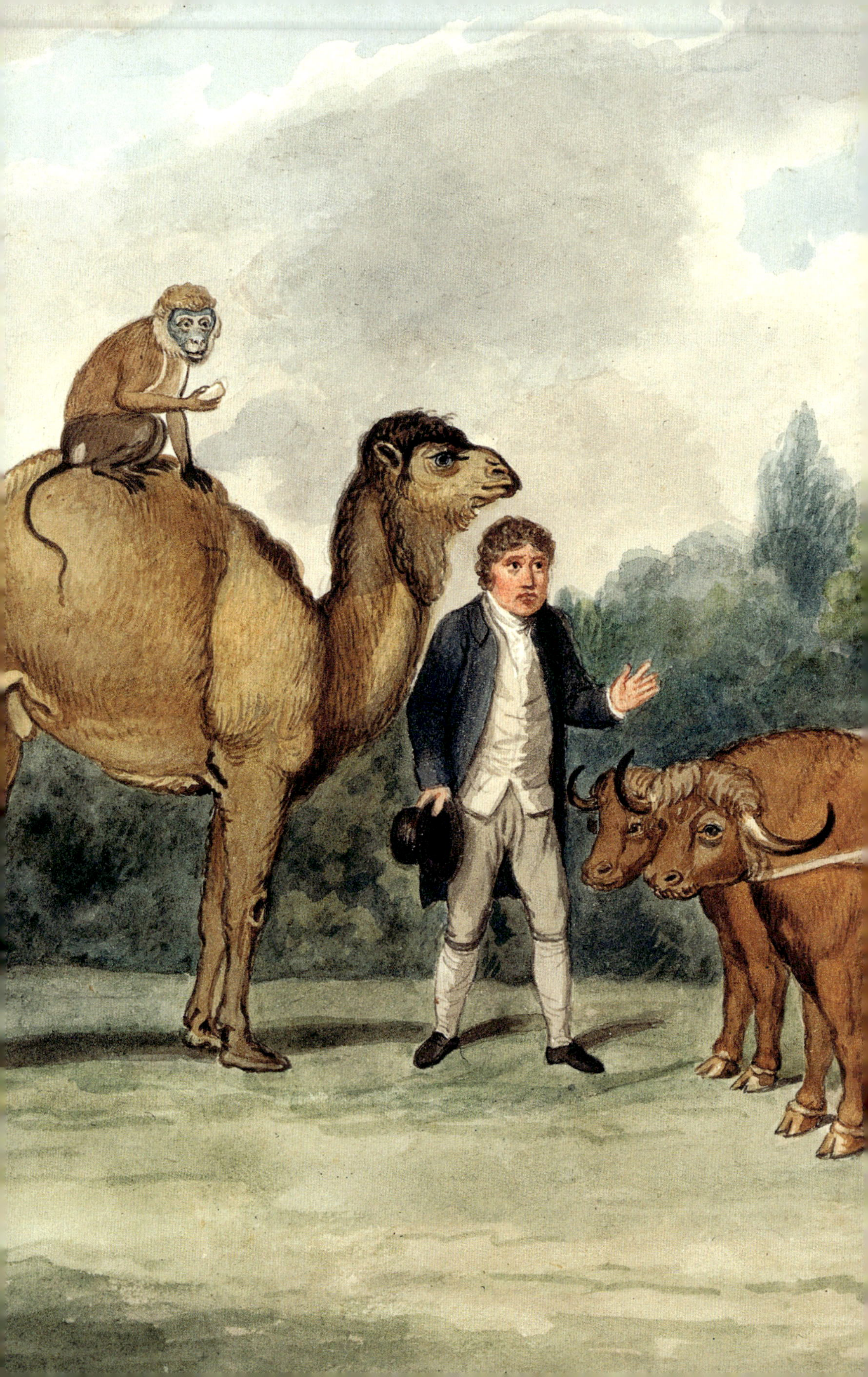

[TEN]

Brookes's Vivarium: 'A Curious Assemblage of Life and Death'

Rocks are generally considered as parts of the foundation of the earth, and their general character is that of grandeur, sometimes mixed with the singular fantastique or romantique. Their expression forms a fine contrast to that of perishable vegetation, and therefore they have been eagerly sought after in gardens, both on this account, and as forming a suitable habitation for certain descriptions of plants. Plant rock-works are protuberant surfaces, or declivities irregularly covered with rocky fragments, land-stones, conglomerated gravel, vitrified bricks, vitrified scoriæ, flints, shells, spar, or other earthy and hard minerals bodies. Such works are, in general, to be looked on more as scenes of culture than of design or picturesque beauty.

Rock-works, for effect or character, require more consideration than most gardeners are aware of ... [and their] ... execution is more a matter of labour than of skill.[1]

JOHN LOUDON, THE GREAT ENCYCLOPAEDIST OF GARDENING, considered 'rock-works' garden structures, and categorised them as 'Characteristic Decorations' – that is, items that were 'purely decorative, without any pretensions to convenience': 'they should ... be very sparingly employed, and only by persons of judgment and experience. A tyro in gardening will be more apt to render himself ridiculous by the use of decorations, than by any other point of practice, and most easily by the use of characteristic decorations.'[2] What, one wonders, must Loudon have made of a letter and accompanying illustration he received in the post from Dr Brookes in early summer 1830 advertising the sale of his 'very large and picturesque piece of Rockwork, formed chiefly of considerable masses of the Rock of Gibraltar, adapted to the purpose of a Vivarium, at present inhabited by an Eagle and several smaller rapacious Birds' [fig. 86]?[3]

86
Charles Hullmandel
after George Scharf,
*A View of the Vivarium,
Constructed principally
with large Masses of the
Rock of Gibraltar, in the
Garden of Joshua Brookes
Esq., Blenheim Street, Great
Marlborough Street*, 1830,
lithograph. London
Picture Archive.

THE VIVARIUM,
f GIBRALTAR, *in the Garden of Joshua Brookes Esq.*
Great Marlborough Street.

Dr Joshua Brookes (1761–1833) was, by all accounts, 'somewhat an eccentric character'.[4] He was the son of a prominent and successful bird trader who owned and operated menageries across the metropolis, and counted among his clients aristocrats and men from the professional classes, including the anatomist and surgeon John Hunter.[5] Having obtained 'an excellent classical education', Joshua junior studied anatomy and surgery in London under William Hunter (John Hunter's brother), William Hewson, Andrew Marshall and John Sheldon, and completed his studies at the Hôtel-Dieu in Paris. On his return to London, he began to teach anatomy, and became 'deservedly, and generally esteemed as one of the best – if not the best – teacher of practical anatomy in London' [fig. 87].[6]

If Brookes 'worked diligently and honourably', and was an assiduous and demanding teacher, he was 'less than fastidious' in his personal habits:[7] the surgeon John Flint South remarked that he was 'without exception the dirtiest professional person I have ever met with … all and every part of him was dirt.'[8]

The anatomist's greatest achievement was his Museum Brookesianum – a vast collection of comparative anatomical material, inspired by John Hunter's anatomical museum.[9] He displayed it in his premises in Blenheim Street, Great Marlborough Street, not far from Oxford Circus, which he leased from 1784 from the natural philosopher Henry Cavendish, who had occupied a large building in its garden as his laboratory or workshop.[10] Brookes converted this to form his Theatre of Anatomy and his museum – which comprised 'an almost endless assemblage of every species of Anatomical, Pathological, Obstetrical, and Zootomical Preparations, as well as subject in Natural History, of the choicest and rarest Species in every department'.[11]

South tells us the doctor lavished great sums on developing his museum: 'it was his pet lamb, and he sacrificed everything to its improvement.'[12] Brookes was in fact so omnivorous that by the turn of the century his collection was 'justly ranked as second to that of the late John Hunter',[13] and the museum was 'so crammed with skeletons and other zoological specimens that it was hardly possible to move without knocking down something with one's coat-tail'.[14]

Given the museum's encyclopaedic contents it is not surprising that during Brooke's long professional career, 'no zoologist, or foreigner of distinction, ever came to this kingdom without paying him a visit.'[15] The noted French natural historian Georges Cuvier pronounced it to be 'the next to that preserved at the Jardins des Plantes' in Paris.[16]

Although the doctor is generally thought to have spent most of his time in the dissecting room, he also pursued town gardening. Horwood's *Map of London* (1813 edn) indicates that his plot was modest, enclosed on two sides by buildings, abutting a neighbouring garden to the east and opening into Blenheim Street on the west. Within this space the anatomist created a garden like no other in London's West End. His efforts are commemorated in a drawing he commissioned in 1830 from the topographer George Scharf, which was to form the basis for the advertisement to promote the sale of his rockwork and his pilgrim's cell. This drawing, inscribed 'at Mr Brookes's Blenheim Street', was made into a lithograph entitled 'A View of the Vivarium, Constructed principally with large Masses of the Rock of Gibraltar, in the Garden of Joshua Brookes Esq., Blenheim Street, Great Marlborough Street'. The print was produced by Brookes's neighbour, the lithographer Charles Hullmandel, published privately by the doctor and circulated with a covering letter to potential purchasers. We do not know how many individuals the doctor approached, but his missives addressed to Sir John Soane and John Loudon survive; indeed, the latter published the letter in the *Gardener's Magazine*.[17]

Brookes's correspondence to Soane on 30 April 1830 supplies a detailed description of his 'Rock':

87
James Fittler after Thomas Phillips, *Joshua Brookes*, 1815, mezzotint.
Wellcome Collection, London.

The structure is excavated in different parts for the seclusion of its residents. The four principal entrances of the Adyta,[18] are ample, and arched with rude portions of Rock; there are likewise many small Cryptae arranged irregularly for various animals; and subterranean passages intersecting each other for their convenience and retirement.[19]

The anatomist's references to *adyta* and *cryptae* suggest that the design of the 'Rock' was informed by the Jesuit polymath Athanasius Kircher's *Mundus Subterraneus* (1665) and *Oedipus Aegyptiacus* (1652–4). In the former Kircher sets out 'before the eyes of the curious reader all that is rare, exotic, and portentous contained in the fecund womb of nature',[20] and covers a large variety of subjects related to the Earth's interior, including fossils, animals, dragons, men and demons, the art of metals, and alchemy; and in *Oedipus Aegyptiacus* he reveals the 'Ancient Mysteries' of Egypt, Greece and Rome. Brookes's rockwork – the profile of which resembles an artificial volcano [fig. 88] – is, however, a very peculiar and bizarre assemblage including both rockworks and waterworks.

88
Anon., 'Typus Montis Ætnæ', etching, in Athanasius Kircher, *Mundus Subterraneus* (1678 edn). Wellcome Collection, London.

His letter to Soane continues:

The whole covers an area of about thirty feet, and is upwards of ten feet in height, somewhat in [the] shape of a truncated cone, on the surface of which there is a spacious reservoir for Fish, aquatic Plants, and oceanic Birds, with a Jet d'Eau in the centre, ascending through an interesting specimen of Rock, considerably elevated above the level of the water, which is prevented from overflowing by a syphon which conveys it through the mouth of an antique head of a large animal nearly resembling that of an Ichthyosaurus.

The interstices of the Rock are occupied by Alpine and appropriate indigenous Plants; these, descending over the stones, embellish and augment the pleasing appearance of the fabric, which would form a beautiful object in an Arboretum, or at the termination of a Vista.

The presence of alpine and indigenous plants is particularly fascinating, as is the way in which they are mixed with the rock's artificial curiosities and exotic fauna. The effect echoes, but surpasses in grotesque splendour, the alpine 'rockwork' at the Chelsea Physic Garden. This latter, created by William Forsyth in 1774 and formed from geological specimens brought back from Iceland by Sir Joseph Banks, interspersed with surplus stone from repairs to the Tower of London, is generally regarded as Britain's first rock garden.[21]

The anatomist continued to elaborate upon the rockwork and its most distinguished avian inhabitants, and concluded his letter with an account of the Gothic 'Pilgrim's Cell' which sat adjacent to and overlooked the Rock:

The four chief Caverns were for many years the residence of a Vulture, a white-headed Eagle, an Ossifrage, and a magnificent auriculated Owl, all natives of the most inhospitable Climes, and such, however, as may be readily obtained. Those that remain are domesticated, and will be given to the purchaser. The two former birds were presented to the Zoological Society, and are now living.

Occupying an angle in the Garden, is a Pilgrim's Cell [fig. 89], constructed principally of the jaws of a Whale, having furniture of the same material, and lighted by a stained glass Window. This structure is also attainable.

Mr. Brookes hopes Mr Soane will accept his apology for troubling him with this detail, but conceives that many Gentlemen having occasion to consult him on horticultural arrangements, might avail themselves of this, perhaps the only means of constructing a noble rural ornament with several tons of the Rock of Gibraltar.[22]

Brookes does not reveal how he came to acquire his 'masses of rock'. It is likely that his interest in Gibraltarian stone began as early as the 1770s when

William Hunter acquired 'two masses of bones ... blended with pieces of the marble' from the peninsula.[23] He and his friends certainly had a scientific, if sometimes rather playful, interest in the stone, which was renowned at the time as 'osseous' or 'bone breccia' – a limestone rich in fossil organic remains [fig. 90].[24]

As for the fauna that inhabited the Blenheim Street vivarium, much of this appears to have come from his father and latterly his brothers. His brother Paul had 'travell'd for several Years to various parts of the Globe, for the Purpose of collecting ... the most Rare and interesting animals ... curious Quadrupeds, and Birds ... as well as Pheasants of every variety, Poultry, Pigeons &c'.[25] Brookes's ingenious and unusual comingling of flora and fauna can also probably be attributed to his familiarity with his father's trade and experimentation: from 1772 Joshua senior collaborated with William Young – botanist to

89
George Scharf, At Mr Brooke's, Blenheim Street (detail), 1830, grisaille watercolour.
© The Trustees of the British Museum.
James Montgomery remarked in Prose by a Poet (1824) that whale jawbones were frequently seen in the 'northern counties, generally forming a kind of Gothic arch over the humble entrance into a field'. Brookes's use of jawbones to frame his pilgrim's cell was unusual.

90

Sarah Stone, A *calcarious Stone full of Bones of Land Animals taken from the Rock of Gibraltar*, 1772, watercolour. Natural History Museum, London. Natural History Museum/Alamy Stock Photo.

Stone's detailed representation of a fragment of fissure breccia from the Quaternary period shows remains of fossilised mammalian bones.

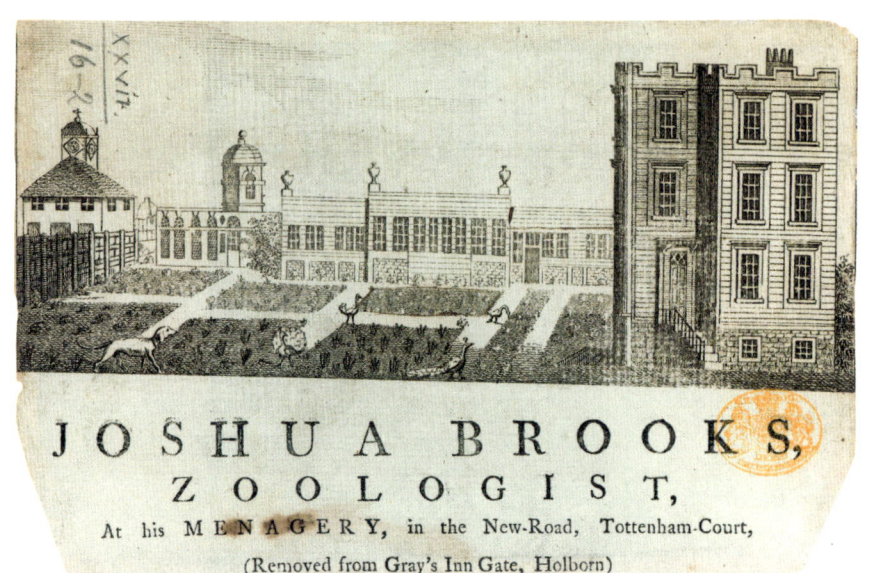

JOSHUA BROOKS, ZOOLOGIST,
At his MENAGERY, in the New-Road, Tottenham-Court,
(Removed from Gray's Inn Gate, Holborn)

91
Anon., fragment of a handbill for Joshua Brookes senior and his Menagerie in New Road, Tottenham Court, c.1776, engraving. © The Trustees of the British Museum.

Brookes's establishment in Tottenham Court contained 'a great collection of very curious Birds from the East Indies, Africa and Southern Parts of America'. He also advertised for sale 'Hundreds of Seedling North American Oak and Tulip Trees, and many flowering Shrubs, and some American Seeds'.

Queen Charlotte at Kew – to supply birds, animals and an astonishing variety of 'shrubs, trees, bog plants, ferns, seeds, acorns and cones' to the wealthy and the fashionable [fig. 91].[26]

The design of Brookes's curious assemblage itself was almost certainly influenced by the garden of John Hunter. Jesse Foot, Hunter's biographer, who was familiar with the surgeon's small country estate in Earl's Court, also made this connection. 'Nobody', he remarked, 'of common curiosity could have ever passed this original cottage, without being obliged to enquire, to whom it belonged. By observing the back of the house, a lawn was found stocked with fowls and animals, of the strangest selection in nature, – as if it had been, another repository belonging to Brook[e]s' [figs 92 and 93].[27]

The similarities continued: the house was flanked by 'two pyramidal collections of shells, of a very contracted base, and mean height – each of them, seeming to conceal a subterraneous entrance to a Golgotha', and 'over the front

92
W.P.S., 'Earle's Court', watercolour included in a grangerised copy of Jesse Foot, *The Life of John Hunter* (1821, first published 1794). Wellcome Collection, London.

The Latin poetic lines translate as 'Here Africa laughs, here Asia – here [are] ravenous tigers, and cruel packs of wolves; the angry lion and lioness with tawny neck pound the sand with swift feet.' The inscription was 'intended to go over the great door where the crocodile was'.

93
Anon., John Hunter with a camel, monkey and two buffaloes, late eighteenth century, watercolour. Science History Images/Alamy Stock Photo.
According to Thomas Baird, who visited Earl's Court House in 1793, 'Hunter caused his buffaloes to be trained to work a cart,' and he drove them through the streets of London.

door was presented the mouth of a Crocodile, gaping tremendously wide.'[28] Hunter's garden also possessed other attributes with a distinctively Brookesian character, including a pond whose margins were 'ornamented with skulls of animals', in which the surgeon bred eels, leeches and freshwater mussels,[29] and a 'Lion's Den' in the form of a tumulus, atop which was a 'little rampart made of bricks and tiles, after the fashion of a castellated tower ... a sort of private fortress', where he kept a gun that he would fire to deter the curious [fig. 94].[30]

There are surprisingly few accounts of Brookes's garden, despite the fact that his premises were 'always open to scientific foreigners, and on certain days in the year (generally one Saturday in a month) to the public at large; while private gentlemen were frequently granted admission on other occasions'.[31]

An exception is a report published in 1829 by a 'Young Surgeon' who described how on one occasion the anatomist was attacked by a 'mad creature':

> He kept a great number of animals in a yard attached to his house, – dogs, and foxes, and rabbits; and amongst the rest a wolf-dog, a savage devil from New South Wales. This beast one day got loose, and was worrying one of the pupils, when some others coming up rescued him. One of the foxes went mad, and jumping at Mr. Brookes bit him on the head, and the injured part was cut out. Besides these creatures, there were all kinds of birds, eagles, owls, &c. Such a curious assemblage of life and death as was here gathered I never saw before.[32]

A neighbour, however, supplies us with the most lurid account of the anatomist's garden: he viewed it in the early hours of 14 January 1792 amidst the 'awful sublimity' of the fire that destroyed the Pantheon in Oxford Street – a conflagration so great that its glare is reputed to have illuminated the sky as far away as Salisbury Plain, and reminded the horrified viewer of 'the temple of Pandemonium, as represented in Milton's poem, when Satan is arraying his troops, on the banks of the fiery lake':

> The country round was illuminated for miles. At this time, spacious iron gates opened into Mr Brookes's garden, through which the passengers could see his collection of living birds and beasts, chained to the artificial rocks, which until

Anon., *The dens in which John Hunter kept his Wild Animals – 1783 – Earl's Court House, 1783*, watercolour. Hunterian Family Album, Royal College of Surgeons of England, London.

95
R. B. Schnebbelie, attrib., *Mr Brookes's, Blenheim off Oxford St*, 1817, watercolour.
Hunterian Family Album, Royal College of Surgeons of England, London.

Brookes's name is boldly inscribed on his gate, and an eagle(?) and the pediment of the pilgrim's cell are visible above the garden wall. The whale jawbone supporting the stained-glass window is guyed to a neighbouring building.

lately, ornamented his plot of ground. The heat was so violent here, that his doors and sash frames were blistered, and the eagle, hawks, racoons, foxes and other animals, terrified by the scene, and incommoded by the heat, were panting and endeavouring to break their chains. The mob assembled, and fancying that the poor animals were roasting alive, kept up an alarming yell, and threatened to pull the house about his ears.[33]

In the event, the doctor and his museum and garden survived. A watercolour attributed to Robert Blemmell Schnebbelie, inscribed 'Sketched on Wednesday 25th June 1817', depicts the premises as seen from Blenheim Street [fig. 95].[34] The gable of the pilgrim's cell and one of the avian denizens of the 'larder-tumulus' are just visible above the brick garden wall.[35] A large pair of gates bearing the inscription 'Dr Brookes' and framed by two piers shows the vantage point from which a crowd of concerned people watched the spectacle of the garden-menagerie as the Pantheon was engulfed in flames.[36]

Sadly, however, though Brookes's extraordinary establishment escaped destruction by fire, it was eventually the victim of changes in medical education which put his thriving anatomy school out of business [fig. 96]. His biographer lamented in 1834 that it was 'to the eternal disgrace of the British nation' that the 'admirable monument of his [Brookes's] industry was, in his declining years, disposed of and dispersed by the hammer of the auctioneer and that collection, which had cost him so much labour and anxiety, and upwards of thirty thousand pounds, was sold for a mere trifle'.[37]

There is no record of what happened to the vivarium and the pilgrim's cell. As for Brookes's proposition that they could be dismantled and re-erected to advantage to form garden eye-catchers, it is unlikely that his idiosyncratic structures would have appealed to many garden improvers. They were, in all likelihood, broken up and their remains scattered or reassembled to create, in Loudon's words, 'characteristic decorations' of a more restrained kind, but doubtless less 'fantastique or romantique'.[38]

96
Anon., cover of 'A Descriptive and Historical Catalogue of the Remainder of the Anatomical & Zootomical Museum of Joshua Brookes, Esq.', 1830. Wellcome Collection, London.

A DESCRIPTIVE AND HISTORICAL CATALOGUE

OF THE REMAINDER OF THE

ANATOMICAL & ZOOTOMICAL MUSEUM,

OF

JOSHUA BROOKES, Esq. F.R.S. F.L.S. F.Z.S. &c.

COMPRISING NEARLY ONE HALF OF THE ORIGINAL COLLECTION,

AND EMBRACING AN ALMOST ENDLESS ASSEMBLAGE OF EVERY SPECIES OF

ANATOMICAL, PATHOLOGICAL, OBSTETRICAL,

AND ZOOTOMICAL PREPARATIONS,

As well as Subjects in

NATURAL HISTORY,

Of the choicest and rarest Species in every Department:

𝕬𝖍𝖎𝖈𝖍 𝖜𝖎𝖑𝖑 𝖇𝖊 𝕾𝖔𝖑𝖉 𝖇𝖞 𝕬𝖚𝖈𝖙𝖎𝖔𝖓,

BY

MESSRS. WHEATLEY & ADLARD,

At the Theatre of Anatomy, Blenheim Street, Great Marlborough Street,

On MONDAY, the 1st of MARCH, 1830,

AND 22 FOLLOWING EVENINGS, (SATURDAYS & SUNDAYS EXCEPTED,)

AT HALF-PAST SIX O'CLOCK PRECISELY.

The Collection may be viewed by Tickets, which with Catalogues, price Three Shillings, may be had in all the principal Towns of England; at Edinburgh; Glasgow, and Dublin; of Mons. Bossange père, and Messrs. Galignani, Paris; and at the Offices of Messrs. Wheatley and Adlard, 191, Piccadilly, London.

PRINTED BY RICHARD TAYLOR, RED LION COURT, FLEET STREET.

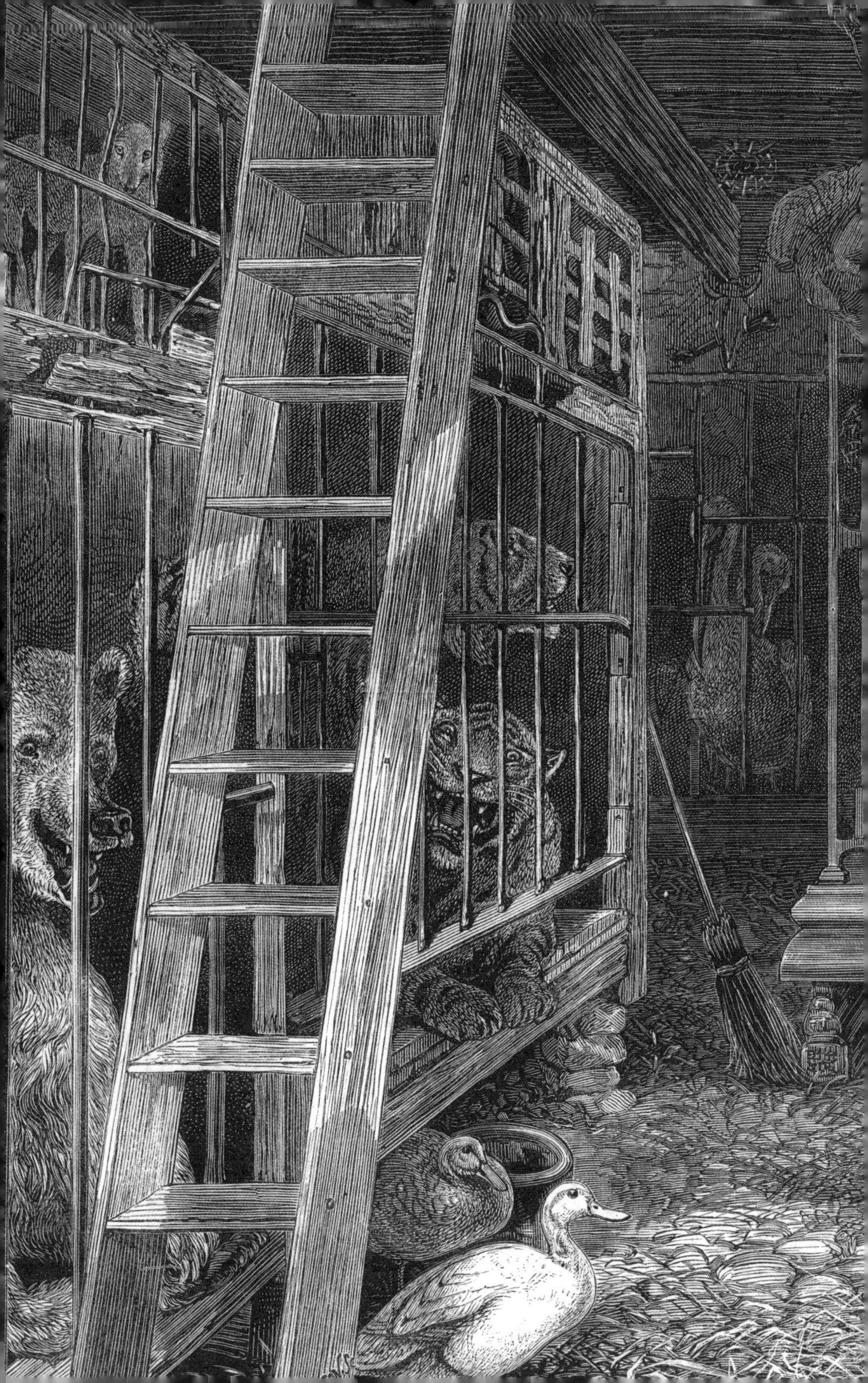

[ELEVEN]

Russell Collett and Sir Robert Heron: Gardens and Goldfish

IN 1826 THE ANTIQUARIAN MAJOR-GENERAL JOHN HENRY LOFT PAID a visit to a then little-known estate in the extra-parochial liberty of Swinethorpe, about 11 km/7 miles south-west of Lincoln, on the Nottinghamshire border.[1] Here, Samuel Russell Collett (1771–1850) had erected a sham-castle, described in The Buildings of England as having a 'folly façade' and being 'Spidery and vegetable-like, an ancestor of Gaudi, if ever there was one' [figs 97 and 98].[2] Loft, who saw the house soon after it had been completed, described it as a 'very singular but tasty and handsome Residence':

> It is composed of over burnt Bricks until they run together in large Masses, these are built up in that rough state forming a Centre and two Circular Corners in the manner of a Castle & has a grotesque but not inelegant appearance. It stands on the Edge but within an inclosure of about 7 A[cres]. in which are a great number of Trees of different Kinds of Timber & Thorns; several Deer of different Kinds are kept here, the American Axis, which has produced a Breed from with the Does; there are also several very fine kangaroos, a male & a female Buffalo (I think) and their young Calf: all these are running loose together.[3]

Loft continues to tell us that the building had 'many good Apartments', and 'the Rear of the House and the Ends' were 'well sheltered from the Wind by large Oaks, Fir & other Trees'.[4] It sat roughly at the centre of its 2.8-ha/7-acre plot, which was divided into three parcels – the largest of which lay west of the house and possessed two ponds. Though there are no surviving early views of the Jungle, Loft's description of its garden 'inclosure' conjures images of an earthly paradise – a bountiful, idealised landscape in which birds and animals co-mingle in a state of harmony and peace, giving the impression of the Garden of Eden before the Fall.

97
Edwin Smith, The Jungle, Eagle, Lincolnshire, 1966, photograph. Edwin Smith/ RIBA Collections.
This 'romantic seat' was described by William White in his *History, Gazetteer and Directory of Lincolnshire* (1856) as 'deeply embowered in wood, and curiously ornamented with clumps of vitrified bricks, having a disorderly and metallic appearance'.

98
Barbara Jones, 'The Jungle, Lincolnshire', drawing, in Barbara Jones, *Follies & Grottos* (1953).
Jones remarks: 'The Jungle is a farmhouse in a remote and tangled district.
It stands without a road in the middle of its fields ... behind a little semicircle of garden
cut from the rough field is a sham castle made of encrustations of over-baked bricks, dark
purple-red ones all run together, a fanged and snarling façade to a plain farmhouse.'

History does not relate what prompted Collett to create such a strikingly picturesque and idiosyncratic ensemble. Born into a prosperous Worcester family, Samuel Russell became a Lieutenant of the Worcestershire Militia, and latterly a yeoman of the Rye or Leasam Cavalry in Sussex (1803–7).[5] In 1797 he married Anne Curteis (1771–1854), daughter of the wealthy solicitor, town clerk and banker Jeremiah Curteis of Rye. The couple appear to have purchased their estate in the village of Eagle in the early 1820s, and entrusted the design of their house to a local and rather eccentric architect, Mr Lovely, of Branston.[6]

It's tantalising to speculate on the origins of the appellation of the Jungle. First described as such in 1826, there were at the time no houses or follies in England with a comparable name. A word of Anglo-Indian origin that came into use in the late eighteenth century, it has a whiff of the emporia that were springing up across the country supplying the 'bounty of empire' to persons of fashion who were eager to acquire, display and sometimes breed rare plants, birds and animals. Collett, as a rich and landed squire, was presumably susceptible to this enthusiasm for exotica, and the fact that he and his wife remained domiciled in Rye after building the Jungle suggests that it was indeed a folly.[7]

Collett's taste for rarities was doubtless in part nurtured by his near neighbour, the eminent menagerist Sir Robert Heron (1765–1854) at Stubton Hall. Described as an 'intelligent but quirky Lincolnshire squire' and 'a good specimen of the best class of English country gentleman', Sir Robert was the only surviving son of Thomas Heron of Chilham Castle, Kent, recorder of Newark, and first wife, Anne, née Wilmot [fig. 99].[8] After graduating from St John's College, Cambridge, he travelled on the Continent between 1784 and 1785 with his tutor Robert Pedley, who, according to Heron, had a 'strange and active imagination' and 'some learning and much ignorance, but being a little mad, his strange ideas taught me to think for myself.'[9] In 1792 he married Amelia, daughter of Sir Horace Mann, 2nd Baronet, and succeeded to the Heron baronetcy in 1794.

Although a Member of Parliament for Grimsby and later Peterborough for over thirty-five years, Heron made little impact on the Commons. He was, by contrast, a seasoned traveller, a 'devoted student of natural history' and the proud proprietor of a 'princely menagerie'.[10] Happily for posterity, Heron published his memoirs: his *Notes* (1850), which were described at the time as 'simply a series of journalistic memoranda of public and private events', supply an overview of his long and active life, including 'spicy bits of scandal and racy personal anecdotes – of the proceedings of the birds and beasts in his menagerie in Lincolnshire – jumbled up with waifs and strays of opinions and judgments, political, literary, and social – the whole mass printed just as

99
Anon., *Sir Robert Heron, 2nd Baronet*, c.1850, etching.
National Portrait Gallery, London.

100
Anon., *The Gold Fish from China*, late eighteenth century, coloured engraving.
Wellcome Collection, London.

it was written, without any pretence to order or arrangement, and forming a sort of artless chaos'.[11]

Heron and Collett shared an interest in kangaroos and Chinese goldfish. Heron remarks in 1836 that he had 'a long possession' of the marsupials, and that he kept a 'flock' of the same; all we know of Collett's mob is that they were 'very fine'.[12] We know considerably more about the gentlemen's collections of goldfish. Loft describes having seen 'a large Pond of Water' at the Jungle, 'in which are kept great numbers of Gold & Silver Fish, with the mixed Breed produced by them', and observes that 'the most singular Thing is they are never removed from this Pond in Winter and do not appear to suffer from the cold' [fig. 100].[13] Sir Robert's collection, on the other hand, was considerably older, larger and more distinguished than his neighbour's: he began breeding goldfish in 1809, and described his 'aquarium' in 1815 as possessing 'about eleven hundred [fish] of all ages'. The 'paved pond' they inhabited was situated in the flower garden by the house, 'which seems to suit them remarkably well, and where they have bred in considerable numbers'. Like most ardent collectors, the baronet was particular about the pedigree of his charges: his original stock came from Burghley House, and 'six from Kendrick's, in Piccadilly'.[14]

101
Anon., Stubton Hall, c.1850, photograph. Fane Collection,
Lincolnshire Archives, Lincoln.

His school of fish was moreover the object of sustained personal study; on at least one occasion Sir Robert presented notes relating to the 'breeding of Gold-fishes in the author's menagerie' to the Zoological Society of London – of which he was an active member and to which he was a generous benefactor.[15]

While the Jungle was a whimsical retreat, Stubton, by contrast, was a country residence worthy of a wealthy landed squire [fig. 101]. In 1813 Sir Robert demolished the early hall to collaborate with the architect Sir Jeffrey Wyattville in building a 'large and handsome modern mansion', and in January 1815 he took especial pleasure in commissioning a conservatory – '60 feet by 20, 21 [feet] high, adjoining to the house'.[16] Heron declared that building was 'a beautiful thing; nothing of the kind ever gave so much satisfaction, and it is planned with the most choice collection of plants. A conservatory is of rather late invention, and it is probably because Jeffrey Wyatt and I had seen so few, that we succeeded so well, our imaginations not being restrained by servile imitation.'[17]

The *Ordnance Survey* (1886) suggests that the gardens and pleasure grounds were very extensive and their layout complex. The approach road formed a large arc traversing the pleasure grounds, terminating in a *rond-point* on the north side of the mansion. The pleasure ground is depicted as being well endowed with a mixture of broadleaf and coniferous trees and criss-crossed by footpaths. From the porte-cochère the visitor looked north to the Green Walk Plantation, and east over the landscape park. The gardens south of the house were more fragmented and less coherent: a south-facing U-shaped terrace, defined by a ha-ha, followed the outline of the house and the conservatory. Beyond this lay the menagerie of several acres, divided into a handful of irregularly shaped paddocks sprinkled with pens, little outbuildings and circular-shaped ponds dotted with central islands for nesting birds [fig. 102].

Heron makes only passing remarks on the gardens in his memoirs, but these attest to his interest in observing and recording the flora and fauna within the park – ranging from reflections on the botanical origins of primroses in his 'green walk plantation' to monitoring the nesting behaviour of birds:

102
After 'The Port Jackson Painter', 'Black Swan', hand-coloured engraving, in G. Shaw and F. P. N. Nodder, *The Naturalist's Miscellany, or Coloured figures of Natural Objects Drawn and Described Immediately from Nature* (1792). Florilegius/Alamy Stock Photo.

In the Islands of my menagerie are wigwams of earth roofed with weeds. At the usual time in January or February last, a black swan made her nest, not in the wigwam, but in the door-way. In about a week, there came a rain which trickled from the roof upon the centre of the nest. The swan, without quitting her nest, with the assistance of her mate, who assiduously brought her the materials, lengthened the nest about eighteen inches from the door-way, and, at night, constantly moved the eggs to the new centre. The operation, which I watched myself, occupied about ten days; the eggs, four in number, were all successfully hatched.[18]

He also describes with enthusiasm the pleasure of planting native and exotic trees:

I was thought foolish by some, for planting, at the age of thirty, trees, which I could never live to see in perfection. I have continued planting all my life; and now, at the age of eighty-three, am planting the newly discovered trees from China and Japan. Many that I have planted are now well grown, and handsome; and have afforded me much pleasure even in their infancy. The soil, so well-adapted to trees, has greatly encouraged me. A grove of cedars of Lebanon is much admired. With my present experience, I could have selected a spot on the river where I might have formed a beautiful domain, with half the expence which this has cost me; true, I should have had to plant every tree, but that has also been the case here; however, I have made it a convenient home, and must be satisfied with it.[19]

Heron's assertion that he was extravagant in his improvement of his gardens is not only corroborated by the extensiveness and diversity of his gardens; a correspondent to the *Gardeners' Chronicle*, writing in 1849, remarked that 'gardening was to be learnt' at Sir Robert Heron's at Stubton and the Duke of Portland's at Welbeck in Nottinghamshire, as these were establishments where, 'as well as gardening and botany, geometry and natural history were taught by such men as McArthur and Thompson.' The Stubton gardeners were furthermore well paid, well treated and took 'pride and interest in their garden'.[20]

Although the baronet found pleasure in gardening and landscape design, the reader gets a sense that these pursuits were secondary to his impulse to collect, breed and exchange exotic fish, birds and animals. He aspired above all to the novelty that was supplied by the battalions of beasts that found their way into his private zoological garden [fig. 103]:

Last Autumn, I sent my large male emu to Cross, of Exeter Change, and received from him a young pair, two years old, and a pair of Poland Cranes. I had before received from him a pair of Balearic cranes, and I have sent him, within two years, two pairs of kangaroos, four pairs of golden pheasants, and a pair of black swans; having besides given of the three last to my friends ... [and] Mrs Chamberlain brought me, from Brazil, a pair of whistling ducks, small and very beautiful, They are different from any I have seen described. She also had for me, a pair of very large black birds, apparently of the genus crux; but of these, one escaped from her on board the ship, and the other pined away. I received only the head.[21]

He was moreover determined that his menagerie should rank among the most exceptional and diverse in the country [figs 104 and 105]:

My menagerie has been, lately, greatly increased, and I am believed to be more successful in rearing animals than others; in fact, I know of no other considerable private collection, except Lord Derby's and Lord Fitzwilliam's. I possess at present llamas, alpacas, nylghaus, tapirs, guanacos, Indian antelopes, Virginian deer, long-tailed lemmus [lemurs], agoutis, common porcupines, hog deer, jerboas, and kangaroos, (macropus major) macropus bennettii, bettongia pencillata, armadillos, and Angora rabbits.[22]

103
William Daniel after John Byrne, 'The Menagerie, Oatlands Park', 1822, etching with engraving. Royal Collection Trust. © Her Majesty Queen Elizabeth II 2021.

In the absence of views of Heron's private zoological garden at Stubton, Byrne's image supplies an evocation of a contemporary menagerie cum aviary that had an equally wide array of exotic birds and beasts.

104
A. T. Elwes, *Jamrack's* [sic] *Wild-Beast Mart, London*, 1875, engraving. Private collection. Heron may have purchased some of his kangaroos from Charles Jamrach, who at the time was widely regarded as 'the world's greatest wholesale dealer in wild beasts', and who, as a breeder as well as an exporter of animals of all kinds, had no rival.

105
J. S. Murdoch after J. Stewart, seven different specimens of kangaroos, including a rabbit-eared perameles, shown with their young in their natural habitat, coloured etching, in Oliver Goldsmith, A *History of the Earth and Animated Nature* (1862). Wellcome Collection, London.

Advancing age did not dampen Heron's impulse to collect and to improve the range and quality of his natural curiosities. In 1853, in his 87th year, he was particularly ambitious in his acquisitions and suffused with pride in them: 'I have just increased my zoological collection by the purchase of Lord Derby's great kangaroos, a large male, a female with young, and a young male for £105. I also obtain[ed] from the same quarter, a pair of smaller kangaroos, and a pair of Egyptian geese. I believe mine is now the only extensive collection in the kingdom, as well as containing the only family of large kangaroos.'[23]

Heron was not only committed to improving his own collection; he was desirous of promoting and expanding those of the new Zoological Gardens in Regent's Park in London [fig. 106]. Over the years he presented gifts of black swans, a common marten, a Virginian opossum, fancy pigeons, and rare and curious freshwater fish; he was, moreover, a regular contributor to the Zoological Society's *Proceedings*.[24]

Collett and Heron may have had different motivations for collecting exotica, but they shared a common purpose: both aspired to create private zoological gardens in the modern landscape taste – that is, using planting to provide the setting in which animals were viewed.[25] In this regard their aims were not dissimilar to those of their contemporaries, the 'enterprising' and 'indefatigable' Edward Cross and the landscape gardener and botanist Henry Phillips, who in 1831 collaborated to establish the Surrey Zoological Gardens [fig. 107]. A correspondent to the *Horticultural Register* (1832) remarked that Cross, 'the well-known keeper of the Menagerie at Exeter-Change, and the King's-Mews', had 'so severely felt the loss of attraction, since the establishment of the Zoological Society [of London]' that he was compelled to 'remove his Collection from a room to a Garden'.[26] That he availed himself of the assistance of Phillips underscores the importance Cross attached to the design of the new garden. Phillips was, as John Constable observed, 'a most intelligent and elegant-minded man'; he was the author of *Sylva Florifera: The Shrubbery Historically and Botanically Treated; With Observations on the Formation of Ornamental Plantations, and Picturesque Scenery* (1823), and had devised the layout of Kemp Town in Brighton, which was credited at the time as possessing 'great novelty and beauty of style'.[27] The resultant scheme, and Phillips's superintendence, received wide acclaim: J. C. Loudon remarked in the *Gardener's Magazine* (1832) that they reflected 'the highest credit upon all concerned', and C. F. Partington declared in *National History and Views of London and its Environs* (1834) that 'the great taste displayed in the arrangement of these gardens, and the careful selection of animals, render it worthy in every respect the extensive patronage it has hitherto received.'[28]

106
George Scharf, *Zoological Gardens, Regent's Park*, 1836, lithograph.
Sir Robert Heron's bird pens and enclosures were probably similar to those in the
London Zoological Gardens.

A contributor to *Paxton's Magazine of Botany, and Register of Flowering Plants* (1834) neatly sums up the then prevailing view of the qualities of a successful modern zoological garden. Having assessed the character and layout of the Surrey Zoological Gardens, the author affirms that though some of his readers might level the criticism that Cross's giant menagerie, with its multifarious birds, beasts, cages and compartments, was 'not much connected with the culture of plants', the 'distance is not so great as at first sight may appear'.[29] The skill of laying out such a piece of ground, 'whether that ground is to be occupied by either plants or animals', was, he believed, to give equal consideration to both with a view to creating a complete work of art.

As a postscript, and to revisit the Jungle, we might consider the proposition that Collett's Lincolnshire retreat was, in fact, a playful exploration of

ENGLISH GARDEN ECCENTRICS
– 172 –

107
F. Alvery, *Surr[e]y Zoological Gardens*, 1836, lithograph. Chronicle/Alamy Stock Photo.
Henry Phillips was praised by a correspondent to the *Horticultural Register* (1832) for his success in transforming a swampy meadow into a pleasure ground.

imaginative possibilities suggested by its geographical location in the village of Eagle. It was the fashion when this quirky edifice was built to create shamcastles or ruins in English menageries for the habitations of eagles. One such set of buildings, the 'ruins' contrived by Phillips for the eagles at the Surrey Zoological Gardens, were described in 1834 as 'rarely surpassed, even where expense has been no object', despite the fact that they were 'merely built out of such rubbish as came in the way'.[30] Though John Henry Loft makes no mention in 1826 of eagles presiding over the pleasure grounds at the Jungle, the folly's rude construction and its curious landscape setting might possibly have invited contemporary visitors to imagine their presence.

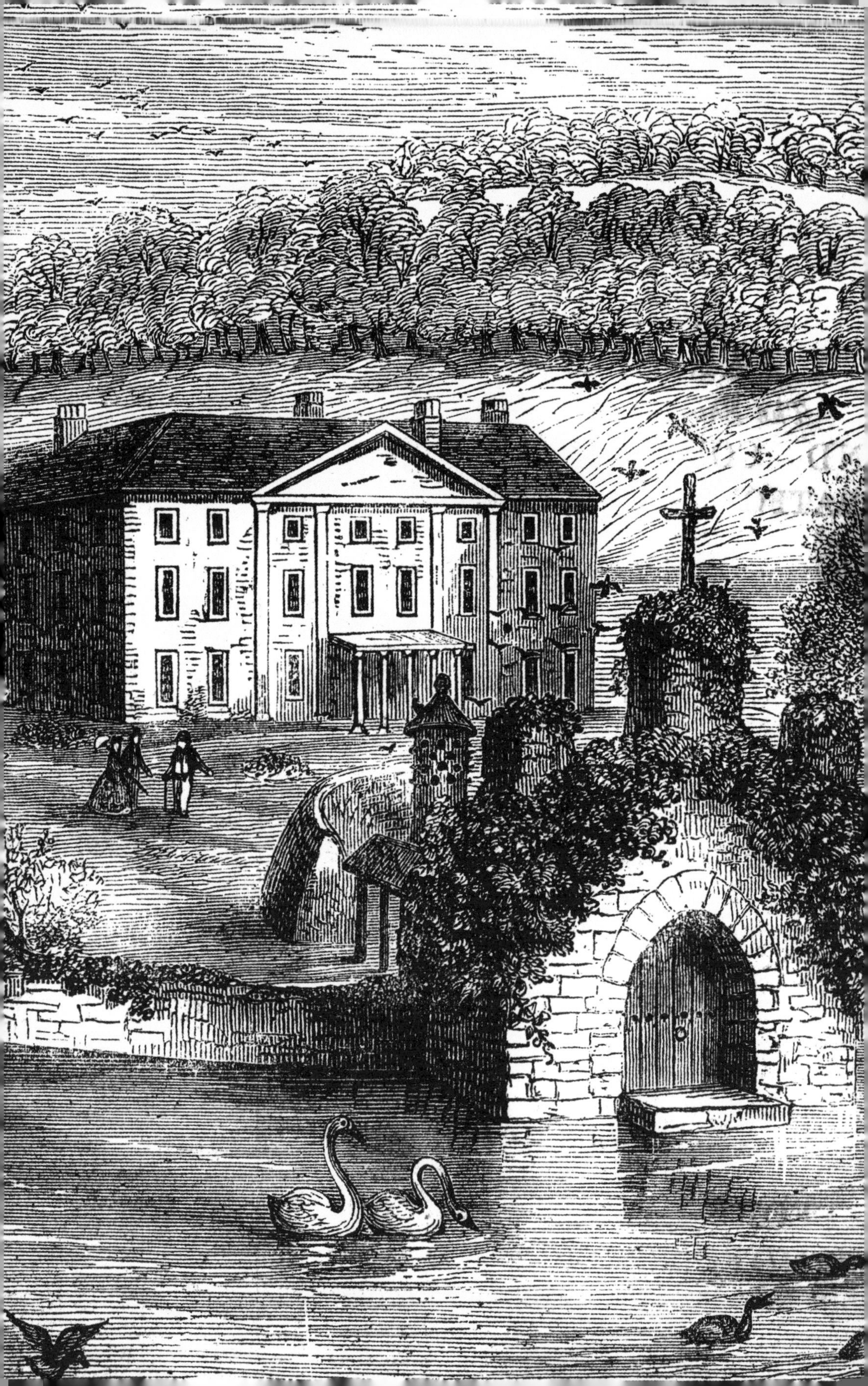

[TWELVE]

Charles Waterton: 'Unwearied Outdoor Observer'

At Stonyhurst there are boundaries marked out to the students, which they are not allowed to pass; and there are prefects always pacing to and fro within the lines, to prevent any unlucky boy from straying on the other side of them. Notwithstanding the vigilance of these lynx-eyed guardians, I would now and then manage to escape, and would bolt into a very extensive labyrinth of yew and holly trees, close at hand. It was the chosen place for animated nature. Birds, in particular, used to frequent the spacious enclosure, both to obtain food and enjoy security.[1]

CHARLES WATERTON'S ACCOUNT IN HIS MEMOIRS OF HIS TRUANT behaviour as a young man at the Jesuit college in the late eighteenth century sets out what he describes as the 'predominant' or 'ruling propensities' of his life: he was to become a keen ornithologist and observer of nature ('my favourite vocation').[2] It also highlights some of the paradoxical qualities of his character; for instance, he was, on one hand, a staunch and old-school English Catholic and, on the other, an adventurous and spirited individualist. The Stonyhurst anecdote also registers some recurrent themes in Waterton's own writing, including the significance of boundaries, enclosure and security. These themes become clear when considering his interest in and approach to gardening and landscape design – an approach quite distinct from any of the improvers we have met thus far.

Charles Waterton (1782–1865) – known more familiarly as Squire Waterton – was born at the family seat of Walton Hall, Sandal Magna, near Wakefield, Yorkshire. He was the eldest son of the six children of Thomas Waterton and his wife, Anne (née Bedingfeld). A man of 'decided character and strong opinions', 'naturally and by habit gentle and kind', he was described by a contemporary writing in the *Wakefield Free Press* (1865) as 'a painstaking and trustworthy naturalist ... [whose] love of birds and beasts and trees and the varied beauties of external nature was intense and delightful'.[3]

As for his personal appearance, it was 'in keeping with his character and ways' [fig. 108]: 'His spare form, vigorous stride, close-cropt hair, odd-shaped blue dress coat with brass buttons and dangling tails, grey trousers, low shoes and worsted stockings, and his umbrella, made the Squire a notable man in our streets.'[4] The twenty-seventh and teetotal lord of Walton was, by his own account, 'pretty well off, as far as breeding goes'.[5] He was proud of his ancient and untitled family, being descended directly from Sir Thomas More through his grandmother; and in remote times some of his ancestors were 'sufficiently notorious' to have had their names handed down to posterity fighting at Crécy and Agincourt and at Marston Moor.[6]

108
Charles Willson Peale, *Charles Waterton*, 1824, oil on canvas.
National Portrait Gallery, London.
Waterton paid a visit to Peale's museum in Philadelphia in 1824.
The American naturalist-artist, who admired Waterton's taxidermical skills,
took the opportunity to paint his likeness.

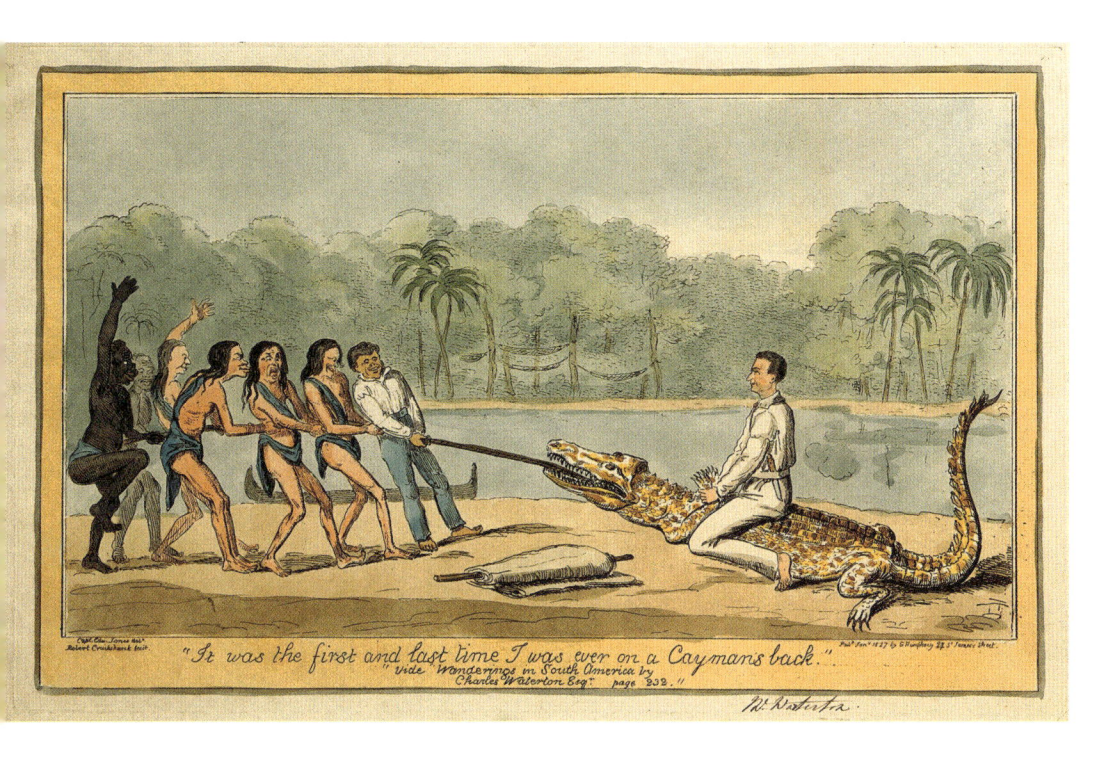

109
Robert Cruikshank after Edward Jones, *It was the first and last time I was ever on a Cayman's back*, 1827, hand-tinted engraving. Wellcome Collection, London.

    The Squire relates that his life of adventure and his 'inordinate relish for ornithological architecture' began at the age of eight when he clambered over the roof of an outhouse to observe a starling's nest. His early years at school 'had scarcely any effect' upon him, and attempts to repress his interest in natural history resulted in the 'warm application' of the birch rod, which 'in lieu of effacing my ruling passion, did but tend to render it more distinct and clear'.[7]

    After two 'mild and cheerful' years at Stonyhurst, he was encouraged by his mother to 'see the world'.[8] This advice precipitated many years of sustained foreign travel (in part inspired by Sir Joseph Banks, with whom he was on friendly terms) which saw the young naturalist observing apes in Gibraltar, fleeing the pestilence at Malaga, and exploring remote and occasionally inhospitable corners of the New World. His barefoot ramblings in the equatorial rain forests of Guyana were published in *Wanderings in South America* (1825), and were immensely popular 'wherever the English tongue has penetrated; and the bold and characteristic deeds therein narrated – the riding of a caiman to death – will at once recur to every mind' [fig. 109].[9]

CHARLES WATERTON

110
'The Cast-Iron Bridge Approach to Walton Hall', steel engraving, in Richard Hobson, *Charles Waterton* (1866).
Waterton often strolled on the bridge to admire 'the rapid flight of the swallows, then skimming the unruffled surface of the lake, and then taking their sundry superficial dips in the water whilst feeding on the wing'.

Waterton succeeded to his family estate in 1806, and in 1829, aged forty-seven, he married Anne Edmonstone, who was thirty years his junior and 'a grand-daughter of the chief of the Arowak Indians'. The marriage was 'supremely happy' but remarkably brief, as she died after giving birth to a son the following year.[10]

Not long after his return from the 'wilds of Guiana' and 'having suffered myself, and learned mercy', the former hunter resolved to halt the persecution of birds and animals on his estate by forming a sanctuary, or what he referred to as a 'place of security', where his charges would be neither encumbered with chains nor restrained by iron bars – a setting to contemplate birds and animals with 'more friendly feelings' and 'under different circumstances'.[11]

Walton Hall had already functioned for several centuries as a sanctuary for the Watertons themselves: the new house and the remains of the family's ancient and venerable 'castellated house' ('reduced to almost a heap of ruins' during the Civil War) sat on a large rock encircled by a 10.5-ha/26-acre sheet of water (formerly a moat), and was accessible only by an iron footbridge [fig. 110].[12] This ensemble stood at the heart of a 121-ha/300-acre park (with neither public roads nor footpaths) generously planted with ancient, gnarled trees, which during the Squire's lifetime was enclosed with a high wall. These circumstances doubtless combined to give rise to the Watertons' insular mentality; the island was both literally and metaphorically a fortress, and the centre of their protected world [fig. 111].

This metaphor began to take shape in the early sixteenth century. As the Squire relates, 'although up to the reign of Henry VIII, things had gone swimmingly for the Watertons', there was a 'sad reverse of fortune', and the 'succeeding reigns brought every species of reproach and indignity upon us.'[13] The once proud and powerful Catholic family was, in the naturalist's words, 'held up to the scorn of a deluded multitude, as damnable idolaters'.[14] This insularity was further enhanced from the late eighteenth century as the estate became increasingly surrounded by coal mines, a new soapworks, iron foundries, cotton and corn mills, factories and slums, all of which polluted the estate's air, land and water, and put enormous pressure on local wildlife.

111
Anon., bird's-eye view of Walton Hall, 1849, engraving.
Private collection.
The presence of a great diversity of birds in this view underscores Waterton's desire that his family estate should provide a 'place of security' for all creatures of the natural world.

Waterton's first step towards establishing his bird and animal sanctuary was to stamp out the 'deep-rooted prejudices' in his household (as in other contexts at the time) against the barn owl, and to restore the habitat of this 'poor, harmless, useful friend of mine' that had had such a 'sad time of it at Walton Hall'. Having a 'great liking for this bird', he decided to form its habitation in the ruins of the family's ancient and abandoned house:

> On the ruin of the old gateway, against which, tradition says, the waves of the lake have dashed for the better part of a thousand years, I made a place with stone and mortar, about 4 ft. square, and fixed a thick oaken stick firmly into it. Huge masses of ivy now cover it. In about a month or so after it was finished, a pair of barn owls came and took up their abode in it. I threatened to strangle the keeper if ever, after this, he molested either the old birds or their young ones.[15]

Here the birds could be closely observed at a safe distance from the drawing room windows of the Hall, and he used a 'large telescope to assist his observation'.[16]

James Stuart Menteath of Closeburn Hall visited the Walton Hall estate in 1834, and reported in the Magazine of Natural History and Journal of Zoology that it was 'a place that must, like Selborne, be ever dear to the lover of ornithology, from the many attractive objects it presents in the way of that engaging pursuit'. He commended the 'ivy-clad tower' as both a testament to the house's 'former chivalry' and an ingenious reuse of a historic structure:

> This tower will be visited with no small interest and curiosity by the ornithologist. The days of rapine and violence having happily passed away, never, we hope to return, this tower, by many ingenious devices and contrivances, has been made a commodious and undisturbed habitation for many a family of the feathered race. In a snug corner, thickly grown over with ivy, can be seen in any day of the year, a pair of common white owls taking their nap; and, at night, the ears of the admirer of such music may enjoy their nocturnal serenades.[17]

Menteath continues to explain how the tower rapidly became attractive to other species of birds as well: 'Though the owl finds in this tower an unmolested haunt, the pretty starling, the blackbird, the thrush, the wild duck, the wood pigeon, "sweet sequestered bird," and several others, reposing a confidence in the humane owner which is never abused, resort to this delightful retreat, either to enjoy its shelter or to bring up their young.'[18]

The success of this 'first settlement' encouraged Waterton to form another habitation in the ruins – this time for starlings. Eager to persuade a 'greater number of these pretty lively birds to pass the summer with me', he made

112

Anon., 'Lofty Yew Fence, the Bridge, and Fisherman's Hut, at Walton Hall', steel engraving, in Richard Hobson, *Charles Waterton* (1866).
A dense, clipped yew hedge encompassed the ivy-encrusted ruined gateway, and a 'nesting tower for the starling, jackdaw and white owl'.

twenty-four holes in the 'old ivied tower' – latterly known as the 'starling tower' – adjacent to the ruined gate [figs 111 and 112].[19]

This retreat was later enhanced with the planting of a dense 'yew tree crescent, three hundred feet in extent' to create further shelter for the denizens of the ruins.[20] The Squire treated the trees as 'ornamental yew trees' – that is, they were clipped. He in fact disapproved of the 'modern disappropriation of ornamental planting in lines and circles', but made an exception for formal treatment of yews, not so much on aesthetic grounds as because they 'will always command the sweet warbling of unnumbered songsters, from earliest spring to latest summer: for the yew tree is a kind friend to the feathered race'.[21] The implication here is that clipped yew hedges provide better shelter for birds than unclipped specimen trees because they are denser.

Waterton had a high regard for gardeners and for decorative planting. In his essay 'Flower-Gardens and Song Birds' published in the *Gardener's Magazine* (1842), he praised the operative and his achievements:

How I prize the gardener! He is Nature's primest jeweller; and he has the power of placing within our reach all that is nutritive, and luscious, and lovely, in the enchanting domains of Flora and Pomona. Without his assistance, Nature would soon run out into uncurbed luxuriance; the flowery lawn would disappear, and ere long the hemlock and the bramble, with a train of noxious attendants, would lord it all around. To the industry, then, of the gardener we are indebted for scenes of rural beauty quite unparalleled; and to his science we owe the possession of every wholesome fruit and root ... Hence, the gardener is my friend; and whenever I have an opportunity of surveying lands which bear marks of his interesting labours, I wish him well from my heart, and I hope that he may not fail to receive a remunerating return for his many useful services to us.[22]

He was fond of flower gardens because they, like hedges, had the potential to attract and feed birds: 'Were I asked my opinion of a highly-cultivated English flower-garden, I should say that it is the loveliest sight in rural nature; and, moreover, that if it afforded me an opportunity of listening to the song of birds, I should pronounce it little short of absolute perfection.'[23]

The flower garden at Walton Hall was concealed behind the stables north of the house. It had been described in 1853 as part of the 'ornamental grounds' located in a 'pretty situation in the woods' which had been laid out to receive and entertain visitors.[24] This 'sylvan paradise' was known as the Grotto [fig. 113]:

Through this Elysium runs the stream which flows from the lake, along the valley out of the park, and the banks were adorned with ferns and flower-beds. In the grotto district was a small square house of one room, where the squire was accustomed to sit by the fire in winter when the weather was too keen to allow him to sit outside, and he had the door wide open, that he might talk, as he said, to cock robin and the magpies.[25]

The Grotto was a natural cavern, and an engraved view from 1866 suggests that it was, like the old gatehouse, surmounted by a large and conspicuous cross.

During the summer months the Squire allowed 'pic-nic parties' to make use of his 'grotto-paradise':

He supplied cups and fire, and they made tea in one of the summer-houses. This was a great treat to schools, and all the associations of working people, choral, scientific, or mechanic, which abound in Lancashire, and the West Riding of Yorkshire. Waterton pitied the workers in cotton-mills, pent-up in hot rooms, and he loved to see them enjoying a holiday, and breathing the pure, fresh air. Few men who had walled in a park for the pursuit of a favourite study, would have thought of admitting the poor to share its beauties.[26]

"THE GROTTO," IN THE GROUNDS AT WALTON HALL.

113
J. Fountain, '"The Grotto" in the Grounds of Walton Hall', steel engraving, in Richard Hobson, *Charles Waterton* (1866).
Hobson described the grotto as a 'favourite place of Observation for the Habits of Birds' and a 'fascinating Retreat of Pic-Nic Parties'.

Richard Hobson reports in 1866 that Waterton had invited the inmates at the Wakefield Asylum to have their 'harmless and frolicksome merriment – their dancing, and their dinner, within the grotto'. They were, he continued 'always greatly delighted, and even tranquillised, so as to temporarily forget their pitiable condition, and one and all to declare the grotto to be an elysium'.[27]

Unlike most of his contemporaries who were raising statues, garden buildings and other embellishments in their parks and gardens, Waterton spent most of his time and money planting trees and shrubs and erecting 'accommodations' for 'animal creation', including hanging wooden bird boxes in trees; making 'apartments' for jackdaws; piercing a 'walled bank' in the garden with upwards of fifty holes, fitted with drain-pipes, to provide nesting sites for sand martins; and applying the hammer and the chisel to excavate fungus from rotting trees to form roosts for tawny owls. The aim of these building initiatives was, Menteath affirms, to exculpate a variety of native fauna – ranging from rooks to ravens, magpies, raptors and hedgehogs – from the 'false charges and foul calumnies' levelled against them.[28]

Norman Moore reports that 'all the accommodations provided for animals were kept in admirable order': 'To woodcraft Waterton paid unremitting attention, and he knew the state of health of every tree in his park. If one of the number had suffered in a storm, or looked sickly, we would climb and inspect it. From constant practice he could ascend trees at an age when most men can hardly hobble with a stick, and in his eighty-third year we went up a tall oak together to look at a nest.'[29]

Waterton was especially determined to secure the boundaries of his sanctuary. The east side of the park was moated by the Leeds and Barnsley Canal, and the remainder was defended by a high stone wall: this 5-km/3-mile long 'fortification' took four years to build (1822–6) and cost the Squire £9,000.[30] The enormous fence was intended to 'keep out the poacher and other intruder' [fig. 114].[31]

> As no gun is ever fired within its precincts, that – 'clamour of rooks, daws, and kites, / The explosion of the levell'd tube excites,' is never heard, nor any dog suffered to disturb its peace, it may easily be supposed it will be the favourite resort of many kinds of birds. Abounding in extensive woods and groves, and an ample space of water, every fowl can suit its own taste for a sheltering-place, for a haunt to build its nest, and rear its little brood; all those birds which elsewhere suffer from the gamekeeper's ruthless gun and trap, and from those whom the bird-stuffer employs to take them prisoners, receive protection within the walls of Walton Park.[32]

THE POACHER ENTRAPPED INTO THE LOCK-UP, BY MR. WATERTON.

114
J. Fountain, 'The Poacher entrapped into the Lock-Up by Mr. Waterton', steel engraving, in Richard Hobson, *Charles Waterton* (1866).
Waterton once trapped a renowned poacher within the ruined water gate. Hobson relates that the 'lachrymose prisoner' was detained for several hours until he repented.

Access to the park from the outer world was gained by traversing a narrow bridge over the canal, the entrance guarded by two lodges. Hobson writes in 1866 that 'on passing over this viaduct, and entering within the gates, you are very forcibly struck with the calm serenity and seclusion that instantaneously meet the eye in every direction.'[33] The park's 'complete privacy and security' provided by its high walls were credited, for instance, in having 'attracted a small family of herons ['ancient princes among game'] to form a colony on some of the aged oaks that overhang the lake'; and the 'herons repay their kind landlord's assiduous care of them by destroying numbers of the water-rat, that infest all our waters, and even houses.'[34]

The enclosed woods and grove soon became a refuge for migratory birds: 'among this assemblage are seen the woodcock, the fieldfare with its inseparable dear fellow traveller the redstart, and several others, emigrants from distant

MR. WATERTON AND THE AUTHOR PHOTOGRAPHED BENEATH THE
LOMBARDY POPLAR.

115
J. Fountain, 'Mr. Waterton and the Author [Richard Hobson] photographed beneath the Lombardy Poplar', steel engraving, in Richard Hobson, *Charles Waterton* (1866).

Hobson had intended to photograph Waterton 'standing alone at the base of a tree looking up and into it as if bird-nesting, the province and position of a naturalist', but was foiled by the Squire's unwillingness to face the camera.

lands'. The park and gardens also abounded with waterfowl ranging from kingfishers to wild duck, widgeon, teal and coot, wild goose, common gull and swan.

Menteath was also impressed by some of the measures Waterton had taken to ensure that his grounds provided adequate year-round protection for the park's residents: 'An instance of the human and paternal care and solicitude Mr Waterton evinces for the comfort of the feathered family, during winter, had nearly escaped me. He encourages the growth of ivy around the stems of his trees, which not only shelters many a poor starved benumbed bird, when the storm rages, but offers it an agreeable place for its nest in the spring.'[35]

Waterton was intensely attached to ivy, and recommended planting it alongside holly, yew and other evergreens to create 'suitable shelter' for birds, as they supplied not only shade and shelter but 'food into the bargain'. He also took especial pleasure in clipping these evergreens. A visitor to the gardens in 1853, who found 'the hardy naturalist, mounted on some high, moveable steps, shearing a thick holly hedge', was told: 'I always trim these hedges myself, and I am repaid for my toil in [bird] music, the year round.'[36]

The reception of the park at Walton Hall, both during and after Waterton's life, strikingly exemplifies the ease with which eccentric gardening comes to be interpreted as a form of biography: the story of the garden-maker inscribing her or his quirks of character upon the landscape. Victoria Carroll, examining reactions to Waterton's estate in *Science and Eccentricity* (2008), emphasises that an encounter with the Squire himself was seen as a crucial part of the experience of the place, when sought out as a noteworthy sight within itineraries of domestic tourism [fig. 115]. Thomas Dibdin and his daughter, for example, feel 'sad disappointment' on finding that Waterton is away from home when they visit: 'the master-spirit was wanting, to give pungency to anecdote and truth to conjecture.' Carroll cites two accounts of meetings in which the visitor, misled by the plain clothing that the Squire habitually adopted, mistakes him for a man of humble background: the oddities of the eccentric garden-maker, it is implied, gain added piquancy from the reader's awareness both that Waterton can do as he pleases in his own domain and that his oddity is sufficiently pronounced to baffle conventional expectations of class identity.[37]

Carroll also argues persuasively that Waterton's *Wanderings in South America* played a major role in shaping visitors' expectations of Walton. Her analysis focuses primarily on the house, in which an array of taxidermic specimens and composite creatures were on display [fig. 116] – among the former, the caiman whose capture, as already mentioned, he describes in his travel book. (After leaping on to the creature's back, he 'immediately seized his fore legs ... thus they served me for a bridle'; the hapless amphibian understandably 'began to plunge furiously' and lashed out with its tail.)[38]

Two of the texts and images that Carroll mentions, however, suggest that viewing Walton Hall with reference to *Wanderings*, and perceiving Waterton as the hero of exotic adventures, carry over from the house to the surrounding landscape, despite the fact that the Squire's concern here is with protecting native flora and fauna rather than exotics. His friend Julia Byrne, in her *Social Hours with Celebrities* (1898), tells an anecdote in which she and Waterton, travelling together, encounter an English tourist at Aix-la-Chapelle who guesses the Squire's geographical origins from his Yorkshire accent, but, unaware that he is talking to the man himself, questions him about the eccentric owner of Walton Hall: 'I've heard he lives among a lot of wild beasts and birds and things. Is *that* true?' 'Yes, sir, it's quite true,' Waterton replies, 'but they're very well-mannered and quite harmless beasts, and so is he.' The tourist then enquires as to 'the story

116

T. H. Foljambe, 'A Nondescript', coloured engraving, frontispiece to Charles Waterton, *Wanderings in South America* (1825).

The 'nondescript' was among Waterton's earliest and most celebrated taxidermical confections. He hoped that its appearance in *Wanderings* would 'stimulate to investigation those who are interested in museums'.

about the crocodile', and explains to his puzzled informant: 'Why, that he rides all over the place on a crocodile; that's what I should like to see.'[39]

Waterton's adventures, then, in the inflamed imagination of his acquaintance, assume a visual presence within the whole estate. A similar effect is produced in an unfinished watercolour by Edward Jones portraying Walton Hall and its surroundings: within the park the artist situates not only a number of the taxidermic specimens and composites (as well as some live birds perched on the branch of a tree), but also Waterton himself, astride the caiman, in the posture described in *Wanderings* [fig. 117]. Once again, the landscape around the Hall is presented as a place to which he brings back both objects and experiences assembled on his travels – as he more obviously does when arranging the house itself.[40]

The Squire can be defined as eccentric, moreover, not only with reference to the perceptions of contemporaries, but also as someone whose preoccupations were highly unusual for his time: he pioneered a concern with conservation that was more generally shared in later decades. Nobody in late Georgian or early Victorian England managed his estate like Waterton: the 'unwearied outdoor observer' was in almost every regard an original and an inspired custodian.[41] Julia Blackburn has identified him in *Charles Waterton: Traveller and Conservationist* (1989) as among the first conservationists who fought to protect wild nature against the destruction and pollution of Victorian industrialisation, and John Hemming proclaims him 'Britain's first eco-warrior' in *Tree of Rivers: The Story of the Amazon* (2008).[42]

Gerald Durrell affirms that Waterton's importance as a naturalist, writer, observer and conservationist has been obscured by his 'extreme eccentricity':

> *Of course, Waterton was an eccentric and his life story reads like something invented by Edgar Allan Poe with a certain amount from Richard Jefferies, but we have always needed eccentrics to point the way. It was Waterton who warned the Americans, for example, of the ultimate costs of their profligate destruction of their forests. It was Waterton who fought against the beginnings of pollution in the Industrial Revolution. It was he who turned the grounds of Walton Hall into a sanctuary, even maintaining trees with holes in them in which birds could nest and building a special bank for sandmartins. Is it also to be considered eccentric that this humane man would have what were in those days called lunatics up to the Hall from the local asylum and allow them to view his lake with its birds through his telescope? Nowadays, it would be called excellent therapy. It was Waterton who warned that if we did not mend our ways and respect the world we live in and not ravage it, we would go to hell in a handcart.*[43]

117

Edward Jones, Charles Waterton at home on the Walton estate, c.1864, watercolour drawing. Wakefield Museums and Castles, West Yorkshire.

The drawing is inscribed on the reverse: 'This is an unfinished picture of Walton Hall, by the late Captain E. Jones. He designed it as a present to my Sisters Eliza and Helen Edmonstone; and it was to have contained the monsters, quadrupeds, birds, serpents and insects from South America, killed and preserved by myself. These are now on the staircase at Walton Hall. But he did not live to complete his project. Having nearly lost his eye-sight, Death struck him low by a fatal attack of paralysis. He was esteemed and beloved by a numerous acquaintance: but by none more, than by his octogenarian friend Charles Waterton. Walton Hall. January 10th 1864.'

Whereas Waterton is nowadays identified as a proto-conservationist, his efforts and achievements in his own day defied easy categorisation: there was nothing remotely comparable to Walton Park, and few stewards possessed such 'inbred originality' and unwavering passion for 'animated nature'.[44] Most of Waterton's contemporaries perceived the estate as some novel form of sanctuary [figs 118]. James Menteath was alone in comparing the park to a zoological garden:

> From these few and hastily collected observations while visiting Walton Hall, it will appear that Mr. Waterton possesses the finest and most extensive zoological garden in the kingdom, or perhaps in Europe. Here roaming unconstrained and at free liberty, every bird and animal can be examined in its true character. In possession of a powerful telescope, which is often used, Mr Waterton watches and examines the habits and movements of his varied feathered population. Almost constantly abroad, nothing escapes him.[45]

THE DISTANT MANSION; THE RUIN; THE LITTLE ISLAND; AND THE LOMBARDY POPLAR.

118

J. Fountain, 'The Distant Mansion, the Ruin, the Little Island, and the Lombardy Poplar', steel engraving, in Richard Hobson, *Charles Waterton* (1866).

Hobson reports that Waterton held the Lombardy poplar in 'a sort of reverential esteem'; it had been planted by his father in 1756, and was 'nursed by the Squire with the tenderest care for many years'.

This analogy was partly true in so far as it contained living birds and animals displayed in quasi-natural and contrived landscape settings. Walton Park did not, however, possess the accessories so often found in contemporary zoological gardens – the pens, dens, aviaries, broad sweeping walks, terraces, vases and fountains. Nor did it boast the curious or exotic flora and fauna that was to be found in the greenhouses and conservatories of the most outstanding establishments of the day. Waterton's park was in fact more akin to a *salon des refusés*. The purpose of the vast enclosure was to provide safe habitation for, and to encourage the proliferation of, what his contemporaries perceived as vermin, including weasels, hedgehogs, jays, jackdaws, hawks, kites, ravens, magpies and owls.

Menteath is perhaps closer to the mark when he invokes the metaphor of a laboratory: 'the perfect seclusion of the park enables him to experiment harmlessly on his subjects. In the spring of 1833, he made a carrion crow hatch two rook's eggs, a magpie those of a jackdaw, and the daw those of a pie.'[46] Such mischievous experiments are the product of a quirky, lively and enquiring mind, of a man who was, in Edith Sitwell's estimation, possessed of an irrepressible sense of fun. His was a very agreeable kind of eccentricity: 'It was eccentric to be childlike, but never childish. We might multiply instances of his eccentricity to any extent, and we may safely say that the world would be much better than it is if such eccentricity were more common.'[47]

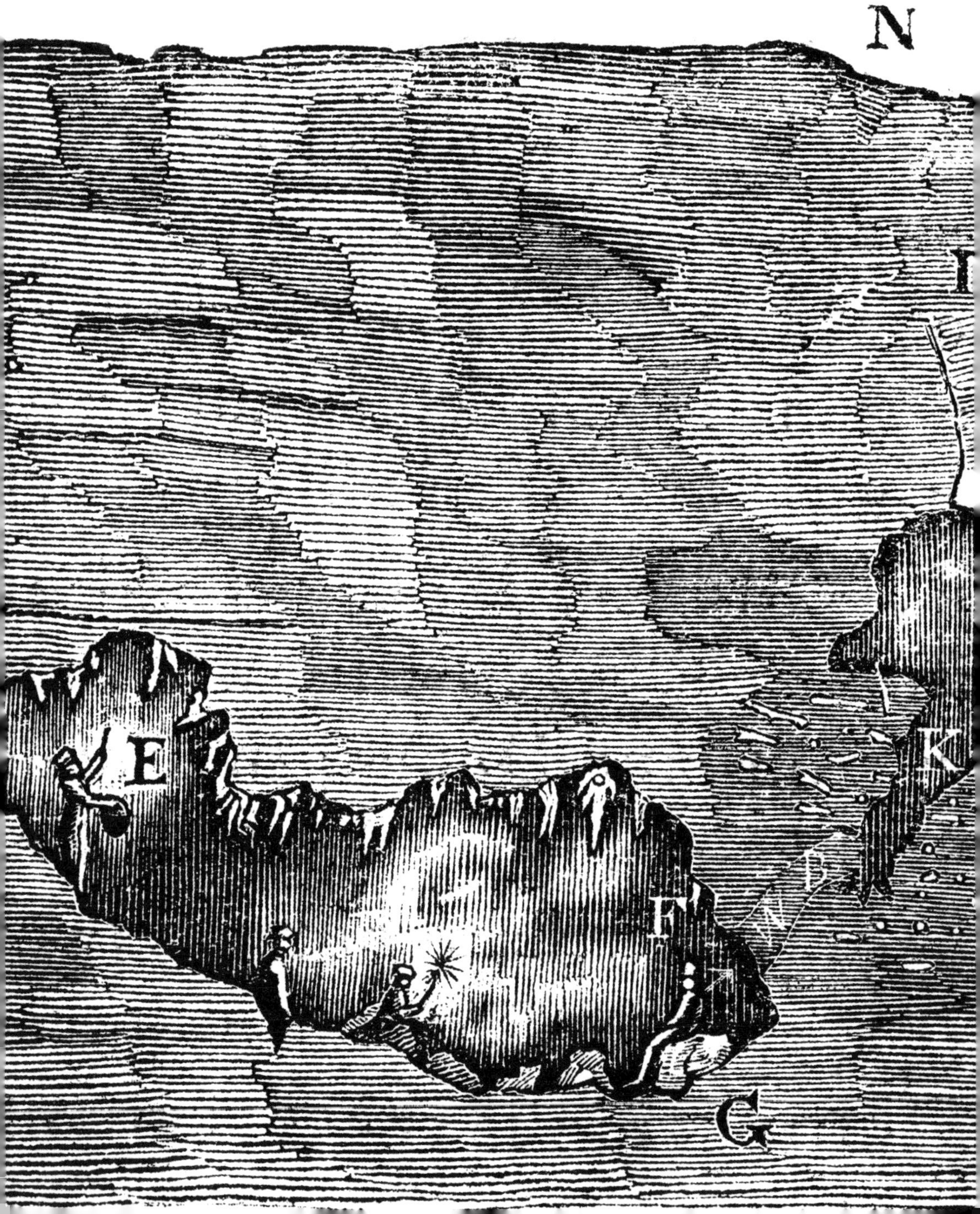

N
E
F
K
G

[THIRTEEN]

Antediluvian Antiquities at Banwell Caves and Pleasure Gardens

Who has not heard of Banwell Bone Caverns? Their fame is world wide, and although our American friends smile at them as 'toys' when compared with their 'Mammoth cave of Kentucky' with its wonderful associations, yet they possess elements of interest which cannot fail both to entertain and to instruct the visitor.[1]

AT THE BEGINNING OF THE NINETEENTH CENTURY THE CAVES OF England – and their fossil fauna in particular – became the object of learned and methodical research. Among the earliest excavations were those of Dr William Buckland at Kirkdale Cave, described in his *Reliquiae Diluvianae; or, Observations on the Organic Remains Contained in Caves, Fissures, and Diluvial Gravel, and on other Geological Phenomena, Attesting to the Action of an Universal Deluge* (1823). Caves and their contents, however, not only interested scholars and antiquaries: they began to appeal to picturesque tourists who were eager to see new and exciting destinations and curious natural phenomena.

The Banwell caves, nestled in the west-facing slope of Banwell Hill, about 19 km/12 miles south-west of Bristol, were in the vanguard of such attractions. The larger of the two, known as the 'Stalactite Cave', was discovered around 1757, and the second, which became known as the 'Bone Cave', was revealed accidentally in 1824 during the course of tunnelling which had been instructed by Revd Francis Randolph, Vicar of Banwell, conjointly with Dr Richard Beadon, Bishop of Bath and Wells and Lord of the Manor of Banwell. The pair resolved to reopen the Stalactite Cave and to 'improve the access to it, for the convenience of visitors from Weston and other adjacent parts, whose donations on viewing it, might increase the funds of a charity school, just then opened in Banwell'.[2]

Although Beadon died in the course of these excavations, his successor to the bishopric proved an enthusiastic patron and a savvy collaborator. George Henry Law, DD (1761–1845) was the thirteenth child and seventh son of Edmund Law, Bishop of Carlisle. Educated at Ipswich and Charterhouse before going up to Queens' College, Cambridge, George Henry attained a series of distinguished ecclesiastical preferments before he was consecrated Bishop of Chester in 1812, and later translated to the See of Bath and Wells [fig. 119]. Law was a high churchman of the old orthodox school who fulfilled the temporal and spiritual duties of the See with energy and ability, and supplied his diocese with 'the stirrings of a new and active life'.[3]

Law was moreover a fellow of the Royal Society and of the Society of Antiquaries, and his keen amateur interest in geology and gardening, business acumen and irrepressible urge to improve doubtless contributed to the great success of the caves. He seized the opportunity at Banwell to indulge both his sacred and his secular interests. Like his friend, the brilliant and eccentric William Buckland, then Reader in Geology at Oxford University and later Dean of Westminster, he was eager to reconcile the newly acquired facts of geology with orthodox religious beliefs; both men shared the conviction that the study of geology had a tendency to confirm the evidences of 'Natural Religion', and that facts developed by it were consistent with the accounts of the creation and deluge recorded in the Mosaic writings.[4] It was the bishop's ambition that the Banwell caves should be pressed into service to illustrate to the public at large the truth of the biblical account of the great deluge.

Buckland very helpfully endorsed the importance of the rediscovery of the caves and their 'Antediluvian Antiquities' in letters that he circulated to the press in early November 1824, many of which were published under the tantalising strapline: 'Discovery of another Cave containing Antediluvian Bones'.[5] His letter to the *Sun* described how an 'immense assemblage of fossil bones' had recently been discovered in a 'cavern of Limestone Rock at Banwell' on the property of the Bishop of Bath and Wells:

> *Many large baskets full of bones have already been extracted, belonging chiefly to the ox and deer tribes ... there are also a few portions of the skeleton of a wolf, and of a gigantic bear. The bones are mostly in a state of preservation equal to that of common grave bones, although it is clear from the fact of some of them belonging to the great extinct species of bear, that they are of antediluvian origin ... There is nothing to induce a belief that it was a den inhabited by hyænas, like the cave of Kirkdale, or bears, like those in Germany: its leading circumstances are similar to those of the ossiferous cavities in the Limestone Rock at Oreston near Plymouth.*[6]

The account continued to report that Buckland had recently examined the cave, operations had commenced for the purpose of 'thoroughly investigating its history and contents', and the bishop had sent collections of bones to Oxford and Cambridge, and proposed to provide a similar supply to the principal public institutions across the country.[7] These announcements did the trick: curious punters became eager to visit the caves.

Soon after the attraction opened to the public in 1825, it was described by a correspondent to the *Bristol Mirror* as comprising 'Antediluvian Caves, and beautiful Woods'.[8] By the following year the attraction had been 'much improved and beautified' and the 'summer-house in the Wood' had been 'tastefully fitted up by the worthy Vicar of the place, for the accommodation of visitors in preparing dinner, tea, &c'.[9] The reporter also praised those 'who have so liberally contributed towards the happiness and pleasures of the neighbourhood', and affirmed that the caves and woods had rapidly become a popular public resort:

> *Above one thousand strangers have visited Banwell within the last year, many of them of the highest rank, fortune, and talent, amongst the most recent of whom were his Grace the Duke of Bedford and his two daughters, Ladies Georgiana and Louisa Russell, who remained inmates of the Vicarage several days. We can only add, that no place in the neighbourhood can afford a man of taste and research more gratification than the one we have now brought before the public.*[10]

William Say after H. W. Pickersgill, *George Henry Law, Bishop of Bath and Wells*, 1820, mezzotint. National Portrait Gallery, London.

John Rutter, who dedicated his booklet *Delineations of the North Western Division of the County of Somerset* (1829) to Law, also generously commended the latter's achievement, declaring that 'Geologists and the Public' were indebted to his 'scientific exertions and liberal patronage ... for the judicious preservation and interesting exhibition of the antediluvian remains at Banwell'.[11]

Visitors approached the cottage and the caves by means of two roads: the lower and 'somewhat circuitous' drive supplied the most picturesque route; the alternative 'direct way', which traversed the domain from east to west, was, however, considered by some as greatly superior as it ran along the declivity of Banwell Hill, and excited an 'additional interest in the mind of the traveller by leading him through potatoe patches, which the benevolent Prelate has allotted to some scores of the labouring poor of Banwell'.[12]

Rutter supplies us with a detailed description of the resort as well as a lithographic view depicting the 'Ornamental Cottage on Banwell Hill' and its pleasure grounds after further enrichments had been made [fig. 120]. The Gothic freestone and pebble-encrusted summer house sits no longer in a wood, but on a grassy expanse above a newly erected thatched cottage. This handsome *cottage ornée*, 'after a plan given by [John] Buckler',[13] was presumably built in 1827 to accommodate the growing number of visitors. The ground around the cottage had also been enclosed and improved; it emerged from a roughly cut bank behind the cottage, was threaded with winding stone-lined paths, and sprinkled with circular shrubberies and juvenile trees. The print also shows the entrance to the caves – 'over which, an appropriate arch has been thrown'[14] – which lies at a short distance below the cottage.

Rutter relates that 'in proceeding from the cottage to examine the caves, visitors usually place themselves under the guidance of Mr. William Beard.' Described in 1837 as 'an upright, intelligent and respectable yeoman', Beard had a long association with the caves, and had been reputed to have initiated the search for and the reopening of the Stalactite Cave, and played a role in the discovery of the Bone Cave [fig. 121].[15] He took up his post in 1825, and 'soon began to be invaded by a host of visitors from all quarters'.[16] His obituary in the *Weston-super-Mare Gazette* (1886) vaunted his achievements:

> It was William Beard's genius and industry which made the discoveries of interest and serviceable to others ... the one object of his life was to unearth and classify the animal remains which had been so long concealed. He gave up farming and let his land to a neighbour. He named his house 'Bone Cottage,' which appellation it richly deserved, for it was soon occupied with cabinets containing his osseous treasures.[17]

120
Anon., 'Ornamental Cottage on Banwell Hill, Erected by the Bishop of the Diocese, who is Lord of the Manor, for the accommodation of Visitors to the Caves', mezzotint, in John Rutter, *Delineations of the … Antediluvian Bone Caverns* (1829). Private collection.

Beard was proud to show and to discourse upon his wonderful collection of bones, and kept a visitors' book in which he recorded 'all the names, with dates, of those who came to inspect his treasures'. So ardent was he in prosecuting his anatomical studies that Bishop Law dubbed him 'Deputy Professor of Geology', and he retained the title of professor until his death.[18]

Beard's tour began with the Bone Cavern, where he explained the 'peculiarities of its contents, having previously caused it to be illuminated'.[19] A rough flight of stone steps led down about 9 m/30 ft to the cavern, which was described as 'consisting of a centre, with three branches, something similar to the palm of the hand, with three expanded fingers':

> The body of the cave, together with the two horizontal branches, was, when first discovered, filled to the depth of eight to ten feet with a confused mass of bones,

121
A. Pocock, *Mr William Beard, Banwell, by whom the caverns in that vicinity were discovered …*, 1841, lithograph. Private collection.

stones, *stiff loam or mud, and coarse gravel, with a small portion of sand. The stones, gravel, and mud, have been cleared out, and the bones arranged on the sides, being piled up into squares, and other more fantastic forms, similar to a charnel house.*[20]

Beard, in his capacity as cicerone, would then describe the course of the discovery, pointing out the bones of various kinds of animals, including ox or buffalo, deer, wolf and bear, and then put forward his theory as to how such a large deposit of bones was found in such a situation. From this cavern visitors traversed a fissure, descending a further 12 m/40 ft, to discover a bank of stones, sand and loam intermingled with bones which had been left undisturbed. The body of this cave was about 9 × 9 m/30 × 30 ft.

Visitors were then conducted to the Stalactite Cavern – the entrance to which was from a much higher level than that of the Bone Cavern, and the descent much greater, more perpendicular and difficult [fig. 122]. They descended first by ladder, and subsequently by a 'very rough flight of rocky and slippery steps' down about 30 m/100 ft to the cavern entrance. The great

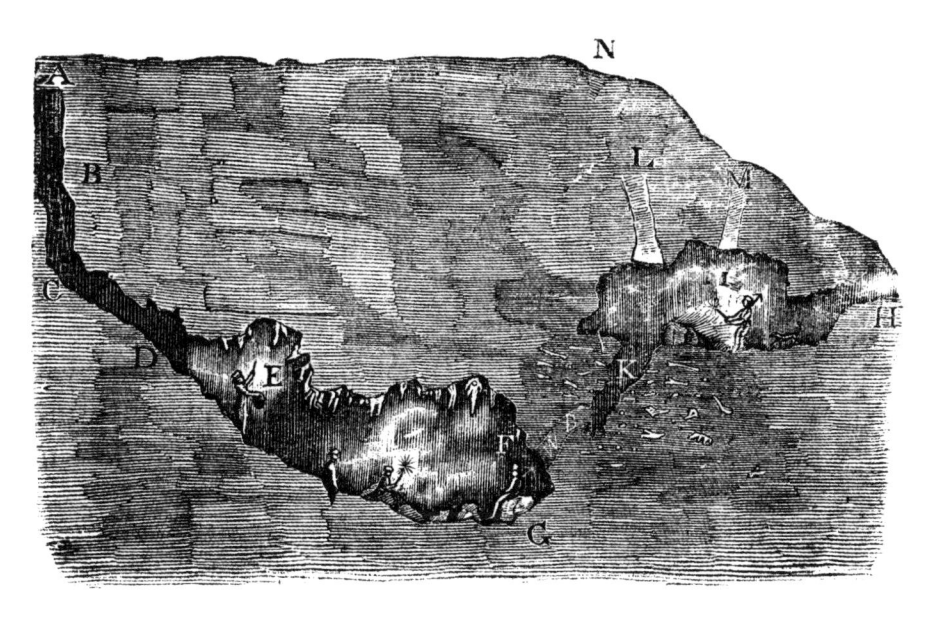

122
Anon., vertical section through the Banwell Caverns, engraving, in John Rutter, Delineations of the ... Antediluvian Bone Caverns (1829). Chris Howes/Wild Places/Alamy Stock Photo.

'F' marks the Stalactite Cave; 'G' the Bishop's Chair; 'I' the Bone Cavern; and 'N' the rough location of the Bishop's Cottage.

'vaulted apartment' of the cavern ranged from 30 to 46 m/100 to 150 ft deep, 11 m/35 ft high, and from 15 to 18m/50 to 60 ft broad, and presented 'a grand and imposing appearance, amply repaying the fatigue and inconvenience of the descent'. The stalactites were exhibited by the aid of the guide's candle, which was fastened to the end of a long pole. Visitors were then led to a further extremity of the cave to be shown the 'Bishop's Chair': 'a rough seat, with a circular back, covered with mamillated carbonate of lime, the seat being formed of a large mass of stalagmite'. This natural chair, which resembled the 'ancient stone crowning chair in Winchester Cathedral', was named in honour of Bishop Law – 'patron of the caves' – who first applied it to its use.[21]

After their fill of gazing at the 'rugged and grotesque' limestone formations, visitors emerged from the caves to repair to the cottage, where, enjoying a short rest, they proceeded by a 'very pleasant [half-mile] walk over the hills' to Mr Beard's house.[22] It was later remarked that visiting Banwell 'without dropping in to see the wonders in and about Mr. Beard's romantic little residence, would be something similar to going to Rome and neglecting to pay a visit to the Vatican and St. Peter's ... an omission not for one moment to be tolerated'.[23]

Crossing a small outdoor court enclosed by a wall surmounted by pieces of stalactites and stalagmites, visitors would enter Bone Cottage to find some of the finest bones found in the caves preserved in a 'curious old carved oak cabinet'. They were placed there 'not only through fear of damage, but lest the number of specimens should gradually be diminished, by the eagerness of collectors overcoming their sense of propriety'.[24]

Here the tour ended; visitors would generally enter their names in the visitors' book, and leave a small gratuity which would be put towards 'increasing the accommodations at the caves, and improving access to them', and the surplus would go to Banwell Charity Sunday School.[25]

As visitor numbers increased year on year, so too did the number of lengthy and flowery verses that either praised or attempted to explain the origins and meaning of the caves' contents: among them the Revd John Skinner's 'Stanzas on Banwell Cave' (c.1828),[26] and T. P. Porch's very curious *The Mysteries of Time: or, Banwell Cave, a Poem in six cantos* (1833), where the poet's imagination, inspired by the 'spectacular catastrophic history implied by the cavern's rock formations', combines geological theory with meditations on the instability of human empires.[27]

The influx of fee-paying 'strangers' also precipitated the construction of a succession of curious structures – several of which were intended to evoke Druidic prehistory – between the early 1830s and the bishop's death in 1845, including the Druid's Temple (1834), the Osteoicon (a receptacle for bones),

123
G. Hollis, 'Banwell Cottage, Somersetshire', mezzotint, *Gentleman's Magazine* (November 1837). Private collection.

the Druid's Circle, the Trilithon and Cromlech (before 1837), and the 'Bishop's Tower' (1835–40, which replaced a short-lived obelisk).[28] Some of these elements are depicted in an engraving of 'Banwell Cottage' published in the *Gentleman's Magazine* in 1837 [fig. 123]. Its correspondent, 'Viator', describes the scene:

> Ascending to the entrance gate, the eye catches the northern face of the hill on which the house is built, with all its rich embellishments; the Druidical circle and trilithon; broad surfaces of verdant turf; parterres of flowers; clusters of flourishing trees; and tasteful fancy structures, of diversified form and designation. The mansion itself stands midway, on the slope of the western extremity of one of the branches of the Mendip hills; sufficiently high to command a glorious view, and protected, at the same time, by the acclivity at its back, from the rage of the south-west gales.

The reporter approved of the idiosyncratic manner in which the mansion had been extended: 'Built at various times, its character has all that variety which forms a prominent feature of the picturesque; but judgment has directed fancy in all the additions; and improvement in comfort as well as appearance, has resulted from every successive enlargement of the structure.'[29]

Beneath the mansion can be seen the Osteoicon, which framed a distant view to Weston-super-Mare, the Bristol Channel and Steep Holm Island. The summer house sits, partially concealed, atop the rough hillside. Viator praised the extent and variety of the scenery as 'seldom equalled' – 'Well does the landscape deserve a poet.'[30]

A later lithographic print entitled 'Ornamental Cottage on Banwell Hill' reproduced in Whereat's Cheddar and Banwell Guide (1847) documents further changes to the setting [fig. 124]. Most striking is the metamorphosis of the former cottage into nothing short of a picturesque episcopal mansion – it had in fact become the bishop's principal residence towards the end of his life. The gardens are more polished and display characteristics of the 'new style' of landscape gardening advocated by Loudon, including an undulating surface, an apparently unlimited extent of smooth lawn, and winding paths; the presence of gesticulating tourists and grazing animals further enlivens the scene.[31]

Whereat's Cheddar and Banwell Guide reports that several of the garden's follies had stone tablets bearing solemn aphorisms – most of which vaunted the triumph of Christianity over paganism. The following verses were, he remarks, found by the entrances to the Druid's Temple and the Bone Cave, respectively:

> *Here once where Druids trod in times of yore,*
> *And stained their altars with a victim's gore;*
> *Here now the Christian, ransom'd from above,*
> *Adores a God of mercy and of love.*
>
> *Here let the scoffer of God's holy word*
> *Behold the traces of a delug'd world;*
> *Here let him in Banwell caves adore*
> *The Lord of Heaven! then go and scoff no more.*

John Whereat was of the opinion that 'the appropriate lines, which occasionally meet the eye in walking through the plantations, are in just accordance with the spirit of the spot, and tend to produce that frame of mind which leads our thoughts from mysterious workings of past ages': 'the marvels of the recesses of the earth, to the majesty of the great God, whose plans are incomprehensible to the limited perceptions of man, and whose wondrous creations are shown in the earth beneath, as well as in the heavens above'.[32]

One could, nevertheless, simply enjoy the spectacle of the caverns and the novelty of the gardens and disregard the site's religious subtext. Law's

124
W. Willis, 'Ornamental Cottage on Banwell Hill', etching, in *Whereat's Cheddar and Banwell Guide* (1847). Private collection.
The Bishop's Tower is visible in the top left of the view.

contemporary, John Loudon, could not abide garden inscriptions, especially if they were religious, as they were 'something superadded to what is or ought to be already complete'.[33] It is likely, in any case, that a 'Druidical inscription' meant nothing to many visitors who had no idea who the Druids might have been. Mary Elton reports in 1837, while visiting Banwell caves, that her friend Emma Eagles heard a young lady in a party of London visitors 'ask her husband (as they read some Druidical inscription), "Who *were* the Druids?"' [fig. 125].[34]

When *Whereat's Guide* was published, Bishop Law had been dead for two years, and the belief in the universal effects of the Noachian deluge had been largely discredited; Charles Lyell's *Principles of Geology* (1830) had begun to put pay to the idea that the Bible was the key to the geological past. These circumstances did not, however, tarnish the celebrity of the antediluvian caverns, as they were now but two of an array of curiosities and 'tasteful fancy structures, of diversified form and designation' laid out in extensive and artfully embellished pleasure grounds.[35] Visitors also came to see the gardens and appreciate the views – they were encouraged to explore the grounds and to ascend the Bishop's Tower to gain delightful and magnificent prospects beyond the gardens' boundaries, over the Bristol Channel:

> It looks round
> Upon the variegated scene of hills,
> And woods, and fruitful vales, and villages,
> Half-hid in tufted orchards, and the sea,
> Boundless, and studded thick with many a sail.[36]

While Bishop Law was landscaping his hilltop estate at Banwell, he was also at the same time engaged in recasting his moated and walled pleasure gardens at the Bishop's Palace in Wells. He is said to have highly improved the grounds through the introduction of a new pond, luxuriant planting, and by levelling the ground to form large smooth lawns studded with enamelled parterres. The scene approached 'horticultural perfection'.[37] It was, however, Law's dramatic approach to the ruins of Bishop Burnell's mediaeval 'new hall' which supplies us with the greatest insight into the essential nature of this improving cleric: he pulled down the east and most of the south walls of the venerable episcopal structure 'for the purpose of giving a more picturesque appearance to these ruins as seen from the adjoining gardens'.[38] As William Phelps remarked in 1836, his alterations to the gardens 'have made even the ruins of the great hall subservient to produce picturesque effect' [fig. 126].[39]

Law's interventions at Wells and Banwell suggest that he possessed strong religious feeling and a picturesque sensibility, and that these sentiments were not only compatible but complementary. But whereas the refurbishment of Wells was a bold and straightforward makeover of an established garden in the new taste, Banwell was something entirely without precedent: what was

125
Mary Elizabeth Elton, 'Banwell Caves', drawing,
in A Few Years of the Life of Mary Elizabeth Elton (1877).
Elton visited Banwell in September 1837, observing, 'The cave was extremely wet and dirty owing to the rains, but well worth seeing, the bones being in such immense quantities.' She described her guide, Mr Beard, as a 'funny little man' who had 'jokes and witticisms ready for all visitors'.

126
L. Keux after W. H. Bartlett, 'Wells Palace: Ruins of the Old Hall & Chapel', etching, in John Britton, *Picturesque Antiquities of the English Cities* (1830). Private collection.

conceived as a fanciful take on the 'sacro monte', or mountain pilgrimage shrine, was incrementally and whimsically elaborated to become what Chris Stringer has recently described in *Homo Britannicus* as 'a solemn reminder of the Flood, a sort of biblical deluge theme park'.[40] If the caverns and their contents engrossed the visitors' attention, they also presumably bewildered their speculations; as Dickens observed in *Household Words* (1853), what was one to make of the Bone Cave with its osseous remains 'piled up against the wall', stuck into the floors and filling up recesses 'in the most fantastic shapes', of a candle 'stuck in the eyeless socket of a skull', of a 'seat composed of horns and leg bones'?[41] Was such a place readily conducive to religious meditation?

To fully comprehend Banwell one must, however, perceive the assemblage – caves, cottage, follies, paths and plantings – as a landscape, and a very innovative one at that. The landscape supplied form, spatial coherence and meaning to the bishop's narrative; it shaped the visitors' experiences, controlled their movements and created a highly specific sense of place. These qualities were reinforced by the fact that visitors had to embark on a special journey to Banwell: its remote position underscored its role as a site of pilgrimage and ensured that when visitors arrived at their destination it was physically and socially distinctive – outside the everyday world.

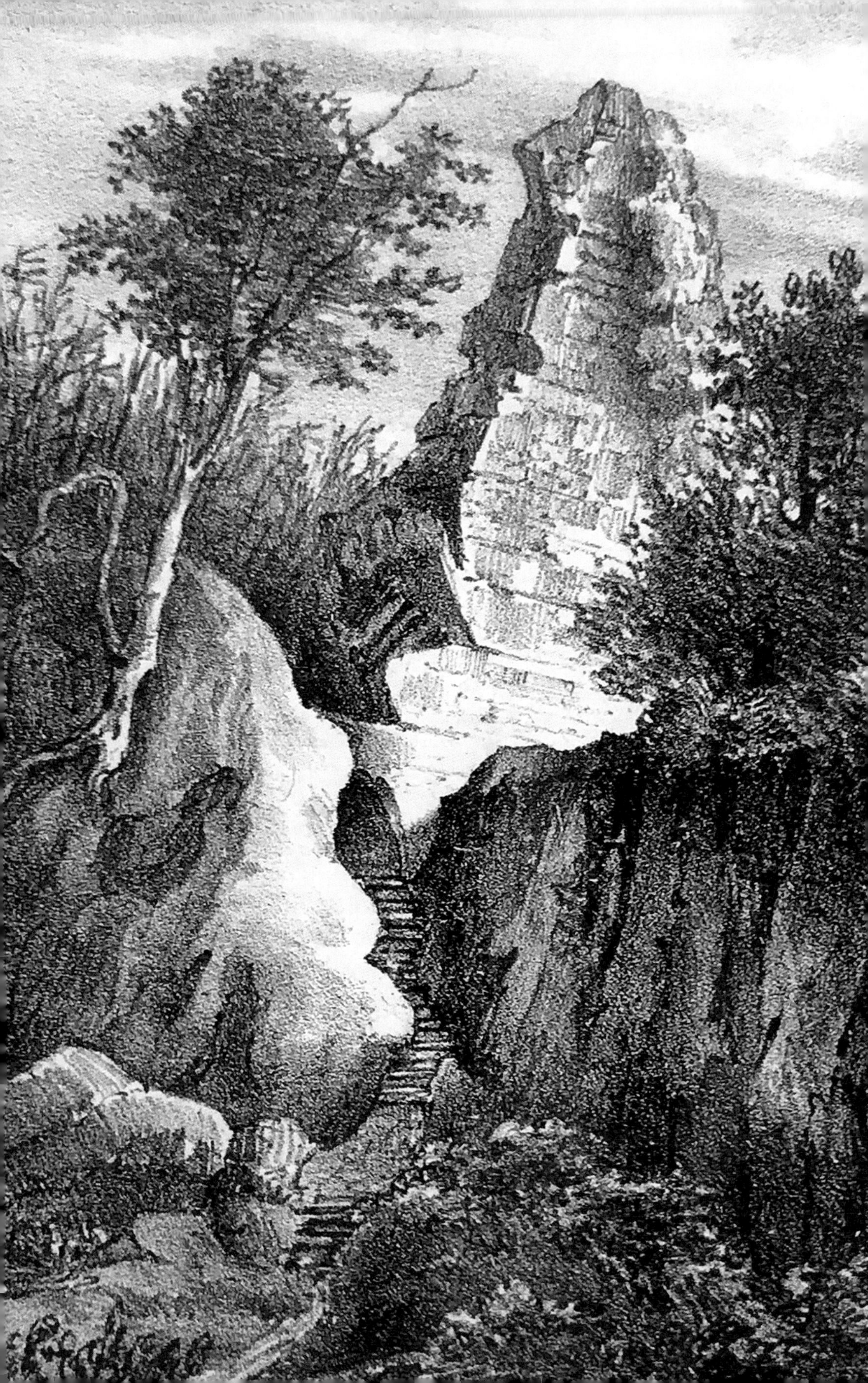

[FOURTEEN]

Hawkstone:
'A Kind of Turbulent Pleasure between Fright and Admiration'

WHEN HESTER THRALE AND SAMUEL JOHNSON VISITED HAWKSTONE in late July 1774, the former remarked that she found it 'upon the whole a place of the first class in this Kingdom'; she also expressed astonishment that a place 'so fine' had 'escaped pompous description'. She continued, 'as words, however, are but poor representations of things I do not much regret the loss of such reputation as words could give. This is a place which should be seen, and when it is seen it is sure to be admired.'[1]

Her companion, Dr Johnson, who, like Thrale herself, had an informed appreciation of landscape and was well versed in the Burkean sublime, painted a picture of the place that emphasised its natural attractions and considered the efforts of the Hill family to enhance them:[2]

> *We saw Hawkstone, the seat of Sir Rowland Hill, and were conducted by Miss Hill[3] over a large tract of Rocks and Woods; a region abounding with striking scenes and terrific grandeur. We were always on the brink of a precipice, or at the foot of a lofty rock; but the steeps were seldom naked: in many places Oaks of uncommon magnitude shot up from crannies of stone; and where there were no trees, there were underwoods and rushes. Round the rocks is a narrow path cut upon the stone, which is very frequently hewn into steps; but Art has proceeded no further than to make the succession of wonders safely accessible. The whole circuit is somewhat laborious; it is terminated by a Grotto cut in the Rock to a great extent with many windings, and supported by pillars, not hewn into regularity, but such as imitate the sports of nature by asperities and protuberances. The place is without any dampness, and would afford an habitation not uncomfortable. There were from space to space seats cut out in the rock.[4]*

127

E. Hill, *Hawkstone Park, Shropshire*, c.1840?, lithograph. Private collection.

This is one of a series of views of the park based on sketches prepared by Elizabeth Hill. The rocky promontory at the centre of this view was known as the Grotto Rock.

HAWKSTONE PARK, SHROPSHIRE.
The Seat of Sir Rowland Hill Bar.^t

128
E. Hill, *Hawkstone Park, Shropshire*, c.1840?, lithograph. Private collection.

Charles Hulbert reported in *Nature's Beauties … in Shrewsbury* (1825) that a decayed piece of wall in the Red Castle bore the inscription, 'See this vast antique Pile, how reverend grey / In hoary age! Its walls and mould'ring towers, / With tufted moss and ivy rudely hung …'

Though Johnson noted that the estate 'wants water', he was impressed by 'the extent of its prospects, the awfulness of its shades, the horrors of its precipices, the verdures of its hollows, and the loftiness of its rocks: the ideas which it forces upon the mind are, the sublime, the dreadful, and the vast. Above is inaccessible altitude, below is horrible profundity' [fig. 127]. 'He that mounts the precipices at Hawkstone, wonders how he came thither, and doubts how he shall return. His walk is an adventure, and his departure an escape. He has not the tranquillity but the horrors of solitude; a kind of turbulent pleasure between fright and admiration … *Hawkstone* can have no fitter inhabitants than "Giants of mighty bone and bold emprise," men of lawless courage and heroic violence.' Hawkstone, he concluded, 'should be described by Milton'.[5]

Hawkstone was the product of generations of improving Shropshire landowners. The estate was acquired in 1549 by Sir Rowland Hill, an enterprising mercer and merchant adventurer who became a very rich man and the first Protestant Lord Mayor of London. His descendant the Revd and Rt Hon. Richard Hill – 'The Great Hill'– who also amassed a considerable fortune, built up the estate and rebuilt the hall following his retirement from public affairs in 1708. It was, however, Richard's nephew, Sir Rowland Hill, 1st Baronet (1705–1783), who enlarged and recast the house in the Palladian taste, and created the landscape that Johnson and Thrale so admired [fig. 129]. He

129
Anon., *Hawkstone Hall*, c.1790, oil on canvas.
Yale Center for British Art, New Haven, Conn.

remodelled the hall and extended the estate through the purchase of lands in neighbouring Redcastle township – which brought the ruined mediaeval Red Castle into the estate – and is thought to have begun extending the pleasure grounds in the 1740s [fig. 128].

The antiquary John Loveday of Caversham was among the early tourists who visited in July 1765 and commented on the park: 'nature indeed has done so much that not to have helpt it somewhat by art would have been unpardonable in a man of fortune ... but the wonder of the place are the great rocks in so cultivated a country, rocks decked in green, nay supporting oaks ... A grotto is now making, to be entered one way through arched passages under ground, turning many ways. The whole of this fine place takes a great circuit.'[6]

The Grotto was described in 1784 as a vast subterraneous cave

curiously beset with costly shells, selected from the remotest regions of the sea, and inlaid with petrifactions and fossils from the deepest recesses of the earth. You will view with amazement, the different dwellings of the briny inhabitants; some burnished with gloss of deepest hue, others rugged with points, and crusted by nature ... These being joined with coral, tinged with ore, spangled with mineral, and receiving light through some exquisitly fine painted glass.[7]

The whole was executed with 'masterly boldness, perfectly characteristic with the scenes around you, without any thing of that diminutive or formal decoration and *petitesse*, by which Grottos are usually rendered more like artificial *baby-houses*, than grand natural and romantic caverns' [fig. 130].[8]

Loveday also observed that the Hermit's Lodge was 'curious indeed, consisting of several apartments, moss and roots the material; by springs the hermit, formed very naturally, has motions that surprise his visitors, who suppose him inanimate.' This automaton was a perennial source of pleasure for visitors, some of whom were critical: Sir Richard Colt Hoare remarked in July 1801 that the face of the 'figure of a hermit who moves and speaks' was 'natural enough' but the figure itself 'stiff and not well managed'.[9] And Thomas Martyn noted in his diary in the autumn of the same year: 'On your putting questions to him, his lips move, and he answers in a hoarse voice, coughs as if almost exhausted' [fig. 131].[10]

Sir Rowland also formed a number of follies and features in the park including the Fox's Knob ('a standing monument' formed by the 'raging billows of the great deluge'), a 'subterraneous passage, called by some, Calcutta', the Vineyard ('laid out in the manner of a fortification'), a menagerie boasting a 'choice collection of Beasts and Birds, both foreign and domestic, among which is a remarkably large Eagle, also a Mackaw, and various sorts of Parrots, with

130
Anon., *The Grotto in Hawkstone Park*, 1854, engraving.
Artocoloro/Alamy Stock Photo.

131
Anon., hermit in his cell at Hawkstone Park, nineteenth century, photograph.
Shropshire Archives, Shrewsbury.

The 'Waxen Hermit' for many years inhabited a cell 'Deep in the grot[to]', and was the subject of a 'descriptive poem' by Charles Ash entitled 'The Hermit of Hawkstone' (1817).

some different species of Monkeys', St Francis's Cave and White Tower.[11] The gardens even contained the residence of Adam and Eve: 'This rural habitation is occupied by a Man and his Wife, who may well be called the Adam and Eve of this delightful Eden. Adam is busily employed in cleaning his ground, whilst Eve bestirs herself about her domestic affairs, and feeds her Poultry, which flock round her in great numbers, on the ringing of a Bell.'[12]

Most striking of all was the 'Awful Precipice' – its name said to have derived from Samuel Johnson's description – from which visitors admired with astonishment 'rugged rocks bulging with terror!' and 'huge pending craggs' that formed the Raven's Shelf.[13]

The landscape was laid out in an extensive and dramatic scenographic 16-km/10-mile circuit linking a series of objects, stations and vantage points set out in a linear sequence intended to supply visitors with opportunities for intellectual, emotional and physical engagement; from 1766 the visitor's passage through the landscape was guided by a small published *Description*, which by 1813 had gone through ten editions, and 'as it is in general the request by all strangers visiting Hawkstone, we hope it will be continually reprinting.'[14] The number of editions is a testimony to the constant novelty and improvements that the Hills introduced to their estate [fig. 132].

When Sir Richard Hill (1732–1808) succeeded to the baronetcy in 1783 he immediately began to undertake 'very many great improvements' [fig. 133].[15] The bachelor baronet, who was well educated and well travelled,[16] and a champion of Calvinistic Methodism, was described by his contemporary Nathaniel Wraxall as 'one of the most upright, disinterested and honest Men who ever sat in Parliament … His Manners were quaint and puritanical; his Address shy and embarrassed. He possessed however a most benevolent Disposition, together with a great Estate, which enabled him to gratify his generous and philanthropic Feelings.'[17] His biographer Edwin Sidney declared in 1839 that under Sir Richard's stewardship the park was 'never traversed without surprise and admiration; but it has the still higher attraction of having been the home of the pious and the brave'.[18]

Among the baronet's first and most 'prodigious' improvements was the creation of 'an immense Piece of Water in the form of a wide navigable River' [fig. 134][19] – begun c.1783 and later extended by William Emes – and the 'Menagerie Pool', both of which were possibly precipitated by Dr Johnson's earlier observation that the landscape lacked water. A postscript in the second edition of the *Description* (1784) described the basin, then in the process of being formed: '[It] is to be about a Mile and a Half in length, and near 100 Yards in breadth, one end of which will lose itself in a thick wood near the Lodge … and the other end will meet all the grand scenery between the Grotto Hill and the Red Castle, in the middle of that fertile and beautiful Valley which separates those two stupendous Rocks.'[20] This three-year improvement, like many of those that followed, was galvanised by the baronet's desire both to enhance the landscape and to keep 'all the industrious poor in the neighbourhood … furnished with bread'.[21]

Some of the other additions made to 'the beauties of Hawkstone' by the 2nd Baronet, which were described in the 1807 *Description* as 'by no means among the least pleasing', included some of the following: a colossal statue of

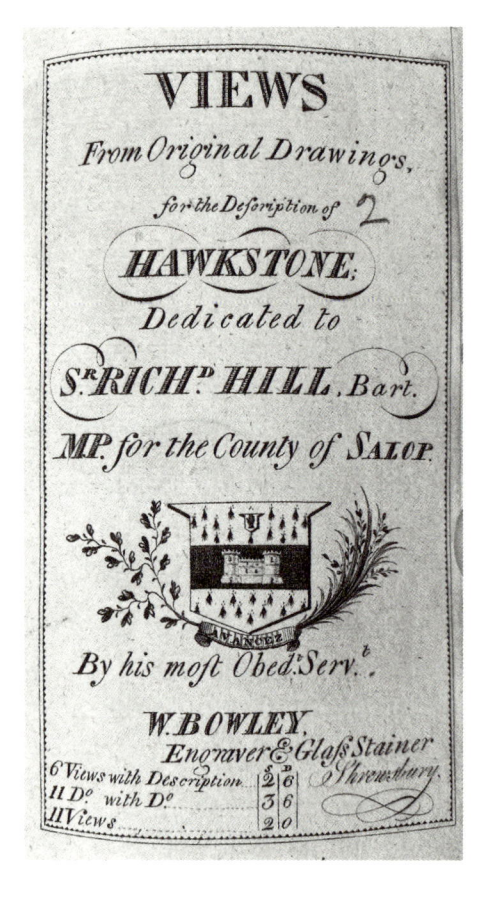

132
W. Bowley, title page for W. Bowley, *Views from Original Drawings for the Description of Hawkstone*, c.1807. © The Trustees of the British Museum.
This pamphlet was published for visitors to the estate and appears to have been sold as a supplement to the official guidebook.

133
John Russell, *Sir Richard Hill, 2nd Baronet*, c.1783, pastel drawing.
National Portrait Gallery, London.

134

John Emes, *The Lake at Hawkstone*, 1790, graphite, watercolour and pen with brown and black ink. Yale Center for British Art, New Haven, Conn.

According to the *Description of Hawkstone* (1807), Hawk Lake was extended by building 'strong high dams which go the whole length of the River Hawk'.

Neptune; a 'whimsical edifice in the exact taste of the houses in North Holland' and a 'windmill ... painted quite in the Dutch style' at the head of Hawk Lake; an Egyptian tent ('taken at the Battle of the pyramids') in 'Amphitrite's flower-garden'; a 'Scene in Swisserland' intended to evoke 'some in that wild romantic country'; a 'Scene at Otaheite' with a low building 'constructed of sticks and reeds, the model of which is taken from one of the prints in Captain Cook's Voyage';[22] and a 'Grand Obelisk' dedicated to Sir Rowland, the lofty gallery of which formed 'a useful observatory for the astronomer either by day or night' [fig. 135].[23] In around 1790 Sir Richard also built a 'handsome, spacious, excellent Inn, with pleasure-grounds, bowling-green, &c.' for the reception of the increasing number of park visitors [fig. 136].[24]

135
W. Bowley, engraver, *Hawkstone House* and *Neptune's Whim*, engraving,
in T. Rodenhurst [pseud.], A *Description of Hawkstone* (1807). © The Trustees of the
British Museum.

Neptune's Whim took its name from a 'fine colossean statue' of the
eponymous god, who was accompanied by Nereïds who threw up a stream of water
to a 'considerable height'.

136
Anon., 'Entrance to Hawkstone Park', steel engraving,
Illustrated London News (December 1854). Private collection.

A scene of the 'great festivity' took place on the estate to mark the coming of age
of the Hon. Rowland Clegg Hill.

The Revd Richard Warner observed that the grounds of Hawkstone in the summer of 1801 were as 'singular as they are beautiful; consisting of a succession of hills and dales connected together in a very small space'. Although critical of the 'artificial ornaments' which he dismissed as 'childish tricks', he was impressed by the 'grandeur of the features ... the majesty of its rocks, and the gloom of its groves'.[25]

The 'parkomaniac' Prince Hermann von Pückler-Muskau, who visited Hawkstone in January 1827, was, however, overwhelmed by what he saw:

> Though I felt perfectly 'blasé' of parks yesterday, and thought I could never take any interest in them again, I am of quite another mind to-day, and must in some respects give Hawkstone the preference over all I have seen. It is not art, nor magnificence, nor aristocratical splendour, but nature alone, to which it is indebted for this pre-eminence, and in such a degree that were I gifted with the power of adding to its beauty, I should ask, What can I add?[26]

Sir Richard would have been delighted by the German prince's assessment of the park as 'a spot whose beauties are so appreciated even in the neighbourhood, that the brides and bridegrooms of Liverpool and Shrewsbury come here to pass their honeymoon'. 'The park seems indeed rather the property of the public than its possessor, who never resides here, and whose ruinous and mean-looking house lies hidden in a corner of the park, like a "hors d'oeuvre".'[27]

The Hills were neither the first nor the only great landed family to open their gardens for public enjoyment: Stowe had welcomed garden tourists from 1717, and the estate's New Inn was purpose-built by Richard Temple, 1st Viscount Cobham, to accommodate them and his guests. The gardens also boasted the country's first guidebook, *A Description of the Gardens at Stowe* (1744).[28] Whereas Stowe was laid out for the delectation of Lord Cobham and his friends, family and visiting dignitaries, however, the park and gardens at Hawkstone appear to have been designed from the onset 'for the Pleasure and Amusement of the Visiters', or as Rodenhurst first remarked in the 1784 edition of the *Description*: 'particularly to those whose curiosity may induce them to visit the beautiful and astonishing scenes of which they treat'.[29] This aim is underscored by the fact that visitors were 'conducted by a guide to the principal walks' and were greeted by an automaton in the Grotto; the Hawkstone Inn – complete with bowling green and pleasure grounds – was described as 'one of the most elegant and spacious Inns in the kingdom, more like a seat of a nobleman than an Hotel'.[30] Yet more hyperbolically, the Methodist local preacher Joseph Whittingham Salmon discerned a spiritual dimension in the public tourism at Hawkstone: he declared in *Moral Reflections in Verse, Begun in Hawkstone Park* (1796) that 'this most charming, romantic, and delightful Park' was an 'Earthly Paradise', and that it furnished its visitors with a means of 'meditating on the Works of their great and good *Creator*' and to observe the 'Operation of his Almighty Power in the visible Works of *Creation*' [fig. 137]. He averred that if visitors explored the gardens with a '*religious* and *Philosophical* Eye, They will then prove to be doubly instructive, as well as doubly blessed, satisfactory and delightful'.[31]

> *Oft have I heard of* HAWKSTONE *Park,*
> *It's Beauties oft defin'd;*
> *But all Description was but dark,*
> *Compar'd with what I find …*
>
> *Let Pope his Windsor Forest praise,*
> *Others of Richmond boast*
> *Of* HAWKSTONE'S *Scenes I tune my Lays,*
> *Because They please Me most …*
>
> *And Oh! That All who come to see*
> *This Earthly Paradise,*
> *May, for their* HAWKSTONE *Visit, be*
> *More happy and more wise;*
>
> *Be struck with such stupendous Things*
> *As Here do please the Eye,*
> *And hence adore the* KING *of* KINGS
> *To all* ETERNITY.[32]

While the first and second baronets deservedly take much of the credit for the most formative landscape improvements at Hawkstone, there is good reason to suggest that Miss Jane Hill (1740–1794) was their éminence grise. It was 'Miss Hill' – daughter of Rowland Hill and Jane Delves Broughton – who was cicerone upon the occasion of Johnson and Thrale's tour, and who according to the lexicographer 'showed the whole succession of wonders with great civility';[33] though Thrale characterised the young guide 'as though she were an odd natural phenomenon', emphasising her lack of metropolitan style in her dress and manners, she found her strangely captivating:[34]

> *In the Lady … there is an odd mixture of sublimity and meanness, Her conversation is elegant, her dress uncommonly vulgar, her manner lofty if not ostentatious,*

137
E. Hill, *Hawkstone Park, Shropshire*, c.1840?, lithograph. Private collection.
The park was celebrated for its 'fine stately Oaks' and 'rugged cliffs'.

and her whole appearance below that of a common house-maid. She is, however, by far the most conversible Female I have seen since I left home, her character, I hear, is respectable, and her address is as polite as can be wished. I shall never see her again probably, and I am sorry for it. One could wish to see her very often.[35]

Miss Hill was not in fact such a shadowy figure at Hawkstone. She remained unmarried and lived on the estate, and therefore witnessed the unfolding of the designed landscape under both her father, Sir Rowland, and her brother, Sir Richard. She travelled periodically with the latter – most notably in 1791, when he was active 'in the improvement of his seat at Hawkstone', they toured Flanders, Germany and France.[36]

Jane was, like her brothers Sir Richard and the Revd Rowland, an ardent Calvinist, and was a 'truly pious sister' who provided 'excellent advice' to her siblings throughout their lives.[37] Much of what we know about her is recorded in the Revd Edwin Sidney's biographies of her brothers,[38] and her correspondence with her friend Willielma, Viscountess Glenorchy (whom she influenced in the latter's decision to become an evangelical activist).[39]

Sidney neatly summarises Hill's pious character:

In addition to gifts of no ordinary kind, Miss Jane Hill was possessed of a spirit of genuine piety, the fervor whereof was effectually regulated, though not at all impaired, by a peculiar sobriety of judgment. Her countenance was altogether the index of the refined qualities of her mind; and its sweet, intelligent expression was graced by an air of sincerity, which ensured the unbounded confidence of those who enjoyed the privilege of her friendship. She read and thought much, but prayed more.[40]

It is difficult to determine to what extent Jane played a part in the design and presentation of the Hawkstone estate. Her 'Hill family pedigree' attests to her family pride,[41] and the landscape paintings she admired by van Ruisdael and Philips Wouwerman presumably reflect her preferred landscape aesthetic of wild irregularity.[42] Jane's role in guiding visitors around the estate – and especially such well-known ones as Dr Johnson and Mrs Thrale – testify to her familiarity with the landscape, its history and its recent and 'considerable alterations and improvements'.[43] Given the above, is it possible that she assumed the pseudonym of T. Rodenhurst, and that she is in fact responsible for the *Description of Hawkstone*? The long-standing and unquestioned attribution of the popular estate guidebook to her father, Sir Rowland, deserves to be re-evaluated, as it seems unlikely that a nobleman who is not known to have produced any notable prose should be credited with what the seasoned topographical writer Joseph Nightingale described in 1813 as 'a little book written with a good deal of fire and fancy'.[44] Miss Hill would not be the only woman in the Hill family to write a book on the estate: her niece, also named Jane Hill, who lived at the Citadel in the park,[45] is credited as the author of the handsomely illustrated *Some Account of the Antiquities of Hawkstone* (1828).

One of the features celebrated in the *Description* – and one of the most enduringly interesting and remarkable features on the Hawkstone estate – is Red Castle Hill [fig. 138]. This lofty and 'delightfully romantic Hill' formed of red sandstone is crowned with an early Iron Age and later Roman hill fort that was described in 1784 as a 'venerable Fortress, long the seat of warriors, and remarkable for its strength' which over time had been reduced to a 'heap

138
Anon., 'Approach to the Highest Part of the [Red] Castle', lithograph,
in *Some Account of the Antiquities of Hawkstone* (1828). © The Trustees of the
British Museum.

The castle was 'al[l] ruin[o]us' and 'decayed' until it was spruced up in about 1780.

139
Anon., 'The Giant's Well', lithograph, in *Some Account of the Antiquities of Hawkstone*
(1828). © The Trustees of the British Museum.

of ruins ... inhabited only by Birds of prey'. According to local folklore it was a matter of common report that the castle was formerly the habitation of two giants by the names of Tarquin and Tarquinius.[46]

While the local legend that the Red Castle had once been inhabited by colossi may have been well established by the late eighteenth century, Rodenhurst was the first to supply its mythical denizens with their Roman names. In the second edition of the *Description* (1784) the author pronounces somewhat equivocally: 'There have been several accounts of this very extraordinary place; the generally received notion, prevalent among all country people in that neighbourhood, that it was formerly the habitation of two huge Giants named Tarquin and Tarquinius, however absurd and ridiculous in itself, is as perfectly correspondent with the place, as the idea of fairies dancing on daisy tops on the verdant plains.'[47]

How and when the giants came to be known as Tarquin and Tarquinius is unknown, but their names suggest that they were a product of a classical education and not of local lore. The names had been paired in classical antiquity: Lucius Tarquinius Collatinus was a Roman nobleman and husband of Lucretia – whose rape by her husband's nephew Sextus Tarquinius (Tarquin) and subsequent suicide led to the overthrow of the monarchy and the establishment of the Roman Republic. Neither man was a giant, though both were in their own ways immensely powerful.

Perhaps Miss Hill – the Calvinist guardian of an Edenic garden, a landscape of great wildness and irregularity undoubtedly, in her eyes, shaped by the hand of God and not by the hand of man – was responsible for naming the giants and invoking the Roman myth – or, since the myth has no obvious relevance to the spot, summoning up the grandeur and violence of Roman antiquity in a more vague and general sense. The apparently random choice of the giants' names and the invention of antique associations for a local landmark are less surprising when considered in the context of the combination of local and de-localising features in the park as a whole. On the one hand, visitors are guided along a route that exploits the 'terrific grandeur' of the natural landscape and ensures that, as Johnson puts it, 'we were always on the brink of a precipice, or at the foot of a lofty rock.'[48] On the other hand, they also take in, for example, the 'whimsical' Dutch house and the Tahitian hut.

The Red Castle was in 1784 the last attraction that visitors to Hawkstone would encounter on their perambulation of the estate; here they would gaze upon its 'solemn scenes', including the Giant's Well [fig. 139] – a 'dreadful profound abyss' – and the 'Stately Lion – a lapidary beast who 'tho' his kingly looks strike terror into the beholder, yet he is so tame and docile, that the most timid may without danger take him by the tooth, and play with him as with a Spaniel'. Having traversed the hill, visitors would pass by the lodge to the 'pretty little village' of Weston, whose 'very good Inn' was genteelly fitted up for their reception. Here, we are told by Rodenhurst, tourists could refresh after their walk and ruminate on the scenes they had 'with so much delight been viewing'.[49]

The *Description* was the official guide and Red Castle Hill was the apogee of the 'romantic scenes, amazing varieties, and natural as well as artificial beauties of Hawkstone-Park'.[50] In its assumption that these beauties demand enumeration, it testifies to a form of eccentricity found in other gardens in this book, such as that of Jonathan Tyers at Denbies: an eccentricity of accumulation. Rather than simply seeking to accentuate and subtly 'improve' the natural qualities of the hilly landscape in which Hawkstone was situated – in Johnson's words, its 'striking scenes and terrific grandeur' – Sir Rowland Hill and Jane Hill, and latterly Sir Richard Hill, treated these advantages of site, relatively unusual in England, as an occasion for constructing increasing numbers of features that refer boldly outwards towards other places and other times. It is hardly surprising that 'Rodenhurst' anticipated visitors might need to rest and ruminate at the local inn.

Alongside its presentation of the garden as constantly acquiring a succession of new sources of wonder and entertainment, the *Description* nonetheless emphasises permanence, punningly presenting the Hills as firmly established in their hilly region. In doing so, it implicitly affirms that a landscape so sublime can easily incorporate and absorb the 'whimsical':

> *O may the* HILLS *for ever live,*
> *Around this pleasant Shore,*
> *Till Rocks shall crumble into Dust,*
> *And Time shall be no more.*[51]

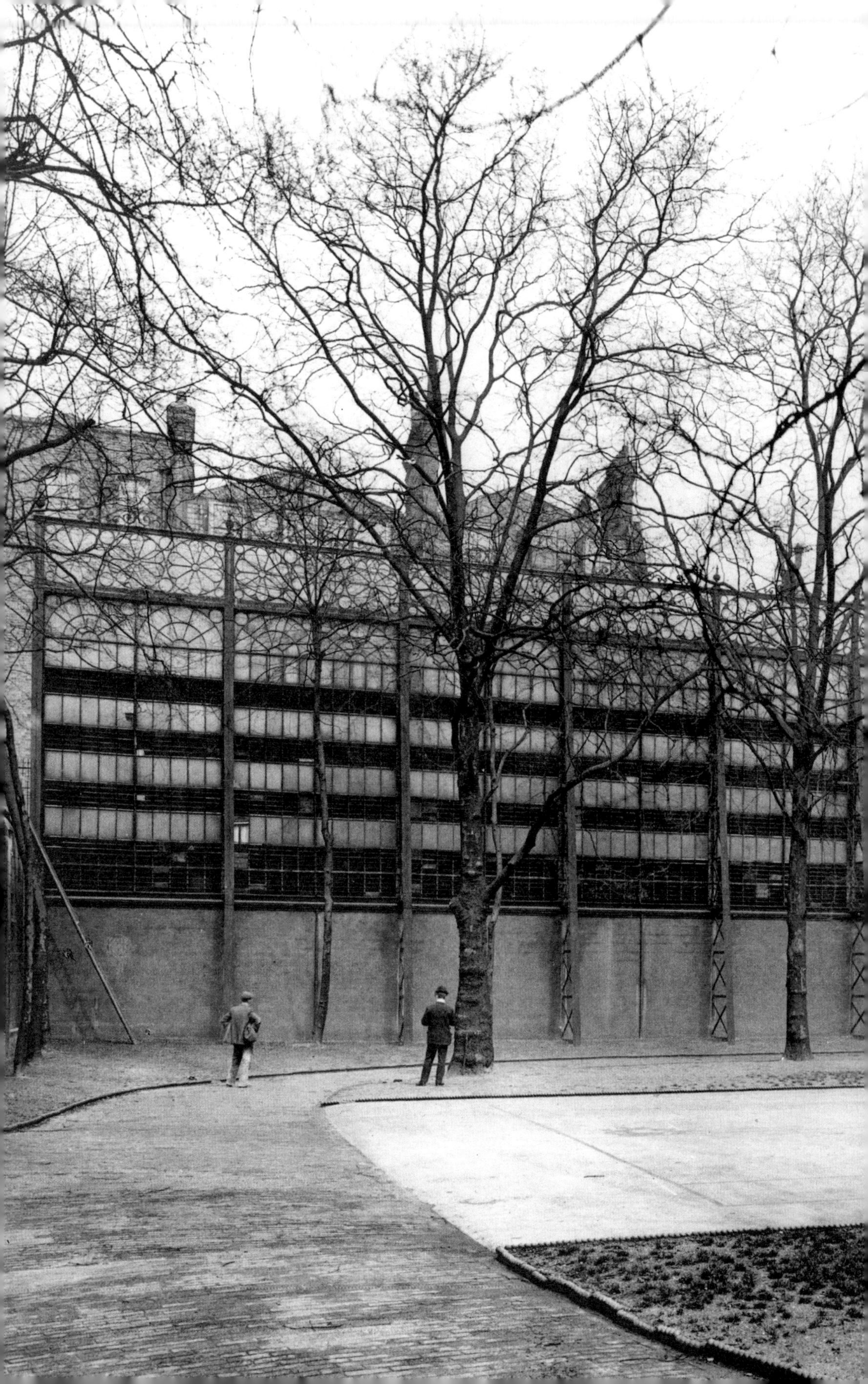

[FIFTEEN]

The Burrowing Duke at Harcourt House

London possesses, on the whole, a fair share of gloomy houses. Some of these are very large. In fact, the larger the house the gloomier very often its appearance. But 'gloomy' would be a mild word to apply to what was Harcourt House, the town house residence aforetime of the Dukes of Portland, in Cavendish-square. Its aspect, from the outside, was absolutely forbidding. But Harcourt House has ceased to be; or, to be precise, it will have ceased to be before many days have passed. For the house-breakers are at work upon it with pickaxe, spade, and shovel, and the west side of Cavendish-square is a mass, partly, of unsightly ruins.[1]

FOR ALMOST TWO CENTURIES HARCOURT HOUSE AND ITS CAPACIOUS garden had the distinction of being among the most private and impenetrable premises in London. Known variously as Bingley, Harcourt and Portland House, it did not evolve slowly and organically to become an inaccessible precinct: it was planned from its earliest days by its occupant cum designer – the amateur architect 'of ability' and former Treasurer to the Household of George II, Robert Benson, the first and last Lord Bingley – with a view to ensuring maximum privacy. Whereas his neighbour, the 'the Grand Duke of Chandos', had taken the whole of the north side of the then newly formed square in pursuit of his wish to build 'a palatial residence, and to purchase all the property between Cavendish-square and his palace of Canons at Edgeware, so that he might ride from town to the country *through his own estate*', Bingley chose to immure himself behind high walls within a large building plot on the western flank of the square.[2]

Between 1726 and 1727, Bingley built what James Ralph described in A Critical Review of the Publick Buildings, Statues and Ornaments in, and about,

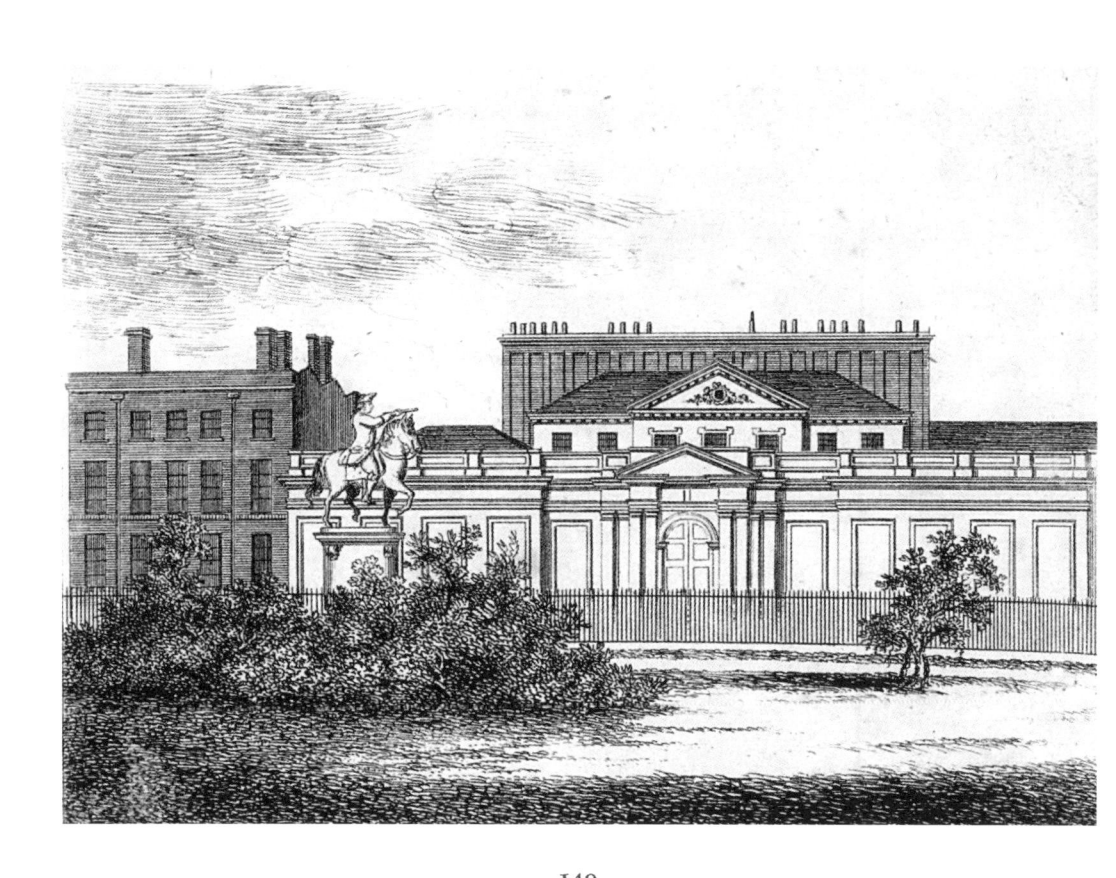

140
J. P. Malcolm, 'The West Side of Cavendish Square', in J. P. Malcolm,
The Anecdotes of the Manners and Customs of London (1808).
T. H. Shepherd remarked in *Metropolitan Improvements; or London in the Nineteenth Century* (1827) that 'the prison-like walls' that closed up the house like a fortress were then necessary 'from its solitary and dangerous situation'.

London and Westminster (1734) as 'one of the most singular pieces of architecture about town'. It was, he opined, 'rather like a convent than a residence of a man of great quality' [fig. 140].[3] He was not the only observer to register the alien character of the ensemble; in 1775 Horace Walpole likened the freestanding mansion lying *entre cour et jardin* to a Parisian *hôtel particulier*. The 'hotel d'Harcourt', he remarked, has 'a *grand air* and a kind of Louis XIV. old fashionhood that pleases me'.[4] This analogy was later reiterated by the architect and archaeologist Samuel Angell in May 1854: 'Harcourt House, presents with its high court walls and "porte-cochere," more of the appearance of a Parisian mansion than any other house in London.'[5]

Although remodelled outside and in by its various occupants, the mansion was always distinguished by what Tim Knox has described as 'a sombre superannuated stateliness'.[6] It certainly cannot be said to have enjoyed its situation overlooking one of the West End's oldest and grandest squares. Instead, it presented to the world 'a dreary expanse of high brick wall, pierced by a pair of stout panelled gates topped by iron spikes [fig. 141]. From behind these fortifications peeped the frowning stucco façade of the mansion itself.'[7] It is no wonder that it is reputed to have informed Thackeray's characterisation of Gaunt House in *Vanity Fair* (1848) – Lord Steyne's cheerless town palace concealed behind a 'vast wall', which occupies nearly a whole side of the dank and 'dreary' Gaunt Square.[8]

141
Anon., The garden walls and the east front of Harcourt House, Cavendish Square, c.1906, photograph. Westminster City Archives.
This photograph was one of several taken shortly before the house was demolished and the grounds built over in 1906.

142

R. Dighton, *William John Cavendish-Bentinck-Scott, 5th Duke of Portland*, c.1830, drawing. Portland Collection, Holbeck. Courtesy of the Portland Collection.

The duke's reputation as an eccentric recluse was posthumously enhanced by the publication of the memoirs of his relative Lady Ottoline Morrell.

143
Anon., 'Tunnels and the Underground Road at Welbeck Abbey',
steel engraving, *Illustrated London News* (1881).

A contributor to *Littell's Living Age* (1884) remarked that the private tunnels built by the 'invisible nobleman' were 'indescribable specimens of costly thought and princely effort, and afford the most astonishing indication of the eccentricity which marked the career of the late Duke of Portland'.

What little we know about the mansion's early garden is largely based upon a reading of contemporary plans. John Rocque's *Plan of the Cities of London and Westminster and Borough of Southwark* (1746) depicts it as a large, walled oblong with a tree-lined exedra forming a terminus at its western end, where it bounds Wimpole Street. The central area is divided into four quadrants radiating from a large central bed. Both the north and south sides of the ground are flanked with what appear to be terrace walks lined with trees. This garden was later recast after the house was taken in 1773 by the 1st Earl Harcourt, Lord Lieutenant of Ireland from 1772 to 1777; Walpole reports to his good friend, the poet and amateur gardener Revd William Mason, in May 1775 that 'there is a large garden and a new *parterre*, and we want some *treillage* if the Irish Exchequer would afford it.'[9] This might be the garden portrayed on Horwood's *Map of the Cities of London and Westminster* (1792), but the latter is more likely to represent improvements made by the 2nd Earl and Countess, both of whom were outstanding gardeners.

The garden does not appear to have changed significantly after 1825, when the lease fell in and the premises reverted to its hereditary landlords, the Dukes of Portland, to become their principal town house. Everything, however, would be dramatically transmuted in 1854 with the accession to the dukedom of the reclusive William John Cavendish-Bentinck-Scott (1800–1879). Within a few years of occupying the house, the 5th Duke transformed the already forbidding pile into what Walter Thornbury later described as 'a dull, heavy, drowsy-looking house', which had about it 'an air of seclusion and privacy almost monastic'. He attributed its increased seclusion to 'three high walls, which have been raised behind the house, the chief object of which appears to be to screen the stables from the vulgar gaze'.[10]

The duke was a perverse and enigmatic man who from the late 1830s lived an isolated life, surrounding himself with 'an atmosphere of the closest mystery' [fig. 142]. Those who caught sight of the aristocrat, who was among the richest men in England, were intrigued by his appearance: 'His hat was of an unusual height, a long old-fashioned wig reached down to his neck. Wet or fine he never stirred out without an umbrella; hot or cold a loose coat was always slung over his arm; and whether the ground was dry or muddy, his trousers were invariably tied up below the knee with a piece of common string, in exactly the same fashion as is adopted by a navvy at his work.'[11]

His ruling passions were the turf, tunnelling and the management of his large estates. At Welbeck in Nottinghamshire, his principal seat – described in 1884 as the '*chef d'œuvre* of human eccentricity, a palace as labyrinthine as Mount Ida, a gorgeous specimen of perverted ingenuity as perplexing as it is astonishing' – the duke made a wide range of costly improvements to the grounds, many of which were to assure 'an unusual amount of privacy to the mansion and the pleasure grounds'.[12] For instance, he constructed a network of gigantic subterranean passages – most 'high and wide enough for carriages to pass along' – that linked suites of underground apartments including a ballroom, hunting stables, a chapel and numerous household offices [fig. 143]. These subterraneous roadways also extended beneath the park 'so that his army of workmen could pass to and fro without disturbing the serene repose he longed for'.[13] The duke's 'strange inclination for subterranean construction' later earned him the sobriquets of the 'Burrowing Duke', the 'Mole Duke' and the 'Invisible Prince'; as his kinswoman Lady Ottoline Morrell, who visited the house in 1879 and found it in a terrible state of dilapidation, remarked in her *Memoirs* (1963): 'Why the house has been allowed to get into this state I do not know, unless it was that the old Duke was so absorbed with his vast work of digging out and building underground rooms and tunnels that he was oblivious to everything else. He pursued this hobby at the cost of every human feeling, and without any idea of beauty, a lonely self-isolated man.'[14]

The duke's desire for privacy also had a considerable impact on the layout of the lawn and garden at Harcourt House: in April 1862 he commenced the erection of an immense glass screen on the north and south sides of his garden to provide privacy for a path round it for 'carriage exercise' [figs 144 and 145].[15] When finished, this formed a translucent barrier 'consisting of a range of strong upright stancheons, filled in with iron sashes, and glazed with fluted glass'. The pair of screens were 'upwards of 22 feet in height above the inclosing fence wall of the garden of Harcourt-house, and about 35 feet from the ground'.[16] Unsurprisingly, several of the duke's immediate neighbours who backed on to his garden (all of whom were his tenants) expressed opposition to the corrugated glass screens. In June 1862 one Mr Radcliffe filed an injunction for 'alleged obstruction of light and air' in an attempt to prevent the completion of the ducal screen.[17] It was, as the legal proceedings record, a case of 'considerable novelty' because the nature of the obstruction was unprecedented: 'a screen of transparent materials, with louvres or openings at intervals for nearly half ... of the whole space covered by it for the admission of air'.[18] In the event, the High Court of Chancery could find no grounds for reproaching the duke's conduct, which was deemed to be 'liberal and considerate'.[19] The injunction was refused.

The screens were not the only visual barriers to be erected by the duke in his garden: he also commissioned the building of a colossal stable block at the western end to occlude views into Wimpole Street [fig. 146].[20] The structure, which masked an earlier range of stables put up in the 1820s, was as high and

144
Anon., glass screen on the northern boundary of Harcourt House, Cavendish Square,
c.1906, photograph. Westminster City Archives.

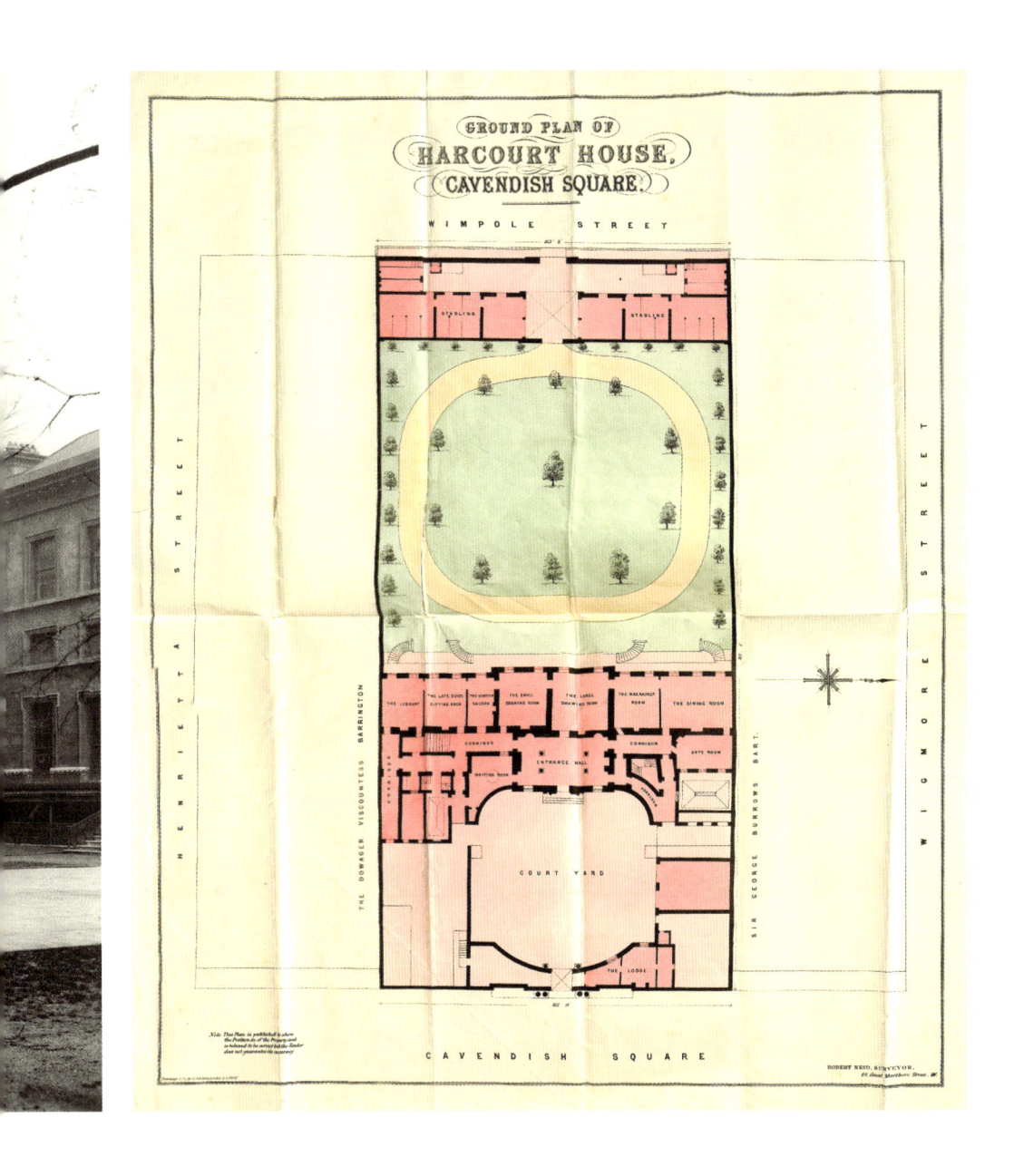

145
Anon., *Ground Plan of Harcourt House, Cavendish Square*, c.1870, lithograph.
Portland Collection, Holbeck. Courtesy of the Portland Collection.

146
Anon., stables at Harcourt House, c.1906, photograph. Westminster City Archives.

The stables faced Wimpole Street.

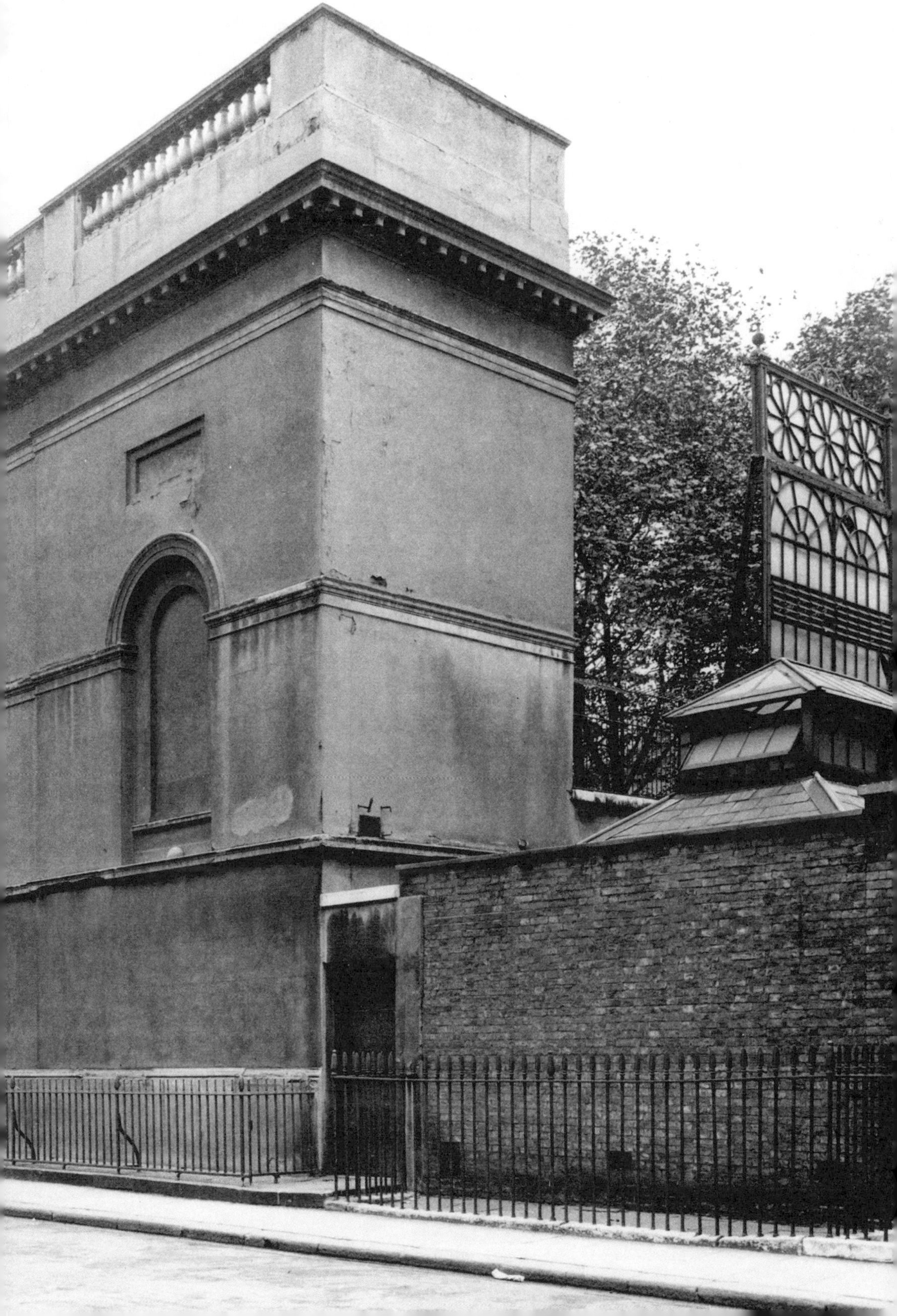

imposing as the glass erections, and was described in 1907 as 'stabling enough to accommodate the stud of a monarch'.[21]

The most notorious of all the duke's garden improvements was a short tunnel that was excavated to link Harcourt House to its stables. Although built with the benign purpose of providing subterranean access for staff to cross the garden without being seen, it became associated, after his death, with more bizarre and nefarious activities. In 1896 a celebrated legal battle known as the Druce–Portland case dragged the late duke and Harcourt House into the very 'vulgar gaze' that he had striven to elude. For eleven years the courts considered the extraordinary allegations that the 5th Duke led a double life as Thomas Charles Druce, co-owner of a London upholstery business called the Baker Street Bazaar, and that Druce's death in 1864 was faked. The claimants, Druce's descendants, hoped to win a share of the ducal estates. The case, which became an international sensation, finally collapsed in December 1907 with the exhumation of Druce's mortal remains.

About eighteen months before the close of the civil action, the Harcourt House garden tunnel was discovered by workmen employed in the demolition of the mansion's cellars. It was mooted at the time as a potentially 'important development' in the case which threatened to deepen the 'mysterious and repellant' aspects of the proceedings: 'in some minds such a discovery as that of this tunnel … will inevitably connect itself with the Druce case … and that the duke was in the habit of passing between Harcourt House and the Baker-street Bazaar by subterranean passage.'[22] Subsequent excavations, however, revealed that it was merely an underground garden passage, and allegations that it may have served any sinister purposes were unfounded. It is a curious but inevitable irony that it was the duke's very proclivity for burrowing, through which he tried so assiduously to conceal himself during his lifetime, that made him the object of such intense public interest and scrutiny after his death.

While many contemporary observers may have had an unflattering view of the 5th Duke – regardless of the outcome of the posthumous court case – one Scottish-born novelist and former secretary to the Bank of England found him a source of inspiration. It has been plausibly argued that Mr Badger in Kenneth Grahame's *Wind in the Willows* (1908) – that amiable and solitary denizen of the 'long tunnel-like passages branching, passages mysterious and without apparent end' – is none other than the burrowing duke himself [fig. 147].[23]

Grahame recounts that when Mole finds himself placed next to his host Mr Badger at lunch, he takes the opportunity to tell him how 'comfortable and home-like' he finds his sett:

'Once well underground,' he said, 'you know exactly where you are. Nothing can happen to you, and nothing can get at you. You're entirely your own master, and you don't have to consult anybody or mind what they say. Things go on all the same overhead, and you let 'em, and don't bother about 'em. When you want to, up you go, and there the things are, waiting for you.'

The Badger simply beamed on him. 'That's exactly what I say,' he replied. 'There's no security, or peace and tranquillity, except underground.'[24]

147
Arthur Rackham, 'Crossing the Hall, they [Badger and Mole] passed down one of the principal tunnels', in Kenneth Grahame, *The Wind in the Willows* (1908; 1951 edn). Private collection.

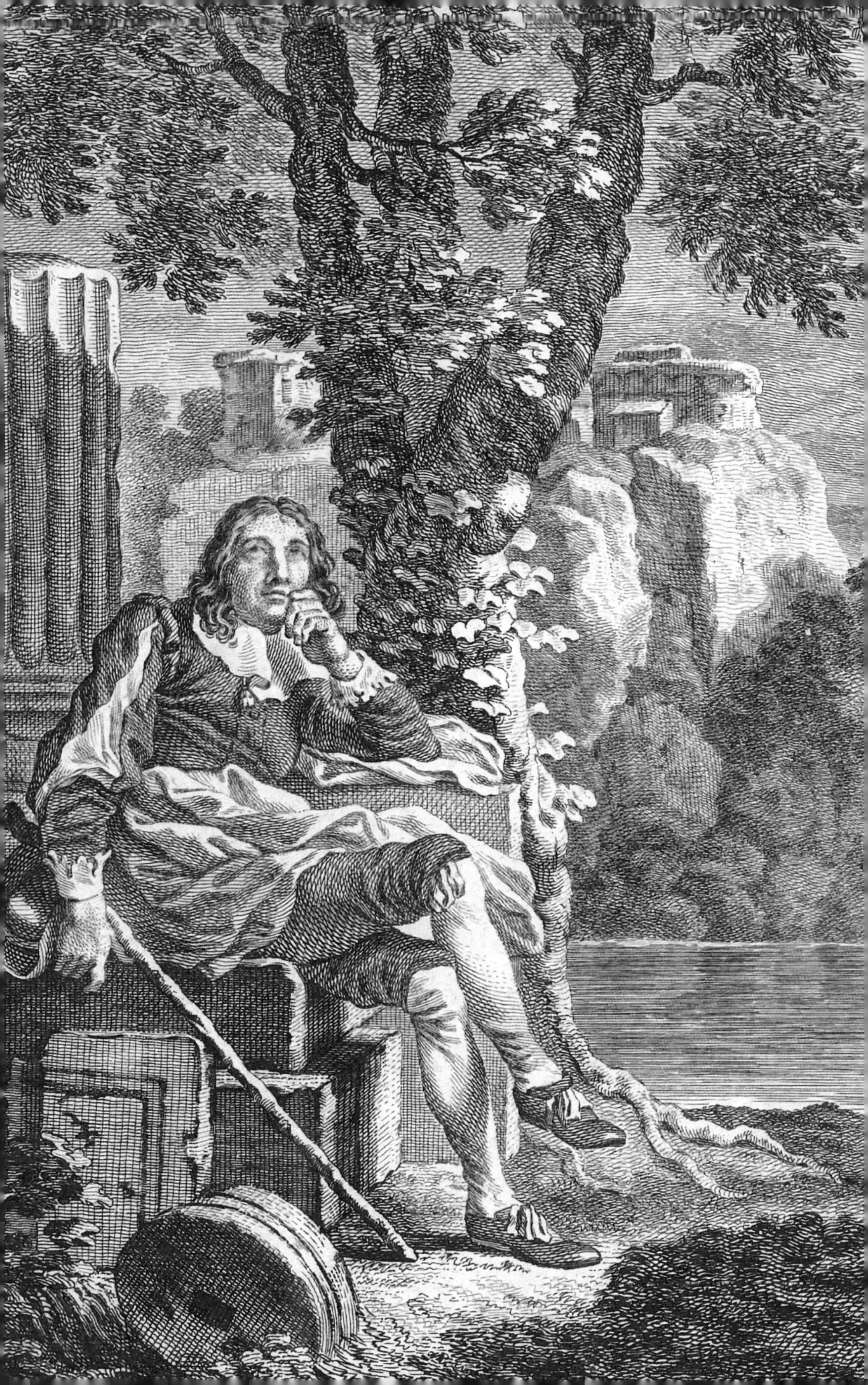

[SIXTEEN]

Denbies:
'A Persuasive Penitentiary'

Few English garden makers have created a garden as singular and idiosyncratic as Jonathan Tyers at Denbies, near Dorking in Surrey. John Timbs remarked in 1822:

> [this] ingenious and eccentric gentleman ... passed much of his time in planning several theatrical allusions and devices, and rendering in his spot a perfect contrast to the bewitching routine of gaiety and merriment, with which he electrified his metropolitan votaries in his role as the 'Master' of Vauxhall Gardens. The anomaly is said to have been conducted with strict adherence to that effect. Here every object tended to impress the mind with grave contemplation, and led to a conviction of the frivolity of the celebrated resort at Vauxhall, then in the zenith of its success.[1]

Jonathan Tyers (1702–1767) was born in Bermondsey, Surrey, the son of Thomas Tyers, woolstapler, and his wife, Ann [fig. 148]. We know little about his life until 1728 when he purchased the lease of Spring Gardens (est. 1661) on the south bank of the Thames, opposite what is now Tate Britain. Here he suppressed what John Lockman described in 1751 as a 'much-frequented rural Brothel' to create a commercial pleasure garden of 'the most rational, elegant, and innocent Kind' – or what Samuel Johnson later characterised as something 'peculiarly adapted to the taste of the English nation: there being a mixture of curious show, gay exhibition, musick, vocal and instrumental, not too refined for the general ear, – for all which only a shilling is paid; and though last, not least, good eating and drinking for those who choose to purchase that regale'.[2]

Tyers was more than the mere 'Master' of this celebrated resort: he was its chief scenographer. As a man of broad and informed cultural interests, he brought them to bear on the redevelopment of what became known as Vauxhall

Gardens, employing a circle of acquaintances to contribute to the visual arts and music, including George Frideric Handel, Thomas Arne, William Hogarth, Hubert François Gravelot, Louis-François Roubiliac and Francis Hayman. The pleasure ground was a richly theatrical garden teeming with life, resplendent in emblematic garden art, and patronised by all levels of society [fig. 149].

Our interest lies not, however, in Vauxhall but in Denbies – its private and extraordinary rural counterpart, and among the wittiest dismal demesnes in Georgian England. When in 1734 Tyers acquired this 'small country-seat', he presumably did so with the intention of rebuilding its 'simple farmhouse' and remodelling its setting.[3] Denbies was perched atop the highest part of Ranmore Hill in the county of Surrey, the view from which was 'as extensive as that from Boxhill'; indeed, it commanded exceptional panoramic vistas extending as far as the pinnacles of St Paul's Cathedral and Westminster Abbey at a distance of 40 km/25 miles, and the 'royal heights' of Windsor Castle 'towering in the horizon' [fig. 150].[4]

148
Anon., *Jonathan Tyers, Proprietor of Vauxhall Gardens*, c.1740, watercolour.
© The Trustees of the British Museum.

149
S. Wale, *The Triumphal Arches, Mr. Handel's Statue &c. in the South Walk of Vauxhall Gardens*,
1751, hand-coloured etching. © The Trustees of the British Museum.

150
Anon., *Denbies, Seat of W. J. Denison, Esq. MP*, 1840, hand-coloured engraving.
Private collection.

There are no known depictions of Denbies during Tyers's tenure. This print shows the
wide and panoramic views that were gained from the house.

It is generally assumed that Tyers did not give 'full scope to his eccentric tastes, in his disposal of the grounds' until at least the mid-1740s, after he succeeded in realising a 'large fortune' at Vauxhall.[5] His house within the precincts of Vauxhall would, in any event, always remain his principal residence, as he only retired to Denbies on Sundays – 'to a place which Nature has wonderfully diversified to his hands; and so far does this surpass the other, that, as Sannazarias said on a less proper occasion, *the one seems the work of man, the other of God.*'[6]

The earliest and only surviving account of the estate published during Tyers's lifetime appeared in the *Gentleman's Magazine* in May 1763. This *amuse bouche* was later supplemented by two further authoritative descriptions, prepared in 1764 and 1767 respectively. The authors of these accounts – all of whom appear to have experienced the gardens at first hand – tell us almost everything we presently know about this short-lived landscape before it was dismantled almost immediately after Tyers's death.

James Barry, study for the etching *Milton dictating to Ellwood the Quaker*, c.1804–5, reed pen and brown ink over black chalk. © The Trustees of the British Museum.

We are told that the 'celebrated master of *Vauxhall*' supplied 'daily proofs of his good taste'; the house was 'greatly inlarging' ('a modern stuccoed edifice') and the garden's 'noble Terrace of near a Quarter of a Mile in Length ... may vie with anything of the Kind in England'.[7] The gardens lay on the side of a hill 'covered thick with a grove of young trees': this 3.25 ha/8-acre plantation, called Il Penseroso, was cut into a 'labyrinth of walks; some descending, some ascending; in some parts easy, smooth, and level, in others rugged and uneven; a proper emblem of human life!'[8] The prospects from these walks were directed over the River Mole at the bottom of the hill towards 'the Wild, then to the South Downs in Sussex'.[9]

The very name of the wood emphasises the role of the garden as a pendant to Vauxhall – not only because of Milton's composition of 'L'Allegro' and 'Il Penseroso' as a rhetorical exercise, alternately supporting two sides of the same question or theme, but because the very first lines of 'Il Penseroso' reject the kind of frivolity with which Vauxhall was associated until at least the mid-1740s [fig. 151]:

> *Hence vain deluding joyes,*
> *The brood of folly without father bred,*
> *How little you bested,*
> *Or fill the fixed mind with all your toyes;*
> *Dwell in som idle brain,*
> *And fancies fond with gaudy shapes possess,*
> *As thick and numberless*
> *As the gay motes that people the Sun Beams,*
> *Or likest hovering dreams,*
> *The fickle Pensioners of Morpheus train.*[10]

The moralising allusion to the 'rugged and uneven' aspects of 'Human Life', however, marks a departure from Milton's two poems, in which gaiety and pensiveness are made to seem equally attractive. This vacillation between the kind of pleasing melancholy celebrated in 'Il Penseroso' and a darker, more puritanical note is also evident in other aspects of the garden – as some of the further observations published in the *St James's Chronicle* in September 1767 might suggest. The author continues to chart a journey through the garden, where 'in some periods of which we pass on easily, and free from incumbrances, and in others drag heavily along':

> Almost at every turn, there are flags hanging out, with some moral Sentences and Admonitions, inscribed on them for our Instruction, and to give a serious

Turn to the Thoughts. Not far from the Entrance, over which is inscribed Procul este profani! [keep away you uninitiated] there is a Sort of Hermitage, called the Temple of Death, wherein is a Monument to the Memory of Lord Petre; on one Side, in which is a Desk for Reading and Meditation, to which we are called by the melancholy striking of a Minute-Clock, and by the Presence of a large white Raven; to assist us therein the walls are covered with the finest Sentiments of our best Writers and Poets, as Dr. Young, &c. &c. to peruse them all would employ [a] great Part of a Day.[11]

The Temple of Death was a small square 'aweful edifice', thatched with reeds, and its interior was 'divided within into small stalls, which are wainscoted in imitation of stone-work after the Gothic manner; as the windows also at the entrance are formed like the rose windows in our cathedrals'.[12] The books chained to the sloping desk were Edward Young's *The Complaint: or, Night-Thoughts on Life, Death, & Immortality* (1742–5) and Robert Blair's *The Grave* (1743) – works that promised readers not so much a sense of their own doomed unworthiness as a pleasing melancholy and a frisson of Gothic horror. The clock, more grimly, was intended incessantly to admonish visitors that 'Time is fleeting, and even the least portion of it [is] to be employed in reflections on Eternity.' The panels around the room were filled with verses containing 'serious reflections on vanity, shortness, or insufficiency of human pleasures'.[13]

The most important attribute of the temple was its stucco monument by the sculptor Louis-François Roubiliac, dedicated to the memory of Tyers's 'great and much honoured friend' Robert James, 8th Baron Petre, who died from smallpox, aged twenty-nine, in July 1742. The dramatic composition depicted an 'angel blowing the last trump, at which the stone pyramid falls to pieces, and the corpse inclosed in it with a mixture of joy and astonishment, throwing aside the grave cloathes, prepares to arise'.[14] On the right-hand side of the monument was an 'Ode to Melancholy' by Dr William Broome. Sadly, we know nothing about Tyers's friendship with Petre. The baron was a garden designer and distinguished patron of botany who played an important role in the botanical and horticultural revolutions of the early eighteenth century. Although it is tempting to credit the peer with a role in the redevelopment of Denbies, there is no surviving evidence to suggest his involvement.

Leaving the temple, the visitor proceeded to the 'awful conclusion of the whole [garden]', a more gruesomely moralising one than might have been anticipated when encountering the Miltonically inspired wood earlier in the tour:

for having finished the tedious Journey of Life, in the close of all we are conducted to the iron gate which leads to the Valley of the Shadow of Death; at the entrance of which, instead of columns for a portico, two stone coffins are erected, with human Skulls placed upon them, and both of them full of inscriptions proper to the different sexes ... These we are informed are the real skulls, one of a celebrated courtezan in the neighbourhood of Covent-garden, the other of a noted highwayman.[15]

The skulls were reported to be in the attitude of addressing those who enter: one proclaiming that 'Men at their best state, *are altogether vanity;* the other pronouncing on all Female accomplishments, that *favour is deceitful, and beauty is vain*'.[16]

> WROTE ON A TOMB-STONE,
> WHERE IS LAID THE SKULL OF A WOMAN
>
> *Blush not, ye fair, to own me, but be wise,*
> *Nor turn from sad mortality your eyes.*
> *Fame says, and fame alone can tell, how true,*
> *I once was lovely, and belov'd like you.*
> *Where are my vot'ries' – where my flatt'rers now?*
> *Gone with the subject of each lover's vow.*
> *Adieu the roses red, and lilies white,*
> *Adieu those eyes which made the darkness light.*
> *No more, alas! that coral lip is seen,*
> *Nor longer breathes the fragrant gale between.*
> *Turn from your mirror, and behold, in me*
> *At once what thousands can't, or dare not see.*
> *Unvarnish'd I the real truth impart,*
> *Nor here am plac'd but to direct the heart.*
> *Survey me well, – ye fair-ones, and believe,*
> *The grave may terrify – but can't deceive.*
> *On beauty's fragil base no more depend,*
> *Here youth and pleasure, age and sorrow end;*
> *Here drops the mask, – here shuts the final scene,*
> *Nor differs grave threescore from gay fifteen.*
> *All press alike to that same goal the tomb,*
> *Where wrinkled Laura smiles at Chloe's bloom.*
> *When coxcombs flatter, and when fools adore,*
> *Learn here the lesson, to be vain no more,*
> *Yet virtue still against decay can arm,*
> *And even lend mortality a charm.*[17]

152

After Francis Hayman, *The Bad Man at the Hour of Death*, c.1783–90, hand-coloured mezzotint. © The Trustees of the British Museum.

153

After Francis Hayman, *The Good Man at the Hour of Death*, c.1783–90, hand-coloured mezzotint. © The Trustees of the British Museum.

WROTE ON A TOMB-STONE,
WHERE IS LAID THE SKULL OF A MAN

Why start! The case is yours, or will be soon,
Some years, perhaps – perhaps, another moon.
Life in its utmost span is but a breath,
And they who longest dream, must wake in death.
Like you I once thought ev'ry bliss secure,
And gold, of ev'ry ill a certain cure;
Till steep'd in sorrows and besieg'd with pain,
Too late I found all earthly riches vain.
Disease with scorn threw back the sordid see,
And Death still answer'd What is gold to me?
Fame, titles, honours next I vainly sought;
And fools obsequious nurs'd the childish thought.
Circled with brib'd applause and purchas'd praise,
I built on endless grandeur endless days;
But Death awak'd me from a dream of pride,
And laid a prouder beggar by my side.
Pleasure I courted, and obey'd my taste,
The banquet smil'd, and smil'd the gay repast.
A loathsome carcase was my constant care,
And worlds were ransack'd but for me to share.
Go on, vain Man, in luxury be firm;
Yet know I feasted, but to feast a worm.
Already sure less terrible I seem,
And you like me can own that Life's a dream;
Whether that dream may boast the longest date,
Farewel[l], remember lest you wake too late.[18]

The effect of awe and melancholy intensified as the visitor descended deeper into the 'gloomy Vale' to discover a 'young wood, which forms a gloomy amphitheatre, entered into through portal made ... of grey Sussex marble'.[19] Here there was a large alcove divided into two compartments, on one side of which the 'Unbeliever' was depicted 'dying in the greatest Distress and Agony, crying. "Oh! Whither am I going?"'[20] Opposite this life-size painting was its equally grim counterpart, representing 'the dying Christian meeting the dart with a pious resignation' [figs 152 and 153]. In this picture the Good Christian or Believer was portrayed in his dying moments: 'calm and serene; taking a decent, solemn Leave of the World, as it were, anticipating the Joys of another Life, with the following Label subjoined "I know that my Redeemer liveth," &c.'[21]

Both of the moralising narrative paintings were the work of Francis Hayman ('who painted the Pieces so much admired at Vauxhall'), and they were praised in the St James's Chronicle in 1767 for the manner in which they expressed 'the Situation of the Persons, their different Sentiments and Passion, very much to the Life'.[22]

The final element of the garden circuit, which was contrived to direct the spectator's gaze to Hayman's canvases, was a 'large Image, on a Pedestal, taking its Vizor off, with this Inscription, TRUTH'. This statue, too, is thought to have been a work of Roubiliac, and was intended to convey the message that 'as soon as the Disguise of this Life shall be taken off, the Picture before it, the Truth must appear at last; when the Wicked will be driven away in his Wickedness, but the Righteous have only hope in Death.'[23]

The contributor to the Gentleman's Magazine in 1763 summed up his impression of the garden: 'The whole, with the entrance to the place, which has something in it very particular, is truly striking to a contemplative mind.'[24] Rather less gently, it was remarked in the Monthly Magazine in 1821: 'Such eccentric imageries, wrought up as irrefragable appeals to the frowardness and contumacy of the dissolute debauchee, might form a persuasive *penitentiary*, and urge the necessity of amendment with better effect than all the farcical frenzies of mere formalists and fanatics.'[25]

What is going on in a garden that seems to be moving in such different directions? That is, in one sense it is a place of calm pleasure and in another almost an attempt to erase and deny the possibility of pleasure. Tyers, when manipulating space commercially rather than privately, was certainly not unaware that contemplation might be compatible with hedonism; Lockman describes how even in Vauxhall (in the area known as 'the Downs') the garden-maker managed to include a statue of Milton in thoughtful mood (actually composing 'Il Penseroso'!), and notes how such a spot proved no enemy to flirtation [fig. 154]:

> *These Downs, where Lambs were seen sporting, are cover'd with Turf; and pleasingly interspers'd with young Cypress, Fir, Yew, Cedar, and Tulip Trees. On one of the above Eminences in these Downs, is a Statue representing our great Poet Milton, as drawn by himself in his Il Penseroso, seated on a Rock; and in an Attitude listening to soft Music. Two Sides of these Downs are bordered with a gravel Walk, (fenced by a Net,) whence we have a delightful View of St. Paul's Cathedral, Westminster Abbey, Lambeth, &c. A View far unlike the rest seen*

154
After Francis Hayman, 'Il Penseroso',
in Thomas Newton's edition of Milton's Il *Penseroso* (1752).

from the other Parts of these Gardens. The Company were very fond, last Season, of straying in the Hollow or Descent of these Downs. This Spot seemed to be the Rendezvous of Cupid; it being as much crouded in an Evening with Lovers, as the Royal Exchange is at two o'Clock, with Men of Business.[26]

One element in Denbies that is worth considering is its perverseness, in the sense that Tyers allows an obsession (in this case, with sin and mortality) to displace expected pleasures – here, the pleasures that a garden of rational delight, away from the giddy temptations of Vauxhall, might have been expected to offer. In this sense, he is more thoroughly eccentric than any of the other gardeners considered so far, none of whom positively aimed to create anti-pleasure gardens.

There is, however, another way of viewing Denbies. Many or most of the gardeners discussed in the present work were collectors: of plants, of minerals, of sculptures and fragments. Tyers too was a collector: he made of his garden an assemblage of literary extracts in a manner analogous to eighteenth-century anthologies such as *The Beauties of Sterne*. His extreme eccentricity is displayed less in his choice of extracts (which were of a fairly conventional and predictable kind) than in the strange air of guilty gloom that he shed over them, through the visual assemblages in which they were incorporated, and also by the sheer effect of accumulation: like other garden eccentrics, Tyers was an impassioned and indefatigable collector.

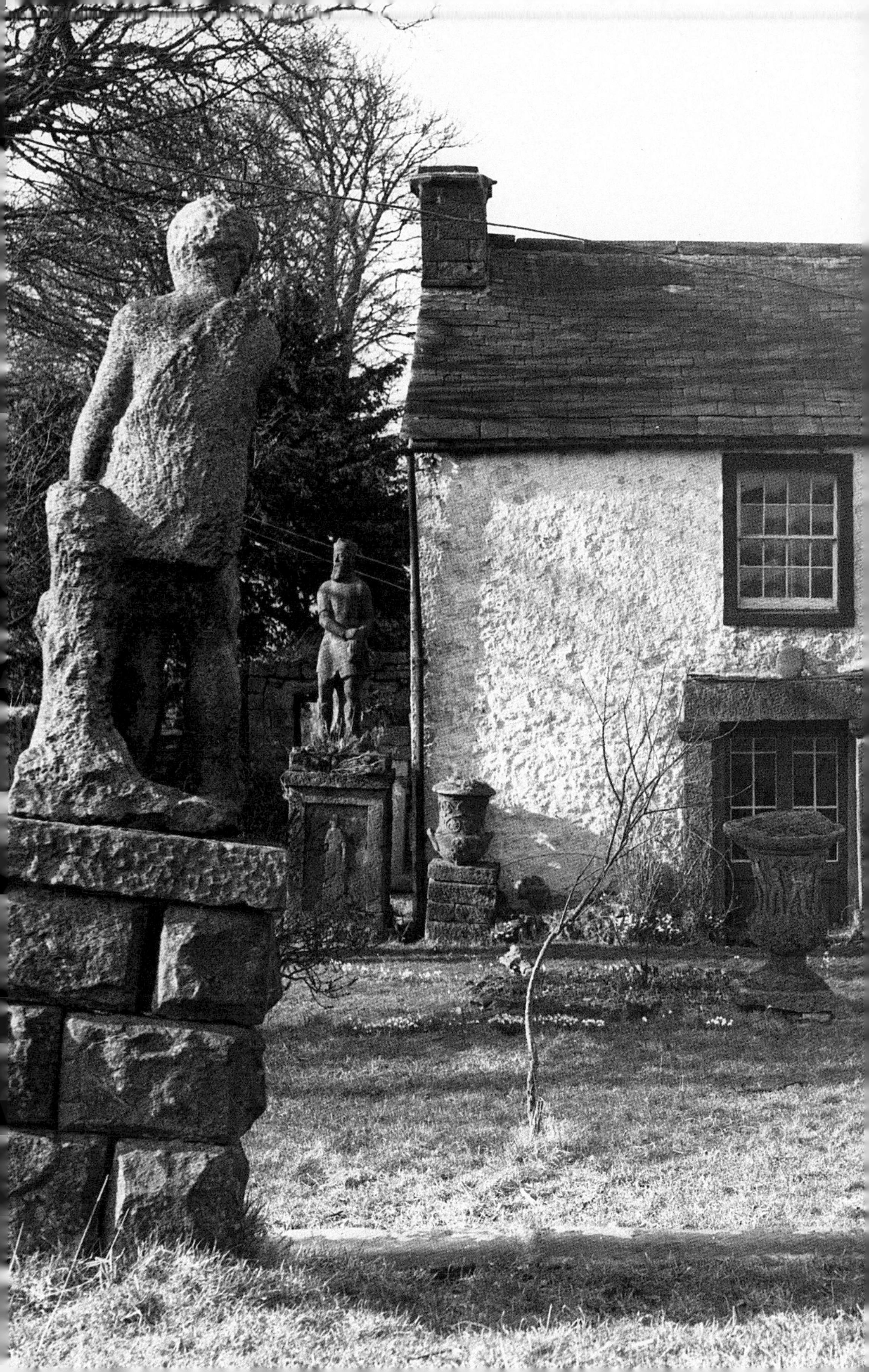

[SEVENTEEN]

'Do You Know Thomas Bland?'

A stranger, passing through the village of Reagill [Westmorland], was surprised to find such a remarkable garden in this out-of-the-way district. Seeing a labourer working at a drain with pick-axe and shovel, he proceeded towards him, and enquired – 'Whose place is this?' 'Thomas Bland's' was the prompt reply. 'Who sculptured the vases and figures which I see in the garden?' 'Thomas Bland.' 'And who is Thomas Bland?' 'I am,' said the man with a pick-axe and shovel; at which the stranger opened his eyes in amazement, and the reader may imagine the rest.[1]

THERE IS VERY MUCH WE DON'T KNOW ABOUT THIS EXTRAORDINARY figure.[2] Thomas Bland (1798–1865) of Yew Tree Farm, Reagill, Cumbria, was described in 1858 by a local journalist as a 'natural genius, ... born and bred amidst the primitive wilds of Shap Falls', who 'has, by the force and energy of his character, earned a notoriety that will long live in the annals of this sequestered district'.[3] The 'worthy yeoman', he continued, was 'a remarkable instance of what may be accomplished by industry and talent, unaided by the advantages that fall to the lot of those who are not thus isolated from the world'.[4] F.M.H. Parker, writing half a century later, also credited the artist with 'a certain amount of eccentricity, though this may have been due to a commonplace reading of unusual gifts and vigorous originality; but it is certainly the case that he was highly esteemed as a man of warm heart and kindly disposition, which attracted all with whom he came in contact.'[5]

Bland was described by his friend Canon George Frederick Weston, then vicar of Crosby Ravensworth, as 'short & of somewhat insignificant figure; but he had a finely formed head & very brightest of eyes ... He was quick in reading character & had a great contempt for anything mean or upstart or pretentious & would often expose what was low or false in terms of withering scorn or ridicule' [fig. 155]. He was, he continued, also 'very appreciative of the beauties of nature', attained 'considerable proficiency' in geology and agricultural chemistry, was 'fond of conchology & there was scarcely a relic of antiquity in the two counties of Cumberland and Westmoreland that he had not visited.'[6]

Although Bland 'worked at art for its own sake, [and] cared nothing for fame', he became a local celebrity during the course of his lifetime, and his renown can be attributed almost entirely to his extraordinary half-acre garden at Yew Tree Farm, which was 'kindly thrown open to the public gratuitously' and served annually in June from at least the early 1840s until the artist's death in 1865 as a site of special entertainments.[7]

The aptly named 'Image Garden' or 'Italian Garden' lay off the village street and was like no other in the county: it was richly adorned with sculpture,

155
Anon., Thomas Bland, n.d., photograph. Penrith and Eden Museum, Cumbria. Reproduced by permission of Penrith and Eden Museum (© Eden District Council).

Bland was described in his obituary published in the *Westmorland Gazette* (23 September 1865) as a 'local celebrity, spending his spare time in sculpture ... Although rather eccentric, he possessed a kind disposition and a warm heart.'

156
John Salkeld Bland, Yew Tree Farm, Reagill, c.1950,
photograph. Bridgeman Images.

paintings and other works of art, primarily the 'products of his brush & chisel'. It also boasted a bandstand, 'little museums' and at least two 'galleries'.[8] The museums contained collections of 'ancient arms and ornaments' mingled with 'specimens of the rocks and fossils of the district'; the 'Local Gallery' displayed Bland's 'best landscapes' depicting local scenes, and the 'Shakespeare Gallery' exhibited scenes from his plays to 'direct attention to the works of that immortal bard' [fig. 156].[9]

The grounds bristled with an array of bas-relief and full length statues that commemorated local worthies (Lancelot Addison and the self-taught Scottish geologist, folklorist and lay theologian Hugh Miller), popular literary figures (Robert Burns and Sir Walter Scott) and historical figures drawn from their work (including Rob Roy, Bois-Guilbert and Bonnie Prince Charlie).[10] A correspondent to the *Westmorland Gazette* who toured the grounds in 1853 was struck by the 'amazing amount of labour Mr Bland has bestowed on his garden' and the 'endless number of works of art' that were scattered about it in 'wonderful profusion': carved sandstone lions and sphinxes flanked flights of steps; terraces were garnished with 'numberless panels adorned with spirited paintings of battles, naïads, and gods which of old sported on the tops of Helicon'; and the walks were lined with 'sculptured warriors, vases supported by nymphs, [and] columns around which are twisted serpents'.[11] Surviving pen and ink drawings by Bland himself illustrate with spirited clarity how his lapidary productions were displayed on the green terrace and under the 'shady sycamores' of his 'Elysian retreat' [figs 157 and 158].[12]

Bland's garden was, however, more than a mere receptacle for the display of an original and idiosyncratic collection of works of art and local antiquities – it was a private performance space laid out for public enjoyment. From the early 1840s Bland began to give fêtes.[13] His initial events honoured his 'favourite authors' – Sir Walter Scott, Robert Burns and Hugh Miller – and at each respective gathering he would unveil 'a few special additions to the statuary & pictures suitable to the occasion ... speeches were arranged and delivered; & many hundreds from far and near came to the entertainment.'[14] By the early 1850s these modest annual celebrations metamorphosed into 'a festival of a somewhat unique character' to mark the anniversary of Queen Victoria's accession to the throne.[15] His interest in commemorating this event may have been first piqued in the early 1840s when he carved a monumental 'affecting piece of work' in honour of the queen, which was erected on a hill north of Shap Wells. P. J. Mannex, writing in 1849, described the composition as the 'production of a reflective and comprehensive mind'. The 'bass-relievos and statue' were, he continued, the 'work and gratuitous contribution of Mr Thomas Bland of Reagill'.[16]

The annual gatherings began to draw ever larger crowds of all classes 'from the titled lady to the humble servant girl'; the proceedings were, Weston said firmly (as though to reassure his readers that the distinction of the gardens neutralised the risks of such social mixing), characterised by the 'greatest propriety'. This account of the fetes suggests that Bland's pleasure in assembling diverse people was an extension of his delight in collecting anything that struck him as singular and noteworthy. Weston relates that Bland was visited by 'all classes from the Earl of Lonsdale down to tramps; all were welcomed, even tramps if there was anything original or queer about them and this he would often draw out.'[17] According to a contributor to the *Kendal Mercury* (1857), the object of the festival was 'to supply, in some measure, that great want in an agricultural district – the opportunity of social intercourse, and the chance of making new friends'. It was, furthermore, established with a view to combining 'instruction with amusement, intellectual with physical enjoyment'. Bland's gardens, 'filled as they were with paintings and statuary, offered great

157
Thomas Bland, *Garden*, n.d., pen and ink. Penrith and Eden Museum, Cumbria. Reproduced by permission of Penrith and Eden Museum (© Eden District Council).

Bland's productions were reported at the time to have been intermingled with a rare collection of local antiquities.

158
Thomas Bland, *Addison Statue* (*Garden*), n.d., pen and ink. Penrith and Eden Museum, Cumbria. Reproduced by permission of Penrith and Eden Museum (© Eden District Council).

159
Thomas Bland, *Garden*, n.d., pen and ink. Penrith and Eden Museum, Cumbria.
Reproduced by permission of Penrith and Eden Museum (© Eden District Council).
Bland may have been in part inspired by William Shenstone's landscape garden,
The Leasowes, which was laid out for public access and filled with temples, seats, urns
obelisks and inscriptions to encourage picturesque contemplation.

facilities for carrying out this experiment; and the proprietor, with a public spirit worthy of all praise, has never ceased to experiment; and adding to, and adorning his grounds, until they appear to have been arranged for the purpose of such a gathering.' The paintings were placed throughout the grounds and were arranged 'mostly in sets, and intended to illustrate some favourite author, or teach some moral lesson'. In one part of the grounds, tables were laid out 'covered with etchings, engravings and sketches of the most remarkable places in the neighbourhood'.[18]

Accounts of Bland's 'Grand Fetes' abound in the local press. One of the more memorable assemblies took place on 30 June 1853 and was recorded by a correspondent from the *Westmorland Gazette*. There was, he observed, 'an unusual degree of bustle and excitement … the youth and beauty for many miles around were there met together, dressed in their holiday garb, and numbering a little less than six hundred people. An excellent band being in attendance, the pleasure was heightened by many a spirited air.'

> In front, spanning the road leading from the unpretending village school, was a tastefully planned triumphal arch, formed of fir and other branches. On all sides 'banners were beaming,' each bearing a suitable motto, and forming a sight worthy of a day of greater pretensions. The Sunday scholars formed into procession, and the band leading them were followed on all sides by the well pleased visitors. Accompanying the throng we at length reached a garden, which Mr. Thomas Bland in his usual kind manner had set apart for the sole use of the congregated multitude … as the ranks marched onward they passed under a second triumphal arch flanked on the right by a picture representing Christ blessing little children, and on the left by an allegory inculcating faith in the cross.[19]

The gardens were also decked with royal emblems, and the 'joyous assembly' of visitors of all ages gave 'hearty cheers for the sovereign', partook of 'tea, coffee, and cake … of very superior quality', and 'regaled themselves with the viands so plentifully arranged'.[20]

The correspondent was particularly attentive to the layout and embellishments of Bland's gardens, remarking that he knew many readers of the *Gazette* 'will be fully aware that Reagill contains a *genius* of no common order of merit' [fig. 159]: 'He at once combines the painter with the sculptor, adding interest to both these accomplishments, by possession of a well stored mind, and a most benevolent and hearty disposition. Years of industrious application must have been spent in decorating this garden of his. Few could visit the neatly laid out spot without calling to mind the poet Shenstone.'[21] Bland, like the celebrated eighteenth-century bard and rural improver William Shenstone, took pleasure in showing strangers around his grounds, regaling them with curious anecdotes and apprising them of his intended improvements; and as he spent much of his time absorbed by his creative pursuits, visitors invariably discovered him in the midst of chiselling, modelling, drawing or 'resting from his labours, bedaubed with clay, without coat, on a block of stone, enjoying his pipe'.[22]

Parker reports that while some visitors came to see Bland 'only from idle curiosity', most sought his company, 'for besides much useful local knowledge which he possessed he had a fund of droll stories, which he told with much point & cleverness in the dialect that was natural to him, & his opinions & remarks always shewed observation and were often illustrated by local proverbial sayings & peculiarities of speech which rendered them very amusing & caused him to be considered very good company.'[23]

Not everyone who paid a visit to the Italian Garden, however, was, according to contemporary accounts, able to identify its maker. Because Bland was a man of 'somewhat wayward habits of life' and 'utterly regardless of his personal appearance, when at work no day labourer could have looked dirtier', some garden visitors mistook him for a rustic operative (as related in the epigraph). Weston relates how 'on many an occasion as he shewed visitors round his garden he was taken for the servant man, & receiving a shilling for his trouble would tell of it afterwards with great glee to his friends as a good joke.'[24] Such anecdotes, like those about Charles Waterton (see Chapter 12), emphasise both the eccentricity of the gardener and his role as an especially unpredictable – and therefore especially intriguing – part of the scenery.

Bland's shabby appearance and his impulsive and energetic activities doubtless contributed to the public perception that he was a creative genius.[25] Weston relates how, 'seized' by a 'wandering fit', Bland, 'with little more than his sketch-book to encumber him would … start off on foot, & walking from village to village, would make rapid pencil outlines of every object of interest that came in his way'.[26] One such sight that he selected as worthy of depiction was a lion that had arrived in the county as part of a travelling circus [fig. 160]. His creative process was even more frenzied when he was confined to working in his studio:

> He would at once stretch & prepare a canvass, & rapidly sketching in some scene which had excited his fancy he would proceed to fill it in … [an] impetuous manner, using palette knife or finger to lay on his colours. A bold effect was produced, but nothing was elaborated, nothing finished. He would work for many hours at a stretch, scarcely taking time for more than a hasty snatch of food, until he had realised to some extent his conception, & was tired. The work would then be set aside & most likely never touched again. In like manner with sculptures, an idea would seize him, once figured better to be realized in stone than on canvass, a suitable freestone block would be at once hewn out of a quarry on his own land. Transported to his yard, it would be at once attacked with frantic blows of hammer, pick & chisel, & would rapidly be transformed into a fair semblance of the creature real or mythical, woman, beast or reptile that had fired his imagination.[27]

It is remarkable that Bland dedicated so much time, energy and personal expense to his various private and public projects. Weston suggests that he was able to do so because he inherited the family property after his father's death:

160
Thomas Bland, *Wombwels Mengarie* [sic], n.d., pen and ink. Penrith and Eden Museum, Cumbria. Reproduced by permission of Penrith and Eden Museum (© Eden District Council).

Bland's carved lions were based on an *ad vivum* sketch he made of a lion in Wombwell's Travelling Menagerie.

161
Thomas Bland, *Garden*, n.d., pen and ink. Penrith and Eden Museum, Cumbria. Reproduced by permission of Penrith and Eden Museum (© Eden District Council).

Elements of this Claudian *capriccio*, such as the stone pines and mountains, echo the Westmorland landscape.

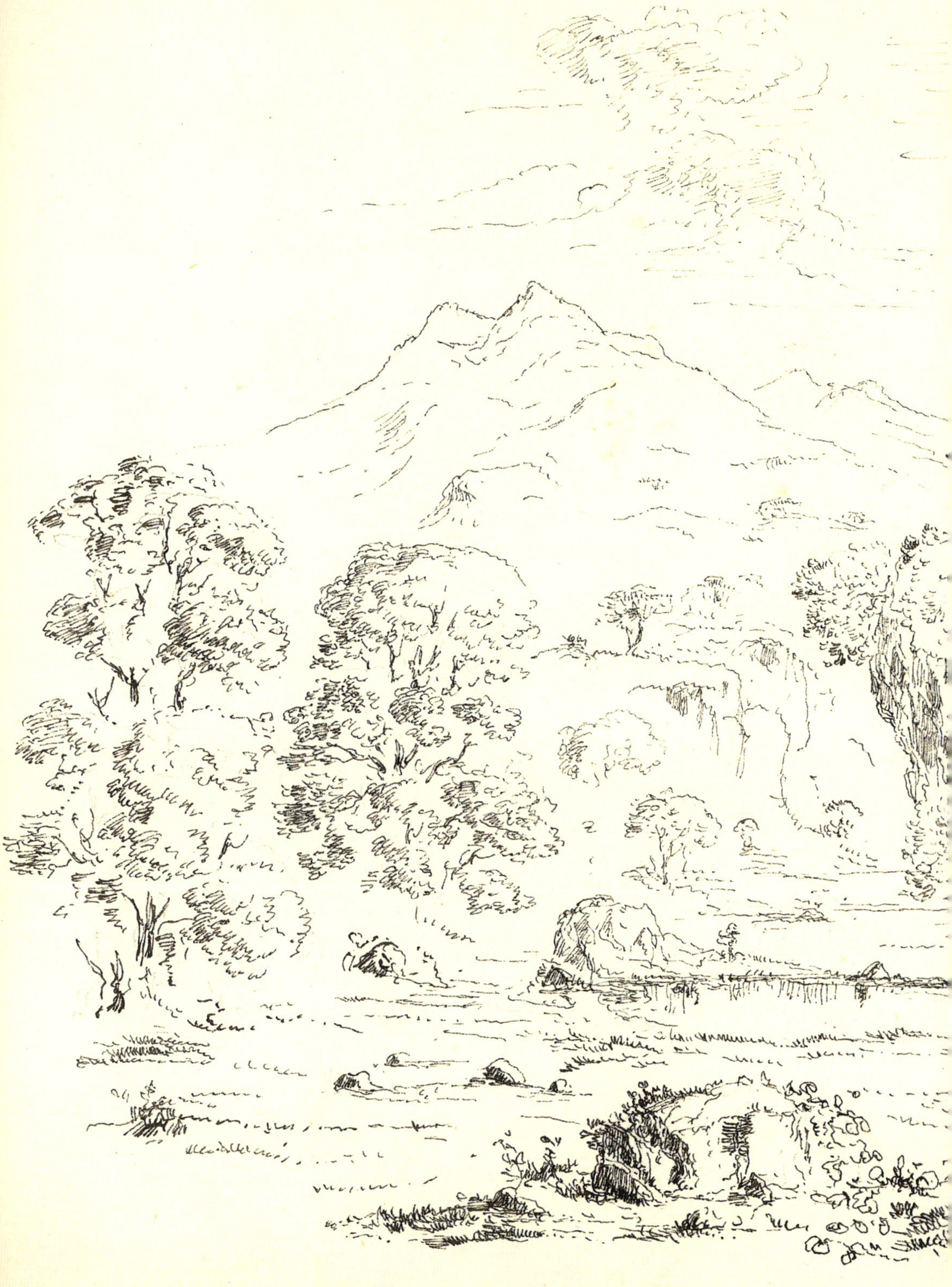

Garden

162 *previous pages*
Thomas Bland, *Garden*, n.d., pen and ink. Penrith and Eden Museum, Cumbria.
Reproduced by permission of Penrith and Eden Museum (© Eden District Council).
In this view Bland makes the local 'mountains' appear especially majestic.

163 *above*
Thomas Bland, *The Italian Garden*, n.d., pen and ink. Penrith and Eden Museum,
Cumbria. Reproduced by permission of Penrith and Eden Museum
(© Eden District Council).

'the house & a comfortable dwelling with a good-sized, old-fashioned garden fell to him.' Thomas at first farmed his little estate himself, 'but being very fond of art & some scientific pursuits, & not caring for the trouble & restraints of business, he let his land to a respectable tenant, reserving a part of the house & garden for his own use. He then devoted himself to the various occupations now one & now another in which he took delight, but not keeping to any one long together.'[28]

Although Thomas did not reveal what inspired him to transform his family's 'old fashioned garden' into an Italianate garden – or what a recent historian has labelled a 'shrunken, home-made echo of some grand Italian villa-garden, though not one of any definable period' – it is possible that this impulse was in part galvanised by his antiquarian interests.[29] He had a great and informed interest in the 'abundant memorials' in the vicinity connected with the Roman, Saxon, Danish and Norman conquests.[30] It is also possible that although he appears never to have travelled abroad, the local scenery – and the view from his garden to the Cross Fell range in particular – conjured up, before his mind's eye, an image of Italy. At least one of the artist's known pen and ink *capricci* depicts clusters of Claudian narrative figures animating a theatrical Italianate landscape teeming with stately stone pines and picturesque rocky outcrops within a mountainous setting [fig. 161]. In another drawing, Bland imparts a strongly Italianate air to the range by framing it within classicising sculptures on a parapet and placing two urns in the foreground. These beguiling images may be more than a whimsical reimagining. In portraying his surroundings in such a manner, Bland was implicitly drawing upon an established etymological association: the magnificent range of hills that encompassed his gardens – 'unsurpassed as they are in quiet grandeur and sublimity by any thing with[in] the United Kingdom' – had long been referred to as the 'English Apennines' [fig. 162].[31]

What is most striking about Bland's drawings is that they show his gardens as if they were an abandoned archaeological site, evoking a lyrical, melancholic atmosphere: many of the classically inspired statues are headless, limbless or fragmentary; monumental walls, pillars and pedestals are clad in ivy or shown crumbling into picturesque decay; and trees and shrubs emerge haphazardly from what appears to be a ruinous landscape [fig. 163].

Though Bland was the driving force behind his garden's design and the chief impresario of the Reagill fetes, his endeavours were enriched by some of his closest friends and relations. He took 'great delight' in the companionship of his nephew John Salkeld Bland (1839–1867), who accompanied him on 'Archaeological & Geological excursions, finding one of his chief pleasures in instructing him in all the knowledge he himself possessed'.[32] Although Thomas was self-taught and John studied botany, geology and chemistry, the two were paired and praised in the contemporary local press as 'two Westmorland "worthies" (born geniuses ...)'.[33] No less influential were, however, Canon Weston and the Revd James Simpson, first president of the Cumberland and Westmorland Antiquarian and Archaeological Society, who was for a time the incumbent of Shap; both men for many years played an important role in entertaining and educating the throngs who attended the annual fetes.

None of Bland's friends, however, was as original as his fellow Reagillian Anthony Whitehead, 'a labouring man ... of no mean powers'.[34] This bard of the Westmerian dialect described Bland in 'The Antiquary' (c.1865) as the 'auld Antiquary cramfull o' queer nwoations', who 'knew aw the history o' t' world's creation, / Fraw 't making of Adam t' birth o' Tom Thumb'; and his earlier poem 'An Address to Tourists' (1859) paints a vivid picture of the work of 'the famous *Thomas Bland*' who 'At't fine arts he oft' tries his hand / Wi[th] good success', and supplies us with further evidence – if any was needed – why his gardens were considered a 'far-famed pleayce throughoot the land' – a 'garden truly grand'. Some of the verses read almost as an inventory of the diverse elements included in the grounds at Reagill; in their sheer enumerative exuberance, they emphasise Bland's range of visual and cultural reference:

> But it wad tak a week var near,
> To tell of aw the things that's here:
> The sphynxes, tigers, wolves an deer,
> T' twa dogs o' Burns,
> An laal neayked lads carved oot sea queer
> O' top of urns.
>
> An things howked oot o' cairns an reaynes,
> At's cost t' chap many tifts an greaynes,
> Auld tip horns, an sowder'd beaynes.
> Girt fossil shells,
> Auld Roman mills, an gowks o' steaynes.
> An Celtic mells.
>
> An girt men's busts stuck up in niches.
> Dogs, an divvils, fiends an witches.
> First rate men, and low born wretches,
> Wad mak ye laugh;
> An then hissel wi' roven britches,
> To finish off ...[35]

These stanzas above all affirm that, as already suggested, Bland, 'a great admirer of good acting & oratory', in his 'roven britches ... a chap [th]at likes a joke, / Or a good crack; / An[d] tellin[g] teayles [a]'boot queer auld fwoak', was in fact the greatest of all the garden's many attractions.[36] They also testify to Bland's disposition to accommodate local and more exotic elements in easy continuity: not only 'twa dogs o' Burns', but also 'laal neayked lads carved oot sea queer / O' top of urns'. Other eccentric gardens, of course, often do this, but in some of them there is a greater tension between the indigenous and the relatively remote: one of the pleasures offered by encountering Lady Broughton's miniature copy of the Swiss glaciers in Cheshire or Frank Crisp's copy of the Matterhorn at Henley-on-Thames is that of surprise. Bland's antiquarian awareness of the material relics of Roman presence in Westmorland, as well as his sense of continuity between the Pennines and the Apennines, allow local and Italian features to coexist without producing any great effect of anomaly; Whitehead lists 'auld Roman mills' as though they must be acquired through forays into the surrounding countryside, since they are names alongside 'gowks o' steaynes / An Celtic mells'.[37]

Eves bower 30 july 1776

[EIGHTEEN]

Stukeley's Travelling Gardens

AFTER WILLIAM STUKELEY DIED IN 1765, WILLIAM WARBURTON, Bishop of Gloucester, remarked of his 'oldest acquaintance':

> There was in him such a mixture of simplicity, drollery, absurdity, ingenuity, superstition and antiquarianism, that he often afforded me that kind of well-seasoned repast, which the French call an ambigu, I suppose from a compound of things never meant to meet together. I have often heard him laughed at by fools, who had neither his sense, his knowledge, nor his honesty; though, it must be confessed that in him they were all strangely travestied.[1]

The Reverend William Stukeley (1687–1765) still remains curiously enigmatic, complex and eccentric. A man of considerable intellectual and physical enthusiasm, he pursued archaeology, antiquarianism and architecture while sustaining two professional careers: first as a doctor of medicine and subsequently as a clergyman of the Church of England [fig. 164].

Like many late seventeenth-century antiquarians, Stukeley believed that antiquities and countryside were part of a common field of intellectual enquiry and aesthetic response: all natural and man-made phenomena could be pragmatically observed, objectively recorded, ordered and classified. Such a method suited the young enthusiast, who had a restless scientific curiosity, a profound love of nature, and a penchant for archival organisation of his findings. Above all, Stukeley had had a well-developed appreciation of the English landscape, which he perceived in terms of his own particular, if unconventional, topographical and historical propriety. He was acquainted with translations of the Roman histories concerning Britain (the *Agricola* of Tacitus and the *Gallic Wars* of Julius Caesar), which cultivated in him an earnest desire to celebrate the sentiment of place, whereby specific localities visited or

164
William Stukeley, *Self-portrait*, coloured engraving, in *Itinerarium Curiosum* (1724).
Wellcome Collection, London.

165
John Harris after William Stukeley, *The Great Temple & Grove of the Druids at Trerdrew in Anglesey*, c.1720, etching. © The Trustees of the British Museum.

explored prompted reflections upon the greatness of past achievements. This sensibility was, however, intensified by his extensive and methodical open-air fieldwork, survey and mensuration. What began as an effort 'to perpetuate the vestiges' of celebrated wonders such as Avebury and Hadrian's Wall ('for I forsee that it will in a few years be universally plowd over & consequently defacd') was, in his later life, distorted and enhanced by fanciful speculations, culminating in his creation of a fantastical Druidic geography.[2] The historian John F. H. Smith has recently speculated that the most important influence on Stukeley's intellectual processes was the belief that the Druids (along with the Egyptians and Plato) held the 'divine truth' of the 'doctrine of the Trinity' [figs 165 and 166]. This conviction made it possible to see the Druids as a native expression of proto-Christianity, and thus meant that their surviving physical works could be reconciled generally with Christianity and particularly with eighteenth-century Anglicanism: 'A garden "temple of the druids" could therefore be seen as a celebration and recognition of this unique fact and a reconciliation of antiquarianism with religion.'[3]

Notwithstanding the vagaries of his beliefs, what is remarkable about Stukeley is that he had such a developed sense of place – for him, the cultural landscape of every layer of every region of the country was mapped, or was capable of being mapped. In short, history and culture could be archived and understood in topographical terms.

Paradoxically, however, Stukeley treated the sense of place as something which in the context of gardening could be regarded as transferable. The gardens of his houses were full of diverse objects – curious plants, 'mechanical artificialls', 'old reliques', antiquities and utensils plundered from (often threatened) landscapes – which, although invested with precise associations by their original siting, were nonetheless unhesitatingly transplanted from one garden to the next. The desire to take these objects with him as he moved about the country was, in fact, strongly endorsed by contemporary assumptions about the symbolic ordering of gardens – as opposed to that of landscape. A garden was a space that permitted specifically personal forms of intervention, and was expected to bear the imprint of its owner's personality. The various 'curiositys' which Stukeley collected not only preserved their original associations, but acquired new meanings as a result of their place in his life. Unlike other eccentrics who managed their grounds on a larger scale, Stukeley warmed to the possibilities that a relatively intimate space opened up.

When Stukeley settled in Grantham in 1726–7, he was sceptical about 'the earnestness & pure nature' of country life and the 'innocent pleasures there only to be met withal, of the green fields, the shady woods, the brooks, the fresh streams arising from corn & grass, the odorous exhalations of flowers & flowering shrubs, & a thousand more charming topics of that sort'.[4] Nevertheless, he quickly conceded that 'never [a] man tasted them with greater delicacy'. Reflecting on his new lifestyle, he remarked that ''tis no less than a divine admonition that drew me insensibly to my truest felicity … that removed the gilded prospect of imaginary enjoyment, & gave me in its stead solid content.'[5] He continued:

Last summer I spent in fitting up part of my house, & levelling my ground for gardening, in which I am at this very time intent. I am planting greens, flowers, alcoves, herbs, fruit trees, & what not? I am laying out the stations of dyals, urns, & statues, inoculating mistletoe, & trying vegetable experiments. Within doors I am fitting up my study, which has a most charming prospect over my garden & adjacent valley, pretty much like that over Amesbury, & just within hearing of a great cascade of the river, which is very noble & solemn.[6]

166
Anon., 'Druidis Britanni Effigies', etching, in Samuel Clarke's edition of
Observations upon Caesar's Commentaries (1712). Private collection.

He claims to have 'worked so hard in my garden as to sweat out all the London fog, [and] ... become vastly athletic':

> My antient country complexion is returned to my cheeks, the blood flows brisk through every anastomosis, my lips recover their pristin red, & my own locks, moderately curled, resemble the Egyptian picture of Orus Apollo, or the emblem of rejuveniscence. It would ravish you to think with what pleasure I take a book in my hand & walk about my garden, my own territorys, mea regna, as Virgil calls it, surrounded with the whole complication of natures charms.[7]

In his walled orchard he made a grove-like 'temple of the druids', which he planted in a series of concentric rings in imitation of the lapidary sanctuary at Stonehenge. The outermost ring was a broad path ('the portico'), which was described on the inside by a circle of 'tall filberd trees in the nature of a hedg', 21 m/70 ft in diameter. The walk gradually descended each way to an entrance which led to a smaller circle, defined by pyramidal evergreens, at the centre of which was an 'antient appletree oregrown with sacred mistletoe'. The 'angles' of the composition – alongside the walls – were 'filled up with fruit trees, plumbs, pears, walnuts and apple trees, & such are likewise interspersed in the filberd hedg & borders, with some sort of irregularity to prevent a stiffness in the appearance, & make it look more easy & natural'.[8] Closer to the house he constructed a 'hermitage vineyard' [fig. 167]. Here he erected the first of many small structures that he was to build in his various gardens over the next thirty-eight years – structures that incorporated (and reused) elements from his ever-expanding cache of curiosities. The symbolic value that he attributed to these fragments is evident in a letter to his good friend Samuel Gale in which he describes the hermitage as a setting for a poignant ritualisation of personal loss when his wife, Frances Williamson, suffered a miscarriage soon after their marriage. He informed his friend: 'my wife miscarried 3 days after your letter to me, the 2d time':

> The embrio, about as big as a filberd, I buryd under the high altar in the chappel of my hermitage vineyard; for there I built a niche in a ragged wall oregrown with ivy, in which I placed my roman altar, a brick from Verulam, & a waterpipe lately sent to me by my Lord Colrain from Marshland. Underneath is a camomile bed for greater ease of the bended knee, & there we enterred it, present my wives mother, & aunt, with ceremonys proper to the occasion.[9]

Six months later Stukeley decided on ordination in the Church. According to his biographer, Stuart Piggott, the decision 'forms the essential turning-point of his whole life, and comes as a culmination of a series of impulsive

167
William Stukeley, *The Hermitage Vineyard 7. June 1727. Granth[am]*, drawing with watercolour wash. Bodleian Libraries, University of Oxford, Gough Maps 230, fol. 412.

moves – [such as] leaving London and getting married, both unexpected to his friends'.[10] In July 1729 he was ordained, and presented in October to the living of All Saints at Stamford in Lincolnshire. Here the parson spent much time embellishing his garden with the assistance of his wife. The most notable building work, however, was only commenced after Frances's death in 1737, and coincided with an active period of restoration of the city's churches which provided him with barrows full of discarded painted glass.[11] The following year he built 'Merlin's Cave' – a rockwork which consisted of a stone alcove, a small cascade and a jet, joined by a decayed wall pierced by a pointed window, and surmounted by a precariously perched arch bearing a Roman altar above which he placed a ball finial [figs 168 and 169]. The whimsically contrived 'hermitage grotto', adorned with adroitly placed vegetation, was based on the eponymous hermitage at Richmond that William Kent created in the early 1730s for Queen Caroline, 'the Architecture of which, is … very Gothique, being a Heap of Stones thrown into a very artful Disorder, and curiously embellished with

168
William Stukeley, *Merlin's Cave in the … hermitage Stamford 3. Dec. 1737*, drawing with watercolour wash.
Bodleian Libraries, University of Oxford, Gough Maps 16, fol. 50v, b.
Stukeley dismantled and reconfigured this structure several times.

169
William Stukeley, *The Hermitage, Austin Street, Stamford*, c.1738, drawing with watercolour wash.
Bodleian Libraries, University of Oxford, Gough Maps 16, fol. 53, a.
The rockwork of Merlin's Cave can be seen in the right-hand foreground.

Moss and Shrubs, to represent *rude Nature*'.[12] Although Stukeley dismissed the claim of the English bishop and chronicler Geoffrey de Monmouth, in *Historia Regum Britanniae* (*c*.1136), that Merlin transported African stones from Ireland to build Stonehenge on Salisbury Plain, he clearly found Geoffrey's reinforcement of the link between Britain and the Trojan and Roman civilisations very appealing, as he did the wizard of Arthurian legend's reinvention of the ancient monument. Stukeley's own rude construction in Stamford was also created with symbolically charged salvage: the Roman altar and its spherical finial had been relocated from his 'hermitage vineyard' at Grantham, where, as we have seen, they had been assembled to commemorate first the burial site of the miscarried 'embrio'; they had latterly also marked the memory of Frances herself.

Shortly after the death of Frances, and studying 'how I may best improve this dispensation of Providence for His glory & my own comfort', Stukeley married Elizabeth Gale, 'a Lady of Great Beauty, and a Fortune of 10 000 l.', who was the sister of his closest friend.[13] This marriage portion, and the addition of a living at Somerby, were a welcome boost to the parson. Within eighteen months he purchased a more capacious house at Barnhill, on the edge of Stamford, remarking that 'though old, [it] will be comfortable, & not inelegant, just suited to my gusto'.[14] He immediately began laying out his orchard – refining and enhancing the garden designs that he had executed at Grantham and Stamford. He planned to cut into the perimeter wall (the town wall) to build a grotto, and a mount or tumulus was projected for the easternmost corner. A 'Temple' garden was also formed in the orchard, this time, however, with intersecting concentric rings – a configuration which may owe less to his antiquarian interest than to a latent sacred geometry, or possibly the optical phenomenon known as 'Newton's rings' – so-called in honour of his fellow Lincolnshire-born friend Sir Isaac Newton.[15]

In 1744 Stukeley demolished a number of outbuildings of the 'great farmyard' and formed a garden on the 'bare rock'.[16] Here he erected his 'curious and useful instrument called a spot dyal',[17] a variety of carved stones from the Queen's Cross (excavated from a tumulus near the Stamford turnpike), a hermitage (possibly a converted building) and a series of small mixed plantations; in a neighbouring area, he laid out a bowling-green close and 'Rosamund Bower' [fig. 170]. Some of the stones from the Cross, as well as the bricks, a doublet-lancet window, plaques, shells, 'cherubims of oak, as big as the life ... like caryatides to support the 4 corners of the arch of the grot', and other decorative baubles – many from his Stamford town garden – were assembled to form a new construction: a Gothic rockwork.[18] Another innovative creation

The Hermitage

Animas quie

170
William Stukeley, *The Hermitage Barnhill 1744* …, drawing with watercolour wash.
Bodleian Libraries, University of Oxford, Gough Maps 230, fol. 410.

The author's Latin inscription is a misquotation of 'animas fieri sapientiores quiescendo', which may be translated as 'Souls grow wiser by resting.'

was the Temple of Flora, wherein his wife was to put 'her numerous pots of elegant curiositys in nature': 'The work is gothic, that suits the place best. Four demi-columns stand in the front. It faces the rising sun. The statue of Flora in pure statuary marble, as big as life, which the Duke of Montagu gave me, is placed before it.' He continues to describe the interior as 'theatrical' (staged for potted plants), and bedecked with 'Several bustos, & other curiositys, in proper places', including stained glass windows and a cupola with a 'dumb bell … which I ring every morning, a most agreeable exercise'.[19]

In 1748 Stukeley left Stamford for a life in London, being tired of the provinciality of the town and craving the literary conversation of the 'fumopolis'.[20] He departed 'exceedingly' grieved by the death of his cat 'Tit' – who, buried by his gardener under the mulberry tree at the entrance to Rosamund's Bower, caused Stukeley to remark that 'I have almost taken a dislike to the garden: never car'd to come near that delightful place: nor so much as to look toward it.'[21]

After more than a decade as rector of St George's, Queen Square, the seventy-two-year-old retired to his last home, which he described as 'a most agre[e]able rural retreat at Kentish-town … clearly out of the influence of the London smoak, a dry gravelly soil, and air remarkable wholsom'. His poem 'The Druid', composed soon after his arrival here in 1759, encapsulates his sense of the peaceful old age that he anticipated in this spot:[22]

> Grant me, ye Fates, a calm retreat
> where I may pass my days
> far from the low, mean follys of the Great
> free from the Vulgars envious hate
> & careless of their praise.
> blessd with a faithful female friend
> thus let my time slide on
> but when my evening sun shal downward tend,
> I'le quietly be gone.
> Just so some tender blossom, that has stood
> in the recesses of Caeus silent wood,
> unruffled by the winds feels slow decay
> hangs down its head, & gently dyes away.[23]

Here Stukeley indulged his Druidic interests unrestrainedly: he blazoned his Druidical name on the front of his bedchamber, and formed a range of curious features in the garden including concentric circles, a Druid walk, a temple, 'Eve's Bower', a hermitage, a grotto, a mausoleum and a tumulus [figs 171–3]. The mausoleum was not a tomb chamber, but a place in which 'to make a retrospect into ones life; and make some provision for ones affairs; after we quit this present stage of being ... it was erected as wel for the plesure of retirem[en]t. & contemplation, as to keep my pictures in.'[24] Stukeley also embellished his gardens with natural and antique 'curiositys' and a great variety of flowering plants and trees including 'yellow curld lilly' (*Lilium pyrenaicum*), evening primrose, primrose, 'white Mezereons' (*Daphne mezereum*), carnations, alpine gentians, roses, Christmas roses, liverwort, snowdrops and winter wolfsbane (*Eranthis hyemalis*). Among the trees and shrubs recorded are almond, holly, Cornelian cherry (*Cornus mas*), blackthorn, whitethorn, cherry, white cedar (*Thuya occidentalis*), 'great hawthorn of Canada' (*Crataegus canadensis*), silver pine and gorse.[25]

In his *Itinerarium Curiosum* (1724) Stukeley scrutinises the terrain of Great Britain for the marks of past human cultures that are inscribed upon it. Within his gardens, he employs material fragments to construct affiliations between this wider cultural context and his own personal history. Through his disposition of these fragments, he creates a series of spaces that echo the larger space of his native country – the country that, he laments, 'lies like a neglected province' while his contemporaries needlessly turn to the rival allurements offered by 'the genteel and fashionable *tours* of France and Italy'.[26]

171
William Stukeley, *The garden view of my house at Kentish town. 28 apr. 1759*, pen and ink.
Bodleian Libraries, University of Oxford, Gough Maps 230, fol. 352.
Druidical circular layouts recur in Stukeley's gardens.

172
William Stukeley, *Eves bower 30 july 1762*, drawing with watercolour wash.
Bodleian Libraries, University of Oxford, Gough Maps 231, fol.107.

The bower may have been inspired by Milton's *Paradise Lost* in Adam and Eve's Prelapsarian nuptial bed, where the 'roofe / of thickest covert was interwoven shade, / Laurel and Mirtle, and what higher grew/ Of firm and fragrant leaf …'

173
William Stukeley, *The hermitage garden, Kentish town … august 1760*,
drawing with watercolour wash. Bodleian Libraries, University of Oxford,
Gough Maps 230, fol. 350.

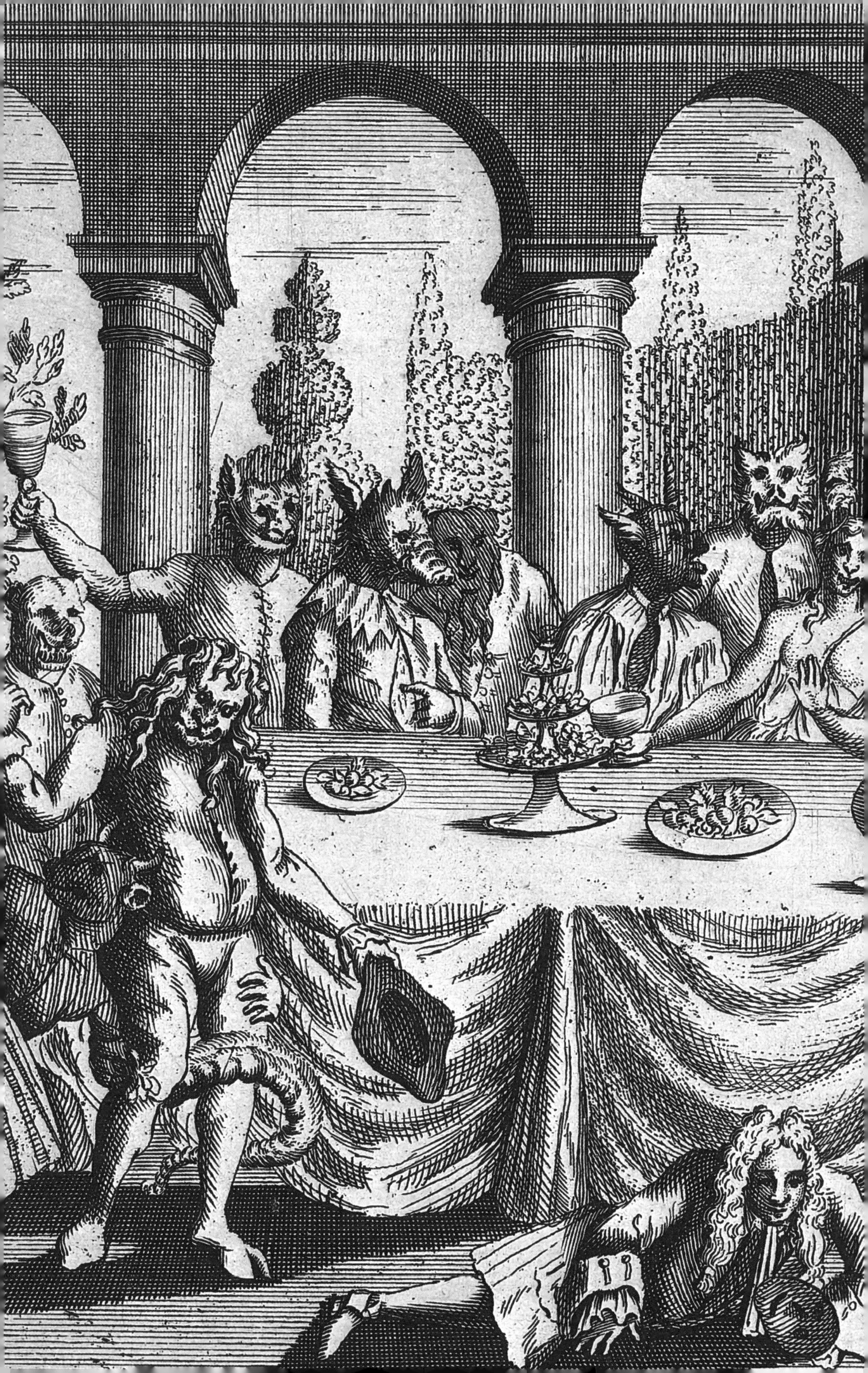

[NINETEEN]

West Wycombe Park: 'Pretty, but very Whimsical'

I am in this House as much at my Ease as if it was my own: and the Gardens are a Paradise. But a pleasanter Thing is the kind Countenance, the facetious and very intelligent Conversation of mine Host, who, having been for many Years engaged in publick Affairs, seen all Parts of Europe, and kept the best Company in the World, is himself the best existing.[1]

BENJAMIN FRANKLIN THUS DESCRIBED HIS CLOSE FRIEND SIR Francis Dashwood while staying with him in August 1773 at West Wycombe Park in Buckinghamshire. The Boston-born statesman, writer and scientist, later to become one of the founding fathers of the United States, had 'come hither to spend a few Days and breathe a little fresh Air', and to collaborate with his host on a 'moderate' abridgement of the Book of Common Prayer – now known as the 'Franklin Prayer Book'.[2] Franklin later reported that Dashwood had requested him to assist with the contraction of the Catechism and the reading and singing Psalms. Although the two men appear to have enjoyed the exercise, Franklin observed ruefully in 1785 that the book was 'never much noticed ... Some were given away, very few sold, and I suppose the bulk became waste-paper.'[3]

Sir Francis Dashwood, 2nd Baronet, later 11th Baron Le Despencer (1708–1781), was a complex, flamboyant and paradoxical character who is now best known as a rake, an aesthete, an amateur architect and an innovative garden builder [fig. 174].[4] Born in London, he was the only son of the East India merchant Sir Francis Dashwood, 1st Baronet – who made his fortune trading porcelain from China and silk from Smyrna – and the second of his four wives, Mary Fane, eldest daughter of Vere Fane, 4th Earl of Westmorland and 7th Baron Le Despencer. His biographer remarks in the *Oxford Dictionary of National Biography* that Dashwood's 'range of interests and achievements was unusual and highlighted his intelligence, discriminating taste, and inquisitive interest in new ideas': 'Contemporaries with whom he worked noted his capacity for diligent administration, his generosity of spirit, his honesty, and his courage, which rendered him careless of popularity. He consequently made powerful political enemies, whose attempts to discredit him were facilitated by the manner in which he flaunted his lecherous proclivities.'[5]

The baronet was unusually well travelled: he embarked on his first of six Grand Tours in 1726, visiting France and Germany; subsequent travels would take him to Italy (1729, 1733 and 1739, visiting Leghorn and the excavations at Herculaneum and staying in Florence and Rome), to Russia (1733), and finally to Greece and Asia Minor (*c*.1735). Though he was edified by his travels, Dashwood – 'Un des plus comiques hommes du monde', as he was described in 1740 – found irresistible the allure of 'wine, general debauchery and mayhem'.[6] Horace Walpole later quipped that the baronet was one who was 'seldom sober'

174
William Hogarth, *Sir Francis Dashwood at his Devotions*, *c*.1751, oil on canvas. Private collection. Picture Art Collection/Alamy Photo.

175
Anon., *The Diabolical Maskquerade, Or the Dragon's-Feast as Acted by the Hell-Fire-Club, at Somerset House in the Strand*, 1721, engraving. © The Trustees of the British Museum.

the whole time he was in Italy, and records in his memoirs how on his travels Dashwood earned a 'European reputation for his pranks and adventures' as he 'roamed from court to court in search of notoriety'.[7]

On his return from his wanderings in 1732, Dashwood and a handful of his fellow well-heeled and convivial English Grand Tourists founded the Society of Dilettanti, a dining club that was initially formed for frivolous revelry, but that incrementally came to promote the knowledge and appreciation of classical art in England, including the sponsorship of archaeological expeditions to Greece and Asia Minor. Horace Walpole disapproved of the society and the bawdiness of some of its members, remarking in 1743 that it was a 'club for which the nominal qualification is having been to Italy, and the real one, being drunk'.[8]

Dashwood's 'pronounced animal spirits' also found an outlet in other circles: he was a member of the Beefsteak and Hellfire clubs, as well as the 'Bucks' or 'Bloods'; and as leading light of the Divan Club, he was able to indulge his love of exotic spectacle and his proclivity for fancy dress [fig. 175].[9] His membership of this is commemorated by a jaunty portrait depicting him as 'Il Faquir Dashwood Pasha'.

As he was an ardent improver, the park and gardens at West Wycombe were in a constant state of flux during the course of his tenure: on the whole, what began as baroque was swiftly transmuted into rococo and finally into a more natural style. His immense energies were also directed into public works, ranging from the realignment of public roads to the building of a lighthouse and public pleasure grounds on a Lincolnshire heath. Everywhere he intervened, the range of interventions was uncompromisingly bold and remarkably original.

When in 1698 the Dashwoods acquired their West Wycombe estate, the house built by their precursors, the Dormers, sat in a modest garden, and the landscape that lay beyond it was meagrely embellished with two short avenues. The park as we know it only began to take shape from the 1730s under the stewardship of the 2nd Baronet. Lord Grimston described it as 'small but pleasant … part of which was laid out in 1739, into walks which are beautified with water and wood'.[10]

Dashwood's first round of improvements is recorded in a series of maps and topographical views, including Maurice-Louis Jolivet's detailed estate survey of 1752 which documents the lake, cascade, the fret-work Walton Bridge, and Venus's Temple and Parlour. Although his early improvements doubtless owe a debt to the contemporary layouts and attributes at the magnificent landscape gardens at Wanstead and Stowe – both of which he knew at first hand and through engraved views – the developments at West Wycombe were invariably more eclectic and perverse.[11]

The lake, praised in the late eighteenth century as 'a fine memorial of lord le Despencer's taste and judgment', sat at the heart of the early pleasure grounds; it was probably formed between 1735 and 1739. The sheet of water is purported to have been an enlargement of an earlier octagonal basin, and its irregular profile has long been compared to the shape of a swan: the emblem of Buckinghamshire since Anglo-Saxon times and sacred among birds to the goddess Venus. William Hannan's views of 1750–51 show small vessels plying the lake, the masts of which, 'rising above the trees', were praised by the agricultural writer Arthur Young as adding 'greatly to the landscape' [figs 176 and 177].[12]

176
After William Hannan, *A View of the Walton Bridge, Venus's Temple, &c, in the Garden of Sir Francis Dashwood Bart. At West Wycomb in the County of Bucks*, 1757, etching.
© The Trustees of the British Museum.

177
After William Hannan, *A View of the Lake &c. taken from the Center Walk in the Garden of Sir Francis Dashwood Bart. At West Wycomb in the County of Bucks*, 1757, etching.
© The Trustees of the British Museum.

Thomas Phillibrown, who visited in 1754, noted in his diary that the lake was at least on one occasion pressed into service for a *naumachia*, or 'sham fight': the aquatic drama featured various vessels, including a 'Snow ...[of] about 60 Tun' ('kept in proper order' by a full-time sailor), completely rigged and bearing carriage guns taken from a French privateer; a '2 mast vessel, a little in the Venetian manner'; and a '1 mast vessel like a sloop'. The observer also notes the incongruous presence of swans at the scene of the battle to 'add to ye beauty'. In the event, an accident put a premature end to the engagement as a 'Capt. who commanded ye Snow comeing to[o] near ye battery received damage from ye wadding of a gun which occasioned him to spit blood'.[13]

Among the first garden buildings to be raised was the overtly erotic ensemble comprising the Temple of Venus and Venus's Parlour (1745–8), possibly to the designs of the architect John Donowell [fig. 178]. Its construction coincided with the baronet's advantageous marriage to the wealthy widow Sarah Ellys, whom Walpole described as 'a poor forlorn Presbyterian prude'.[14] The temple took the form of a domed elliptical rotunda containing a lead statue of the Venus de' Medici, and surmounted by a statue of Leda and the Swan. It was perched atop a grassy knoll which concealed a grotto or cave flanked by curved walls. The ensemble brings to mind the anatomist Samuel Collins's description of 1685 of the vagina as a 'Temple of Venus' and the *mons veneris* as Venus's cushion.[15] John Wilkes reports that the entrance to the subterraneous parlour was 'contrived to shadow out to us the entrance by which we all come into the world, and the door is made to represent what some idle wits have called *the door of life*.'[16] A statue of Mercury was stationed above the entrance to the 'parlour', possibly to guide the souls of men to paradise. Wilkes remarks, rather mischievously, that his sworn enemy, the Earl of Bute, 'particularly admired this building', and advised the baronet to lay out the £500 bequeathed to him by Lord Melcombe's will '*for an erection*, in a Paphian column, to stand at the entrance, to be made of Scottish pebbles,' to the Temple.[17]

The temple cum parlour adjoined a grove bearing twenty-five small lead figures 'in different attitudes', some of which Wilkes avers were of a lewd nature: 'In these gardens no bust even is to be found of Socrates, Epaminondas, Hampden, or Sydney, but there is a most indecent statue of the unnatural satyr.'[18]

The notorious Hell-Fire Caves were excavated in the early 1750s as a means of alleviating local unemployment after a succession of failed harvests. The flints removed from the labyrinthine burrowings were used to surface the public highway on the north side of the park. The entrance to the caves was dressed with an imposing flintwork facade resembling a ruined church nave.

178
After William Hannan, detail of fig. 176 showing the bridge and the Temple of Venus.
© The Trustees of the British Museum.

The caverns were much the same as those at Hawkstone (see Chapter 14), except for the fact that they latterly gained a (groundless) reputation as a setting for dissolute behaviour. Benjamin Franklin – 'Brother Benjamin of Cookham' – remarked in 1771: 'His Lordship's imagery, puzzling and whimsical as it may seem, is as much evident below earth as it is above.'[19]

Dashwood also embarked on landscape initiatives further afield: at the ruins of Medmenham Abbey, a property that he leased, roughly 16 km/10 miles south-west of West Wycombe, he created unrestrainedly erotic gardens as a meeting place for the Knights of St Francis of Wycombe [fig. 179]. The brotherhood, also known as the Monks of Medmenham, had a small membership comprising illustrious, high-spirited 'wits and humorists', among them Frederick, Prince of Wales, the 4th Earl of Sandwich, the 3rd Earl of Bute,

179
Francis Grose, *Medmenham Abbey, Henley-on-Thames, Oxfordshire*, 1783, etching.
Antiqua Print Gallery/Alamy Stock Photo.

George Bubb Dodington, the painter William Hogarth and Thomas Potter, the son of a former archbishop of Canterbury; the poet Paul Whitehead acted as secretary and steward, and Dashwood served as grand master.[20] Captain Edward Thompson described the club in 1777 as 'a set of worthy, jolly fellows, happy disciples of Venus and Bacchus'.[21] Others, however, condemned the depravity of the 'un-holy fraternity'. Sir Nathaniel Wraxall, for instance, writing in 1781, declared that Dashwood 'far exceeded in licentiousness of conduct, any thing exhibited since Charles the Second': 'Rites, of a nature so subversive of all decency, and calculated, by an imitation of the ceremonies and mysteries of the Catholic church, to render religion itself an object of contumely, were there celebrated, as cannot be reflected on without astonishment. Sir Francis himself officiated as High Priest, habited in the dress of a Franciscan Monk.'[22]

That we know anything at all about these intriguing, intensely private and short-lived gardens can be attributed to a very bitter public spat between Dashwood, then chancellor of the exchequer, and his one-time political ally, the radical journalist and former fellow Monk, John Wilkes. (Even the relatively neutral comments by Wilkes quoted so far register a hint of malice.) The two men fell out over the baronet's proposals for economic reform, which in turn galvanised the disgruntled Wilkes to publish in 1763 'sardonic and sexualised accounts' of the baronet's gardens at Medmenham Abbey and their alleged 'secrets' with a view to ridiculing and embarrassing his former ally.[23]

The garden in question lay in a situation 'remarkably fine' on the banks of the Thames near Marlow, in Buckinghamshire, and was described at the time as comprising 'Beautiful hanging woods, soft meadows, a crystal stream, and a grove of venerable old elms'; the abbey itself was a former ruin which had been converted by the fraternity into a convivial resort. The 'retiredness' of the mansion made it 'as sweet a retreat as the most poetical imagination could create'.[24] Wilkes supplies tantalising accounts of the abbey's grounds:

> *The garden, the grove, the orchard, the neighbouring woods, all spoke the loves and frailties of the younger monks, who seemed at least to have sinned naturally. You saw in one place – Ici pâma de joie des mortels le plus heureux [here the happiest mortals died of joy] – in another very imperfectly – mourut un amant sur le sein de sa dame [a lover dies on the bosom of his lady] – in a third – en cet endroit mille baisers de flamme furent donnés, & mille autres rendus [in this place a thousand kisses of fire were given, and a thousand others returned]. – Against a fine old oak was – Hic Satyrum Naias victorem victa subegit.*[25]

Wilkes was quoting from erotically charged inscriptions which were fixed to the garden's trees, seat and buildings. Some of the epigrams derive from Jean de la Fontaine's La Fiancée du roi de garbe (1665), a licentious tale that charts the journey of Alaciel to the court of her father, Zaïr, in the course of which she has a series of sexual encounters with eight suitors.

Wilkes continues to describe the scene unfolding before him: 'at the entrance of a cave was the Venus, stooping to pull a thorn out of her foot. The statue turned from you, and just over the two nether hills of snow [her buttocks] were these lines of Virgil':

> *Hic locus est, partes ubi se via finditur in ambas:*
> *Hac iter Elyzium nobis: at laeva malorum*
> *Exercet poenas, & ad impia Tartra mittit*[26]

Inside the artificial rockwork, on a 'mossy couch', was the following exhortation:

> *Ite, agite, o juvenes; partier sudate medullis*
> *Omnibus inter vos; non murmura vestra columbae,*
> *Brachia non hederae, non vincant oscula conchae*[27]

Wilkes's description of the garden concludes with what must have been its most provocative and sexually explicit statue: 'The favourite doctrine of the Abbey is certainly not *penitence*; for in the centre of the orchard was a very grotesque figure, *and in his hand a reed stood flaming, tipt with fire*, to use Milton's words, and you might trace out

> PENI TENTO
> *non*
> PENI TENTI.'[28]

This description presumably refers to a statue of Priapus, the flaming reed, 'tipt with fire', being his large erect penis.

On the statue's pedestal was a 'whimsical representation of Trophonius's cave, from whence all creatures were said to come out melancholy':

> Among the strange dismal group, you might however remark a cock crowing, and a Carmelite laughing. The words –
>
> gallum gallinaceum & sacerdotem gratis were only legible.*

* *Omne animal post coitum triste est, praeter gallum gallinaceum, et sacerdotem gratis fornicantem.*[29]

The landscape historian Wendy Frith proposes that Wilkes's representations of the baronet's gardens were deliberately ambivalent:

> On one hand, he was clearly representing Dashwood and his gardens in terms of notions of sexuality at odds with those advocated as the norm, otherwise these 'revelations' would have had little political effect. Yet, on the other hand, Wilkes had to identify and be identified with what allegedly occurred at Medmenham in order to authenticate his account, making it unlikely that he would have articulated anything he did not at least tacitly endorse. Moreover, overt condemnation would have sat uneasily with his reputation as a libertine and discredited his own libertarian agenda ... Hence the tone in which the 'secrets' are 'revealed' is one of tongue-in-cheek amusement and relish.[30]

The second phase of improvements at West Wycombe took place from the early 1760s, and coincided with Dashwood's accession to the Barony of Le Despencer and his appointment as Lord-Lieutenant of Buckinghamshire.

180
William Hannan, *West Wycombe House and Garden*, c.1757, preparatory drawing for a print study. © The Trustees of the British Museum.

At first he concentrated his energies on remodelling the house [fig. 180], rebuilding the church and building the mausoleum; from the 1770s he turned his attention to the park and gardens – extending the park eastwards and building a profusion of ornamental buildings, including the Temple of St Crispin (a shoemaker's cottage disguised as a sham chapel), the Temple of Flora, the Music Temple, the Pepperbox Bridge and Sawmill House; many more (including a mosque) designed by the baronet in collaboration with his 'amiable drudge', the architect John Donowell, remained unrealised.[31]

The mausoleum is among the most singular structures at West Wycombe. The large, roofless hexagonal shell sits atop a high hill overlooking the park [fig. 181]. Built with a bequest from his friend Bubb Dodington, Baron Melcombe Regis, this 'eccentric, somewhat nightmarish structure faced with flint, is more akin to a Scottish "lair" or sepulchral enclosure than to any conventional mausoleum'.[32] Like so many of the buildings across the estate, it has classical antecedents. Tim Knox has pointed out that it is a hybrid of two

181
Humphrey Spender,
'The Mausoleum,
West Wycombe,
Buckinghamshire',
c.1935, photograph.
Trinity Mirror/
Mirrorpix/Alamy
Stock Photo.

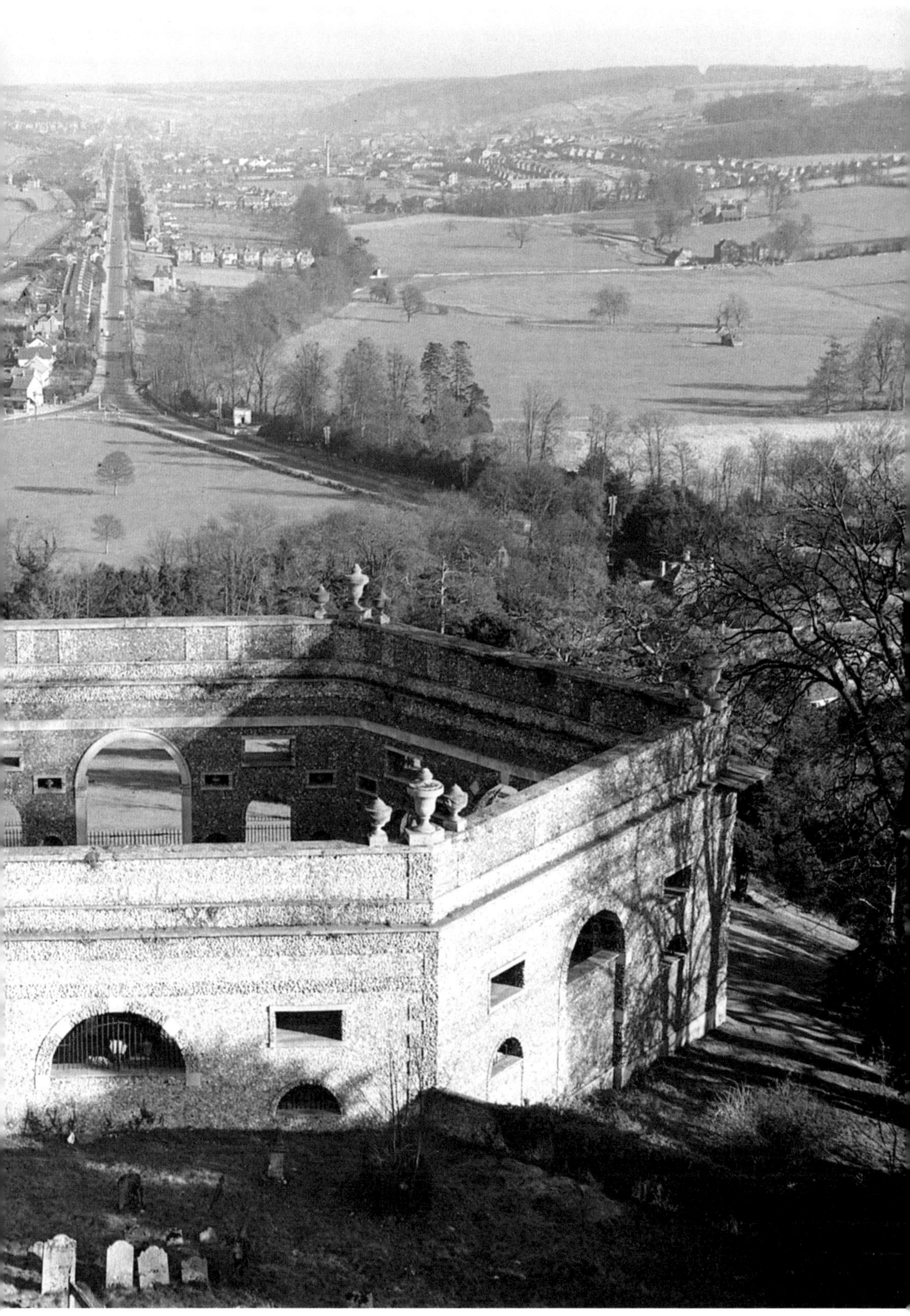

imperial mausolea in ancient Rome: the mausoleum of Augustus in the Campus Martius and the tomb of the household of Augustus on the via Appia (28 BC) [fig. 182]. Here the baronet placed the remains of his family and raised monuments to his ancestors, servants and friends, including a bust of Dodington and a 'very elegant urn of curious variegated marble' which entombed the shrivelled heart of his friend Paul Whitehead.[33]

The Temple of Bacchus ranks among the baronet's most important contributions to West Wycombe, since it was designed to serve as both the principal entrance to the mansion and a very superior garden temple – a bridge between the house and garden. The architect Nicholas Revett's giant portico-like structure was the first serious reconstruction of a Greek temple in England, and underscores Dashwood's fascination with the past and his eccentric and imaginative appropriation of antiquity. It was also possibly the first building of its type to have been consecrated with a procession *à la grecque ancienne* – a bizarre and extravagant ceremony that encapsulated Dashwood's love of magnificent spectacle.[34]

The *Gentleman's Magazine* reported that Lord Le Despencer held a 'Grand Jubilee' at West Wycombe Park in September 1771 to mark the completion of the temple. The festivities at the 'terrestrial paradise' took place over five days, and included rehearsals and concerts 'of those masterly compositions of Mr Handel, the Oratorios of Jephtha and Sampson', 'plenteous elegancies of the table' and masques in the gardens, with actors who, 'supporting their various characters with great spirit, wit and humour, added greatly to the entertainment of this rural and poetic scene'.[35]

On one evening a 'new and unexpected scene presented itself':

These delightful gardens were opened for the amusement of the public in general, and a rural walk exhibited, in which a very novel and pleasing representation was introduced. You must know, a fine portico at the west end of the house has been lately erected, in imitation of that belonging to the ancient temple of Bacchus [at Teos, near Smyrna in Turkey], for the dedication of which a Bacchanalian procession was formed, consisting of Bacchanals, Priests, Priestesses, Pan, Fawns [sic], Satyrs, Silenus, &c. all adorned in proper habits, and skins wreathed with vine leaves, ivy, oak, &c. in the most picturesque manner imaginable.[36]

The dedication of the temple itself was superintended by Sir Francis in the guise of the High Priest:

This procession arriving in the portico, the High Priest addressed the statue in an invocation, which was succeeded by several hymns and other pieces of music, both

182

'Mausoleum of Augustus, Campus Martius, Rome', engraving, in Etienne du Perac, I vestigi dell'antichità di Roma (1575). Private collection.

The circular mausoleum was initiated in 28 BC by Augustus. The top of the structure was planted with a garden.

183

Giuseppe Borgnis, detail of a ceiling painting depicting the Banquet of the Gods in the Music Room, West Wycombe Park, Buckinghamshire. ©National Trust Images/John Hammond.

The artist's composition, derived from one of Raphael's cycle of ceiling paintings at the Villa Farnesina, doubtless appealed to Dashwood's sense of theatre and love of the antique.

vocal and instrumental, suitable to the occasion; and having finished the sacrifice, proceeded through the groves to a tent pitched among several others at the head of the lake, where the Pæans and Libations were repeated; then ferrying to a vessel adorned with colours and streamers, again performed various ceremonies accompanied by the discharge of cannon, and bursts of acclamations from the populace, who surrounded the shore.[37]

At the close of the evening, the procession, 'which consisted of ladies and gentlemen', returned to the temple to finish the ceremony with a 'congratulatory ode to the Deity of the place' [fig. 183].[38] As Gervase Jackson-Stops remarks: 'this precedence of landscape over house marks a climax of the cult of the Picturesque, and one can imagine few better to stage manage it than an actor manqué such as Sir Francis Dashwood.'[39]

It is revealing that Lord Le Despencer called his extravagant apotheosis a 'Grand Jubilee' – a term that was then synonymous with 'Popish pageantry'. In the Catholic Church, jubilees were special years of remission of sins and universal pardon; they were described at the time as 'of origin, half Jewish, half Pagan', and were purported to have been 'designed to succeed the *Ludi Sæculares* or secular games of the *Romans*, and that in order to divert the Christians from this Pagan ceremony, it was the intention of Boniface VIII. to substitute a better, accompanied with several shining acts of piety. It was he who had the first grand jubilee celebrated.'[40]

We should perhaps expect no less from a man who spent years in Italy, and who was in equal measure fascinated and repelled by the Catholic Church, its liturgical ritual and pageantry; who in Rome in 1740 took part in a mock English conclave impersonating Cardinal Ottoboni ('c'était un vrai scandalum magnatúm'); who reputedly, on Good Friday in the same year, in a darkened Sistine Chapel, took a horsewhip to devout flagellants; and whose likeness was in more than one instance portrayed as a lascivious friar or saint (for example, in the 1742 portrait by George Knapton).[41]

Was Lord Le Despencer, in the tradition of the grand jubilees, dispensing penance? What is certain is that the gregarious, mischievous and fun-loving baronet was in his element when he was in fancy dress, performing a ceremonious act, had a captive audience and was the centre of attention. The gardens of West Wycombe – his 'pagan masterpiece' – were more than a vivid declaration of his beliefs in beauty, humour and pleasures both sensual and sexual; they were his private stage where every element, from its miniature fleet on the lake to its eye-catching cobbler's tower, was intended to be animated, to be pressed into the service of his idiosyncratic *theatrum mundum*.[42]

Though Dashwood opened his gardens to the 'public in general' on the occasion of his Grand Jubilee, and he was immensely proud of them, they were not, unlike many of the period, generally open to picturesque tourists. An anecdote from 1780 suggests, however, that those who were invited to inspect the demesne could expect great hospitality and an exhaustive tour.

Francis North, 1st Earl of Guilford, relates in a letter addressed to Mary Delany in July 1780 that, having recently met Lord Le Despencer at Beaconsfield, he decided to indulge his wish to pay him a visit at West Wycombe: 'I was taken with a curiosity just to look into his garden, and in the afternoon went boldly up to the house, and sent a servant to desire leave of the gardener for me just to look into the garden, when the answer was he had not dared to do it without telling my lord I was there, and his lordship was coming out to meet me. At this I was thunderstruck, and concluded I should be fatigued to death, but there was no remedy.'[43]

The septuagenarian baronet immediately appeared in an open portico and began to show his equally elderly visitor his 'curiositys': 'He was but just risen from table, and the hour very inconvenient. He pressed me to drink tea, which in my confusion I accepted. This brought down Mrs Parker (Barker, or Darker) [Dashwood's female companion Mrs Barry] in an elegant dishabille, whom it had *not* been *at all* my intention to visit, and I thought the water a *great while before it boiled*, but both she and my lord overwhelmed me with politeness!'[44]

A lengthy conversation ensued, and when Guilford eventually ordered his carriage, 'my lord sent it to a garden door, and was to show me a great deal in walking to it':

> To this I made a violent resistance, but with no effect. My lord said it was all down hill, and he walked it every day, so we hobbled out, and I was to admire everything I passed, which I did very awkwardly, looking upon it as probably the last walk I should ever take. But with labour and sorrow I arrived at my carriage, much rejoiced to put an end to a visit the most inconvenient and troublesome, both to the visitor and visited, that ever was made! My lord had been so polite as to conduct me to the door of my carriage, when we both seemed to have had enough, and I was in pain to think how he would ever get up the hill again.[45]

The earl declared to his correspondent that his 'distress' was, at the time, '*serious*, but now it was over, and I am alive, I give you leave to laugh at it'. His assessment of West Wycombe was perceptive and to the point: 'pretty, but very whimsical'.[46]

MRS PHENE'S HOUSE CHELSEA

[TWENTY]

Dr Phené's 'Senseless and Bewildering Accumulation of Incongruous Things'

On 12 March 1912 the *Pall Mall Gazette* reported the death of the 'wealthy and eccentric' Dr John Samuel Phené, known as 'the owner of the "mystery house" in Oakley-street, Chelsea':

> The strange residence stands at the corner of Oakley-street and Upper Cheyne-row. It is a high, square building of substantial type. Its Cheyne Row front is decorated in the most bizarre fashion. From pavement level to sloping roof it is a jumble of twisting columns and quaint symbolic figures. There are cupids, ancient goddesses, mermaids, imps, and the rest without end. Surmounting them all are two rampant dragons. Over the pillared doorway are set the words 'Renaissance du Château de Savenay'. The front door is covered with dirt of so many years, the windows are shuttered, the doors boarded up.[1]

We are told that Phené was reconstructing the house for his wife, but when she died in 1901, he suddenly gave up the task. It was nearly thirty years since the house had been occupied, and twelve years since the front had been 'prepared in its present style'. The garden of this 'silent, shuttered house' was 1.6 ha/4 acres in extent and 'decorated with scores of statues and figures, many now broken and weather-worn, which the doctor collected during journeyings on the Continent or from curiosity dealers'.[2]

Before the year was out, a two-day sale was conducted in the doctor's 'mournful garden'.[3] The auctioneers cleared 348 lots from the 'mysterious nightmare mansion', including 'South Sea idols, Gothic stonework, abbey choirstalls rich with goblins and poppy heads carved by craftsmen of the Middle Ages, plaster busts of Prince Albert and the Queen Victoria of 60 years ago, arches from Norman churches, wrought iron gates from old châteaux, weather vanes and bells of bronze green with age, a Roman marble bath, [and] loads of moss-grown bricks' [fig. 184].[4]

184
Anon., statues in Dr Phené's garden, photograph, *Daily Mirror* (19 November 1912). Royal Borough of Kensington & Chelsea.

This photo was taken when the 'Mystery House' and its garden were thrown open for public inspection for the sale of its contents.

185
Anon., statues in Dr Phené's garden, photograph, *Daily Mirror* (19 November 1912). Royal Borough of Kensington & Chelsea.

Phené brought these statues back from his travels in Indo-China.

186
Anon., 'Sale at Chelsea's Mystery House', photograph, *Daily Graphic* (20 November 1912). Royal Borough of Kensington & Chelsea.

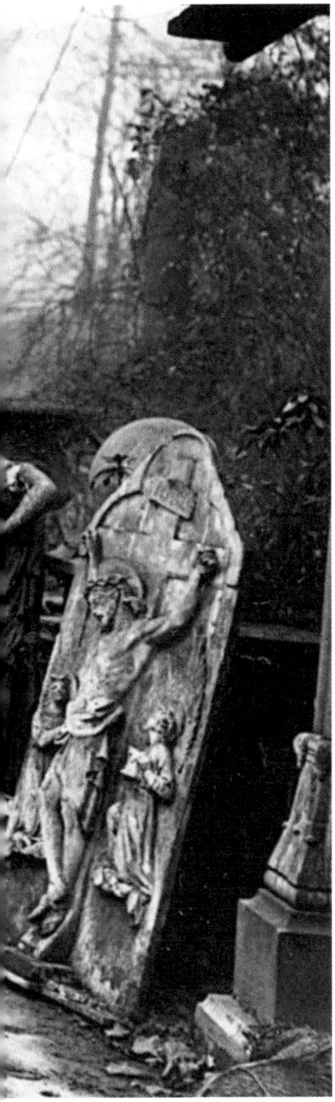
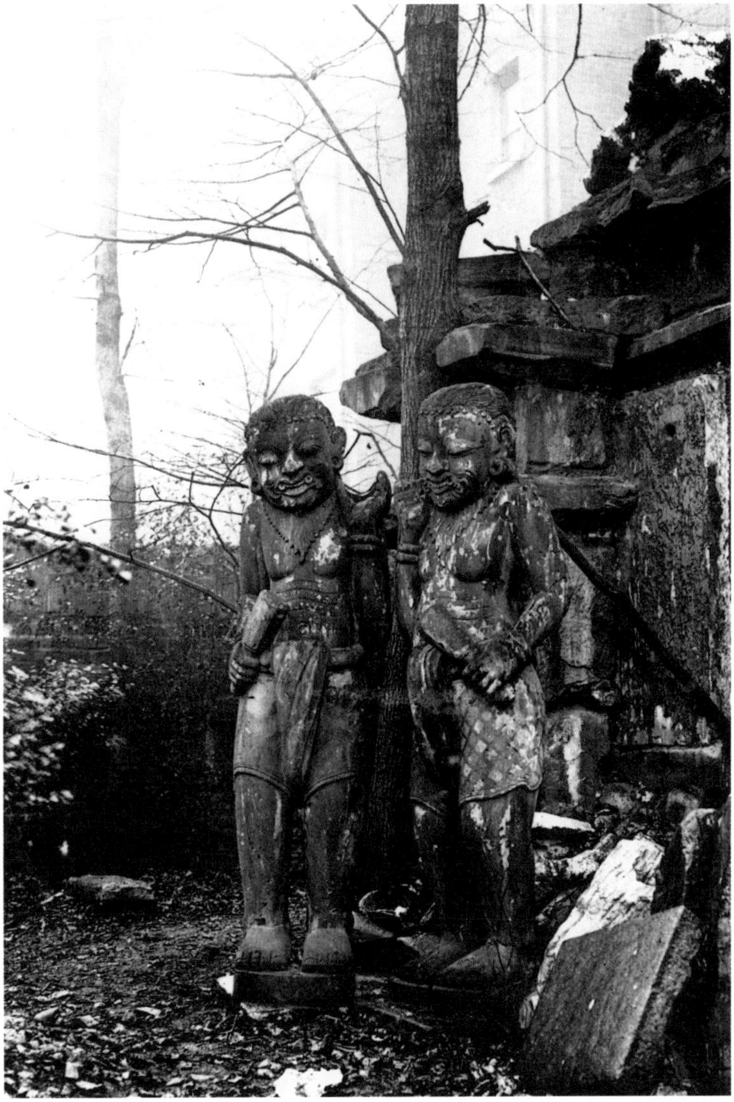
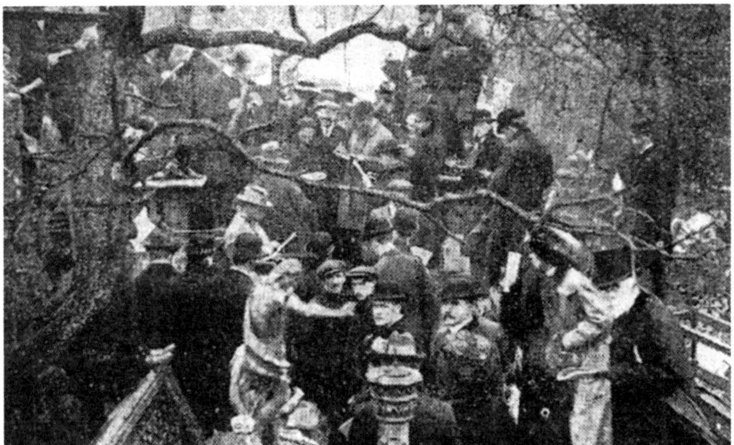

And there were even stranger things to be had in the 'sad garden, with tangled, dripping trees, and weed-grown paths':

Maimed statues, headless and handless, stained by the weather, crumbling into decay. Here again plaster busts; long groves of them – Nelson and Julius Caesar, Pitt and Fox; strange heads in classic draperies and side whiskers; two more statues of Queen Victoria standing up in the wilderness; Gothic doorways propped up with great baulks of timber, cromlechs built of carved stone from churches, mural tablets with strange inscriptions, fountains with a green crust at the bottoms of their basins, gargoyles, stone calvarys – all piled in chaotic disarray, wet and moss-grown'.[5]

The garden possessed a 'central Terrace running North and South', a 'Mound', a 'covered way', a blacksmith's forge, several fountains, and a 'Greek temple with small stone cairn adjoining' that marked the burial spot of 'a thirty-seven years' old, long blind pony which he brought from Iceland forty years ago'.[6] Although the garden was purported to be rather lifeless and a 'receptacle for dead cats', it possessed a 'fowl-run with particularly lively hens'.[7] A correspondent for the *Daily Mail* suggested that for his garden Dr Phené 'seems to have had the terrace gardens of the Isola Bella (Lake Maggiore) in mind. But whereas on the Isola Bella, whatever one may think of the taste of this sculpture garden, everything is order and harmony, the garden in Oakley-street is an indescribable confusion and disorder.' It was, he concluded, 'a senseless and bewildering accumulation of incongruous things' [figs 185 and 186].[8]

This 'Jumble Sale of Many Lands' clearly baffled the throng of visitors – the 'furniture dealers and curio connoisseurs, ladies of title and elderly clubmen with a taste for bric-à-brac, stonemasons, builders and architects, collectors of old prints, artists and sculptors from the neighbouring colony of studios'.[9] All were 'a little awed' crossing the threshold: it was 'a nightmare of incongruities in marble and stone and terra-cotta – Gustave Doré at his wildest pitch – Madame Tussaud gone raving mad! There was just room to squeeze through the crowded avenues of dingy statuary.'[10] A correspondent to the *Daily News & Leader* put it best: the garden was 'a Classical Rubbish Heap' and the sale of its 'mildewed wonders' at auction was a 'Prosaic End to a Doctor's Splendid Dream'.[11]

Some years before, Phené is reported to have remarked, when opening the door to his Oakley Street house:

This is the dream of my life ... People say I'm mad. But it is London herself who is mad and blind to the possible beauties of architecture. In this home I have attempted to reproduce some of the beauties of my beloved Italy, but somehow the fragile charm of Italia loses its effect when transplanted to London. That is why I am constantly building and rebuilding – that is the simple and only explanation of this 'house of mystery' ... and all I get for my efforts is the ribald laughter of the superlatively ignorant![12]

John Samuel Phené was born in 1824 in London [fig. 187]. His grandfather was purported to be librarian at Kew to George III, 'who marked his sense of merit by giving him a long lease of a residence in Cambridge-place, Kew Green'.[13] We know with greater certainty that his father, William Phené, was a cook and confectioner, and his mother, Mary Anna Jones, was a well-known painter.[14] John studied at King's Lynn Grammar School and Durham University, and completed his studies at Trinity College, Cambridge. After leaving Trinity he was awarded a travelling tutorship which enabled him to embark on the 'inexpressible pleasure' of a Grand Tour of the Continent.[15] This experience generated in Phené a great love for travel, and he spent much of his life travelling 'over practically all the world, and as an explorer of remote regions he had few equals':[16]

187
Elliott and Fry, *Dr. John Samuel Phené*, photograph, *The Graphic* (1 December 1906).

During his pilgrimages he systematically pursued a series of studies in comparative archaeology. One branch of investigation took him from Iceland to South Africa, and in America from Lake Superior to the Gulf of Mexico. His journeys were always undertaken with a definite purpose: he once followed carefully the various places in Byron's 'Childe Harold's Pilgrimage.' In another he followed the missionary journeys of St. Paul, while later he visited the Seven Churches in Asia, mentioned in Revelation. In Greece he went to all the spots of classic fame, and in Asia, with Troy as a base, he followed the exploits of the Homeric heroes. In China and India he studied particularly the ancient routes of traffic and the ethnology of the various races. He spent some time in Japan, exploring its many caves and tumuli, to aid him in elucidating the ancient religion of that country ... [and] he loved wild tribes and untrodden tracks.[17]

The doctor was later articled under the architect Philip Hardwick and became a fellow of the Royal Institute of British Architects in 1872.[18] He later became one of the founder fellows of the Huguenot Society and the Japan Society, a fellow of the Royal Archaeological Society at Athens and a corresponding member of the Academy of Sciences of New York.

According to one of his obituaries, Phené had a 'peculiar type of mind that takes pleasure in the study of serpent worship [as had his grandfather] and such by-ways of religious belief', and 'his views and practice on the subjects of art and architecture were equally remote from the normal' [fig. 188].[19] He also had an ardent interest in his 'ancient descent', of which he was ferociously proud, and which he traced back from the Phoenicians through India, Persia, Troy and Italy.[20]

There was little doubt that the doctor was a polymath with an exceptionally lively intellect: the breadth of his scholarship is reflected in the variety of lectures he presented to countless learned societies across the globe on subjects as diverse as 'parallel incidence in mythology and science', the construction of mural and architectural works by the builders of 'Cyclopean and other masonry' in Troy and Mycenae, 'On the Sanitary Results of Planting Trees in Towns', and a history of Icelandic native costume. Those who knew Phené personally affirmed that he was 'a good man little understood',[21] and 'had a heart of gold ... That he had the misfortune to outlive the time when such great and gracious qualities he possessed in abundance were duly appreciated was indeed his misfortune. He himself was the very soul of all that was chivalrous.' Though friends of the doctor refuted claims that he was a hermit ('The Chelsea Hermit') and a recluse, these allegations 'amused his vacant thoughts'.[22]

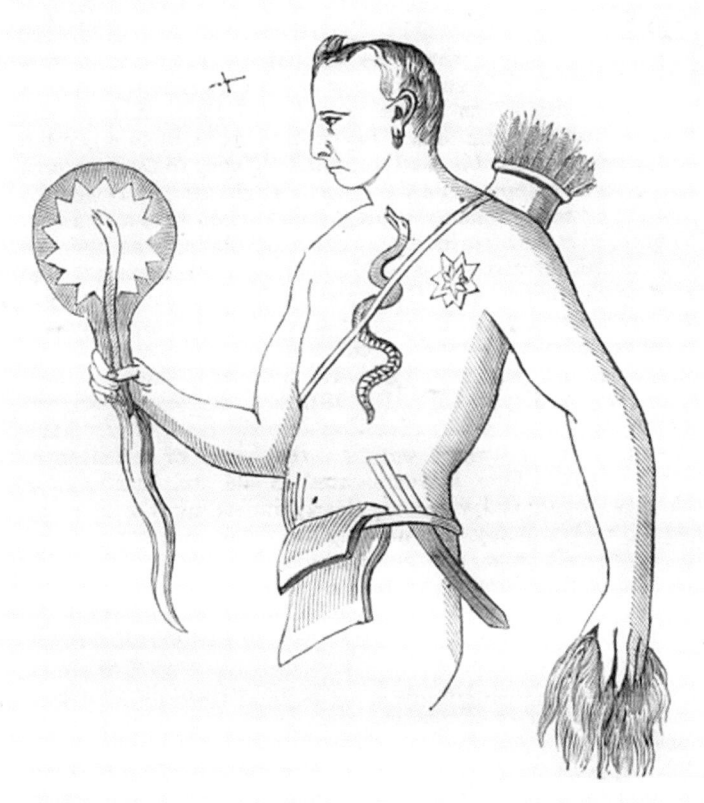

Fig. 12.

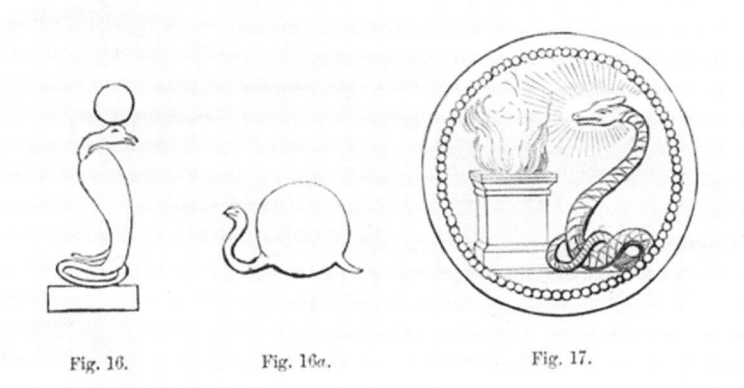

Fig. 16.   Fig. 16a.   Fig. 17.

188
Anon., engraving reproduced in J. S. Phené, On Prehistoric Traditions and Customs in Connection with Sun and Serpent Worship (1875).

Phené alleged that 'American Indians as late as 1741 tattooed a serpent on the chest, and a star on the left breast, and had sun and serpent emblems.'

Phené came to live in Chelsea after inheriting the leasehold of extensive glebe land from his elder brother, who had died suddenly while travelling in India. Chelsea was then a fairly unfashionable and slightly shabby western suburb. The doctor swiftly began to develop streets of houses – and in an innovative manner: he laid out Margaretta Terrace (named in honour of his wife, Margaretta Forsyth) along with Phené and Oakley Streets in 1850.[23] Margaretta Terrace was an exemplary development: 'a row of prettily proportioned, snug little houses, with dainty garden forecourts'.[24] In accordance with his belief in the value of urban greenspace, he planted London planes – specially imported from Holland – on both sides of Oakley Street and Margaretta Terrace – 'in the style of the French boulevards'.[25] The tree species was selected because of its 'special oxygenating properties'.[26] According to Mark Johnston writing in *Street Trees of Britain* (2017), these now 'leafy and affluent suburban streets with their charming houses of classical architecture soon attracted much praise. Prince Albert thought the addition of trees along the footway an excellent idea and it motivated him to support further street tree planting in London.'[27]

Two of the terraced houses Phené built on his Oakley Street estate were destined to become his own homes: he lived on the south side of the street at no. 32, and faced no. 76 across Upper Cheyne Row. The latter was the house the doctor's neighbours referred to as the 'silent house of mystery', and the 'Gingerbread Castle' on account of the curious encrustations which, between 1901 and 1912, accrued sporadically and unceasingly on its hitherto unornamented south-facing front [fig. 189].[28] Both houses had their principal entrances in Upper Cheyne Row, and both initially had substantial gardens. While the grounds of no. 32 were cut up into small lots and leased for development by the early 1890s, those opposite at the chateau remained densely planted with trees.[29] This garden had special historical significance, as it occupied the 'secluded grounds' of Old Cheyne House (formerly the property of the Earls of Shrewsbury)[30] and an ancient cottage 'stated to have been originally a Hunting Lodge of King Henry VIII'.[31] It was described in 1892 by Alfred Beaver as 'the most interesting private garden in Chelsea': 'Some of the trees are of considerable age: there is a mulberry supposed to date from Tudor times, the stump of a cedar, which flourished years ago, a beautiful catalpa, still vigorous, planted when this tree was very rare in England, and some old hollies.'[32]

This is a rare account of the garden when it was perceived as being both historically interesting and attractive. Few of Phené's friends recorded their observations of the grounds, and although passers-by frequently registered their surprise at observing the house and its walled garden from the street, there is only one report of a tentative trespass:

Certainly no thought would ever have come to us of bothering Dr Phené, had we not suddenly collided with him, one hot day, when the gloom of his dank weed-yard showed not unpleasantly through the palisade gate, for once half-open. Who could have resisted a look in? As we looked the owner alarmingly shot out ... and made a gesture of welcome. We accepted. We advanced. For a moment we stood still in that overgrown desert. For a moment only; because, having made a vague gesture of explanation ... the eccentric remarked explosively: 'This is the garden. Good-bye!'[33]

The most flattering description is supplied in a reminiscence by the doctor's old friend Annesley Owen, Recorder of Walsall, published in the *Daily Chronicle* in March 1912. Owen recounts how the amiable 'hermit' marked his year of office as Master of the Clothworkers' Company by hosting a 'Fête à la grecque ancien[ne], in his grounds'[34] to acquaint his guests with his 'Italian Renaissance Chateau now in progress of being finished':

> *A pavilion formed of matwork, like the dwellings of the Gabii, an ancient Greek colony in Italy, was erected for the distinguished company of guests, to whom Dr. Phené gave an address, describing his archæological travels in Italy, Greece, and Asia Minor, and how the results of his studies were synthesised in the renaissance in Chelsea of his ancient family home, the Château de Savenay, on the Loire.*[35]

He conducted his guests through the garden, which was arranged in avenues of statues of the personages of Latin, Greek and Scandinavian mythology, to heroes of Tudor times, and ending in a gigantic statue of Queen Victoria. Alternating with the statues were ancient vases of brilliant flowers and pedestals showing the progress of civilisation from corn-grinding querns, flint celts and arrowheads, onwards.

The doctor also explained to the visitors that the front of the house – facing into Upper Cheyne Row – represented 'the struggle between the Greeks and Trojan before Troy', and inside the house some of the ceilings exhibited 'in high relief' the countries he had visited, with their 'flora, fauna, buildings, and civic and religious ceremonies', while others depicted 'the interior of the earth, with the mythological persons supposed to have lived in Hades' [fig. 190].

One wonders how Phené's house and gardens could have suffered such spectacular decline between his fete in 1907 and his death five years later. Perhaps the premises always had the air of a builder's yard? Perhaps the freakish facade of the house did not bear close scrutiny; was it in reality a piecemeal assemblage of cheap, curious and tatty ornament? Contemporary photographs of the property lend support to this view: the house gives the impression of a

189
Anon., 'Dr Phene's House Chelsea', c.1910, photograph.
Private collection.

190
R. A. Inglis, Dr Phené on the steps of his house in Upper Cheyne Row, Chelsea, c.1907, photograph. Royal Borough of Kensington & Chelsea.
The lintel above the porch bears the inscription 'Renaissance du Chateau de Savenay'.

spirited but clumsy pastiche – or even, as it was so often rather uncharitably described, a 'nightmare medley in gilt and plaster and terra-cotta' – and its garden was in fact a dank jungle sprinkled with a reckless profusion of 'meaningless iron and marble, ecclesiastical symbols, baths, allegorical nymphs and cupids, and church furniture, which Dr Phené made it his absorbing mission in life to collect' [fig. 191].[36]

The images of the house in these photographs are poignantly at odds with the ambitions expressed by Phené in a rare interview with the press in 1901; soon after he had begun to embellish the south-facing front of his chateau, he spoke to a journalist about his plans for it. He remarked that it was 'going to be the most wonderful in London! Style – Italian Renaissance! All my own designs, all my own models ... All round the place I'm going to fix statues – reputable statues of reputable gods, goddesses, fighting men, poets, and so on.'[37] He did not, however, explain why, in his late seventies, he decided to embark on refacing a single facade of his then four-sided, free-standing house. Perhaps the doctor, in his later years, was prompted to use his house as a vehicle for consolidating his own sense of self; the extraordinary decorations were thought to be an evocation in gilt and painted plaster, stone and terracotta of his own lineage, which he felt to be long and distinguished.

At the same time, Phené's interest in his garden appears to have waned. With the exception of the fete, when the garden was dressed for the occasion, it appears to have been little used and almost wholly neglected – indeed, so much so that when the public was finally admitted to the mystery house and its even more mysterious garden in late November 1912 – on the occasion of his house-breaking sale after the 'old Phoenician's' death – most expressed a sense of disappointment. 'The Londoner', writing in the *Evening News*, summed up the general sentiment: now that one could see the well-guarded secrets of this long-standing Chelsea landmark, it was 'only a mad lumber-room after all ... The mystery flew out of this rubbish heap as soon as the auctioneer turned the key in the front door.'[38]

The doctor's garden was, however, never intended to be a public resort. It was a rich man's very idiosyncratic and very personal oasis. Mr Roote, who had been in the service of Dr Phené, reported after the doctor's death that he 'always put into one of the windows of no. 32 a notice when he wanted me. I knew the meaning of that notice: it was that I was to call and guide him across the street to no. 75 and let him into the empty house.' The house had a 'strange and complicated lock on the front door and a peculiar key, both of his design. I always went in with him and conducted him into the grounds, where he would sit for hours in a deck chair, dreaming.'[39]

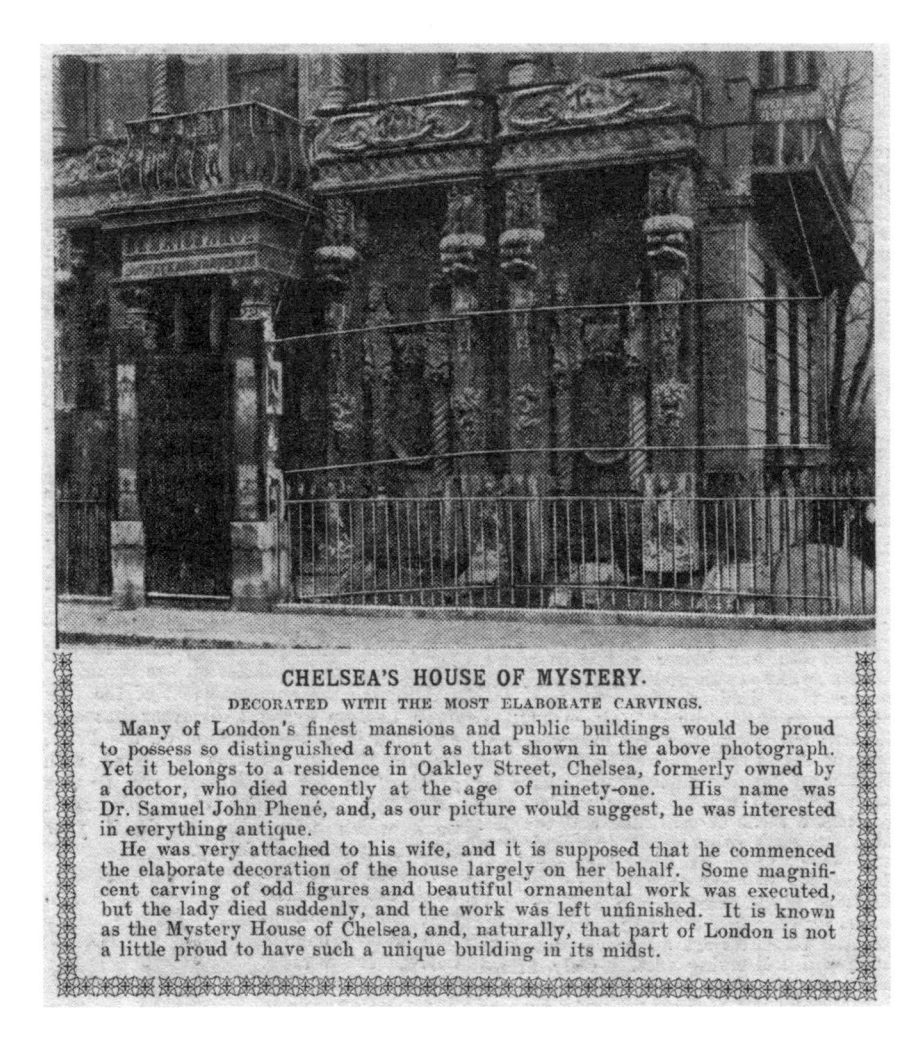

> **CHELSEA'S HOUSE OF MYSTERY.**
> DECORATED WITH THE MOST ELABORATE CARVINGS.
> Many of London's finest mansions and public buildings would be proud to possess so distinguished a front as that shown in the above photograph. Yet it belongs to a residence in Oakley Street, Chelsea, formerly owned by a doctor, who died recently at the age of ninety-one. His name was Dr. Samuel John Phené, and, as our picture would suggest, he was interested in everything antique.
> He was very attached to his wife, and it is supposed that he commenced the elaborate decoration of the house largely on her behalf. Some magnificent carving of odd figures and beautiful ornamental work was executed, but the lady died suddenly, and the work was left unfinished. It is known as the Mystery House of Chelsea, and, naturally, that part of London is not a little proud to have such a unique building in its midst.

191
Anon., 'Chelsea's House of Mystery. Decorated with the Most Elaborate Carvings', c.1912, newspaper clipping. Private collection.

Despite the seclusion in which he enjoyed the chateau gardens, Phené was not the only regular visitor to them. An account published in the *Builder* in November 1879 that reported on a paper read by Phené 'On the Sanitary Results of Planting Trees in Towns' at the Social Sciences Congress, Manchester, reveals that Thomas Carlyle was among the very few people whom the doctor had been able to persuade of the benefits of planting trees in streets. The celebrated man of letters had 'joined in his plans', and not only had planted trees in front of his house in Chelsea, but was accustomed to take 'daily walks under those on Dr Phené's property'.[40] Carlyle lived around the corner in Cheyne Row, was a 'conscientious gardener' and the original 'Chelsea Hermit'.[41] He was moreover, like Phené, a man with unorthodox views, and one who argued that factual accuracy was less important than getting to the heart and soul of the subject. According to the *Oxford Dictionary of National Biography*, in writing *The French Revolution*, Carlyle wished 'more than anything else ... to create a work of art rather than of expository logic or historical fact, a visionary and revelatory book that expressed the power of the supernatural within the natural, the patterns of providence within the facts of history'.[42]

Discrepancies between different accounts of Dr Phené's garden – and between the doctor's grandiose visions and the shabby condition of the garden as a whole apparent in photographs – reveal something about the relation between gardening, collecting and eccentricity. Both gardening and collecting open up a space for the play of eccentricity; they provide an occasion for the expression of individual idiosyncrasy, which may or may not be endorsed by the rest of the world. Gardens and collections, moreover, lend themselves to haphazard, irregular modes of procedure – unless or before they are hauled into the more sedate, rule-bound realm of public life. This irregularity, in both cases, can readily acquire an extra charge from an element of theatricality that resists a sense of permanence: the two activities occupy an uneasy, marginalised role in relation to the arts as commonly understood, both in the last few centuries and in contemporary culture. Those outside the inner world of the gardener and collector become unsettled by a feeling of lurking transgression, unleashed in a more overt form once the energies of the eccentric are no longer there to endorse and protect the garden-collection.

N
BEDFORD
B E D F O R
Catworth
Lit Catworth
Long Stow
Spaldwick
Easton
Grafham
Covington
Hargrave
Chelveston
Shelton
Kimbolton
Tilbrook
Upper Dean
Yelden
Newton Bromswold
Melchbourne
Swineshead
Pertenhall
Gt Staughton
Little Staughton
Wymington
Riseley
Bolnhurst
Colmworth
Thurleigh
Bletsoe
Odell
Harrold
Milton Ernest
Oakley
Stevington
Clapham
Ravensden
Wilden
Renhold
Great Barford
Blunham
Goldington
Bromham
Willington
Cople
Cardington
Elstow
Stagsden
Wootton
Kempston
Wilshamstead
Haynes
Cranfield
Marston Moretaine
Lower Shelton
Northill
Old Warden
Southill
Houghton Conquest
Ampthill
Lidlington
Millbrook
Higham Ferrers
Raunds
Stanwick
Irthlingborough
Turvey
Carlton
Pavenham
Sharnbrook
Souldrop
Keysoe
Knotting
Astwood
Salford

[TWENTY-ONE]

Bedford's Modern Garden of Eden

It was here [in Bedford] that the Lord God made that beautiful garden in which He used to talk in the cool of the day, and it was HERE, *that through sin the joys of Paradise turned to the misery of hell, so they saw that it is here that everything must be put straight.*[1]

OUR SURVEY OF ENGLISH GARDEN ECCENTRICS CONCLUDES WITH a very personal and very English take on the Garden of Eden. Mabel Barltrop (1866–1934) was born in Peckham, South London [fig. 192]. The only daughter of Augustus Charles Andrews, a banker's clerk, and his wife, Katherine Anne, née Buxton, as a young woman she was influenced in equal measure by her mother's Anglo-Catholicism and her aunt Fanny's Low Church belief; the former gave her a taste for High Church ceremonial and the latter for doing good works. Mabel married the deacon and priest Henry Barltrop in 1889, had four children, and settled in Bedford around 1905. At the time of her husband's death in 1906 she was a patient at a local asylum suffering from melancholia.

In 1914, feeling increasingly disillusioned with conventional Christianity, Barltrop embraced the spiritual philosophy of the early nineteenth-century prophet Joanna Southcott and enthusiastically adopted her millenarian beliefs. A key element of Southcott's sect was its insistence that a female figure would bring about millennial change. In February 1919 Mabel was identified as 'Shiloh' – the messenger and daughter of God whose appearance was foretold by Southcott (the self-proclaimed Mother of Shiloh) – and was given the name 'Octavia' because she was believed to be the eighth prophet in the Southcottian line [fig. 193]. As her biographer Jane Shaw remarks: 'the Trinitarian God of orthodox Christianity was now reconfigured to become "foursquare": God the Father, God the Mother (the Holy Spirit), Jesus the Son, and Octavia the Daughter.'[2]

Octavia appointed twelve female apostles from her loose network of followers – one from each sign of the zodiac – and washed their feet in imitation of Jesus. Initially known as the Community of the Holy Ghost and latterly as the Panacea Society, the community rapidly grew in numbers, attracting between fifty-five and seventy like-minded, wealthy, self-taught, middle-class women and a handful of men, who became resident members and who shared a handful of terraced houses and communal gardens, mostly clustered on one street, and a chapel in central Bedford.

These new Southcottians were attracted to the Society as, according to Shaw, it gave women a 'distinctive role in the redemption of the world, teaching that if Eve had been the cause of the Fall, only Woman could be the final redeemer'.[3] On a practical level, Southcottianism gave women active roles in the leadership and running of the movement.

The community eagerly anticipated the second coming of Christ and believed that he would return to their modest town garden because in their view Bedford was the site of the original Garden of Eden. Octavia had a vision that when Jesus returned he would stroll with her around the garden in Albany Road,[4] converse on a first-name basis, and they would break bread together in the garden in the company of the resident members of the community.

Octavia first referred to Bedford as the site of Eden in a sermon she delivered in July 1924 entitled 'The Original Garden of Eden'.[5] Presumably this proposition had been gestating for some time, as her secretary Jessie Johnson had mooted it as early as 1918: she predicted in her 'Plan of the Lord' that when Christ came again the world would be 'turned into a beautiful garden studded with jewels, divided into ten-mile-square sections'.[6] Bedford was, in her estimation, 'the place of God's glory' and was destined to be 'the Centre of the world's work'.[7]

Eager to establish a residential community and familiar with Bedford, Mabel endorsed Johnson's assertion, affirming in 1919 that 'really devoted believers could take up nice houses in Bedford, which is a most lovely place & is going up by leaps and bounds. Selfridges is coming [&] has taken a huge block in High St & Vickers-Maxim are coming.'[8] Her followers evidently agreed that it was a 'Land of Goshen', as by the early 1930s there were over fifty resident members living in and around Albany Street (later Road) in houses owned by the Society.[9] A hand-coloured plan of c.1950 shows the extent of their Bedford estate.

Vicki Manners suggests in '"The Garden of Eden": The Impact of the Panacea Society on Bedford 1919–1949' (2019) that there do not appear to be any scriptural or Southcottian reasons why the historic market town of Bedford

192
Anon., Mabel Barltrop with her pet jackdaw, c.1930, photograph. Panacea Charitable Trust, Bedford. Copyright and image supplied courtesy of The Panacea Charitable Trust.

193
Thomas Rowlandson, *Joanna Southcott*, c.1812, pen, ink and watercolour. Courtesy Bonham's, London.

Baltrop was profoundly influenced by Southcott's millenarian visions.

was made a place of theological significance, or why it was designated as the site of the original Garden of Eden.[10]

Though the Panaceans owned several small gardens and a large allotment in central Bedford – referred to collectively as the Estate of Jerusalem – only the garden at no. 12 Albany Street, Mabel's home and the Society's headquarters, appears originally to have been designated as the Garden of Eden [fig. 194]. The garden was a very modest affair as much of the ground was in fact occupied by a shed that in 1920 was converted into a chapel capable of holding upwards of fifty worshippers. Sadly, there are no surviving views of Mabel's original earthly paradise.

Over the years the boundaries of the garden fluctuated as neighbouring properties were annexed to form a large communal pleasure ground. The first extension took place in the mid-1920s when Kate Firth, an old friend of Mabel's and a founding member of the Society, made available her house called The Haven in Newnham Street for the Society's use. Its large garden was very conveniently connected to Octavia's own in Albany Street, so the two were thrown together by forming an opening in their shared garden wall.

194
Anon., Mabel Barltrop's house at 12 Albany Street, Bedford, c.1930, photograph. Panacea Charitable Trust, Bedford. Copyright and image supplied courtesy of The Panacea Charitable Trust.

The fate of this welcome addition to Eden was, however, for a short time in jeopardy on account of Firth's romantic dalliance with fellow resident Leonard Tucker Squire. As liaisons between Society members were forbidden, and neither Firth nor Squire agreed to submit to the will of the Divine Mother (Miss Emily Godwin, who was 'Eve' embodied), they repudiated the Society, quit the community, and Firth repossessed her house and garden. Octavia was vexed to lose a member and The Haven, but 'yet more upsetting' was that Firth had requested that the opening between the gardens should be bricked up. As Shaw remarks: 'For Octavia, who never went more than 77 paces from her house [lest Satan should attack her], this represented a serious loss of space (and view), and the loss of part of the Garden of Eden, and it was thus a very severe blow.' In May, the resident member Peter Rasmussen 'duly bricked up the openings, using cement made with the blessed water. For good measure, the assembled members threw a spider (a sign of poison) into The Haven's garden and gathered in the Garden Room (now bricked up on one side) to sing the hymn "Jerusalem the Golden".'[11]

In the event the Society was able to buy The Haven in August 1926, shortly after Firth and Squire moved to London: the garden wall came down once again, and the two grounds were reunited. Eden was restored, and in the words of Octavia the premises had 'entered into the Estate of Jerusalem'.[12]

The most significant addition to the garden took place in late 1930 with the annexation of Castleside. The capacious red-brick Victorian house in Newnham Road – opposite the ruins of Bedford Castle – had an unusually long and broad garden, the largest portion of which adjoined Octavia's home and the original Garden of Eden. Soon after its acquisition Peter Rasmussen set about joining its grounds to those of Octavia's house and The Haven to form a single pleasure ground. The new enlarged Eden was embellished with decorative treillage (to supply privacy), a terrace, fishpond, birdbath and conservatory;[13] soon thereafter a clock tower, built by members of the Society, was erected beside the chapel. Contemporary photographs suggest that most of the garden was given over to lawn, with a view to providing as much space as possible for entertaining.

Occasionally, ephemeral features were erected in the gardens for special events or ceremonial activities, the most striking of which was a makeshift altar formed of blockwork which was used to burn members' confessions. Confession was among the most important rituals in the Panacean practice of Overcoming – spiritualised group therapy, or the active process of 'trying to rid oneself of one's personality, of one's very self'.[14] A photograph survives showing Peter Rasmussen, Octavia's right-hand man, officiating at one of these rituals in the presence of a toy lamb symbolising Christ, the lamb of God [fig. 195]. Although the garden was important in both social and ceremonial events, we know little about its use from day to day: how much the residents were permitted or encouraged to use it and how it was governed. There were presumably stringent garden rules, which would have been rigorously enforced, as they were in every other aspect of residents' lives, from the eating of sweets to the scrunching of toast.[15]

It is paradoxical that Octavia – a woman of such idiosyncratic and outré ideas – appears to have had a very conventional approach to the design of the Garden of Eden. Whereas most of the eccentrics we have examined thus far have mined exotic models and points of reference to elaborate their gardens, Baltrop borrowed hers from a sphere with which she was familiar – the Edwardian suburban garden. Her interest in the garden lay less in its visual qualities than in its symbolic role as a place that offered the promise of returning to the original state of being in the Garden of Eden – that is, a place where the chosen could once again partake of the tree of life and live forever.

It is not, therefore, surprising that the Yggdrasil – a large weeping ash tree beside the chapel – was among the most conspicuous elements of the garden [fig. 196]. Thomas Carlyle had earlier popularised this 'world-tree' of Norse mythology, which was a symbol of cosmic unity:

> *Igdrasil, the Ash-tree of Existence, has its roots deep-down in the kingdoms of Hela or Death; its trunk reaches up heaven-high, spreads its boughs over the whole Universe: it is the Tree of Existence. At the foot of it, in the Death-kingdom, sit Three Nornas, Fates, – the Past, Present, Future; watering its roots from the Sacred Well. Its 'boughs,' with their buddings and disleafings, – events, things suffered, things done, catastrophes, – stretch through all lands and times. Is not every leaf of it a biography, every fibre there an act or word? Its boughs are Histories of Nations. The rustle of it is the noise of Human Existence, onwards from of old. It grows there, the breath of Human Passion rustling through it; – or stormtost, the stormwind howling through it like the voice of all the gods. It is Igdrasil, the Tree of Existence. It is the past, the present and the future; what was done, what is doing, what will be done; 'the infinite conjugation of the verb To do' … I find no similitude so true as this of a Tree. Beautiful; altogether beautiful and great.[16]*

The members of the Panacea Society believed that their modern Garden of Eden was harnessing the power of this pagan symbol.

The canopy of the ash was sufficiently capacious in the mid-1920s that 'a meeting of fifty or sixty people could easily be held beneath its branches.'[17]

195
Anon., Peter Rasmussen burning members' confessions on a makeshift altar in the
Panacea Society's garden, c.1925–7, photograph. Panacea Charitable Trust, Bedford.
Copyright and image supplied courtesy of The Panacea Charitable Trust.

196
Anon., members of the Panacea Society dancing round the Yggdrasil tree
(large weeping ash) in the garden, c.1925–7. Panacea Charitable Trust, Bedford.
Copyright and image supplied courtesy of The Panacea Charitable Trust.

Rachel Fox described the first of the parties: 'Octavia gave a Garden Party to all at the Centre, in the Garden of *The Haven*, on the 18th [*c*.1925] – a most perfect day. Tea was served under the big weeping ash-tree named Yggdrasil. After the Meeting, twelve of the party danced country dances, dressed as country people in smocks and panier dresses.'[18]

Octavia also described the same event 'under the shade of the wonderful tree Yggdrasil', observing that 'we have advanced from such a small affair, to the beautiful gardens in which we have just been having tea ... Most of us have been taught that we must not enjoy ourselves too much; but we are now beginning to find that God wills us to enjoy His gifts as much as we can.'[19]

From sometime in the mid-1920s the Panaceans began to believe that the Garden of Eden was in fact much larger than their own communal gardens: it extended for a 4.8-km/3-mile radius from their Bedford chapel. The land contained within this precinct had 'never belonged to Satan' and was a place where 'the Lord retained a pied-à-terre or foothold'.[20] Even this increase in the Estate of Jerusalem, however, was deemed too small by Octavia, who, in August 1925, eager to expand the boundaries of her area of control, announced in *The Writings of the Holy Ghost* that she had begun to investigate 'all records which point to the importance of the statement that the ground upon which we meet and a distance of twelve miles in all directions ... comprises the original Garden' [fig. 197].[21] As a result of this exercise, in October of the same year, a 'very special bit of protection work was done to protect the Garden of Eden and its environs.'[22] The Panaceans designated all the land encompassed within a 19-km/12-mile radius of their chapel as the Royal Domain – that is, the Daughter of God took possession of a great swathe of Bedfordshire with a view to creating an 'ark of protection' for all those who resided within it. The boundaries of the Domain were sanctified by the burial of eight small consecrated linen sections at eight equidistant points along the circumference of this large circle. The Society's gardener Evelyn Gillett played a crucial role in this operation, supplying the transportation and covering the consecration points with soil.

Although my survey of eccentric gardeners does not set out to analyse the qualities that characterise them as English, the Panaceans have such a strong and explicit sense of Englishness that our reading of their garden would be incomplete without acknowledging that the members retained an imperial mindset, 'drawing on a strong streak for the lost – or dying – sense of Britain's place in the world'.[23] Jane Shaw affirms in 'Englishness, Empire and Nostalgia: A Heterodox Religious Community's Appeal in the Inter-war Years' (2018) that the Society appealed to its members both at home and abroad in three ways: 'through its theology, which put Britain at the centre of the world; by presuming the necessity and existence of a "Greater Britain" and the British empire, while in so many other quarters these entities were being questioned in the wake of World War I; and by a deliberately cultivated and nostalgic notion of "Englishness"'.[24]

The very conventionality of the Panaceans' recreation of Eden – which is in itself eccentric – can be in part explained by Baltrop's desire to create a setting in a way that she knows, using props and furnishings with which she is both familiar and comfortable, to convey a nostalgic notion of Englishness. If, as F. S. Stuart affirms in the Society's journal, *The Panacea* (1924), the members believed that 'Britain's destiny was to become the New Jerusalem', then their new Garden of Eden needed to be recognisably English.[25]

Octavia and the Panaceans had a great enthusiasm for garden parties – that most archetypal English *plein-air* entertainment which was a constellation of class privilege, material luxury and polite sociability. Between 1929 and 1932 the garden was the setting for annual summer parties – coinciding with the

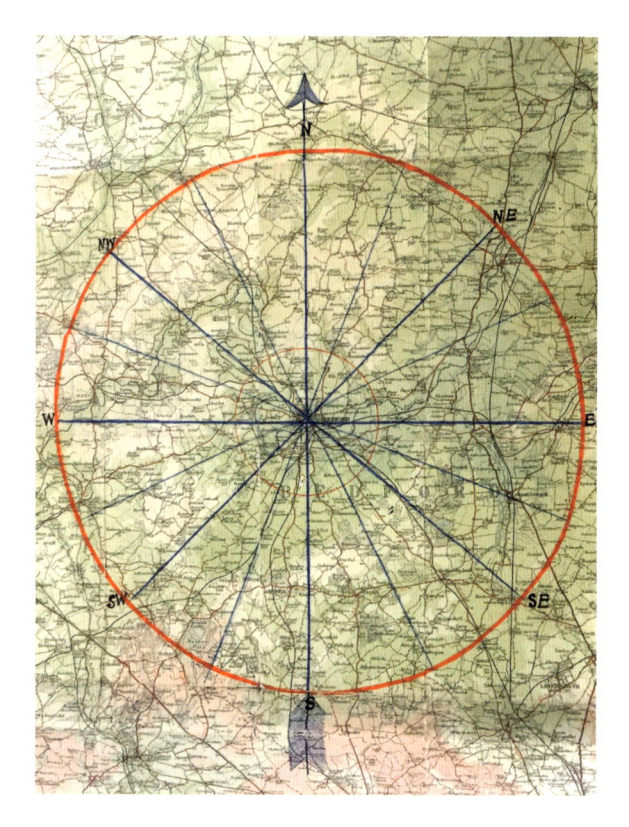

197
Anon., 'The Royal Domain', 1925, annotated plan. Panacea Charitable Trust, Bedford.
Copyright and image supplied courtesy of The Panacea Charitable Trust.
In 1925 the Panaceans designated all the land contained within a 19-km/12-mile radius of their chapel in Bedford as the Royal Domain, providing an 'ark of protection' for all those who lived within it.

Society's General Council meetings – when it was used to stage amateur theatricals, country dancing and organised recreation in the form of games, including potato races, clock golf, tennis, darts, rings and putting, and badminton. Shaw reports that Octavia choreographed all these events down to the last detail [fig. 198].[26]

The garden parties were nevertheless more than mere fetes; they were very special treats for the resident community which served as dress rehearsals for the second coming of Christ: their success would hasten his arrival and would supply a foretaste of their immortal life. Their first garden party was in fact described as being 'only the beginning of the pleasures that would be ours'.[27]

It might seem strange that social rituals that seem so sedate to twenty-first-century eyes should appear to presage eternal bliss to Barltrop and her followers. One way of grasping the apparent lack of any sense of incongruity on the part of these messianic party planners is to see their visions of immortality as invoking the heady symbolic role of the 'long hot summer' and (by implication) its attendant garden parties, both in Edwardian writings themselves and in literature that looks back to the Edwardian era as a golden age of tranquillity before the carnage of the First World War. Sarah Edwards, looking at both earlier and later expressions of wistful fantasy in her essay 'Dawn of the New Age' – in the first instance, works such as Edward Thomas's *The South Country* (1909) and, in the second, for example, Vita Sackville-West's

198
Anon., garden party at The Haven, late 1920s, photograph. Panacea Charitable Trust, Bedford. Copyright and image supplied courtesy of The Panacea Charitable Trust.

The Edwardians (1930) and George Orwell's *Coming up for Air* (1938) – suggests that each of the two genres features 'an exotic, self-contained space which is beyond the realm of the protagonist's ordinary experience: geographically remote, stilled in time, promising heightened adventures and sensory delights'.[28]

The importance of these *plein-air* festivities to the Panaceans partly explains the fact that their garden appears to have been much less visually striking than many of those considered in the preceding chapters. A useful point of reference for understanding the role allotted to horticultural and landscape elements in gardens that needed to accommodate celebrations of this kind is supplied by a short story of the period, Katherine Mansfield's 'The Garden Party' (1920) – a narrative that also delicately indicates the adaptability of the myth of Eden, since the festive garden, however carefully contrived, is a place of joy and childlike innocence in which guests seem to alight 'like bright birds'. (Darker elements threaten to impinge from outside.) The story is set in New Zealand, but the event is implicitly presented as following English models; there are almost no details to evoke an exotic setting.[29]

Vegetation, it is established at the outset, needs to be kept in order: the lawns have been mown and swept until they 'seemed to shine'. When co-operating with human endeavour, plants nonetheless play a crucial role in commanding an elevated attention: 'As for the roses, you could not help feeling that they understood that roses are the only flowers that impress people at garden-parties; the only flowers that everybody is certain of knowing. Hundreds, yes, literally hundreds, had come out in a single night; the green bushes bowed down as though they had been visited by archangels.'[30]

At the same time, other features of the garden present problems. As the narrative begins, Laura Sheridan, an adolescent on the verge of adulthood, is sent out by her mother to supervise some workmen who have come to erect a marquee. Two possible sites are rejected: the 'lily-lawn' is 'not conspicuous enough', and the tennis court has already been partially assigned to a small band. The spot finally chosen is one in which the requirement of entertainment assumes priority over burgeoning nature:

> 'Look here, miss, that's the place. Against those trees. Over there. That'll do fine.
>   Against the karakas. Then the karaka-trees would be hidden. And they were so lovely, with their broad, glistening leaves, and their clusters of yellow fruit. They were like trees you imagined growing on a desert island, proud, solitary, lifting their leaves and fruits to the sun in a kind of silent splendour. Must they be hidden by a marquee?
>   They must.[31]

Later in the narrative, the subordination of the landscape to the demands of the social occasion is wittily echoed when a guest comments facetiously on the 'green-coated' musicians: "'My dear!" trilled Kitty Maitland, "aren't they too like frogs for words? You ought to have arranged them round the pond with the conductor in the middle of a leaf.'"[32]

Octavia's plans for receiving Christ in appropriate style did not extend to marquees and bands, but photographs of her garden parties show that large grass swards were needed for tables and chairs, and for the dancing and other activities that formed part of the events [fig. 199]. Enabling these activities to take place was more important than striving for visual impact or producing an effect of natural beauty and simplicity; as already noted, planting literally had to be consigned to the margins. The emphasis on bustling social life is very different from Charles Waterton's vision of nature protected from human depredation, despite his encouragement of occasional festivities in the grotto. Nevertheless, Mansfield's short story implicitly endorses the view that energetic social organisation and the natural world can combine to induce a state of exaltation. When Laura is under pressure to venture outside her Eden into a more sinister world, she feels for a moment unable to do so, and reflects on the reason why: such features of the party as 'voices, tinkling spoons, laughter, the smell of crushed grass' are 'somehow inside her': 'She had no room for anything else.'[33]

The paradox of seeking to create a new Eden by forming a garden adapted to conventional social rituals is not the only potential contradiction within Mabel Barltrop's millenarian vision and practical programme for realising it. Her decision to limit her own movements to seventy-seven paces from the chapel, concentrating her activities in the house and the garden, seems sharply at odds with her expansionist ambitions: not only the extension of the Estate of Jerusalem to an area radiating 4.8 km/3 miles – and then 19 km/12 miles – from this chapel, but an implicit desire to ensure that the Panaceans' way of life – and enjoyment of a new Eden – should be adopted by the entire world. The Society had in fact by the late 1920s spread its tentacles rapidly and efficiently beyond Britain's shores to welcome members from the colonies and former colonies, including Canada, the United States, New Zealand, Australia, India, South Africa and the West Indies. Such unconcern about contradictory and conflicting elements is less obvious in the gardens of the other eccentrics considered here, but they all seek to establish a space within which such elements can coexist – in which productive forces and idiosyncratic preoccupations are allowed to run riot, sometimes relatively untrammelled by the institutions and social habits of the outside world, sometimes in open defiance of them.

199
Anon., preparations for a garden party at The Haven, late 1920s, photograph.
Panacea Charitable Trust, Bedford. Copyright and image supplied courtesy of
The Panacea Charitable Trust.

200
Anon., the garden at Castleside, Bedford, c.1930, photograph. Panacea Charitable Trust,
Bedford. Copyright and image supplied courtesy of The Panacea Charitable Trust.

All of the garden eccentrics included within this book were passionate in their pursuit of their own enterprises. While they were able to pursue their aspirations by virtue of the clearly established boundaries that marked out a protected space for private experimentation, they nonetheless looked beyond these boundaries towards a world from which elements of multifarious cultures and geographies could be appropriated: at Hawkstone, a Dutch house and windmill and Egyptian tent, a 'Scene in Swisserland' and a 'Scene at Otaheite', and for Thomas Bland, at Reagill, an Italian garden that resembles contemporary prints of Herculaneum and Pompeii.[34] A correspondent for the Daily Mail suggested that Dr Phené's garden in Chelsea was inspired by the terrace gardens of the Isola Bella at Lake Maggiore (though rather less orderly than its precursor).[35] In some cases, the elements assimilated within the English countryside are so unexpected that the gardeners produce the impression that they are testing out their ambitions against recalcitrant reality, whether reducing the Mer du Glace to a tiny cordillera in a Cheshire villa garden and the Matterhorn to a miniature rockwork in Oxfordshire, or fabricating Druidical monuments at the mouths of Somersetshire caves to proclaim the triumph of Christianity over paganism.

In their defiance of the limitations of their native terrain, such gardeners display the quality of a certain rigidity – 'some exaggeration of the attitudes common to Life' – that Edith Sitwell notes at the beginning of English Eccentrics: 'This attitude, rigidity, [or] protest ... has been called eccentricity by those whose bones are too pliant.'[36] In the topiary gardens considered in early chapters, the quality of rigidity is literalised in the formal attributes of trees and bushes subjected to human control. It is the preponderance of determination over flexibility (as in Lady Reade's assumption that she can travel with a vast assemblage of wildlife) that gives some of the projects surveyed here an air of inadvertent comedy; in eschewing the compliance of more conventional gardeners with the demands of the terrain and the dictates of practicality, they produce the effect of humour that Henri Bergson, in Le Rire (1912), has identified as 'du mécanique plaqué sur le vivant' – the sense of something rigid, and therefore in a sense mechanical, where what is expected is something living and flexible.[37]

Some of these projects would have been incomprehensible to outsiders in the absence of their makers, who often and willingly served as ciceroni to strangers and interlopers. Miss Jane Hill impressed Johnson and Thrale with the 'great civility' with which she showed them round Hawkstone, despite the fact that 'her whole appearance' was 'below that of a common housemaid'.[38] Several eccentrics resorted to erecting signage and directions to explain their programmes to the outside world: at Denbies, Tyers placed 'flags' at 'almost every Turn ... with some Moral Sentences and Admonitions, inscribed on them for our Instruction, and to give a serious Turn to the Thoughts', and at Lamport, Sir Charles Isham positioned small handwritten placards throughout his rockery to apprise visitors of the goings-on of the bizarre diminutive tableaux that unfolded before them.[39] These signs took the form not only of flags and placards, but of miniature models; at Hoole these were preserved within a rosewood commode in the house, and at Friar Park a small bronze model was placed at the foot of the gritstone facsimile.

One of the more common and abiding aims of the gardeners we have examined is their desire to establish versions of paradise – whether explicitly as at Walton and Lamport Halls or West Wycombe Park, or implicitly as at the Jungle, where Loft's description of its garden 'inclosure' conjures images of an earthly paradise – a bountiful, idealised landscape in which birds and animals mingle in a state of harmony and peace, giving the impression of the Garden of Eden before the Fall. The word 'paradise' crops up very often indeed in accounts of the gardens discussed here; to cite just one example, Benjamin Franklin, at West Wycombe, acclaims the results of Sir Francis Dashwood's efforts by remarking, simply, 'the Gardens are a Paradise.'[40]

The paradisal qualities that eccentric gardeners pursue extend not only to the happy coexistence with animals – as they do for Charles Waterton and for Lady Reade, for example – but also to an untroubled fellowship among humans. Waterton not only allowed 'pic-nic parties' of workers to enjoy his 'sylvan paradise', or grotto, but also invited the inhabitants of the local lunatic asylum to indulge in 'harmless and frolicsome merriment' in this same pastoral setting, where they are able 'to temporarily forget their pitiable and frequently unhappy condition, and one and all to declare the grotto to be an elysium'.[41] Dr Phené held an acclaimed 'Fête à la grecque ancien[ne]', and Thomas Bland provided a 'Grand Fete' for throngs of villagers.[42]

Though most of the eccentrics considered here created gardens with paradisal elements, only Mabel Barltrop perceived events that took place within her terrestrial paradise as possessing special significance: she equated the defection of Kate Firth and the temporary loss of part of the Estate of Jerusalem with the Fall. As Jane Shaw remarks, 'Octavia made theological sense of what had happened in the way she knew best: by casting the figures that surrounded her back into the biblical narrative, and giving the happenings in the community a cosmic significance.'[43] Having established their paradise in Bedford and rediscovered the Garden of Eden, the Panaceans 'now *had* to experience the Fall'.[44] The troubling events were, as Rachel Fox put it, 'ravages in her [Octavia's] paradise', but Octavia exhorted the members of her community to remain 'loyal, contented and obedient': 'You are not to be any longer as merely people "following the Woman" or "on Octavia's side". No, that is too small. You are the children of the Great I AM, sent down to form the Kingdom, THE Garden, Paradise in Earth – and I, the Daughter, am with you on the side of the Great Father and Mother.'[45]

Mabel's version of paradise was clearly not a conventional one [fig. 200]. Its oddities, however, draw attention to a striking aspect of paradisal elements in eccentric gardens: on the one hand, they intensify the sense of an individual psyche at grips with the terrain, and ineluctably removing it from a shared domain of day to day existence, but on the other hand, in registering a desire to create an earthly paradise, they draw upon a dream horticultural milieu, readily respond to it and, even in the midst of highly unusual garden elements, grasp it as a point of familiarity.

Such an aspiring vision could hardly fail to have its mournful side. While Mabel considered her Bedfordshire Eden an eternal estate, many of our eccentrics (who did not, like Barltrop, expect to live forever) were content to see their intensely personal gardens as ephemeral creations. They were in their minds living biographies – sanctuaries so inextricably entangled with their personae that they could not in their absence survive them – nor did they consider the long term survival of the gardens as important. As Lieutenant Hammond remarked in 1635 upon seeing Thomas Bushell's 'maister-peece' at Enstone: 'it seeme[d] strange to me that a Gentleman should be so strangely conceited and humour'd, as to disburse and lay out so much Money as he has done, in planting, framing, con[s]truing and building vpon another Mans Freehold, to reare a Paradise and then to loose it. A mad gim-cracke sure, yet hereditary to these Hermiticall and Proiecticall Vndertakers.'[46]

It is in fact the fleeting quality of gardens that makes them so remarkably alluring and poignant. As George Cable remarked in *The Amateur Garden* (1914), there is poetic charm in the evanescence of nature: 'The transitoriness of a sunset glory, or of human life, is rife with poetic pathos because it is a transitoriness which *cannot be helped* ... The only poetic evanescence is evanescence that is inevitable.'[47]

[CODA]

The Present Status of the Gardens

BANWELL CAVES Well Lane, Banwell, North Somerset BS29 6NA
George Henry Law, Bishop of Bath and Wells
The caverns and gardens are open to the public and are a Site of Special Scientific Interest (SSSI). Many of the garden's buildings have undergone incremental repairs since the 1970s.

BARN HILL HOUSE (FORMERLY BARNHILL) Barn Hill, Stamford, Lincolnshire PE9 2AE
William Stukeley
The extent of Stukeley's house and garden can still be determined, though few of the original features are intact; those that remain include the Great Gate (now known as King Charles's Gateway) and a commemorative plaque from 1733 dedicated to Dr Rogers.

DENBIES London Road, Dorking, Surrey RH5 6AA
Jonathan Tyers
The early gardens were dismantled soon after Tyers's death in 1767. The house has been much modernised. Much of the surviving estate land has been given over to vineyards and is currently run by a winery.

ELVASTON CASTLE Borrowash Road (A6120), Elvaston, Derby, Derbyshire DE72 3EP
Major-General Charles Stanhope, 4th Earl of Harrington, better known as Viscount Petersham
The house and some of the gardens – and their topiaries – survive. Purchased in 1969 by the then Derby Corporation and opened in 1970 as one of the first country parks in England, it is now owned and managed by Derbyshire County Council.

– 335 –

THE 'ENSTON ROCK' The Drive, Enstone, Chipping Norton, Oxfordshire
OX7 4NF
Thomas Bushell
Largely destroyed; known primarily through archaeological remains. It is possible that some elements of the former Rock were re-erected in the village – the most notable of which is a so-called 'grotto', now converted into a dwelling.

FRIAR PARK 16 Church St, Henley-on-Thames, Oxfordshire RG9 1SE
Sir Frank Crisp
The garden – complete with its miniature Matterhorn – survives and was restored by George Harrison (of Beatles fame) from the 1970s. The estate is private and not open to the public.

HAWKSTONE PARK Shrewsbury, Shropshire SY4 5UY
Sir Richard Hill and Miss Jane Hill
The 40.5-ha/100-acre park, which lies 19 km/12 miles from Shrewsbury, is open to the public and remains remarkably picturesque. Hawkstone Park Hotel is open to paying guests.

THE HERMITAGE Austin Street, Stamford, Lincolnshire PE9 2QR
William Stukeley
This garden has vanished.

THE HERMITAGE VINEYARD Grantham, Lincolnshire NG31 6SQ
William Stukeley
This garden no longer exists.

HOOLE HOUSE Hoole Road, Chester, Cheshire CH2 3LR
Dame Eliza Broughton
Hoole House and gardens formerly sat at the corner of Hoole Road and Piper's Lane, near the A56/A41 roundabout. All traces of the garden have vanished.

THE JUNGLE Harby Lane, Eagle, Lincolnshire LN6 9DT
Russell Collett
While the rustic sham-castle facade of the Jungle survives, the interior has been gutted and extensively redeveloped (most recently in the late twentieth century). The ponds remain, but the grounds have been redesigned.

LAMPORT HALL Lamport, Northampton NN6 9HD
Sir Charles Isham, 10th Baronet
The house and gardens are managed by the Lamport Hall Preservation Trust. Both house and gardens are open to the public on a regular basis. The rockwork remains a curious and commanding structure.

LONDON Harcourt House, 19a Cavendish Square, London W1G 0PN
William John Cavendish-Scott-Bentinck, 5th Duke of Portland
The house was pulled down in 1907 and rebuilt as a block of flats. The garden has been redeveloped.

LONDON Junction of Oakley Street and Upper Cheyne Row, Chelsea, London SW3 6SQ
Dr Samuel Phené
The house has been replaced with an early twentieth-century redbrick dwelling. Much of the garden has been covered with development. Dr Phené's memory is preserved in the eponymous public house in Phené Street which was designed by him and named in his honour.

LONDON Various Middlesex churchyards
John Saxy
The ancient churchyard yews survive unclipped at St Peter & St Paul, Harlington (High St, Harlington, Hayes UB3 5DN) and St John the Baptist, Hillingdon (Royal Lane, Uxbridge UB8 3QP). The Peacocks at St Mary the Virgin, East Bedford (Hatton Rd, Feltham TW14 8JR) remain pruned and in excellent order.

LONDON Ramillies House, 1–2 Ramillies Street (formerly Blenheim Street), Soho, London W1F 7LN
Dr Joshua Brookes
Dr Brookes's garden was built over by the middle of the nineteenth century. It is now occupied by the London College of Beauty Therapy. There is no record of the fate of the Vivarium.

LONDON 124 Kentish Town Rd, Kentish Town, London NW1 9QB
William Stukeley
Stukeley's villa and estate lay on the east side of Kentish Town Road, more or less on the site of the present Abbey Tavern (junction of the present Bartholomew Road). No trace remains of either the house or estate, both of which were redeveloped in the nineteenth century.

PANACEA SOCIETY (PANACEA MUSEUM) 9 Newnham Rd, Bedford, Bedfordshire MK40 3NX
Mabel Barltrop
The house and gardens are now run by the Panacea Society Charitable Trust. The gardens were recently refurbished and remain reasonably intact.

Reagill (Image Garden) Yew Tree Far, Reagill, Shap, Cumbria CA10 3ER
Thomas Bland
Much of Thomas Bland's sculpture survives in situ. In 1999 it was proposed to sell the premises and its remaining sixty-seven sculptures. Following strong and wide public objection, Chris Smith, then Secretary of State for Culture, Media and Sport, supported the listing of the property as a site of special architectural and historic interest (Grade II). Access by appointment only with the present owners.

Shipton Court High Street, Shipton Under Wychwood, Chipping Norton, Oxfordshire OX7 6DG
Dame Harriott Reade
The house has been divided into flats. Much of Dame Harriott's garden legacy was destroyed in the nineteenth century.

Stubton Hall Fenton Rd, Stubton, Newark, Lincolnshire NG23 5DD
Sir Robert Heron
Now a wedding venue. Little remains of the early gardens.

Walton Hall Waterton Park Hotel, Walton, Wakefield, West Yorkshire WF2 6PW
Charles Waterton
Walton Hall is now occupied by the Waterton Park Hotel. The house, park and gardens have been significantly altered. Little remains of Squire Waterton's original gardens or landscape improvements.

West Wycombe Park High Wycombe, Buckinghamshire HP14 3AJ
Sir Francis Dashwood, 2nd Baronet
The park and gardens are owned and managed by the National Trust. The house is occupied by Sir Francis's successor, Sir Edward Dashwood, 12th Baronet. The Mausoleum and the Hell-Fire Caves are open to the public on a regular basis.

Witley Court Worcester Road, Great Witley, Worcestershire WR6 6JT
Rachel Anne Gurney, Countess of Dudley
The countess's garden has disappeared. The mansion was gutted by fire in 1937 and is now a spectacular and consolidated ruin. The property is owned and managed by English Heritage.

[ENGLISH GARDEN ECCENTRICS]

Notes

Introduction pages 1–11

1 Victoria Carroll, *Science and Eccentricity: Collecting, Writing and Performing Science for Early Nineteenth-Century Audiences* (London: Pickering & Chatto, 2008), 35.

2 Paul de Man, *The Rhetoric of Romanticism* (New York: Columbia University Press, 1984), 70, 67–8.

3 Dr Phené's invitation to his 'Fête in the Ancient Greek Style', in *Chelsea Scraps* (Chelsea Reference Library, Local History Scrapbook, hereafter CRL/LHS), 631; The Londoner, 'To-night's Gossip', *Evening News*, 20 November 1912. Some aspects of the relation between the public and the intimate in collecting are explored by John Forrester in 'Mille e tre: Freud and Collecting', in *The Cultures of Collecting*, ed. John Elsner and Roger Cardinal (London: Reaktion Books, 1994), 224–51, 248–9.

4 Charles Isham, *Emily* (Lamport: Lamport Hall, 1899), n.p.; 'The Londoner', in the passage just cited, takes a similar view of Dr Phené's house and grounds, commenting cruelly: 'The mystery flew out this rubbish heap as soon as the auctioneer turned the key in the front door' ('To-night's Gossip').

5 Sophie Aymes-Stokes and Laurent Mellet, eds, *In and Out: Eccentricity in Britain* (Cambridge: Cambridge University Press, 2012), 7.

6 Malcolm Andrews, 'Dickens, Turner and the Picturesque', in *Imagining Italy: Victorian Writers and Travellers*, ed. Catherine Waters, Michael Hollington and John Jordan (Newcastle-upon-Tyne: Cambridge Scholars Publishing, 2010), 181; William Hazlitt, 'On the Picturesque and Ideal' [1822], in *Table Talk*, 2 vols (London: Henry Colburn, 1824), 2:371.

7 Quoted in *A Description of Hawkstone, the Seat of Sir R. Hill, Bart M.P.* (Shrewsbury: printed at the Chronicle Office, 1840), 44. Dr Johnson is more concerned with the sublime than with the picturesque in his account of Hawkstone, but his emphasis on irregularity here nonetheless implicitly invokes the latter; in the essay just quoted, Hazlitt declares that 'the picturesque may be considered as something like an excrescence on the face of nature.' Hazlitt defines picturesque surprise in his declaration that this quality 'surprises … the mind', whereas the ideal 'satisfies' it ('On the Picturesque and Ideal', 371).

8 H. W. Sargent, 'Impressions of English Scenery', *Magazine of Horticulture, Botany,*

and *All Useful Discoveries and Improvements in Rural Affairs*, 31 (1865), 328.

9 Sue Jourdan, 'Lady Harriet Reade (1727–1811) of Shipton Court', *Wychwoods History*, 12 (1997), 50.

10 Donald Winnicott, *Playing and Reality* (Harmondsworth: Pelican Books, 1974), 76.

11 F.M.H. Parker, *The Vale of Lyvennet: Its Picturesque Peeps and Legendary Lore* (Kendal: Titus Walker, 1910), ix.

12 Timothy Green, 'Remarkable Dame Sitwell: I am an unpopular electric eel set in a pond of catfish', *Life Magazine*, 54, no. 1 (4 January 1963), 61.

1 The 'Enston-Rock' pages 13–25

1 Thomas Bushell refers to what is now generally known as the 'Enstone Marvels' as the 'Enston-Rock' in *A Just and True Remonstrance of His Majesties Mines-Royall in the Principality of Wales* (London: E.G., 1641), n.p. His contemporaries referred to it as 'Mr. Bushells Rock'. Ole Borch was also known as Olaus Borrichius or Olavus Borrichus.

2 Paige Johnson and Matthew Maynard, 'The Garden Notes of Ole Borch: Scientific Traveller and Garden Visitor, 1662–63', *Garden History*, 41, no. 2 (2013), 201.

3 The Earl of Danby founded the Oxford Physic Garden (now the Oxford Botanic Garden) in 1621; the king to Henry Earl of Danby, 3 September 1635, *Calendar of State Papers, Domestic Series, of the Reign of Charles I. 1635*, ed. John Bruce (London: Longman, Green, Longman, Robert & Green, 1865), 366.

4 Thomas Bushell, *The Severall Speeches and Songs, at the presentment of Mr Bvshells Rock to the Qveens Most Excellent Majesty* (Oxford: printed by Leonard Lichfield, 1636), line 74, title page. 'For better enabling Bushell's endeavours, the king desires the Earl [of Danby] to call such as it may concern for disposing the highway to some other place, which may be most convenient to his Majesty's design, trusting he will find no man so refractory as he should have cause to certify his obstinacy to the King.' The king to Henry Earl of Danby, 3 September 1635, *Calendar of State Papers*, 366; Robert Plot, *The Natural History of Oxford-shire, Being an Essay toward the Natural History of England* (Oxford: The Theatre; London: S. Miller, 1677), 236.

5 Andrew Clark, ed., *'Brief Lives,' chiefly of Contemporaries, set down by John Aubrey, between the Years 1669 & 1696*, 2 vols (Oxford: Clarendon Press, 1898), 1:130, 131. William Blundell, *A History of the Isle of Man ... 1648–1656, Printed from a Manuscript in the Possession of the Manx Society*, ed. William Harrison, 2 vols (Douglas: Manx Society, 1876–7), 1:34.

6 Blundell, *History*, 1:34.

7 Blundell, *History*, 1:35.

8 Thomas Bushell, *The First Part of Youths Errors: Written by Thomas Bushel, the superlative prodigall* (London: by T. Harper, 1628); Blundell, *History*, 1:34.

9 Thomas Bushell, *Mr. Bushel's Minerall Overtures* (London: s.n., 1659), A3.

10 Ruth Scurr, *John Aubrey: My Own Life* (London: Vintage Digital, 2015), 60.

11 John Aubrey, *Aubrey's Brief Lives*, ed. Ruth Scurr (London: Vintage, 2016), 43. The discovery of the rock was not perhaps as serendipitous as Aubrey suggests: the name of the village of Enstone derives from the word 'enstone', which in contemporary parlance meant to petrify. Giovanni Florio, *Queen Anna's New World of Words, or Dictionarie of the Italian and the English tongues*, 2 parts (London: printed by Melch. Bradwood for Edw. Blount and William Barret, 1611), 1:258.

12 Lieutenant Hammond, 'A Relation of a Short Survey of the Western Counties made by a Lieutenant of the Military Company in Norwich in 1635', ed. L. G. Wickham Legg, Camden third series, 52, *Camden Miscellany*, vol. 16 (London: Royal Historical Society, 1936), 81–3. We know nothing about Hammond, but scholars have surmised that

he was very likely an antiquary with a legal background.

13 Hammond, 'A Relation', 81.

14 Thomas Bushell, 'Post-Script to the Judicious Reader', in *An Extract by Mr. Bushell of his late Abridgment of the Lord Chancellor Bacons Philosophical Theory in Mineral Prosecutions* (London: Tho. Leach, 1660), 21.

15 Aubrey, *Brief Lives*, 43.

16 Scurr, *John Aubrey*, 61.

17 Hammond, 'Relation', 82.

18 Hammond, 'Relation', 82.

19 Hammond, 'Relation', 82.

20 Paul Woodfield, 'Early Buildings in Gardens in England', in *Garden Archaeology: Papers presented to a Conference at Knuston Hall, Northamptonshire, April 1988*, ed. Anthony Ernest Brown, Research report no. 78 (London: Council for British Archaeology, 1991), 134.

21 Hammond, 'Relation', 82.

22 Hammond, 'Relation', 82–3.

23 Scurr, *John Aubrey*, 60.

24 Hammond, 'Relation', 81.

25 Hammond, 'Relation', 81.

26 Bushell, *Severall Speeches and Songs*, line 101.

27 The hermit also told the story of Bushell's moral transformation and his ambition to continue in his pious ways. The second act entailed a 'Contemplation' upon the rock. This was followed by 'a Sonnet within the pillar of the Table at the Banquet'; a dialogue with Echo; and closed with a farewell song, expressing thanks for the royal visit and sadness at the king and queen's departure.

28 Aubrey, *Brief Lives*, 42.

29 C. E. McGee, 'The Presentment of Bushell's Rock: Place, Politics, and Theatrical Self-Promotion', *Medieval & Renaissance Drama in England*, 16 (2003), 39.

30 C. E. Challis, ed., *A New History of the Royal Mint* (Cambridge: Cambridge University Press, 1992), 282. Bushell was later asked to establish mints at Oxford and Bristol.

31 Aubrey, *Brief Lives*, 43.

32 Scurr, *John Aubrey*, 61.

33 Roy Strong, *The Renaissance Garden in England* (London: Thames and Hudson, 1979), 130.

34 Francis Bacon, *New Atlantis and the Great Instauration*, ed. Jerry Weinberger (Chichester: Wiley Blackwell, 2017), 100.

35 Both Francis Bacon and Salomon de Caus were members of the scientific salon at Prince Henry's court.

36 Translated and quoted in Strong, *Renaissance Garden*, 96, n.10.

37 Lady Charlotte Lee, Countess of Lichfield (née Lady Charlotte Fitzroy, 1664–1718), was the illegitimate daughter of Charles II.

38 Plot, *Natural History of Oxford-shire*, 236.

39 Plot, *Natural History of Oxford-shire*, 236.

40 Scurr, *John Aubrey*, 155.

41 Scurr, *John Aubrey*, 155.

42 Charles Herle, *Worldly Policy and Moral Prudence …* (London: printed for Sa. Gellibrand, at the Ball in St Pauls Churchyard, 1654), 195.

43 Aubrey, *Brief Lives*, 54.

44 John Evelyn, *The Diary of John Evelyn (1620 to 1706)* (London: Macmillan, 1908), 232.

2 Lady Broughton's 'Miniature Copy of the Swiss Glaciers' pages 27–39

1 Joel Elias Springarn, 'Henry Winthrop Sargent and the Early History of Landscape Gardening and Ornamental Horticulture in Dutchess County, New York', in *Year Book of the Dutchess County Historical Society*, vol. 22 (New York: Dutchess County Historical Society, 1937), 10.

2 H. W. Sargent, 'Impressions of English Scenery', *Magazine of Horticulture, Botany, and All Useful Discoveries and Improvements in Rural Affairs*, 31 (1865), 325.

3 'Striking' is the process of taking a piece of the stem or root from a source plant and placing it in a suitable medium, such as moist soil, with a view to creating a new plant independent of the parent.

4 Sargent, 'Impressions', 326.

5 Sargent, 'Impressions', 327.

6 Sargent, 'Impressions', 327–8.

7 Sargent, 'Impressions', 328.

8 [John Loudon], 'Hoole House …', *Gardener's Magazine*, 14 (1838), 353; [John Loudon], 'General Results of a Gardening Tour', *Gardener's Magazine*, 7 (1831), 551.

9 Thomas Moule, *The English Counties Delineated*, 2 vols (London: George Virtue, 1837), 2:271; Cheshire Archives and Local Studies, Chester, DDB/F/17.

10 Brent Elliot, *Victorian Gardens* (London: Batsford, 1986), 47.

11 [Loudon], 'Hoole House', 353.

12 [Loudon], 'Hoole House', 353.

13 *Liverpool Standard*, 21 January 1851. This is a republication of an extract from the *Gardener's Magazine* with commentary. Loudon was not entirely satisfied with the woodcuts: 'On the small scale of our engravings, and without the aid of colour, it is altogether impossible to give an adequate idea of the singularity and beauty of this rocky boundary' ([Loudon], 'Hoole House', 358).

14 [Loudon], 'Hoole House', 359

15 [Loudon], 'Hoole House', 355.

16 [Loudon], 'Hoole House', 355–6.

17 [Loudon], 'Hoole House', 357.

18 [Loudon], 'Hoole House', 357.

19 [Loudon], 'Hoole House', 358.

20 '[Loudon], 'Hoole House', 358–9.

21 '[Loudon], 'Hoole House', 359.

22 Jane Loudon, 'On Rockwork', *Ladies' Magazine of Gardening* (London: William Smith, 1842), 7, 5.

23 Loudon, 'On Rockwork', 7.

24 Loudon, 'On Rockwork', 10.

25 Thomas Raffles, *Letters during a tour through some parts of France, Savoy, Switzerland* (Liverpool: Longman, Hurst, 1818), 192.

26 Mary Wollstonecraft Shelley, *Frankenstein; or, The Modern Prometheus* [1818], ed. D. L. Macdonald and Kathleen Scherf, facsimile of 3rd edn (Peterborough, Ont., and Buffalo, N.Y.: Broadview Press, 2012), 117.

27 Loudon, 'On Rockwork', 7.

28 Sir Philip de Malpas Grey-Egerton, *A Short Account of the Possessors of Oulton* (London: Hatchards for private circulation, 1869), 29; Howard Colvin, *A Biographical Dictionary of British Architects 1600–1840* (London: John Murray, 1978), 874.

29 Will of Dame Eliza Broughton, Widow of Hoole House, Cheshire, National Archives, Kew, ref. PROB 11/2249/182.

30 Edwards was given the generous bequest of nineteen guineas.

31 Will of Dame Eliza Broughton.

32 Thomas A. Hose, ed., *Geoheritage and Geotourism: A European Perspective* (Woodbridge: Boydell Press, 2016), 58.

33 The 'Celtic Cabinet' was acquired from John Britton when the Wiltshire Archaeological and Natural History Society and Devizes Museum were founded in 1853. The megalithic subjects of the watercolours which decorate it are identified; two of the paintings are ascribed to John Sell Cotman; the others are related to topographic artists in John Britton's employment. The models in the cabinet of Stonehenge and Avebury are identified as standard products of Henry Browne, the first guardian of Stonehenge. The cabinet was made, probably about 1824, for George Watson Taylor of Erlestoke Park, Devizes.

34 Browne made several models on different scales, 'and the mould being preserved, these were afterwards sold by his son, together with some of his own drawings equally accurate, to occasional visitors' (William Long, *Stonehenge*

and its Barrows (Devizes: H. F. & E. Bull, 1876), 78n).

35 Sir James Edward Smith, *A Sketch of a Tour on the Continent, in the Years 1786 and 1787 ...* , vol. 3 (London: J. Davis, 1807), 162.

36 William Wordsworth, *The Prose Works of William Wordsworth*, ed. A. B. Grosart, 3 vols (London: Edward Moxon, 1876), 2:235.

37 Susan Stewart, *On Longing: Narratives of the Miniature, the Gigantic, the Souvenir, the Collection* (Durham, N.C., and London: Duke University Press, 1993), 66.

38 Andrew Jackson Downing, *A Treatise on the Theory and Practice of Landscape Gardening* (New York: Wiley & Putnam, 1841), 394n.

39 Downing, *Treatise*, 394n.

3 Friar Park pages 41–51

1 For the chapter title, see 'Alpinism at Home', *The Bystander*, 30 July 1913, 263. The golden age of alpinism was the decade between Alfred Wallis's ascent of the Wetterhorn in 1854 and Edward Whymper's ascent of the Matterhorn in 1865.

2 'Alpine Tourists', *The Times*, 20 September 1865, 10.

3 'Our City Article', *Tatler*, no. 192 (1 March 1905), 349; Jehu Junior, 'Mr Frank Crisp', *Vanity Fair*, issue 1126, no. 471 (31 May 1890), 477.

4 'Sir F. Crisp. Lawyer and Gardener', *The Times*, 1 May 1919, 10.

5 C. H. Curtis, 'Friar Park, Henley-on-Thames', *Gardeners' Magazine*, 41 (1898), 442; Jennifer Sherwood and Nikolaus Pevsner, *The Buildings of England: Oxfordshire* (Harmondsworth: Penguin Books, 1975), 639.

6 Quoted in Sherwood and Pevsner, *The Buildings of England*, 639.

7 'Gardeners at Friar Park', *Surrey Mirror*, 15 August 1913, 5.

8 'Sir Frank Crisp, Bart. LL.B, J.P.', *The Garden*, 30 December 1916, iv. This volume of *The Garden* was dedicated to Crisp.

9 Sir Frank Crisp, 'The Public in Private Grounds: Experiences of Landlords. To the Editor of *The Times*', *The Times*, 21 August 1913.

10 'Friar Park, Henley', *Gardeners' Chronicle*, 26, 3rd series (28 October 1899), 321.

11 'Gardens Old & New: The Alpine Garden, Friar Park, Henley, the Residence of Mr Frank Crisp', *Country Life*, 18 (5 August 1905), 162.

12 'Friar Park', *Gardeners' Chronicle*, 321.

13 'Friar Park', *Gardeners' Chronicle*, 322.

14 'The First Collection of Antique Microscopes Ever Catalogued for Sale: Sir Frank Crisp's Hobby', *Illustrated London News*, 14 February 1925, 250–51.

15 'Friar Park', *Gardeners' Chronicle*, 321.

16 'Gardeners at Friar Park', *Surrey Mirror*, 5.

17 'Alpinism at Home', *The Bystander*, 263; 'Building Imitation Alps of Rocks and Concrete on an English Nobleman's Estate', *Popular Science Monthly*, 93, no. 2 (August 1918), 262–3.

18 'Friar Park', *Gardeners' Chronicle*, 322.

19 'Gardens Old & New', *Country Life*, 162.

20 'Gardeners at Friar Park', *Surrey Mirror*, 5.

21 'Building Imitation Alps', *Popular Science Monthly*, 262.

22 Henry Correvon, 'The Rock Garden at Friar Park', *Country Life*, 33 (3 May 1913), 641–2.

23 Charles T. Druery, 'Friar Park Rock Garden', *Gardeners' Magazine*, 54 (1911), 641.

24 Correvon, 'Rock Garden', 641. Wilhelm Miller, 'What England Can Teach Us About Rock Gardening', *Country Life in America*, 16 (August 1909), 391.

25 Robinson quoted in Brent Elliot, 'The British Rock Garden in the Twentieth Century', *Occasional Papers from the* RHS *Lindley Library*, 6 (Dorchester: Advantage

Digital Print, 2011), 18; Edmund Howard Jenkins, *The Small Rock Garden* (London: Country Life and George Newnes; New York: Charles Scribner's Sons, 1913), 6.

26 Correvon, 'Rock Garden', 641.

27 Correvon, 'Rock Garden', 641.

28 Correvon, 'Rock Garden', 642.

29 Correvon, 'Rock Garden', 641.

30 'Finchley Chrysanthemum Society Outing', *Hendon and Finchley Times*, 26 July 1912.

31 Ottoline Morrell, *Memoirs of Lady Ottoline Morrell: A Study in Friendship, 1873–1915* (London: Faber, 1964), 83.

32 Montague Free, 'The Rock Garden of the Brooklyn Botanic Garden', *Brooklyn Botanic Garden Record*, 20, no. 3 (May 1931), 196.

33 Charles Thonger, *The Book of Rock and Water Gardens* (London and New York: John Lane, 1907), 12.

34 A.T.J., 'The Garden: Gardens in Miniature', *Country Life*, 66 (21 December 1929), xl.

35 'Ice Carnival: The Scene in the Great Hall', *St James's Gazette*, 14 March 1889.

36 Correvon, 'Rock Garden', 644.

4 Sir Charles Isham's Gardens at Lamport Hall pages 53–67

1 For the chapter title quotation, see Arthur Oswald, 'The Gardens at Lamport Hall – II: The Northamptonshire Home of Sir Gyles Isham, Bt.', *Country Life*, 128 (17 November 1960), 1164. For the text quotation, Oswald, 'The Gardens at Lamport Hall', 1166. Sir Charles carried out much of the work in the rockery, but he had between five and seven gardeners assisting him in the rest of the pleasure grounds. Neil Lyon, 'Lamport Hall Gardens', file notes (2016), Lamport Hall Archive.

2 [Charles Isham], *Emily* (Lamport: Lamport Hall, 1899), n.p.

3 'Testimony of Sir Charles Isham', *The Spiritualist*, 3, no. 59 (1 September 1873), 314. Isham served on the Council of the British National Association of Spiritualists (est. 1873).

4 Isham was an Associate of the British Vegetarian Society.

5 John Preston Neale, 'Lamport Hall, Northamptonshire', in *Views of the Seats of Noblemen and Gentlemen, in England, Wales, Scotland and Ireland*, vol. 2 (London: Sherwood, Neely and Jones, 1819), n.p.

6 'Lamport', *Gardeners' Chronicle*, 22 (25 September 1897), 210.

7 Lyon, 'Gardens'.

8 'Lamport', *Gardeners' Chronicle*, 210.

9 'Rambles Round About – No. 14: Lamport', *Northampton Mercury*, 4 September 1869.

10 [Isham], *Emily*. Presumably named in honour of the celebrated London-based importer of wild beasts: 'Mr Jamrach's College for Young Beasts', *Leisure Hour*, no. 338 (17 June 1858), 377–80.

11 Lyon, 'Gardens'.

12 'Lamport', *Gardeners' Chronicle*, 210.

13 Robert Fish, 'Lamport Hall', *Journal of Horticulture, Cottage Gardener and Country Gentleman*, 22, new series (20 June 1872), 502–3.

14 Fish, 'Lamport Hall', 503.

15 Fish, 'Lamport Hall', 503.

16 'Lamport', *Gardeners' Chronicle*, 209.

17 'Lamport', *Gardeners' Chronicle*, 209.

18 'Lamport', *Gardeners' Chronicle*, 209.

19 'Lamport', *Gardeners' Chronicle*, 209.

20 'Lamport', *Gardeners' Chronicle*, 209.

21 'Lamport', *Gardeners' Chronicle*, 209.

22 'Lamport', *Gardeners' Chronicle*, 209.

23 'Lamport', *Gardeners' Chronicle*, 210–11.

24 Lyon, 'Gardens'.

25 Herbert Pratt, 'A Wonderful Rock Garden', *Strand Magazine*, 19 (January–June 1900), 225;

H. O. Nethercote, *The Pytchley Hunt: Past and Present* (London: S. Low, Marston, Searle & Rivington, 1888), 321–2.

26 Pratt, 'A Wonderful Rock Garden', 229; 'Obituary: Sir Charles Isham, Bart.', *The Garden*, 63 (18 April 1903), 270.

27 Richard Potter, 'Unique Alpine Garden', and Mrs Newsham, 'A Tribute to the Lamport Rockery', both reproduced in *Emily*; 'Obituary', *The Garden*, 270. Potter directed the installation and planting at many of James Backhouse's best-known rock gardens, including those at Warley and Friar Park.

28 Quoted in 'Lamport', *Gardeners' Chronicle*, 209.

29 [Charles Isham], 'Notes on Gnomes and Remarks on Rock Gardens: The Lamport Rockery' (Lamport: Lamport Hall, 1888 edn). The publication was updated and reprinted almost annually from 1884 until the late 1890s.

30 [Isham], 'Notes' (1888 edn).

31 [Isham], 'Notes' (1894 edn), Lamport Hall Archive, ref. NRO YZ 7777.

32 See Walter Scott, *The Talisman* (Edinburgh: A. Constable and Co.; London: Hurst, Robinson and Co., 1825); Lyon, 'Gardens'.

33 First published in the occultist journal *Medium and Daybreak* (November 1889), and reprinted in *Emily*.

34 [Isham], *Emily*; [Isham], 'Notes' (1884 edn).

35 Pratt, 'A Wonderful Rock Garden', 229.

36 'Grand Fete at Lamport Hall Gardens', *Northampton Mercury*, 11 September 1869.

37 'Let all who feel dejected and at a loss for explanation, / Instead of taking psychic, take a pass to Lamport Station / A lovely path, but much too short, leads to Elysian ground, / Where much to cheer the heavy heart is visible around. / E'en those who suffer from hard times, bowed with excess of grief, / Will frequently experience miraculous relief.'

Charles Isham, 'Delights of Lamport' [n.d.], reproduced in *Emily*.

38 Nethercote, *The Pytchley Hunt*, 322.

39 [Isham], *Emily*.

40 Samuel Reynolds, *The Memories of Dean Hole* (London: Edward Arnold, 1893), 209.

5 Topiary on a Gargantuan Scale
pages 69–81

1 This chapter is based on Todd Longstaffe-Gowan, 'Topiary on a Gargantuan Scale: The Clipped "Yew-trees" at Four Ancient London Churchyards', *London Gardener*, 11 (2005–6), 70–86. For the quotation, see Richard Brinsley Peake, *Memoirs of the Colman Family*, 2 vols (London: Bentley, 1841), 2:290.

2 In Hood's version, the two sisters both display general vanity and hauteur – the latter not merely in response to the 'unfruitful sighs of young men', but also, for example, in 'frowning reluctant duty from the poor' ([Thomas Hood], 'The Two Peacocks of Bedfont', *London Magazine*, October 1822, 304, line 19).

3 David Jacques, 'English Topiary', *Topiarius*, Autumn 2000, 10–14; Charles H. Curtis and W. Gibson, *The Book of Topiary* (London and New York: Bodley Head, 1904); and Miles Hadfield, *Topiary and Ornamental Hedges* (London: Adam & Charles Black, 1971).

4 Joseph Addison, unnamed essay originally published in the *Spectator*, no. 414 (25 June 1712), in *The Works of the Late Right Honourable Joseph Addison, Esq.*, 4 vols (London: printed for Jacob Tonson, 1721), 3:497.

5 See W. A. Lawson, *A New Orchard and Garden* (London: R. Æsop for R. Jackson, 1618), 58; Robert Plot, *The Natural History of Oxford-shire* (Oxford: The Theatre, 1677), 260–61; and Alexander Pope, 'An Essay on Verdant Sculpture', *The Guardian*, 173 (29 September 1713).

6 Peter Razzell, ed., *The Journals of Two Travellers in England in Elizabethan and Early*

Stuart England: Thomas Platter and Horatio Busino (London: Caliban, 1995), 68.

7 Joseph Addison's term for commercial nursery plants grown for sale to the 'great Modellers of Gardens' who marshalled 'Magazines of Plants' to create new gardens (Addison, *Spectator*, no. 414 (25 June 1712)).

8 'Cits' is eighteenth-century London slang for 'citizens', or members of the urban mercantile classes.

9 Pope, 'Essay on Verdant Sculpture'. The 'Giants' are sixteenth-century stone figures of Gog and Magog that formerly stood in front of the Guildhall in the City of London (and are now inside the same). The statues commemorated two legendary giants, originally known as Gogmagog and Corineus (the former an ancient inhabitant of Britain and the latter a Trojan invader), representing warriors in a supposed conflict which resulted in the founding in 1,000 BC of Albion's capital city, New Troy.

10 See T. Longstaffe-Gowan, *The Gardens and Parks at Hampton Court Palace* (London: Frances Lincoln, 2005), 46, 88, 192–4, for an account of a similar antiquarian inspired phenomenon at the royal gardens in the late eighteenth and early nineteenth centuries.

11 These yews were commemorated in two ballads: [Edmund Gayton], 'Upon Mr Bobards Yew-men of the Guards to the Physick Garden' (1662), and John Drope, 'Upon the most hopefull and ever Flourishing Sprouts of Valour, the indefatigable Centryes or Armed *Gyants* cut in Yew at the *Physick Garden* in *Oxford*' (London: W. Hall, 1664). Gayton also refers to the 'Highgate-*Hercules*, / In [the] Garden of the good Marquess'. The location and appearance of this yew giant remains unknown.

12 'Mould' was the eighteenth-century term commonly used to describe soil.

13 The Earls of Arlington took their name from Harlington. Henry Bennet (son of Sir John Bennet of Dawley) was raised to the peerage in 1663 as Viscount Thetford and Earl of Arlington.

14 See Francis Clive-Ross, *The Church of St Mary the Virgin, East Bedfont, Middlesex* (Bedfont: The Vicarage [the author], 1978), 15–16.

15 'Account of the Village of Bedfont', *Gentleman's Magazine*, September 1825, 201–2. The article is accompanied by an engraving of the Peacocks in the churchyard.

16 The earliest record of payments for 'Cutting the Yew' in the churchwarden's accounts date from 1756. Messrs Hawkins and Phillips carried out the cutting between 1756 and 1768.

17 Three pencil drawings, formerly in the collection of Sir J. Gardner D. Engelheart, KCB, photos of which are included in a nineteenth-century Sherborn Family Scrapbook compiled by Charles Davies Sherborn, now deposited in the English Heritage National Monuments Record, Swindon.

18 Peake, *Memoirs of the Colman Family*, 2:290.

19 J. Norris Brewer, *London and Middlesex; or, An Historical, Commercial, & Descriptive Survey of the Metropolis of Great Britain* (London: J. Harris, 1816), 514–15.

20 The bench was present from at least 1731. See David Pam, *A History of Enfield, Volume One – before 1837: A Parish near London* (London: Enfield Preservation Society, 1990), 293.

21 Richard Steele and Joseph Addison, *Selections from the Tatler and the Spectator*, ed. Angus Ross (Harmondsworth: Penguin Books, 1988), 380, from Joseph Addison, 'The Pleasures of the Imagination, 5: Primary Pleasures: The Effects of Nature and Art Compared and Contrasted', *Spectator*, no. 414 (25 June 1712).

22 Although Wordsworth recalls that the 'spread' of the tree was 'much diminished by mutilation': Michael G. Baron and Derek Denman, eds, *Wordsworth and the Famous Lorton Yew Tree* (Lorton & Derwent Fells Local History Society, 2004), 13.

23 'Yew-Trees' (1815), published in *Wordsworth and the Famous Lorton Yew Tree*, 12.

24 Loudon included the Harlington yew in his 'biography of celebrated yew trees', and published an illustration of it. He remarked: 'the tree ceased to be clipped, we are informed by a present clerk, about 1780 or 1790; and it is now suffered to assume its natural shape.' J. C. Loudon, *Arboretum et Fruticetum Britannicum*, 8 vols (London: printed for the author, 1838), 4:2076–7. Loudon also illustrated the yew in its 'natural shape' (8:293).

25 Philip Sherwood, *Harlington and Harmondsworth: A History and Guide* (Stroud: Tempus Publishing, 2002), 91.

26 James Thorne, *Handbook to the Environs of London; Alphabetically Arranged … pt.1* (London: John Murray, 1876), 318. In 1875 the tree measured in circumference 5.44 m/17ft 10 inches at 1.25 m/4 ft from the ground.

27 W. Dallimore, *Holly, Yew and Box: With Notes on Other Evergreens* (London and New York: John Lane, 1908), 188–9.

28 In 1990 a survey of ancient yew trees conducted by the Conservation Foundation estimated the Harlington yew to be over 1,000 years old.

29 Clive-Ross, *The Church of St Mary the Virgin*, 15–16.

30 Walter Jerrold, *Highways and Byways in Middlesex* (London: Macmillan and Co., 1909), 199–200.

31 Dallimore, *Holly, Yew and Box*, 190.

32 Clive-Ross, *The Church of St Mary the Virgin*, 15–16; Barry D. Cripps, 'A Brief History of East Bedfont' (1960), typescript, ex Derek Sherborn Collection, Bedfont House, deposited with the National Monuments Record (English Heritage) 2005.

6 Lord Petersham's Gardens at Elvaston Castle pages 83–97

1 Princess Dorothea Lieven, *The Private Letters of Princess Lieven to Prince Metternich*, ed. Peter Quennell (London: John Murray, 1937), 132; Joseph Knight, rev. K. D. Reynolds, 'Maria Foote [Married Name Maria Stanhope, Countess of Harrington] (1797–1867), Actress', *Oxford Dictionary of National Biography* (online edn), Oxford University Press, 2004, www.oxforddnb.com.

2 'Memoirs of Celebrated Actresses: Maria Foote, Countess of Harrington', *Bow Bells: A Weekly Magazine of General Literature and Art*, 20 (1874), 546.

3 Knight, 'Maria Foote'.

4 W. H. Mallock, *Memoirs of Life and Literature* (London: Chapman & Hall, 1920), 116–17.

5 'Charles (Stanhope), Earl of Harrington', in George Edward Cokayne and Vicary Gibbs, eds, *The Complete Peerage*, vol. 6 (London: St Catherine Press, 1926), 327; 'William Barron', *Gardeners' Chronicle*, 25 April 1891, 523, 522; R. Glendinning, 'Elvaston Castle, the Seat of the Earl of Harrington', *Gardeners' Chronicle*, 8 December 1849, 773.

6 Glendinning, 'Elvaston Castle', 8 December 1849, 773.

7 'William Barron', *Gardeners' Chronicle*, 25 April 1891, 522.

8 William Barron, *The British Winter Garden: Being a Practical Treatise on Evergreens …* (London: Bradbury and Evans, 1852), 1.

9 Barron described his techniques in *The British Winter Garden*.

10 R. Glendinning, 'Elvaston Castle, the Seat of the Earl of Harrington', *Gardeners' Chronicle*, 9 February 1850, 84.

11 Glendinning, 'Elvaston Castle', 9 February 1850, 84. 'Barron provides very little information concerning the source of these trees and seems to have been unconcerned with the effects of denuding places of well-established specimens' (Paul Elliott, Charles Watkins and Stephen Daniels, 'William Barron (1805–91) and Nineteenth-Century British Arboriculture: Evergreens in Victorian Industrializing Society', *Garden History*, 35, supplement (2007), 142).

12 'William Barron', *Gardeners' Chronicle*, 523.

13 Note by J. C. Loudon, in William Barron, 'List of the Species and Varieties of Coniferous Plants in the Pinetum at Elvaston Castle, Derbyshire, the Seat of the Earl of Harrington', *Gardener's Magazine*, 14 (1838), 79.

14 Note by Loudon, in Barron, 'List', 79.

15 'William Barron', *Gardeners' Chronicle*, 523.

16 'The Flower Garden', *Quarterly Review*, 70 (1842), 234; R. Glendinning, 'Elvaston Castle, the Seat of the Earl of Harrington', *Gardeners' Chronicle*, 15 December 1849, 789.

17 The Conductor [J. C. Loudon], 'Recollections of a Tour … made in May, 1839', *Gardener's Magazine*, 15 (1839), 458.

18 George Cockburn, A *Voyage to Cadiz and Gibraltar: Up the Mediterranean to Sicily and Malta in 1810 and 11*, 2 vols (London: J. Harding, 1815), 1:373–4.

19 William Turner, *Journal of a Tour in the Levant*, 3 vols (London: John Murray, 1820), 1:21.

20 Robert Stuart [pseud. Robert Stuart Meikleham], A *Dictionary of Architecture … alphabetically arranged …*, 3 vols (London: Jones & Co. [1830]), n.p., under 'Antics' ('fancies that have no foundation in nature').

21 [Loudon], 'Recollections', 458–9.

22 [Loudon], 'Recollections', 459.

23 [Loudon], 'Recollections', 460.

24 Janet Myles, *L. N. Cottingham 1787–1847: Architect of the Gothic Revival* (London: Lund Humphries, 1996), 8.

25 Mark Girouard, *Return to Camelot* (New Haven and London: Yale University Press, 1981), 88.

26 Girouard, *Return to Camelot*, 88.

27 Edmund Spenser, *The Faerie Queene*, book 2, canto 12. See Joseph Black et al., eds, *The Broadview Anthology of British Literature, Volume 2: The Renaissance and the Early Seventeenth Century*, 3rd edn (Peterborough, Ont.: Broadview Press, 2016), 281.

28 'Brief Remarks: Opening of Elvaston Gardens', *Floricultural Cabinet, and Florist's Magazine* (1852), 183–4.

29 Glendinning, 'Elvaston Castle', 15 December 1849, 789; Mark Girouard, *A Country House Companion* (London: Magna Books, 1993), 199.

30 'William Barron', *Gardeners' Chronicle*, 523.

31 Brent Elliot, *Victorian Gardens* (London: Batsford, 1986), 84; Glendinning, 'Elvaston Castle', 8 December 1849, 773.

32 Thomas Baines, 'Elvaston Castle', *Gardeners' Chronicle*, 30 December 1876, 838.

33 Glendinning, 'Elvaston Castle', 15 December 1849, 789.

34 E. Adveno Brooke, 'Elvaston Castle, Derbyshire … The Seat of the Right Hon. the Earl of Harrington', in *The Gardens of England* (London: T. McLean, [1858]).

35 Elliott, Watkins and Daniels, 'William Barron (1805–91)', 131.

36 Robert Buist, 'Elvaston Castle', *Horticulturist and Journal of Rural Art and Taste*, 7 (May 1857), 209.

37 Mark Johnston, *Street Trees in Britain* (Oxford: Windgather Press, 2017), 123.

38 Buist, 'Elvaston Castle', 211.

39 Thomas Appleby, 'Coniferae', *Cottage Gardener*, 15 July 1852, 244.

7 The Countess of Dudley's 'Stop and Buy' Topiaries *pages 99–109*

1 'A Plucky Vice Queen', *The Sketch*, 41 (11 February 1903), 130.

2 'Panic in the City – Stoppage of Overend, Gurney, and Co.'s Bank', *Reading Mercury*, 12 May 1866, 4.

3 'Our Ladies' Pages', *The Sketch*, 41 (18 March 1903), 345.

4 'Death of Lady Dudley', *The Times*, 28 June 1920, 16.

5 Laura Troubridge, *Memories and Reflections* (London: William Heinemann, 1925), 123, 133.

6 See Amanda Andrews, 'The Great Ornamentals: New Vice-Regal Women and their Imperial Work', D.Phil. thesis, School of Humanities, University of Western Sydney, 2004, 290–352.

7 'Garden Memorandum', *Gardeners' Chronicle and Agricultural Gazette*, 19 November 1864, 1111.

8 Brian Dix, '"Barbarous in its Magnificence": The Archaeological Investigation and Restoration of W. A. Nesfield's Parterre Design for the East Garden at Witley Court, Worcestershire', *Garden History*, 39, no. 1 (2011), 51. W. A. Nesfield (1794–1881) was commissioned in the late 1850s by William Humble Ward, later 1st Earl of Dudley.

9 'The South Fountain, Witley Court', *Illustrated London News*, 40 (15 March 1862), 275.

10 Brent Elliot, *Victorian Gardens* (London: Batsford, 1986), 144 caption, fig. 56.

11 Anon., 'Witley', *Journal of Horticulture, Cottage Gardener, and Home Farmer*, 19, 3rd series (24 September 1889), 263.

12 'The South Fountain, Witley Court', *Illustrated London News*, 275.

13 Bill Pardoe, *Witley Court and Church: Life and Luxury in a Great Country House* (Gloucester: Peter Huxtable Designs, 1986), 22.

14 D. T. Fish, 'The Fountain at Witley Court', *Gardeners' Chronicle*, 14 June 1873, 812.

15 Charles H. Curtis and W. Gibson, *The Book of Topiary* (London and New York: Bodley Head, 1904), 36. Curtis also rated the garden as foremost among the country's topiary gardens in 'An Ancient and Curious Craft: Revival of the Art of Topiary', *The Garden*, 84 (1920), 112.

16 S. Leonard Bastin, 'The Revival of Topiary', *Country Home*, 5 (1910), 122.

17 William Cutbush & Son ('Cutbushes at Cutbush') of Barnet and Highgate; Cheal & Sons of Crawley; and Richmond Nurseries, Windlesham.

18 Pardoe, *Witley Court*, 21.

19 Miss Gratienne Violette Charton was described in 1929 as 'a woman of remarkable and versatile ability ... a talented linguist, with a wonderful memory, abounding energy, and a mind stored with varied knowledge. She wrote well in both prose and poetry, having contributed under the name of "Hackleplume" many articles on social and political topics to the journal of the National Citizens' Union, and was author of *My Lady's Garden*' ('In Memoriam', *Literary Guide and Rationalist Review*, no. 391, new series (January 1929), 75).

20 Vivien Newman, *Tumult & Tears: The Story of the Great War through the Eyes of its Women Poets* (Barnsley: Pen & Sword Books, 2016), p. 68.

21 Lady Dudley was appointed CBE in 1918 and awarded a Royal Red Cross medal later that year. She established in France the Australian Voluntary Hospital, funded by Australians and staffed by Australian doctors and nurses. She also worked as a hospital superintendent, Voluntary Aid Detachment nurse and anaesthetist.

22 John Klinkert, 'Sculpted Verdure', *The Globe*, 5 February 1920, 12.

23 [Shirley Hibberd], 'Topiary Gardening', *Littell's Living Age*, 141 (April–June 1879), 255.

24 [Hibberd], 'Topiary Gardening', 256.

25 Quoted in Curtis and Gibson, *Book of Topiary*, frontispiece.

26 Donald Winnicott, *Playing and Reality* (Harmondsworth: Pelican Books, 1974), 76. The Countess of Dudley had been very unhappy with her husband during their time in Ireland between 1902 and 1905.

8 Lady Reade and her 'Gaudy Natives of the Tropics' pages 111–125

1 W. F. Mavor, A New Description of Blenheim (Oxford: Munday & Slatter, 1817), 65.

2 Harriet Reade, widow of Sir J. Reade, 5th Baronet, of Barton, Berkshire: letters relating to her will, 1811–12; and Woodstock, Oxfordshire: letters relating to aviary at Blenheim Palace, 1811–12, British Library, London, Add. MS 61674, fols 107–17. Known as 'Dame Harriott Reade of Shipton under Wychwood' in her Last Will and Testament, though often referred to in the press as Dame Harriet Reade.

3 Dr Thomas Brookes's account is published in full in Sue Jourdan, 'Lady Harriet Reade (1727–1811) of Shipton Court', Wychwoods History, 12 (1997), 48–51. Brookes's account was first published, in part, in 'Singular Account of Lady Reade, of Shipton, in Oxfordshire, from the unpublished MS. of a Tourist', Saturday Magazine, 1, new series (1821), 197–9.

4 George Spencer, 4th Duke of Marlborough (1739–1817); Symonds mistakenly refers to Queen Charlotte. Dame Harriott's will makes clear that it was her intention to bequeath her 'Little quadruped animals' to Princess Frederica Charlotte, Duchess of York (1767–1820).

5 Jourdan, 'Lady Harriet Reade', 50.

6 Athalaricus [pseud.], 'Lady Reade's Remarkable Aviary', Gentleman's Magazine, 94 (June 1802), 494.

7 Athalaricus, 'Lady Reade's Remarkable Aviary', 494.

8 The generous legacies left by Lady Reade on her death to the vicar and his children suggest that they were on good and intimate terms. Will of Dame Harriott Reade, Widow of Shipton under Wychwood, Oxfordshire, National Archives, Kew, PROB 11/1529/218 (the will is twenty-nine pages long and numbered sequentially from 300r to 313r, including one additional leaf 304a r–v); the Revd Thomas Brookes DD was born, bred and died in Shipton under Wychwood.

9 Jourdan, 'Lady Harriet Reade', 48.

10 The whereabouts of Sir Joshua Reynolds's portrait of Harriet Lady Reade is presently unknown. There is no known portrait of the sitter by the artist; it may, however, be an unidentified work.

11 Jourdan, 'Lady Harriet Reade', 48.

12 Jourdan, 'Lady Harriet Reade', 49. There are some inaccuracies in the vicar's narrative, one of which seriously undermines his interpretation of Lady Reade's life: Thomas Reade in fact survived his mother. Dame Harriott was, as previously noted, married to the 5th Baronet and had twin sons in 1762. Their son John, 6th Baronet, married Jane Chandos Hoskyns in 1784 and they also had twins: one of these two little girls, Harriet, died a few days before her father, and her sister, Louisa, died shortly thereafter.

13 Jourdan, 'Lady Harriet Reade', 49.

14 Jourdan, 'Lady Harriet Reade', 49–50.

15 Jourdan, 'Lady Harriet Reade', 50.

16 Jourdan, 'Lady Harriet Reade', 50.

17 Jourdan, 'Lady Harriet Reade', 50.

18 Among the few notices in the press is the following published in the Gazetteer and New Daily Advertiser on 30 March 1791: 'Lady Reade is said to have received a slight wound in her hand from a dog; that soon afterwards died, with some symptoms approaching to madness. Her Ladyship is now by the sea side, and such precautions have been used, as will no doubt prevent any ill effects.'

19 J. P. Losty, 'Mary Impey, née Reade, Lady Impey', Oxford Dictionary of National Biography (online edn), Oxford University Press, 2004, www.oxforddnb.com.

20 Will of Dame Harriott Reade, 303r–v.

21 One of the five daughters of the barrister William Boscawen (1752–1811).

22 Will of Dame Harriott Reade, 309v.

23 Thomas Raikes, A Portion of the Journal Kept by Thomas Raikes, Esq.: From 1831 to 1847, 2 vols (London: Longman, Brown, Green & Longmans, 1856), 1:147.

24 Raikes, Journal, 1:147.

25 John Wilson Croker, The Croker Papers: The Correspondence and Diaries of the Late Right Honourable John Wilson Croker, Secretary to the Admiralty from 1809 to 1830, 3 vols (Cambridge: Cambridge University Press, 2012), 1:122.

26 Will of Dame Harriott Reade, 309v.

27 'Memoirs of the Life of Warren Hastings, first Governor-General of Bengal …', Edinburgh Review: Or Critical Journal, 74 (October 1841–January 1842), 252.

28 Sir Charles Lawson, The Private Life of Warren Hastings: First Governor-General of India (London: Sonnenschein, 1895), 166.

9 Lady Dorothy Nevill and her Ephemeral 'Exotic Groves'
pages 127–141

1 Edmund Gosse, 'Three Experiments in Portraiture: Lady Dorothy Nevill, An Open Letter', in Some Diversions of a Man of Letters (New York: Charles Scribner's Sons, 1920), 187.

2 Gosse, 'Three Experiments in Portraiture', 183. The letter was addressed to Baroness Winifred Anne Henrietta Christine Herbert Gardner Burghclere in January 1914.

3 'Lady Dorothy Neville', Country Life, 46 (1 November 1919), 563; Gosse, 'Three Experiments in Portraiture', 184–5.

4 Guy Nevill, The Reminiscences of Lady Dorothy Nevill (London: Edward Arnold, 1906), 59.

5 Gosse, 'Three Experiments in Portraiture', 186.

6 'Death of Lady Dorothy Nevill, Prominent Society Figure', Gloucester Journal, 29 March 1913, 3.

7 'Court and Society', Graphic, 21 September 1907, 382. Lord Zouche was Sir Cecil Augustus Bisshopp, 10th Baronet of Parham (1821–1849).

8 Ralph Nevill, The Life and Letters of Lady Dorothy Nevill (London: Methuen, 1919), 301.

9 Guy Nevill, Reminiscences, 77.

10 Benjamin Disraeli to Lady Dorothy, 21 April 1864, cited in Guy Nevill, Reminiscences, 209.

11 'Garden Memoranda', Gardeners' Chronicle and Agricultural Gazette, 27 September 1856, 647.

12 D. Deal [pseud. H. H. Dombrain], 'Dangstein', Journal of Horticulture, 5 January 1864, 9.

13 William Robinson, 'Garden Memoranda: Dangstein', Gardeners' Chronicle, 4 November 1865, 1039.

14 Dorothy Nevill, Under Five Reigns (London: Methuen, 1910), 80.

15 Deal, 'Dangstein', 9.

16 'Garden Memoranda', Gardeners' Chronicle and Agricultural Gazette, 647.

17 Walter G. Gaiger, 'The Late Mr James Vair', Journal of Horticulture, 14 (10 March 1887), 193.

18 [D.], 'Dangstein', Gardeners' Chronicle, 31 August 1861, 794; Gaiger, 'The Late Mr James Vair', 193; Obituary notice, Journal of Horticulture, 3 March 1887, 170.

19 See W. R. Trotter, 'The Glasshouses at Dangstein and their Contents', Garden History, 16, no. 1 (Spring 1988), 72–3, for an analysis of Dangstein's various hothouses.

20 Lady Dorothy Nevill to Sir Joseph Hooker, n.d., Directors' Correspondence, DC 36, fol. 326, Library and Archives, Royal Botanic Gardens Kew.

21 Guy Nevill, Reminiscences, 77.

22 Charles Darwin, Insectivorous Plants (London: John Murray, 1875), 282: 'one of the bits of meat excited so much secretion … that it flowed some way down the medial furrow, causing the inflection of the tentacles on both sides as far as it extended.'

23 Arthur Symons, *The Symbolist Movement in Literature* (New York: E. P. Dutton & Co., 1919), 250. Symons's essay 'Joris-Karl Huysmans' was first published in the *Fortnightly Review* (1892).

24 Charles Darwin to Dorothy Fanny Nevill, 12 November [1861], in Charles Darwin, *The Correspondence of Charles Darwin, Volume 9: 1861*, ed. Frederick Burkhardt et al. (Cambridge: Cambridge University Press, 1994), 338.

25 Charles Darwin, *The Various Contrivances by which Orchids are Fertilised by Insects* (London: John Murray, 1877), 158.

26 Guy Nevill, *Reminiscences*, 56.

27 'Garden Memoranda', *Gardeners' Chronicle and Agricultural Gazette*, 647.

28 Gosse, 'Three Experiments in Portraiture', 182.

29 Guy Nevill, *Reminiscences*, 80, 81.

30 Lady Dorothy Nevill to Sir Joseph Hooker, 24 April 1866, Directors' Correspondence, DC 97, fols 41–2, Library and Archives, Royal Botanic Gardens Kew.

31 'Occasional Notes', *Pall Mall Gazette*, 5 May 1879, 9.

32 Lady Dorothy Nevill to Sir Joseph Hooker, 1 May [1878], DC 97, fol. 45, Kew; Trotter, 'The Glasshouses at Dangstein', 88; Charles III was possibly advised to acquire the plants by the celebrated French plantsman and landscape improver Édouard André.

33 Gosse, 'Three Experiments in Portraiture', 194. Lady Dorothy Nevill to Sir Joseph Hooker, 19 June 1879, DC 97, fol. 49, Kew.

34 Lady Dorothy Nevill to Sir Joseph Hooker, n.d [1878], DC 97, fol. 47, Kew; Lady Dorothy Nevill to George Maw, 16 December 1879, letters to George Maw, RHS Lindley Library, London, GB 803 MAW/1/284 (Album 3).

35 For 'The Memoirs of Lady Dorothy Nevill', see Virginia Woolf, *The Essays of Virginia Woolf, Volume I: 1904–1912*, ed. Andrew McNeillie (London: Hogarth Press, 1986), 178–83; 'Behind Bars' (1919) was later republished as 'Outlines' (1925). See Virginia Woolf, *The Essays of Virginia Woolf, Volume IV: 1926–1928*, ed. Andrew McNeillie (London: Hogarth Press, 1994), 200–4.

36 Alex Zwerdling, *Virginia Woolf and the Real World* (Berkeley, Los Angeles and London: University of California Press, 1986), 96.

37 'Outlines', 'Lady Dorothy Nevill', in Woolf, *Essays*, 4:201.

38 'Outlines', 203.

39 Ralph Nevill, *Life and Letters*, 300; quoted in 'Outlines', 204.

40 Ralph Nevill, *Life and Letters*, 300.

41 'Outlines', 202–3.

42 Dorothy Nevill, *Leaves from the Note-Books of Lady Dorothy Nevill* (London: Macmillan, 1907), 234.

43 Dorothy Nevill, *Leaves*, 238.

44 'Outlines', 203.

45 Ralph Nevill, *Life and Letters*, 108.

46 Ralph Nevill, *Life and Letters*, 291.

10 Brookes's Vivarium pages 143–159

1 For the chapter subtitle, see 'The Young Surgeon, No. 1', *New Monthly Magazine*, 25 (1829), 346–7. For the epigraph, see J. C. Loudon, *An Encyclopaedia of Gardening* (London: Longman, Hurst, Rees, Orme and Brown, 1822), 404.

2 Loudon, *Encyclopaedia*, 403.

3 Letter from Joshua Brookes to John Loudon, 24 June 1830, published in 'A Picturesque Mass of Rock-work', *Gardener's Magazine*, 6 (1830), 491.

4 William Jerdan, *National Portrait Gallery of Illustrious and Eminent Personages of the Nineteenth Century*, 5 vols (London: Fisher, Son & Jackson, 1830–34), 5:9.

5 Christopher Plumb, *The Georgian Menagerie: Exotic Animals in Eighteenth-Century London* (London and New York: I. B. Tauris, 2015), 29.

6 John Flint South, *Memorials of John Flint South: Twice President of the Royal College of Surgeons, and Surgeon to St. Thomas's Hospital … collected by Rev. Charles Fett Feltoe, M.A.* (London: John Murray, 1884), 103.

7 P. E. Kell, 'Joshua Brookes (1761–1833), Anatomist', *Oxford Dictionary of National Biography* (online edn), Oxford University Press, 2004, www.oxforddnb.com.

8 South, *Memorials*, 104.

9 Now the Hunterian Museum at the Royal College of Surgeons of England, London.

10 Ratebooks for Great Marlborough Street and Marlborough Mews, St James's, Westminster, Westminster City Archives, D 1263–65.

11 *Museum Brookesianum: A descriptive and historical catalogue of the remainder of the anatomical & zootomical museum, of Joshua Brookes, Esq.* FRS FLS FZS &c. (London: Richard Taylor, 1830).

12 South, *Memorials*, 106.

13 'Joshua Brookes, Esq.', *The Annual Biography and Obituary*, vol. 18 (London: Longman, Rees, Orme, Brown, Green & Longman, 1834), 288.

14 South, *Memorials*, 106.

15 Jerdan, *National Portrait Gallery*, 5:11.

16 'The Young Surgeon, No. 1', *New Monthly Magazine*, 347.

17 A Picturesque Mass of Rock-work', *Gardener's Magazine*, 491.

18 An adytum was the most sacred place of worship in an ancient Greek temple, from which the laity was excluded.

19 Private correspondence, ref. I.B.18.1, Soane Museum Archive, London.

20 John Glassie, 'Athanasius, Underground', *Public Domain Review*, 1 November 2012, https://publicdomainreview.org/essay/athanasius-underground.

21 Richard Gorer and John H. Harvey, 'Early Rockeries and Alpine Plants', *Garden History*, 7, no. 2 (1979), 69.

22 Private correspondence, ref. I.B.18.1, Soane Museum Archive.

23 William Hunter, 'Account of Some Bones Found in the Rock of Gibraltar', *Philosophical Transactions of the Royal Society of London … Abridged*, 13 (1809), 65.

24 In a list of organic remains discovered in the Gibraltar breccia, Cuvier enumerates the fossil elephant, cave bear, ox, deer, antelope, sheep, rabbits, water-rats, mice, horse, ass, snakes, birds and land shells. Frederick Sayer, *The History of Gibraltar and of its Political Relation to Events in Europe* (London: Chapman & Hall, 1865), 450.

25 'Original Menagerie, New Road, Near Fitzroy Square, London', 1780, trade card, British Museum, London.

26 Plumb, *The Georgian Menagerie*, 29–30.

27 Jesse Foot, *The Life of John Hunter* (London: T. Becket, 1794), 241.

28 Francis Trevelyan Buckland, *Log-book of a Fisherman and Zoologist* (London: Chapman & Hall, 1876), 380. The garden in fact possessed a 'cloister dug about six feet into the earth' that ran all about the house which served as a 'grand place for keeping live stock'. Foot conjectured that within this cloister Hunter kept 'many of his smaller animals used for experiments, such as dormice, hedgehogs, bats, vipers, snakes and snails'. Leading off the cloister there was another subterraneous passage, 'very dark, and like an enlarged fox's earth'. At one end of this burrow there was a small room with a 'largish-sized copper boiler' that he presumed was used for macerating bones of large specimens – among them, 'O'Brien [Charles Byrne], the Irish Giant' (pp. 382–3).

29 Stephen Paget, *John Hunter, Man of Science and Surgeon (1728–93)* (London: T. Fisher Unwin, 1897), 87.

30 'John Hunter's Residence at Kensington', *Antiquary*, 1 (1871), 214.

31 Jerdan, *National Portrait Gallery*, 5:8.

32 'The Young Surgeon, No. 1', *New Monthly Magazine*, 346–7.

33 Henry Angelo, *Reminiscences of Henry Angelo, with Memoirs of his Late Father and Friends* (London: Henry Colburn, 1828), 95–6. Angelo's published account was supplied by 'a friend of the Wyatt family' who lived in Great Marlborough Street – 'only two doors from the back of the Pantheon' – at the time of the fire.

34 Tim Knox, 'Another Glimpse of Brookes's Vivarium', *London Gardener*, 10 (2004–5), 107–9.

35 Tim Knox, 'Joshua Brookes's Vivarium: An Anatomist's Garden in Blenheim Street, W1', *London Gardener*, 3 (1997–8), 34.

36 It is not known whether any of the animals were set free or survived the blaze.

37 Jerdan, *National Portrait Gallery*, 5:8.

38 Loudon, *Encyclopaedia*, 404.

11 Russell Collett and Sir Robert Heron pages 161–173

1 An 'extra-parochial' is an area considered to be outside any parish. It was therefore exempt from payment of the poor or church rate and usually tithe.

2 Nikolaus Pevsner and John Harris, *The Buildings of England: Lincolnshire* (Harmondsworth: Penguin, 1964), 521.

3 *General Loft's Lincolnshire Notebook c.1826–1844* (Lincoln: Lincolnshire Family History Society, 2007), 33. The American Axis is also known as spotted deer or chital deer; it is native to the Indian subcontinent.

4 *General Loft's Lincolnshire Notebook*, 33.

5 Collett was commissioned 29 May 1794: *List of Officers of the Several Regiments and Corps of Fencible Cavalry and Infantry: Of the Officers of the Militia; Of the Corps and Troops of Gentlemen and Yeomanry; And of the Corps and Companies of Volunteer Infantry* (1795), 106.

6 Mr Lovely was later responsible for other *bizarrerie* including the zebra-striped Stonefield House in Branston, the garden piers of which are formed of a conglomerate of rough stone and surmounted by squat carved monkeys. See Nikolaus Pevsner, John Harris and Nicholas Antrim, *The Buildings of England: Lincolnshire* (New Haven and London: Yale University Press, 2002), 180.

7 Russell and Anne Collett were domiciled at Leasam House, a stately pile on the outskirts of Rye. The house had been built for them *c.*1800 by Anne's father.

8 'Reviews of New Books: Notes by Sir Robert Heron', *The Atlas*, 14 February 1852, 106.

9 Robert Heron, *Notes: Printed but not Published* (Grantham: S. Ridge, 1850), 264, 291.

10 'Reviews of New Books', *The Atlas*, 106; 'Poultry Literature', *Littell's Living Age*, 30 (12 July 1851), 51.

11 'Reviews of New Books', *The Atlas*, 106.

12 'Proceedings of the Learned Societies: Zoological Society', *London and Edinburgh Philosophical Magazine and Journal of Science*, 9 (July–December 1836), 67.

13 *General Loft's Lincolnshire Notebook*, 33.

14 Heron, *Notes*, 55. George Kendrick was a wireworker and animal dealer based in Piccadilly.

15 Minutes of the Meeting of the Zoological Society, 25 May 1841, *Proceedings of the Zoological Society of London*, pt IX (London: printed for the Society by R. and J. E. Taylor, 1841), 42.

16 William White, *History, Gazetteer, and Directory of Lincolnshire* (Sheffield: printed by R. Leader, 1856), 393; Heron, *Notes*, 41.

17 Heron, *Notes*, 41. Wyatt changed his surname to Wyattville after having received a knighthood.

18 Heron, *Notes*, 261.

19 Heron, *Notes*, 326–7.

20 Home Correspondence, 'Gardeners' Wages', *Gardeners' Chronicle & New Horticulturist*, 9 (13 January 1849), 22.

21 Heron, *Notes*, 157.

22 Heron, *Notes*, 329.

23 Heron, *Notes*, 3rd edn (1853), 344.

24 'Zoological Gardens, Regent's Park', *Morning Post*, 23 May 1853.

25 See, for example, 'Zoological Society', *The Mirror*, xiv (1829), 13. The author of this article wished to see a greater variety of trees, shrubs and herbaceous plants introduced in the London Zoological Gardens. See also Ruth Guilding, '"The most delightful lounge in the Metropolis": London's Zoological Gardens from 1825–2000', *London Gardener*, 5 (1999–2000), 38–45.

26 'Remarks on the Surrey Zoological Garden, established by Mr. Cross', *Horticultural Register, and General Magazine*, 1 (1832), 219.

27 Alice M. Coats, 'A Forgotten Gardener: Henry Phillips, 1779–1840', *Garden History Society Newsletter*, no. 14 (1 September 1971), 2–3.

28 'Miscellaneous Intelligence', *Gardener's Magazine*, 8, no. 40 (1832), 594; Charles Frederick Partington, *National History and Views of London and its Environs* (London: Allan Bell, 1834), 213.

29 'Plan of a Flower Garden', *Paxton's Magazine of Botany, and Register of Flowering Plants*, 1 (1834), 186.

30 'Plan of a Flower Garden', *Paxton's Magazine*, 186.

12 Charles Waterton pages 175–193

1 For the chapter subtitle, see Charles Waterton, *Essays on Natural History … with a Life of the Author*, ed. Norman Moore (London: Frederick Warne; New York: Scribner, Welford, 1871), 133. For the epigraph, see Charles Waterton, *Essays on Natural History chiefly Ornithology by Charles Waterton, Esq … with An Autobiography of the Author* (London: Longham, Brown, Green & Longmans, 1838), xxiv–xxv.

2 Waterton, *Essays* (1838), xxvii.

3 'Charles Waterton, Esq.', *Wakefield Free Press*, 3 June 1865.

4 'Charles Waterton, Esq.', *Wakefield Free Press*.

5 Waterton, *Essays* (1838), xv.

6 Waterton, *Essays* (1838), xvi.

7 Waterton, *Essays* (1838), xx–xxi.

8 Waterton, *Essays* (1838), xxiii, xxviii.

9 'Death of Charles Waterton, the Naturalist', *Westmoreland Gazette and Kendal Advertiser*, 3 June 1865.

10 Waterton, *Essays* (1871), 62.

11 Waterton, *Essays* (1838), 10, 105, 9.

12 James Stuart Menteath, 'Some Account of Walton Hall, the Seat of Charles Waterton, Esq.', *Magazine of Natural History and Journal of Zoology, Botany, Mineralogy, Geology, and Meteorology*, 8 (1835), 29.

13 Waterton, *Essays* (1838), xvi, xviii.

14 Waterton, *Essays* (1838), xvii–xviii.

15 Waterton, *Essays* (1838), 7, 9, 10–11.

16 Waterton, *Essays* (1871), 123.

17 Menteath, 'Some Account', 29–30. Menteath's published letter is dated 22 November 1834.

18 Menteath, 'Some Account', 32.

19 Waterton, *Essays* (1871), 125. A second 'starling tower' was later erected.

20 Waterton, *Essays* (1871), 451.

21 Charles Waterton, *Essays on Natural History, chiefly Ornithology … with a continuation of the Autobiography of the Author* (London: Longman, Brown, Green & Longmans, 1844), 61.

22 Charles Waterton, 'Flower-Gardens and Song Birds', *Gardener's Magazine*, 18, new series (1842), 254

23 Waterton, 'Flower-Gardens', 254.

24 'Walton Hall', *Leeds Intelligencer*, 10 September 1853.

25 Waterton, *Essays* (1871), 122.

26 Waterton, *Essays* (1871), 122. For instance, the visit of the West Riding Education Board ('West Riding Educational Board', *Leeds Intelligencer*, 11 June 1864); 'Walton Hall and its Late Owner', *Barnsley Times and South Yorkshire Gazette*, 29 May 1875.

27 Richard Hobson, *Charles Waterton: His Home, Habits and Handiwork* (London: Whittaker, 1866), 88.

28 Waterton, *Essays* (1871), 122; Menteath, 'Some Account', 32.

29 Waterton, *Essays* (1871), 122–3.

30 Waterton, *Essays* (1871), 119.

31 'The Naturalist', *Mirror of Literature, Amusement and Instruction*, 25 (1835), 22. Abridged from the *Magazine of Natural History* (cited above).

32 Menteath, 'Some Account', 32.

33 Hobson, *Charles Waterton*, 56.

34 Menteath, 'Some Account', 34.

35 Menteath, 'Some Account', 34, 35. Waterton became aware of the value of ivy in 1817 when he paid a visit to the pheasant preserve of the Duke of Tuscany at the Cascine Park in Florence.

36 'Walton Hall and its Late Owner', *Barnsley Times and South Yorkshire Gazette*.

37 See Victoria Carroll, *Science and Eccentricity: Collecting, Writing and Performing Science for Early Nineteenth-Century Audiences* (London: Pickering & Chatto, 2008), 210, n.151; quoted in Carroll, 159, 155.

38 See Carroll, *Science and Eccentricity*, 149, n.100. The pieces of composite taxidermy include the well-known *Nondescript* (see fig. 116).

39 Julia Byrne, *Social Hours with Celebrities*, 2 vols (London: Ward & Downey, 1898), 2:76–7.

40 Carroll, *Science and Eccentricity*, 161.

41 Waterton, *Essays* (1871), 133.

42 John Hemming, *Tree of Rivers: The Story of the Amazon* (London: Thames & Hudson, 2008), 134.

43 Gerald Durrell, foreword to Julia Blackburn, *Charles Waterton: Traveller and Conservationist*, new edn (London: Vintage, 1997).

44 Waterton, *Essays* (1871), 134, 365.

45 Menteath, 'Some Account', 35.

46 Menteath, 'Some Account', 35.

47 Edith Sitwell, *English Eccentrics* (Harmondsworth: Penguin Books, 1971), 246.

13 Antediluvian Antiquities at Banwell Caves and Pleasure Gardens *pages 195–207*

1 'Remarkable Places of Easy Access from Weston-super-Mare', *Weston-super-Mare Gazette*, 28 August 1886, 3.

2 John Rutter, *Delineations of the North Western Division of the County of Somerset and of its Antediluvian Bone Caverns* (London: Longman, Rees and J. & A. Arch, 1829), 148. The money raised was to go towards the Banwell Sunday Charity School; see 'Bristol Institution', *Bristol Mirror*, 4 December 1824, 4.

3 William Hunt, *Diocesan Histories: The Somerset Diocese, Bath and Wells* (London: Society for Promoting Christian Knowledge, 1885), 241.

4 W. Buckland, *Vindiciæ Geologicæ: or The Connexion of Geology with Religion Explained* (Oxford: University Press for the author, 1820), dedication. Mosaic authorship is the traditional belief that the Torah – the first five books of the Old Testament – were dictated to Moses by God.

5 For instance, William Buckland, 'Discovery of another Cave containing Antediluvian Bones', *Morning Advertiser*, 18 November 1824, 4; 'Discovery of another Cave containing Antediluvian Bones', *Cambridge Chronicle and Journal*, 19 November 1824, 2; and 'Discovery

of another Cave containing Antediluvian Bones', *Derby Mercury*, 24 November 1824, 4.

6 'Antediluvian Antiquities', *Sun* (London), 16 November 1824, 3.

7 'Antediluvian Antiquities', *Sun* (London).

8 'Weston-super-Mare', *Bristol Mirror*, 5 August 1826, 3.

9 'Weston-super-Mare', *Bristol Mirror*.

10 'Weston-super-Mare', *Bristol Mirror*.

11 Rutter, *Delineations*, iii.

12 Law had in fact innovated a 'system of Cottage gardening' or 'field garden allotments' at Banwell and Wells. He did this by apportioning tracts of church land into small lots which were let 'to promote industry, and better the condition of the labouring classes' (A Working Man, 'Wells, Field Garden Allotments', Letter to the editor, *Wells Journal*, 25 April 1857, 8); Viator [pseud.], 'Banwell Cottage, Somersetshire: The Seat of the Bishop of Bath and Wells', *Gentleman's Magazine*, 8, 2nd series (1837), 467.

13 Andrew Foyle and Nikolaus Pevsner, *Buildings of England: Somerset, North and Bristol* (New Haven and London: Yale University Press, 2011), 90.

14 Rutter, *Delineations*, 150.

15 Viator, 'Banwell Cottage', 468; D. J. Irwin and C. Richards, 'Banwell Bone and Stalactite Caves 1757–1826', *Proceedings of the University of Bristol Spelaeological Society*, 20, no. 3 (1996), 201.

16 'Sketch of the Life of the Late William Beard, of Bone Cottage, Banwell', *Weston-super-Mare Gazette*, 6 February 1886, 5.

17 'Sketch of the Life', *Weston-super-Mare Gazette*.

18 'Sketch of the Life', *Weston-super-Mare Gazette*.

19 'Sketch of the Life', *Weston-super-Mare Gazette*.

20 Rutter, *Delineations*, 150.

21 Rutter, *Delineations*, 152–3.

22 Rutter, *Delineations*, 153.

23 *Beedle's Popular Sixpenny Handbook of Weston-Super-Mare and its Vicinity* (Weston-super-Mare: T. Beedle; London: Tallant; Bristol: R. W. Bingham, 1863), 67.

24 Rutter, *Delineations*, 154.

25 Rutter, *Delineations*, 154.

26 Revd John Skinner, 'Stanzas on Banwell Cave, Somerset', *Bath Chronicle and Weekly Gazette*, 21 August 1828, 4.

27 Quoted in Siobhan Carroll, *An Empire of Air and Water: Uncolonizable Space in the British Imagination, 1750–1850* (Philadelphia: University of Pennsylvania Press, 2015), 242, n.118.

28 Sam Smiles says in *The Image of Antiquity: Ancient Britain and the Romantic Imagination* (New Haven and London: Yale University Press for the Paul Mellon Centre for Studies in British Art, 1994) that 'the image of the Druid was beginning to take shape' in England in the seventeenth century (p. 78), and that by the first half of the eighteenth century, 'the Druids' presence was securely established in literature' (p. 80). The Revd Edward Ledwich remarked in 'A Dissertation on the Religion of the Druids … Read November 11, 1784': 'On no subject has fancy roamed with more licentious indulgence than on that of the Druids and their institutions' (*Archaeologia: Or Miscellaneous Tracts Relating to Antiquity*, 7 (1785), 304).

29 Viator, 'Banwell Cottage', 467.

30 Viator, 'Banwell Cottage', 467.

31 J. C. Loudon, *The Suburban Gardener, and Villa Companion* (London: Longman, Orme, Brown, Green and Longmans, 1838), 739.

32 John Whereat, *Whereat's Cheddar and Banwell Guide* (Weston-super-Mare: J. Whereat, 1847), 7–8.

33 J. C. Loudon, *Encyclopaedia of Gardening* (London: Longman, Hurst, Rees, Orme and Brown, 1822), 405.

34 Letter from Mary E. Elton to A. H. Elton, 11 September 1837, in A. H. Elton, ed., A Few Years in the Life of Mary Elizabeth Elton (Clevedon Court, Somerset: printed for the author, 1877), 154.

35 Viator, 'Banwell Cottage', 468.

36 Whereat, *Whereat's Guide*, 7.

37 A Working Man, 'Wells, Field Garden Allotments'; Viator, 'Banwell Cottage', 467.

38 Augustus Charles Pugin and A.N.W. Pugin, *Examples of Gothic Architecture*, 3 vols (London: printed for the author, 1831–8), 2:46.

39 William Phelps, *History and Antiquities of Somersetshire* (London: printed for the author, 1836), 142.

40 Chris Stringer, *Homo Britannicus: The Incredible Story of Human Life in Britain* (London: Penguin Books, 2006), 166.

41 Charles Dickens, 'Old Bones', *Household Words*, no. 183 (24 September 1853), 442.

14 Hawkstone *pages 209–225*

1 Samuel Johnson and Hester Lynch Piozzi, *Dr Johnson & Mrs Thrale's Tour of North Wales 1774*, ed. Adrian Bristow (Wrexham: Bridge Books, 1995), 99. Since Hester Lynch Piozzi's first husband, Henry Thrale, did not die until 1781, she was still Mrs Thrale when she visited Wales. She became Mrs Piozzi in 1784 when she married Gabriele Piozzi.

2 Ronald Paulson, review of Morris R. Brownwell, *Samuel Johnson's Attitude to the Arts*, *Eighteenth-Century Studies*, 23, no. 3 (1990), 362.

3 Jane Hill (1740–1794), daughter of Rowland Hill and Jane Delves Broughton.

4 Quoted in T. Rodenhurst [pseud.], *A Description of Hawkstone, the Seat of Sir R. Hill, Bart M.P.* (Shrewsbury: printed at the Chronicle Office, 1840), 44.

5 Rodenhurst, A *Description* (1840), 45.

6 Sarah Markham, *John Loveday of Caversham 1711–1789: The Life and Tours of an Eighteenth-century Onlooker* (Salisbury: Michael Russell, 1984), 446.

7 T. Rodenhurst [pseud.], A *Description of Hawkstone*, 2nd edn (London: T. Wood, 1784), 15–16.

8 Rodenhurst, A *Description* (1784), 15.

9 John Loveday, quoted in Gordon Campbell, *The Hermit in the Garden: From Imperial Rome to Ornamental Gnome* (Oxford: Oxford University Press, 2013), 75; Richard Colt Hoare, *The Journeys of Sir Richard Colt Hoare through Wales and England, 1793–1810*, ed. M. W. Thompson (Gloucester: Alan Sutton, 1983), 194.

10 Thomas Martyn, quoted in Campbell, *The Hermit in the Garden*, 71.

11 Rodenhurst, A *Description* (1784), 24–33.

12 Rodenhurst, A *Description* (1784), 34.

13 Rodenhurst, A *Description* (1784), 19.

14 Revd Joseph Nightingale, *The Beauties of England and Wales: Original Delineations, Topographical, Historical, and Descriptive*, vol. 13, pt 1 (London: Longman, 1813), 292. From the mid-1820s, but possibly much earlier, visitors were 'conducted by a guide to the principal walks' (J. P. Neale, *The Seats of Noblemen and Gentlemen …*, 2nd series, vol. 3 (London: Sherwood, Gilbert and Piper, 1826), 'Hawkestone Park, Shropshire', n.p.).

15 Rodenhurst, A *Description* (1840), 37.

16 Sir Richard, 2nd Baronet, travelled around the Continent in 1756–7 with Charles, 5th Earl of Elgin, visiting Genoa, Parma, Milan, Bologna, Florence, Pisa, Lucca, Massa and Carrara. John Ingamells, *A Dictionary of British and Irish Travellers in Italy 1701–1800* (New Haven and London: Yale University Press for the Paul Mellon Centre for Studies in British Art, 1997), 498, 334.

17 N. William Wraxall, *Historical Memoirs of My Own Time*, 3 vols (London: printed for T. Cadell and W. Davies, 1818), 3:712–13.

18 Edwin Sidney, *The Life of Sir Richard Hill, Bart.* (London: Seeley and W. Burnside, 1839), 3.

19 Rodenhurst, A *Description* (1784), 47.

20 Rodenhurst, A *Description* (1784), 47–8.

21 Rodenhurst, A *Description* (1784), 48.

22 T. Rodenhurst [pseud.], A *Description of Hawkstone* (London: printed for John Stockdale, 1807), 50, 51–2, 62–4.

23 Rodenhurst, A *Description* (1807), 66.

24 Rodenhurst, A *Description* (1807), 43.

25 Richard Warner, A *Tour through the Northern Counties of England, and the Borders of Scotland*, 2 vols (Bath: R. Cruttwell, 1802), 2:181–2.

26 [Prince Hermann von Pückler-Muskau], *Tour in England, Ireland, and France, in the Years 1826, 1827, 1828, and 1829* (Philadelphia: Carey, Ley & Blanchard, 1833), 81.

27 [Pückler-Muskau], *Tour*, 81–2.

28 The Leasowes in Shropshire opened to the public and published a guidebook by 1764 (William Shenstone, *The works in verse and prose, of William Shenstone, Esq; most of which were never before printed. In two volumes, with decorations …*', 2 vols (London: printed for R. and J. Dodsley, 1764); Hagley in Worcestershire did the same by 1777 (Joseph Heely, A *Description of Hagley Park* (London: printed for the author and sold by R. Baldwin, 1777).

29 Joseph Whittingham Salmon, *Moral Reflections in Verse, Begun in Hawkstone Park, May 20th and 21st. 1794* (Nantwich and Drayton: E. Snelson, 1796), ix; Rodenhurst, A *Description* (1784), vi.

30 Charles Hulbert, *Nature's Beauties Displayed, in Shrewsbury, Hawkstone Park, Runcorn, Halton and the Isle of Man* (London: W. Baynes, and Son, [1825?]), 9.

31 Salmon, *Moral Reflections*, xvii, ix. Salmon had been a local Methodist preacher and an admirer of Swedenborg's writings – 'a man distinguished for his eminent piety and zeal in the cause of divine truth' (Robert Hindmarsh, *Rise and Progress of the New Jerusalem Church in England, America, and Other Parts* (London: Hodson & Son, 1861), 64).

32 Salmon, *Moral Reflections*, ix, xvi.

33 James Boswell, *The Life of Samuel Johnson, LL.D., including a Tour to the Hebrides*, 5 vols (London: John Murray, 1831), 3:133.

34 Catherine Ingrassia, *The Cambridge Companion to Women's Writing in Britain, 1660–1789* (Cambridge: Cambridge University Press, 2015), 203.

35 Johnson and Piozzi, *Dr Johnson & Mrs Thrale's Tour*, 100.

36 Sidney, *Life of Sir Richard Hill*, 368. Chapter XV of this book contains excerpts from the journal of Jane Hill during a Continental tour with her brother, including a first-hand account of Louis XVI and Marie Antoinette dining in public at Versailles ('the king ate heartily, but the queen did not touch a morsel … the king has a countenance of all others the most vacant and bloated. He is fat and very awkward – quite destitute of the graces'). She took a particular interest in Voltaire, whom she considered a depraved infidel and an enemy of the species (as one 'whose life was spent in the happy enjoyment of true piety, [she] made anxious inquiries as to tend of this dreadful enemy of religion, in order to confirm the assurance she always expressed, that the strongest infidelity must yield before the terrors of approaching dissolution') (pp. 368–91, 375, 390). Her 'incidents and anecdotes' make it clear that she had an informed interest in literature and a lively sense of observation.

37 Edwin Sidney, *The Life of the Rev. Rowland Hill, A.M.* (London: Baldwin & Cradock, 1834), 19, 8.

38 Sidney, *Life of the Rev. Rowland Hill*, and *Life of Sir Richard Hill*.

39 Thomas Snell Jones, *The Life of … Willielma, Viscountess Glenorchy* (Edinburgh: printed for William Whyte, 1824), 6.

NOTES

40 Sidney, *Life of Sir Richard Hill*, 62.

41 Jane Hill, 'Hill family pedigree', [n.d.], Shropshire Archives, XHIL/838/83.

42 'Ticket; This painting – a landscape by Ruysdael belongs to Miss Jane Hill …', Shropshire Archives, XHIL/838/5/95; 'This Painting – a landscape by Wouverman – belongs to Miss Jane Hill if she survives me – If not – to her Heir. Eleanor Vickers', [n.d.], Shropshire Archives, XHIL/838/5/94.

43 Rodenhurst, *A Description* (1784), v.

44 Nightingale, *The Beauties of England and Wales*, 292.

45 The Citadel is a dower house in the guise of a sham castle, built in 1824–5 to the designs of Thomas Harrison of Chester. John Newman and Nikolaus Pevsner, *The Buildings of England: Shropshire* (New Haven and London: Yale University Press, 2006), 294–5.

46 Rodenhurst, *A Description* (1784), 39, 40.

47 Rodenhurst, *A Description* (1784), 40.

48 Quoted in Rodenhurst, *A Description* (1840), 45.

49 Rodenhurst, *A Description* (1784), 42–5.

50 Rodenhurst, *A Description* (1784), iv.

51 Rodenhurst, *A Description* (1784), 46.

15 The Burrowing Duke at Harcourt House pages 227–239

1 'Harcourt House: A Strange Discovery', *Daily Telegraph and Courier*, 19 June 1906, 9. I am grateful to Tim Knox for allowing me to pillage his article and research on the duke and his proclivity for burrowing. See Tim Knox, 'Precautions for Privacy: The "Mole Duke's" Secret Garden at Harcourt House, Cavendish Square', *London Gardener*, 2 (1996–7), 27–33.

2 John Timbs, *Curiosities of London* (London: David Bogue, 1855), 680.

3 [James Ralph], *A Critical Review of the Publick Buildings …* (London: printed for C. Ackers by J. Wilford and J. Clarke, 1734), 107.

4 Horace Walpole to the Revd William Mason, 7 May 1775, in Horace Walpole, *The Letters of Horace Walpole, Earl of Orford*, ed. Peter Cunningham, 9 vols (London: Henry G. Bohn, 1861), 6:212.

5 Samuel Angell, 'On the Open Spaces of Our Metropolis', in *Papers Read at the Royal Institute of British Architects, Session 1853–54* (London: published at the rooms of the Institute, 1854), 111.

6 Knox, 'Precautions for Privacy', 27.

7 Angell, 'Open Spaces', 111.

8 W. M. Thackeray, *Vanity Fair*, ed. J.I.M. Stewart (Harmondsworth: Penguin Books, 1968), 545.

9 Horace Walpole to Revd William Mason, 7 May 1775, in Walpole, *Letters*, 6:212. Simon Harcourt, 2nd Earl Harcourt, son of Simon Harcourt, 1st Earl, was to become one of Mason's closest friends and patrons. Mason recast his gardens at Nuneham Courtney in Oxfordshire.

10 Walter Thornbury, *Old and New London: Westminster and the Western Suburbs* (London: Cassell, 1891), 446

11 'The Late Duke of Portland: His Eccentricities', *Derby Mercury*, 17 December 1879, 7.

12 'Welbeck Abbey', *Littell's Living Age*, 161 (April–June 1884), 574; White Francis & Co., *Nottinghamshire: History, Gazetteer, and Directory of the County, and of the Town and County of the Town of Nottingham …* (Sheffield: White Francis & Co., 1864), 702–3.

13 'Welbeck Abbey', *Littell's Living Age*, 574.

14 Ottoline Morrell, *Memoirs of Lady Ottoline Morrell: A Study in Friendship, 1873–1915*, ed. Robert Gathorne-Hardy (New York: Alfred A. Knopf; London: Faber, 1964), 7.

15 Portland Papers, Nottinghamshire Archives, ref. DD 4P 70/32/4, 5 July 1862. The duke had created a similar 'gallery made of iron and glass … a quarter of a mile in length' at Welbeck in order that his horses might be

exercised in damp weather. 'The Late Duke of Portland', *Derby Mercury*, 7.

16 'Radcliffe v. The Duke of Portland – Injunction – Alleged Obstruction of Light and Air – Glass Screen', *Law Times Reports, containing All the Cases Argued and Determined*, vol. 7 (London: Law Times Office, September 1862 to March 1863), 126.

17 'Radcliffe v. The Duke of Portland', 126.

18 'Radcliffe v. The Duke of Portland', 127.

19 'Radcliffe v. The Duke of Portland', 127.

20 The new stables were 13 m/42 ft high (replacing an earlier 5.5-m/18-ft high 'fence wall'). J. W. de L. Giffard, *Reports of Cases Adjudged in the High Court of Chancery*, 5 vols (London: Wildy & Son, 1862), 3:703.

21 Charles J. Archard, 'A Romance of the Peerage', *Lowestoft Journal*, 15 June 1907, 3.

22 'Druce Case Development', *Sevenoaks Chronicle and Kentish Advertiser*, 22 June 1906; 'Harcourt House and the Druce Case: A Strange Discovery', *Nottingham Evening Post*, 19 June 1906.

23 Kenneth Grahame, *The Annotated Wind in the Willows*, ed. Annie Gauger (New York and London: W. W. Norton, 2009); Kenneth Grahame, *The Wind in the Willows* (London: Methuen & Co., 1908), 71.

24 Grahame, *Wind in the Willows* (1908 edn), 85.

16 Denbies pages 241–253

1 John Timbs, *A Picturesque Promenade round Dorking, in Surrey* (London: J. Warren, 1822), 31.

2 [John Lockman], 'A Sketch of the Spring-Gardens, Vaux-Hall, in a Letter to a Noble Lord' (London: printed for and sold by G. Woodfall, [1751]), 27–8; James Boswell, *The Life of Samuel Johnson*, LL.D., 5 vols (London: John Murray, 1831), 1:304.

3 John Shenton Bright, *The History of Dorking and Neighbouring Parishes* (Dorking: R. J. Clark; London: Simpkin, Marshall & Co., 1884), 133.

4 'Some Account of the Parish of Dorking, and its Environs', *Gentleman's Magazine*, 33 (May 1763), 222; Timbs, *A Picturesque Promenade*, 52.

5 [John Dennis], *A Hand Book of Dorking* (Dorking: John Roe; London: G. Willis, 1855), 26. Robert Chambers, ed., *Book of Days*, 2 vols (London and Edinburgh: W. & R. Chambers, 1879), 1:69; Brian Allen, 'Jonathan Tyers's Other Garden', *Journal of Garden History*, 1 (1981), 218.

6 'Singularities at the late Mr. Tyers's Villa ...', *Gentleman's Magazine*, 51 (March 1781), 123. This account was apparently written *c*.1764. Jacopo Sannazaro (pseud. Actius Sincerus Sannazarias) was an Italian poet whose *Arcadia* (published 1504) was the first pastoral romance and, until the rise of the Romantic movement, one of the most influential and popular works of Italian literature.

7 Timbs, *A Picturesque Promenade*, 30; 'Some Account of the Parish of Dorking', 220; 'Short Description of the late Mr. Tyers's Garden at Denbigh, near Dorking in Surr[e]y', *St James's Chronicle; or, The British Evening Post*, 19–22 September 1767, 1.

8 'Short Description', *St James's Chronicle*.

9 'Singularities', *Gentleman's Magazine*, 123.

10 John Milton, *Comus and Other Poems by John Milton* (Cambridge: Cambridge University Press, 1906), 52.

11 'Short Description', *St James's Chronicle*.

12 'Singularities', *Gentleman's Magazine*, 123.

13 'Singularities', *Gentleman's Magazine*, 123.

14 'Singularities', *Gentleman's Magazine*, 123–4.

15 'A Short Description of the late Mr Tyers's Gardens at Denbigh, near Dorking in Surr[e]y', *Scots Magazine*, 29 (October 1767), 456.

16 'A Short Description', *Scots Magazine*, 456.

17 'Wrote on a tomb-stone, where is laid the skull of a woman', *Scots Magazine*, 24 (August 1762), 434.

18 'Wrote on the Tomb-Stone, where is laid the skull of a man', *Sacred and Moral Poems on Deity – Creation – Life –Death – and Immortality* (London: printed for Joseph Wenman, 1789), 196–7.

19 'Singularities', *Gentleman's Magazine*, 124.

20 'Some Account', *Gentleman's Magazine*, 222.

21 'Short Description', *St James's Chronicle*.

22 'Short Description', *St James's Chronicle*.

23 'Short Description', *St James's Chronicle*; Allen, 'Jonathan Tyers's Other Garden', 225.

24 'Some Account', *Gentleman's Magazine*, 222.

25 'Picturesque Promenade near Dorking', *Monthly Magazine*, 51 (March 1821), 124.

26 [Lockman], 'A Sketch of the Spring-Gardens, Vaux-Hall', 20.

17 'Do You Know Thomas Bland?' pages 255–269

1 'Do You Know Thomas Bland?', *Cumberland and Westmorland Advertiser, and Penrith Literary Chronicle*, 16 February 1858, 4.

2 The most comprehensive assessment of Bland and his work is Tim Longville, 'A Terrier at History's Rabbit Holes – Thomas Bland and his Image Garden', *Cumbria Gardens Trust: Occasional Papers*, 2 (2004), 65–113.

3 'Do You Know Thomas Bland?', *Cumberland and Westmorland Advertiser*.

4 'Do You Know Thomas Bland?', *Cumberland and Westmorland Advertiser*.

5 F. M. H. Parker, *The Vale of Lyvennet: Its Picturesque Peeps and Legendary Lore* (Kendal: Titus Walker, 1910), ix.

6 G. F. Weston's biographical account, quoted in Longville, 'A Terrier', 102–3.

7 William Whellan, *The History and Topography of the Counties of Cumberland and Westmorland* (Pontefract: W. Whellan and Co., 1860), 795; and 'Do You Know Thomas Bland?', *Cumberland and Westmorland Advertiser*.

8 Weston, quoted in Longville, 'A Terrier', 103.

9 'Reagill Fete', *Penrith Observer*, 25 June 1861, 5.

10 Lancelot Addison (1632–1703) was the father of the essayist Joseph Addison (1672–1719).

11 'Grand Fete at Reagill', *Westmorland Gazette and Kendal Advertiser*, 9 July 1853, 5.

12 'Do You Know Thomas Bland?', *Cumberland and Westmorland Advertiser*.

13 Weston, quoted in Longville, 'A Terrier', 103. The earliest published account of the annual fete appeared in the *Westmorland Gazette* on 3 June 1843, 3.

14 Weston, quoted in Longville, 'A Terrier', 102.

15 Whellan, *History*, 795.

16 P. J. Mannex, *History, Topography, and Directory, of Westmoreland* (London: Simpkin, Marshall & Co.; Beverley: printed for the author by W. B. Johnson, 1849), 223. In 1843 Bland also carved and erected a rustic obelisk in Crosby Ravensworth to mark the source of the River Lyvennet, where 'King Charles 11. halted and regaled his army, on his hasty march from Scotland, in 1651' (p. 221).

17 Weston, quoted in Longville, 'A Terrier', 103.

18 'Reagill Fete', *Kendall Mercury*, 27 June 1857, 8.

19 'Grand Fete', *Westmorland Gazette*.

20 'Grand Fete', *Westmorland Gazette*.

21 'Grand Fete', *Westmorland Gazette*.

22 'Do You Know Thomas Bland?', *Cumberland and Westmorland Advertiser*. The term *bard* is adopted here, as it is employed from at least the late eighteenth century onwards, to refer to a poet who is perceived as performing verses in the tradition of an ancient order of Celtic minstrels – a tradition that, after the term is idealised by Walter Scott, is increasingly associated with local or national affiliations (see OED).

23 Parker, *Vale of Lyvennet*, ix.

24 Weston, quoted in Longville, 'A Terrier', 103.

25 Bland obituary published in the *Westmorland Gazette and Kendal Advertiser* on 23 September 1865.

26 Weston, quoted in Longville, 'A Terrier', 102–3. Weston describes how Bland tackled archaeological excavations with unfettered enthusiasm: 'The impetuosity with which he would burrow into, & hack away these [burial] mounds' reminded him and his companions of 'a terrier at a rabbit hole'.

27 Weston, quoted in Longville, 'A Terrier', 102.

28 Weston, quoted in Longville, 'A Terrier', 102.

29 Longville, 'A Terrier', 84.

30 'On the Roman Station at Borough Bridge, Westmorland', *Westmorland Gazette and Kendal Advertiser*, 18 August 1860, 6.

31 The 'English Apennines' – also known as the 'Backbone of England' – was the name given to ranges of hills beginning a little north of Cross Fell, in Cumberland, which traversed Westmorland and terminated in the Derbyshire hills. 'A Report of the Quality of Rain which has fallen in Kendal, Westmoreland …', *Magazine of Natural History*, 8 (1835), 345–6.

32 Weston, quoted in Longville, 'A Terrier', 103.

33 'On the Roman Station', *Westmorland Gazette*. John Salkeld Bland is buried in Crosby Ravensworth churchyard in a 'coffin-shaped tomb with painter's pallet and brushes'.

34 'An Address to Shap Abbey', *Ulverston Mirror and Furness Reflector*, 5 July 1862, 3.

35 Anthony Whitehead, *Legends of Westmorland, and Other Poems; with Notes* (Penrith: R. Scott, 1896 edn), 42–3.

36 Weston, quoted in Longville, 'A Terrier', 103; Whitehead, *Legends of Westmorland*, 43.

37 Whitehead, *Legends of Westmorland*, 42–3.

18 Stukeley's Travelling Gardens
pages 271–285

1 James G. Percival, 'Letter CIX: The Bishop of Gloucester to Mr Hurd', in *Elegant Extracts, or Useful and Entertaining Passages*, 6 vols (Boston: Samuel Walker, [1826]), 4:225–6. This chapter is based upon Todd Longstaffe-Gowan, 'Stukeley's Travelling Gardens …', *Architectural Review*, 189 (April 1991), 78–84.

2 Stuart Piggott, *Ancient Britons and the Antiquarian Imagination: Ideas from the Renaissance to the Regency* (London: Thames and Hudson, 1989), 127.

3 John F. H. Smith, 'William Stukeley in Stamford: His Houses, Gardens and a Project for a Palladian Triumphal Arch over Barn Hill', *Antiquaries Journal*, 93 (September 2013), 363.

4 *The Family Memoirs of the Rev. William Stukeley*, M.D., ed. W. C. Lukis, 3 vols, Surtees Society 73 (Durham: Andrews, 1882–7), 1:188.

5 William Stukeley to Samuel Gale, 6 February 1726/7, in *Family Memoirs*, 1:188.

6 Stukeley to Gale, 6 February 1726/7, in *Family Memoirs*, 1:189.

7 Stukeley to Gale, 6 February 1726/7, in *Family Memoirs*, 1:190.

8 Stukeley to Gale, 14 October 1728, in *Family Memoirs*, 1:209.

9 Stukeley to Gale, 14 October 1728, in *Family Memoirs*, 1:208.

10 Stuart Piggott, *William Stukeley: An Eighteenth-Century Antiquary* (Oxford: Clarendon Press, 1950), 84.

11 Frances died on 1 September 1737.

12 'T.G.', *The Flowers of Parnassus: or, the Lady's Miscellany* (London: printed and sold by J. and T. Dormer, 1736), 82.

13 Stukeley to Gale, 2 February 1737/8, in *Family Memoirs*, 1:299; for Mrs Stukeley's marriage portion, see news cutting in Bodleian Library, Oxford, MS Eng. Misc. c.314, dated 13 January 1739.

14 Stukeley to Gale, 5 September 1742, in *Family Memoirs*, 1:336.

15 'Newton's rings' was a pattern of interference caused by two surfaces after reflection of light – a sphere surface and an adjacent flat surface. Although first described by Robert Hooke in his *Micrographia* (1664), its name derives from Sir Isaac Newton, who was the first to analyse the phenomenon.

16 John Drakard, *The History of Stamford, in the County of Lincoln* (Stamford: printed for John Drakard, 1822), 520.

17 Diary entry for 26 December 1748, in *Family Memoirs*, 3:463. A spot dial was 'a sundial in which the time was indicated by the position of a spot, especially a bright spot produced by sunlight shining through a hole or reflected from a mirror' (OED).

18 Stukeley to Gale, 1 August 1746, in *Family Memoirs*, 1:381.

19 Stukeley to Gale, 12 June 1747, in *Family Memoirs*, 1:391–2.

20 Stukeley to Gale, 2 February 1737/8, in *Family Memoirs*, 1:300.

21 Piggott, *William Stukeley*, 152.

22 Diary entry for 26 January 1761, in *Family Memoirs*, 3:20.

23 Bodleian Library, Oxford, MS Eng. Misc. e.138, fol. 48. This verse is a variation on 'The Female Wish' published in the *Gentleman's Magazine* in August 1733 (p. 433).

24 Quoted in John F. H. Smith, 'William Stukeley in Kentish Town, 1759–65', *London Gardener*, 24 (2020), 21–3.

25 Bodleian Library, Oxford, MS Eng. Misc. e.138, fols 66r and 76v; MS Eng. Misc. e.139, fols 1, 3, 47 and 51.

26 William Stukeley, *Itinerarium Curiosum: or, An Account of the Antiquities and Remarkable Curiosities in Nature or Art* [1724], 2 vols (London: printed for Messrs Baker and Leigh, 1776), 1:3.

19 West Wycombe Park
pages 287–303

1 Letter from Benjamin Franklin to William Franklin, 3 August 1773, quoted in Albert Henry Smyth, *The Writings of Benjamin Franklin*, 10 vols (New York: Haskell House Publishers, 1970), 6:111.

2 Lionel Fanthorpe and Patricia Fanthorpe, *The World's Most Mysterious People* (Toronto and Oxford: Hounslow Press, 1998), 143.

3 Richard Meade Bache, 'The So-Called "Franklin Prayer-Book"', *Pennsylvania Magazine of History and Biography*, 21, no. 2 (1897), 228. Letter from Franklin to Granville Sharp, 5 July 1785.

4 Dashwood inherited this title from his uncle John Fane, 7th Earl of Westmorland and 10th Baron Le Despencer (d.1762).

5 Patrick Woodland, 'Dashwood, Francis, eleventh Baron Le Despencer (1708–1781)', *Oxford Dictionary of National Biography* (online edn), Oxford University Press, 2004, www.oxforddnb.com.

6 Charles de Brosses, *Le Président de Brosses en Italie: Lettres familières écrites d'Italie en 1739 et 1740*, 2 vols (Paris: Didier et Co., 1858), 2:422. Quoted in John Ingamells, *A Dictionary of British and Irish Travellers in Italy 1701–1800* (New Haven and London: Yale University Press for the Paul Mellon Centre for Studies in British Art, 1997), 278; letter from Francis Dashwood to Lord Boyne, January 1740, quoted in Ingamells, *Dictionary*, 278.

7 W. S. Lewis, ed., *Horace Walpole's Correspondence*, 47 vols (New Haven: Yale University Press, 1937–83), 18:211; L. Cust and S. Colvin, eds, *History of the Society of Dilettanti* (London and New York: Macmillan, 1898), 9.

8 Lewis, *Horace Walpole's Correspondence*, 18:211.

9 Donald McCormick, *The Hell-Fire Club: The Story of the Amorous Knights of Wycombe* (London: Jarrolds, 1958), 28.

10 *Report on the Manuscripts of the Earl of Verulam, Preserved at Gorhambury*, vol. 64 of the Historic Manuscripts Commission (York: printed by B. Johnson for H.M. Stationery Office, 1906), 243.

11 The garden historian Michael Symes has remarked that the designed landscape ranks among the 'richest and most layered' of eighteenth-century England. Unlike most great pictorial landscapes of the period, it possesses neither a rigid or well-defined iconographical programme, nor a set circuit: it is, he affirms, an associationist garden, where the features within it are visually, spatially or iconographically linked. Michael Symes, 'Flintwork, Freedom and Fantasy: The Landscape at West Wycombe Park, Buckinghamshire', *Garden History*, 33 (Summer 2005), 1–2.

12 William Hannan's views were engraved in 1754–7; Arthur Young, *A Six Weeks Tour through the Southern Counties of England and Wales* (London: printed for Nichol, 1768), 86.

13 Thomas Phillibrown, Diary (MS, 1754), transcript from Sir Edward Dashwood, Dashwood papers, West Wycombe Park.

14 Lewis, *Horace Walpole's Correspondence*, 19:224.

15 Samuel Collins, *A systeme of anatomy* ([London:] Thomas Newcomb, 1685), 564–5.

16 Augustus Henry Fitzroy, Duke of Grafton, *Letters Between the Duke of Grafton, the Earls of Halifax, Egremont, Chatham ... and John Wilkes, Esq.* ([London: s.n.,] 1769), 46.

17 Grafton, *Letters Between*, 46–7.

18 Tim Knox, 'Sir Francis Dashwood of West Wycombe Park, Buckinghamshire, as a Collector of Ancient and Modern Sculpture', in *Collecting Sculpture in Early Modern Europe*, ed. Nicholas Penny and Eike D. Schmidt (New Haven and London: Yale University Press for the National Gallery of Art, Washington, DC, 2008), 402; Grafton, *Letters Between*, 46.

19 Quoted in Tim Knox, *West Wycombe Park, Buckinghamshire* (London: National Trust, 2001), 44.

20 Augustus J. C. Hare, *Memorials of a Quiet Life*, 2 vols (London: Strahan & Co., 1873), 1:78.

21 Samuel Johnson, ed., *The Works of the English Poets*, 21 vols (London: J. Nichols and Son, 1810), 16:203, n.7.

22 N. William Wraxall, *Historical Memoirs of My Own Time*, 3 vols (London: printed for T. Cadell and W. Davies, 1818), 2:253. These memoirs were published posthumously.

23 Wendy Frith, 'Sexuality and Politics in the Gardens at West Wycombe and Medmenham Abbey', in *Bourgeois and Aristocratic Encounters in Garden Art, 1550–1850*, ed. Michel Conan (Washington, DC: Dumbarton Oaks Research Library and Collection, 2002), 288.

24 'Explanatory Note of a Passage in Mr Churchill's Candidate, where he Speaks of Medmenham-Abbey', in *The New Foundling Hospital for Wit: Being a Collection of Fugitive Pieces, in Prose and Verse, Not in Any Other Collection*, 6 vols (London: printed for J. Debrett, 1786), 3:105; Grafton, *Letters Between*, 34–5.

25 Grafton, *Letters Between*, 37. The Sibyl is speaking to Aeneas: 'Here is the place where the road parts: there to the right ... is our way to Elysium, but the left wreaks the punishment of the wicked, and sends them on to pitiless Tartarus.' Virgil, *Eclogues. Georgics. Aeneid I–VI*, trans. H. Rushton Fairclough, rev. G. P. Goold, Loeb Classical Library 63 (Cambridge, Mass., and London: Harvard University Press, 1999), 570–71.

26 Grafton, *Letters Between*, 37. This epigram translates as: Here is the place where the path divided into two; this on the right is our route to Heaven; but the left-hand path exacts punishment for the wicked, and sends them to a pitiless Hell.

27 Grafton, *Letters Between*, 38. This epigram translates as: Go into action, you youngsters; put everything you've got into it together, both of you, let not doves outdo your cooings, nor ivy your embraces, nor oysters your kisses.

28 Grafton, *Letters Between*, 38.

29 Grafton, *Letters Between*, 38.
30 Frith, 'Sexuality and Politics', 288–9.
31 Knox, *West Wycombe Park*, 33.
32 Knox, 'Sir Francis Dashwood', 412.
33 Quoted in Knox, 'Sir Francis Dashwood', 413.
34 Nikolaus Pevsner and Elizabeth Williamson, *The Buildings of England: Buckinghamshire* (New Haven and London: Yale University Press, 2003), 729.
35 'Description of the Grand Jubilee at Lord Le Despencer's, at West Wycombe, in a Letter from Oxford, dated Sept. 22', *Gentleman's Magazine*, 41 (October 1771), 641.
36 'Description of the Grand Jubilee', *Gentleman's Magazine*, 641.
37 'Description of the Grand Jubilee', *Gentleman's Magazine*, 641.
38 'Description of the Grand Jubilee', *Gentleman's Magazine*, 641.
39 Gervase Jackson-Stops, 'The West Wycombe Landscape – II', *Country Life*, 27 June 1974, 1683.
40 Jean-Frédéric Bernard, ed., *The Religious Ceremonies and Customs of the Several Nations of the Known World*, 7 vols (London: printed for Nicholas Prevost, 1731), 1:380.
41 De Brosses, *Le Président de Brosses en Italie*, 2:422; Horace Walpole, *Memoirs of the Reign of King George the Third*, ed. Denis le Marchant, 4 vols (London: Richard Bentley, 1845), 1:173, n.1.
42 Suzanne L. Barnett, *Romantic Paganism: The Politics of Ecstasy in the Shelley Circle* (Basingstoke: Palgrave Macmillan, 2018), 46.
43 Letter from the Earl of Guilford to Mrs Delany, 8 July 1780, in Lady Llanover, *The Autobiography and Correspondence of Mary Granville, Mrs. Delany*, 3 vols (London: Richard Bentley, 1862), 2:549.
44 Guilford to Delany, 8 July 1780, Llanover, *Autobiography*, 2:549. After Lady Le Despencer died in 1769, Dashwood lived at West Wycombe with a Mrs Barry 'who presided over his establishment near eleven years, and was much beloved and respected by all who knew her'. R.F.A. Lee, *A Vindication of Mrs. Lee's Conduct towards the Gordons* (London: Greenland and Norris, 1807), 12.
45 Guilford to Delany, 8 July 1780, Llanover, *Autobiography*, 2:550.
46 Guilford to Delany, 8 July 1780, Llanover, *Autobiography*, 2:550.

20 Dr Phené's 'Senseless and Bewildering Accumulation of Incongruous Things' pages 305–317

1 'Death of Chelsea Hermit. Eccentric Doctor's Life Romance. Mystery Mansion. Bizarre Relics Placed in Silent Home', *Pall Mall Gazette*, 12 March 1912, 7.
2 'Death of Chelsea Hermit', *Pall Mall Gazette*.
3 'Chelsea's House of Mystery: Sale of Dr Phené's Weird Collection', *Daily Chronicle*, 20 November 1912.
4 'Strangest Sale on Record: Chelsea Mystery House', *The Standard*, 20 November 1912.
5 'Strangest Sale on Record', *The Standard*.
6 Tyler & Co, 'Catalogue … For Sale on Tuesday and Wednesday, 19th and 20th November 1912', in *Chelsea Scraps* (Chelsea Reference Library, Local History Scrapbook, hereafter CRL/LHS), 1068–70. E. Annesley Owen, 'The Late Dr Phené: Mr E. Annesley Owen's Reminiscences', *West London Press*, 12 March 1912.
7 'Death of Dr Phené. A Remarkable Chelsea Character. The Story of his Studious Life. Truth about his Ruined Château', *West London Press (Chelsea News)*, 15 March 1912; 'Dr Phené's Collection', *West London Press (Chelsea News)*, 22 November 1912.
8 'Chelsea Mystery House: Jumble Sale of Many Lands', *Daily Mail*, 18 November 1912.
9 'Strangest Sale on Record: Chelsea Mystery House', *The Standard*, 20 November 1912.

10 'Amazing Jumble Sale. Dr Phené's Weird Collection. Artistic Nightmare at Auction', *Daily News & Leader*, 20 November 1912.

11 '"Mystery House" of Chelsea', *Daily News & Leader*, 19 November 1912.

12 '"Mystery House" of Chelsea', *Daily News & Leader*.

13 'Dr John Samuel Phené: Biographical Notes', unpaginated typescript, Dr John Samuel Phené cuttings collection, Kensington Local Studies Library.

14 'William Phene, Watling-street, London', in *The Poll of the Electors for Parliament to Represent the City of Canterbury* (Canterbury: printed for W. Bristow, 1796), 24; 'Society of Arts, Adelphi, May 28th, 1805: The Rewards conferred by the Society', *Agricultural Magazine for 1805*, 12 (January to June 1805), 364.

15 'Obituary. From the *Oxford University Herald*, the *West Middlesex Advertiser*, &c., 21 December 1889' (for the Revd Edward Bradley). Dr Phené folder, Kensington Local Studies Library.

16 'Phené: Biographical Notes'.

17 'Death of Dr Phené', *West London Press (Chelsea News)*.

18 'Dr. John Samuel Phené, 1823 [sic]–1912', unpaginated typescript, Dr John Samuel Phené cuttings collection, Kensington Local Studies Library.

19 'Fellows whom we have lost by death … John Samuel Phené', *Proceedings of the Society of Antiquaries of London*, 24 (London: Society of Antiquaries, 1911), 235. One of his publications included *On Prehistoric Traditions and Customs in Connection with Sun and Serpent Worship* (1875).

20 'Death of Dr Phené', *West London Press (Chelsea News)*.

21 'A Chelsea Hermit's Death', *Beds. Advertiser & Luton Times*, 15 March 1912.

22 Robin H. Legge, 'The Chelsea Hermit', *Pall Mall Gazette*, 13 March 1912; 'The Late Dr. Phené', *West London Press (Chelsea News)*.

23 They married in 1847. The 1871 Census shows that Phené was living on his own at no. 32 Oakley Street, with two servants.

24 'The Late Dr. Phené', *West London Press (Chelsea News)*.

25 'Trees in Town', *Journal of the Society of Arts*, 28 November 1879, 31. 'On the Sanitary Results of Planting Trees in Towns' (an account of Dr Phené's lecture of the same name presented at the Social Science Congress in Manchester in October 1879), *Builder*, 1 November 1879, 1214.

26 'Death of Dr Phené', *West London Press (Chelsea News)*.

27 Mark Johnston, *Street Trees in Britain: A History* (Oxford and Havertown, Pa.: Oxbow Books, 2017), 88.

28 'Hermit's Secrets Revealed: Nightmare in a Chelsea Garden', *Daily Express*, 19 November 1912; '"Mystery House" of Chelsea', *Daily News & Leader*.

29 The 1895 Ordnance Survey (OS London 1:1,056 – Sheet x.20) depicts the ground as impenetrably treed.

30 The oldest surviving portion of the mansion had formed part of Cheyne House, originally built c.1715 for Elizabeth Gerard, Duchess of Hamilton.

31 Tyler & Co., 'By order of the Executrix of the late Dr Phené: Chelsea, Old Cheyne House, The Mystery House, and King Henry VIII's Hunting Lodge', 8 July 1914.

32 Alfred Beaver, *Memorials of Old Chelsea: A New History of the Village of Palaces* (London: Elliot Stock, 1892), 220.

33 'W M', 'An Eccentric', *Daily Mirror*, 12 March 1912.

34 Dr Phené's invitation to his 'Fete in the Ancient Greek Style', in *Chelsea Scraps* (CRL/LHS), 631.

35 E. Annesley Owen, 'Dr Phené and his Fantastic Mansion: Interesting Reminiscences by a Recorder', *Daily Chronicle*, 14 March 1912.

36 'Chelsea's House of Mystery', *Daily Chronicle*.

37 'Death of Dr Phené', *West London Press (Chelsea News)*, 15 March 1912.

38 The Londoner, 'To-night's Gossip', *Evening News*, 20 November 1912.

39 'Death of Chelsea Hermit', *Pall Mall Gazette*.

40 'On the Sanitary Results of Planting Trees in Towns', *Builder*.

41 Sally Williams, 'The Carlyle's Garden in "the Noisiest Babylon that Ever Raged"', *London Gardener*, 9 (2003–4), 74. Carlyle's sobriquet – 'The Chelsea Hermit' – appears to have been applied posthumously.

42 Fred Kaplan, 'Thomas Carlyle (1795–1881), author, biographer, and historian', *Oxford Dictionary of National Biography* (online edn), Oxford University Press, 2008, www.oxforddnb.com.

21 Bedford's Modern Garden of Eden *pages 319–334*

1 'Divine Sealing, Divine Healing, Divine Sealing', PA L130, Panacea Society Archives, Bedford.

2 Jane Shaw, 'Barltrop, Mabel [name in religion Octavia] (1866–1934)', *Oxford Dictionary of National Biography* (online edn), Oxford University Press, 2004, www.oxforddnb.com. The squares were sent free of charge to anyone who requested the healing.

3 Jane Shaw, *Octavia, Daughter of God: The Story of a Female Messiah and her Followers* (London: Jonathan Cape, 2011), 11.

4 Formerly known as Albany Street.

5 Octavia [pseud. Mabel Barltrop], *The Writings of the Holy Ghost*, 16 vols (Bedford: printed for the Panacea Society, 1924), 6:6.

6 Vicki Manners, '"The Garden of Eden": The Impact of the Panacea Society on Bedford 1919–1949', MA thesis, Open University (2019), 10; Shaw, *Octavia*, 36.

7 'Letters from Mabel Barltrop to Rachel Fox Jan – Dec 1918', PA, F.4.3.16, and 'Johnson, JC, Letter from JCJ to R Fox, 22 Jan 1917', F.6.1.9, Panacea Society Archives, Bedford.

8 'Letters from Mabel Barltrop and others to Ellen Oliver Jan – Dec 1919', letter dated 24 Jan 1919, PA, F.4.2.3, Panacea Society Archives, Bedford. Vickers Ltd manufactured armaments, and the Maxim Gun Company was founded with shares owned by Vickers.

9 The Society had acquired eight additional dwellings by the late 1920s. 'Bedford Data 1934–1965', PA, C.3.4.1–3, and 'The Panacea Society, Property History', PA, C.1.1.4, Panacea Society Archives, Bedford.

10 Manners, 'The Garden of Eden', 7.

11 Shaw, *Octavia*, 205.

12 Octavia, *Writings*, 10 August 1926, 8:180.

13 The community banned members from keeping personal pets of their own.

14 Shaw, *Octavia*, 99.

15 Shaw, *Octavia*, 101.

16 Thomas Carlyle, 'On Heroes, Hero-worship, and the Heroic in History' (lecture delivered 5 May 1840), *Monthly Review*, 2 (May 1841), 3.

17 Rachel J. Fox, *How We Built Jerusalem in England's Green and Pleasant Land*, Part II (London: Cecil Palmer, 1937), 107–8.

18 Fox, *Jerusalem*, 107–8.

19 Quote from Octavia in Fox, *Jerusalem*, 107–8.

20 Rachel J. Fox, *The Suffering and Acts of Shiloh-Jerusalem: A Sequel to 'The Finding of Shiloh'* (London: Cecil Palmer, 1927), 382; Shaw, *Octavia*, 119.

21 Octavia, *Writings*, 7:157.

22 Shaw, *Octavia*, 173.

23 Jane Shaw, 'Englishness, Empire and Nostalgia: A Heterodox Religious Community's Appeal in the Inter-war Years', *Studies in Church History*, 54 (2018), 376.

24 Shaw, 'Englishness', 374.

25 F. S. Stuart, 'Wembley and After', *The Panacea*, 1, no. 4 (1924), 80–81. See also Shaw, 'Englishness', 374–92.

26 Shaw, *Octavia*, 119.

27 Fox, *Jerusalem*, 107.

28 Sarah Edwards, 'Dawn of the New Age: Edwardian and Neo-Edwardian Summer', in *Edwardian Culture: Beyond the Garden Party*, ed. Naomi Carle, Samuel Shaw and Sarah Shaw (Abingdon: Routledge, 2019), 15–30; 16.

29 Katherine Mansfield, 'The Garden Party', in *The Garden Party and Other Stories* (London: Constable, 1922), 68–93; 85. The young protagonist initially wants to cancel the garden party when she hears of the death of a carter who lives nearby; at the end of the story she pays a disturbing visit to his wife.

30 Mansfield, 'The Garden Party', 68.

31 Mansfield, 'The Garden Party', 70, 71. The karaka tree, or New Zealand laurel, is the one indication in the narrative that it is set there rather than England.

32 Mansfield, 'The Garden Party', 85.

33 Mansfield, 'The Garden Party', 88–9. Laura remembers 'kisses', which might perhaps have been seen as less innocent at a Panacean party.

34 T. Rodenhurst [pseud.], A *Description of Hawkstone* (London: printed for John Stockdale, 1807), 64.

35 'Chelsea Mystery House: Jumble Sale of Many Lands', *Daily Mail*, 18 November 1912.

36 Edith Sitwell, *English Eccentrics* (Harmondsworth: Penguin Books, 1971), 16.

37 Henri Bergson, *Le Rire: Essai sur la signification du comique* (Paris: Felix Alkan, 1912), 39. Bergson clarifies this definition in a manner that suggests its applicability to many eccentric gardeners, as 'une raideur *quelconque* appliquée sur la mobilité de la vie' (any rigidity applied to the mobility of life).

38 Samuel Johnson and Hester Lynch Piozzi, *Dr Johnson & Mrs Thrale's Tour of North Wales 1774*, ed. Adrian Bristow (Wrexham: Bridge Books, 1995), 100.

39 'Short Description of the late Mr. Tyers's Gardens at Denbigh, near Dorking in Surr[e]y', *St James's Chronicle and the British Evening Post*, 19–22 September 1767.

40 Letter from Benjamin Franklin to Sir Francis Dashwood, 3 August 1773, quoted in Albert Henry Smyth, *The Writings of Benjamin Franklin*, 10 vols (New York: Haskell House Publishers, 1970), 6:111.

41 Richard Hobson, *Charles Waterton: His Home, Habits and Handiwork* (London: Whittaker, 1866), 40; Charles Waterton, *Essays on Natural History chiefly Ornithology by Charles Waterton, Esq … with An Autobiography of the Author* (London: Longman, Orme, Brown, Green & Longmans, 1838), 122. For instance, the visit of the West Riding Education Board (*Leeds Intelligencer*, 11 June 1864, 7); 'Walton Hall and its Late Owner', *Barnsley Times and South Yorkshire Gazette*, 29 May 1875.

42 E. Annesley Owen, 'Dr Phené and his Fantastic Mansion: Interesting Reminiscences by a Recorder', *Daily Chronicle*, 14 March 1912; 'Grand Fete at Reagill', *Westmorland Gazette and Kendall Advertiser*, 9 July 1853.

43 Shaw, *Octavia*, 205.

44 Shaw, *Octavia*, 205.

45 Quotes from Fox and Octavia in Shaw, *Octavia*, 206.

46 Lieutenant Hammond, 'A Relation of a Short Survey of the Western Counties made by a Lieutenant of the Military Company in Norwich in 1635', ed. L. G. Wickham Legg, in *Camden Miscellany*, vol. 16, Camden third series, 52 (London: Offices of the Royal Historical Society, 1936), 81.

47 George Washington Cable, *The Amateur Garden* (New York: Charles Scribner's Sons, 1914), 70.

[ENGLISH GARDEN ECCENTRICS]

Select Bibliography

ALLEN, Brian, 'Jonathan Tyers's Other Garden', *Journal of Garden History*, 1 (1981), 215–38

ANDREWS, Amanda, 'The Great Ornamentals: New Vice-Regal Women and their Imperial Work', D. Phil. thesis, School of Humanities, University of Western Sydney, 2004

ANGELO, Henry, *Reminiscences of Henry Angelo, with Memoirs of his Late Father and Friends* (London: Henry Colburn, 1828)

APPLEBY, Thomas, 'Coniferae', *Cottage Gardener*, 15 July 1852, 244.

ATHALARICUS [PSEUD.], 'Lady Reade's Remarkable Aviary', *Gentleman's Magazine*, 94 (June 1802), 494

A.T.J., 'The Garden: Gardens in Miniature', *Country Life*, 66 (21 December 1929), xl–xlii.

AUBREY, John, *Aubrey's Brief Lives*, ed. Ruth Scurr (London: Vintage, 2016)

BACON, Francis, *New Atlantis and The Great Instauration*, ed. Jerry Weinberger (Chichester: Wiley Blackwell, 2017)

BAINES, Thomas, 'Elvaston Castle', *Gardeners' Chronicle*, 30 December 1876, 838

BARNETT, Suzanne L., *Romantic Paganism: The Politics of Ecstasy in the Shelley Circle* (Basingstoke: Palgrave Macmillan, 2018)

BARON, Michael G. and Derek Denman, eds, *Wordsworth and the Famous Lorton Yew Tree* (Lorton & Derwent Fells Local History Society, 2004)

BARRON, William, 'List of the Species and Varieties of Coniferous Plants in the Pinetum at Elvaston Castle, Derbyshire, the Seat of the Earl of Harrington, in Derbyshire', *Gardener's Magazine*, 14 (1838), 76–9

——, *The British Winter Garden: Being a Practical Treatise on Evergreens; showing their General Utility in the Formation of Garden and Landscape Scenery ... Practised at Elvaston Castle* (London: Bradbury and Evans, 1852)

Beedle's Popular Sixpenny Handbook of Weston-Super-Mare and its Vicinity (Weston-super-Mare: T. Beedle; London: Tallant; Bristol: R. W. Bingham, 1863)

BLACKBURN, Julia, *Charles Waterton: Traveller and Conservationist*, new edn (London: Vintage, 1997)

BLUNDELL, William, *A History of the Isle of Man ... 1648–1656, Printed from a Manuscript in the Possession of the Manx Society*, ed. William Harrison, 2 vols (Douglas: Manx Society, 1876–7)

BOSWELL, James, *The Life of Samuel Johnson, LL.D., including a Tour to the Hebrides*, 5 vols (London: John Murray, 1831)

BREWER, J. Norris, *London and Middlesex; or, An Historical, Commercial, & Descriptive Survey* of the Metropolis of Great Britain (London: J. Harris, 1816)

BRIGHT, John Shenton, The History of Dorking and Neighbouring Parishes (Dorking: R. J. Clark; London: Simpkin, Marshall & Co., 1884)

BROOKE, E. Adveno, 'Elvaston Castle, Derbyshire … The Seat of the Right Hon. the Earl of Harrington', in The Gardens of England (London: T. McLean, [1858])

DE BROSSES, Charles, Le Président de Brosses en Italie: Lettres familières écrites d'Italie en 1739 et 1740, 2 vols (Paris: Didier et Co., 1858)

BUCKLAND, Francis Trevelyan, Log-book of a Fisherman and Zoologist (London: Chapman & Hall, 1876)

'Building Imitation Alps of Rocks and Concrete on an English Nobleman's Estate', Popular Science Monthly, 93, no. 2 (August 1918), 262–3

BUIST, Robert, 'Elvaston Castle', Horticulturist and Journal of Rural Art and Taste, 7 (May 1857), 208–12

BUSHELL, Thomas, The First Part of Youths Errors: Written by Thomas Bushel, the superlative prodigall (London: by T. Harper, 1628)

——, The Severall Speeches and Songs, at the presentment of Mr Bvshells Rock to the Qveens Most Excellent Majesty (Oxford: printed by Leonard Lichfield, 1636)

BYRNE, Julia, Social Hours with Celebrities: Being the Third and Fourth Volumes of 'Gossip of the Century', 2 vols (London: Ward & Downey, 1898)

CABLE, George Washington, The Amateur Garden (New York: Charles Scribner's Sons, 1914)

Calendar of State Papers, Domestic Series, of the Reign of Charles I: 1635, ed. John Bruce (1865; Nendeln, Liechtenstein: Krause Reprint Ltd, 1967)

CAMPBELL, Gordon, The Hermit in the Garden: From Imperial Rome to Ornamental Gnome (Oxford: Oxford University Press, 2013)

CARROLL, Siobhan, An Empire of Air and Water: Uncolonizable Space in the British Imagination, 1750–1850 (Philadelphia: University of Pennsylvania Press, 2015)

CARROLL, Victoria, Science and Eccentricity: Collecting, Writing and Performing Science for Early Nineteenth-Century Audiences (London: Pickering & Chatto, 2008)

CHALLIS, C. E., ed., A New History of the Royal Mint (Cambridge: Cambridge University Press, 1992)

CLIVE-ROSS, Francis, The Church of St Mary the Virgin, East Bedfont, Middlesex (Bedfont: The Vicarage [the author], 1978)

COATS, Alice M., 'A Forgotten Gardener: Henry Phillips, 1779–1840', Garden History Society Newsletter, no. 14 (1 September 1971), 2–4

COCKBURN, George, A Voyage to Cadiz and Gibraltar: Up the Mediterranean to Sicily and Malta in 1810 and 11, 2 vols (London: J. Harding, 1815)

COLLINS, Samuel, A systeme of anatomy ([London]: Thomas Newcomb, 1685)

COLVIN, Howard, A Biographical Dictionary of British Architects 1600–1840 (London: John Murray, 1978)

CORREVON, Henry, 'The Rock Garden at Friar Park', Country Life, 33 (3 May 1913), 641–4

CRIPPS, Barry D., 'A Brief History of East Bedfont' (1960), typescript, ex Derek Sherborn Collection, Bedfont House, deposited with the NMR 2005

CROKER, John Wilson, The Croker Papers: The Correspondence and Diaries of the Late Right Honourable John Wilson Croker, Secretary to the Admiralty from 1809 to 1830, 3 vols (Cambridge: Cambridge University Press, 2012)

CURTIS, Charles H., 'Friar Park, Henley-on-Thames', Gardeners' Magazine, 41 (1898), 442–4

—— AND W. GIBSON, The Book of Topiary (London and New York: Bodley Head, 1904)

——, 'An Ancient and Curious Craft: Revival of the Art of Topiary', *The Garden*, 84 (1920), 112

CUST, L. and S. Colvin, eds, *History of the Society of Dilettanti* (London and New York: Macmillan, 1898)

[D.,] 'Dangstein', *Gardeners' Chronicle*, 31 August 1861, 793–4

DALLIMORE, W., *Holly, Yew and Box: With Notes on Other Evergreens* (London and New York: John Lane, 1908)

DARWIN, Charles, *Insectivorous Plants* (London: John Murray, 1875)

——, *The Various Contrivances by which Orchids are Fertilised by Insects* (London: John Murray, 1877)

——, *The Correspondence of Charles Darwin, Volume 9: 1861*, ed. Frederick Burkhardt et al. (Cambridge: Cambridge University Press, 1994)

DEAL, D. [pseud. H. H. Dombrain], 'Dangstein', *Journal of Horticulture*, 5 January 1864, 9–10

[DENNIS, John,] *A Hand Book of Dorking* (Dorking: John Roe; London: G. Willis, 1855)

DICKENS, Charles, 'Old Bones', *Household Words*, no. 183 (24 September 1853), 441–2

DIX, Brian, '"Barbarous in its Magnificence": The Archaeological Investigation and Restoration of W. A. Nesfield's Parterre Design for the East Garden at Witley Court, Worcestershire', *Garden History*, 39, no. 1 (2011), 51–63

DOWNING, Andrew Jackson, *A Treatise on the Theory and Practice of Landscape Gardening* (New York: Wiley & Putnam, 1841)

DRAKARD, John, *The History of Stamford, in the County of Lincoln* (Stamford: printed for John Drakard, 1822)

DROPE, John, 'Upon the most hopefull and ever Flourishing Sprouts of Valour, the indefatigable Centryes or Armed Gyants cut in Yew at the Physick Garden in Oxford' (London: W. Hall, 1664)

DRUERY, Charles T., 'Friar Park Rock Garden', *Gardeners' Magazine*, 54 (1911), 641–2

ELLIOT, Brent, *Victorian Gardens* (London: Batsford, 1986)

ELLIOTT, Paul, Charles Watkins and Stephen Daniels, 'William Barron (1805–91) and Nineteenth-Century British Arboriculture: Evergreens in Victorian Industrializing Society', *Garden History*, 35, supplement (2007), 129–48

ELTON, A. H., ed., *A Few Years in the Life of Mary Elizabeth Elton* (Clevedon Court, Somerset: printed for the author, 1877)

'Elvaston Castle, the Seat of the Earl of Harrington', *Gardeners' Chronicle*, 9 February 1850, 84

EVELYN, John, *The Diary of John Evelyn (1620 to 1706)* (London: Macmillan, 1908)

An extract by Mr. Bushell of his late abridgment of the Lord chancellor Bacons philosophical theory in mineral prosecutions (London: Thomas Leach, 1660)

The Family Memoirs of the Rev. William Stukeley, M.D., ed. W. C. Lukis, 3 vols, Surtees Society 73 (Durham: Andrews, 1882–7)

FANTHORPE, Lionel and Patricia Fanthorpe, *The World's Most Mysterious People* (Toronto and Oxford: Hounslow Press, 1998)

'The First Collection of Antique Microscopes Ever Catalogued for Sale: Sir Frank Crisp's Hobby', *Illustrated London News*, 14 February 1925, 250–51

FISH, Robert, 'Lamport Hall', *Journal of Horticulture, Cottage Gardener and Country Gentleman*, 22, new ser. (20 June 1872), 501–3

FLORIO, Giovanni, *Queen Anna's New World of Words, or Dictionarie of the Italian and the English tongues*, 2 parts (London: Melch. Bradwood for Edw. Blount and William Barret, 1611)

'The Flower Garden', *Quarterly Review*, 70 (1842), 196–243

FOOT, Jesse, *The Life of John Hunter* (London: T. Becket, 1794)

Fox, Rachel J., *The Suffering and Acts of Shiloh-Jerusalem: A Sequel to 'The Finding of Shiloh'* (London: Cecil Palmer, 1927)

——, *How We Built Jerusalem in England's Green and Pleasant Land* (London: Cecil Palmer, 1937)

Foyle, Andrew and Nikolaus Pevsner, *Buildings of England: Somerset, North and Bristol* (New Haven and London: Yale University Press, 2011)

Free, Montague, 'The Rock Garden of the Brooklyn Botanic Garden', *Brooklyn Botanic Garden Record*, 20, no. 3 (May 1931), 196

'Friar Park, Henley', *Gardeners' Chronicle*, 26, 3rd ser. (28 October 1899), 321–4

Frith, Wendy, 'Sexuality and Politics in the Gardens at West Wycombe and Medmenham Abbey', in *Bourgeois and Aristocratic Cultural Encounters in Garden Art, 1550–1850*, ed. Michel Conan (Washington, DC: Dumbarton Oaks Research Library and Collection, 2002), 285–309

'Garden Memoranda', *Gardeners' Chronicle and Agricultural Gazette*, 27 September 1856, 647

'Gardens Old & New: The Alpine Garden, Friar Park, Henley, the Residence of Mr Frank Crisp', *Country Life*, 18 (5 August 1905), 162–6

General Loft's Lincolnshire Notebook, including Graveyard Misc. 1826–1844 (Lincoln: Lincolnshire Family History Society Trustees, 2007)

Girouard, Mark, *Return to Camelot* (New Haven and London: Yale University Press, 1981)

——, *A Country House Companion* (London: Magna Books, 1993)

Glendinning, R., 'Elvaston Castle, the Seat of the Earl of Harrington', *Gardeners' Chronicle*, 8 December 1849, 773

——, 'Elvaston Castle, the Seat of the Earl of Harrington', *Gardeners' Chronicle*, 15 December 1849, 789

——, 'Elvaston Castle, the Seat of the Earl of Harrington', *Gardeners' Chronicle*, 9 February 1850, 84

Gorer, Richard and John H. Harvey, 'Early Rockeries and Alpine Plants', *Garden History*, 7, no. 2 (1979), 69–81

Gosse, Edmund, 'Three Experiments in Portraiture: Lady Dorothy Nevill, An Open Letter', in *Some Diversions of a Man of Letters* (New York: Charles Scribner's Sons, 1920)

Grafton, Augustus Henry Fitzroy, Duke of, *Letters Between the Duke of Grafton, the Earls of Halifax, Egremont, Chatham … and John Wilkes, Esq.* ([London: s.n.,] 1769)

Grahame, Kenneth, *The Wind in the Willows* (London: Methuen & Co., 1908)

Grey-Egerton, Sir Philip de Malpas, *A Short Account of the Possessors of Oulton* (London: Hatchards for private circulation, 1869)

Hammond, Lieutenant, 'A Relation of a Short Survey of the Western Counties made by a Lieutenant of the Military Company in Norwich in 1635', ed. L. G. Wickham Legg, in *Camden Miscellany*, vol. 16, Camden third series, 52 (London: Offices of the Royal Historical Society, 1936), 1–128

Herle, Charles, *Worldly Policy and Moral Prudence: The Vanity and Folly of the one, the Solidity and Usefulnesse of the other* (London: printed for Sa. Gellibrand, at the Ball in Pauls Churchyard, 1654).

Heron, Robert, *Notes: Printed but not Published* (Grantham: S. Ridge, 1850)

[Hibberd, Shirley,] 'Topiary Gardening', *Littell's Living Age*, 141 (April–June 1879), 255–6

Hindmarsh, Robert, *Rise and Progress of the New Jerusalem Church in England, America, and Other Parts* (London: Hodson & Son, 1861)

Hoare, Richard Colt, *The Journeys of Sir Richard Colt Hoare through Wales and England, 1793–1810*, ed. M. W. Thompson (Gloucester: Alan Sutton, 1983)

Hobson, Richard, *Charles Waterton: His Home, Habits and Handiwork* (London: Whittaker, 1866)

[HOOD, Thomas,] 'The Two Peacocks of Bedfont', *London Magazine*, October 1822, 304–8

HOSE, Thomas A., ed., *Geoheritage and Geotourism: A European Perspective* (Woodbridge: Boydell Press, 2016)

HULBERT, Charles, *Nature's Beauties Displayed, in Shrewsbury, Hawkstone Park, Runcorn, Halton and the Isle of Man* (London: W. Baynes, and Son, [1825?])

HUNT, William, *Diocesan Histories: The Somerset Diocese, Bath and Wells* (London: Society for Promoting Christian Knowledge, 1885)

HUNTER, William, 'Account of Some Bones Found in the Rock of Gibraltar', *Philosophical Transactions of the Royal Society of London … Abridged*, 13 (1809), 64–5

INGAMELLS, John, *A Dictionary of British and Irish Travellers in Italy 1701–1800* (New Haven and London: Yale University Press for the Paul Mellon Centre for Studies in British Art, 1997)

INGRASSIA, Catherine, *The Cambridge Companion to Women's Writing in Britain, 1660–1789* (Cambridge: Cambridge University Press, 2015)

IRWIN, D. J. and C. Richards, 'Banwell Bone and Stalactite Caves 1757–1826', *Proceedings of the University of Bristol Spelaeological Society*, 20, no. 3 (1996), 201–13

[ISHAM, Charles,] 'Notes on Gnomes and Remarks on Rock Gardens: The Lamport Rockery' ([Lamport: Lamport Hall,] 1884)

——, 'Notes on the Lamport Rockery' ([Lamport: Lamport Hall,] 1894)

——, *Emily* ([Lamport: Lamport Hall,] 1899)

JERDAN, William, *National Portrait Gallery of Illustrious and Eminent Personages of the Nineteenth Century*, 5 vols (London: Fisher, Son & Jackson, 1830–34)

JERROLD, Walter, *Highways and Byways in Middlesex* (London: Macmillan and Co., 1909)

JOHNSON, Paige and Matthew Maynard, 'The Garden Notes of Ole Borch: Scientific Traveller and Garden Visitor, 1662–63', *Garden History*, 41, no. 2 (2013), 196–208

JOHNSON, Samuel, ed., *The Works of the English Poets*, 21 vols (London: J. Nichols and Son, 1810)

—— and Hester Lynch Piozzi, *Dr Johnson & Mrs Thrale's Tour of North Wales 1774*, ed. Adrian Bristow (Wrexham: Bridge Books, 1995)

JOHNSTON, Mark, *Street Trees in Britain* (Oxford: Windgather Press, 2017)

JONES, Thomas Snell, *The Life of the Right Honourable Willielma, Viscountess Glenorchy* (Edinburgh: printed for William Whyte, 1824)

'Joshua Brookes, Esq.', *The Annual Biography and Obituary*, vol. 18 (London: Longman, Rees, Orme, Brown, Green & Longman, 1834), 282–95.

JOURDAN, Sue, 'Lady Harriet Reade (1727–1811) of Shipton Court', *Wychwoods History*, 12 (1997), 48–51

KNOX, Tim, 'Precautions for Privacy: The "Mole Duke's" Secret Garden at Harcourt House, Cavendish Square', *London Gardener*, 2 (1996–7), 27–33

——, 'Joshua Brookes's Vivarium: An Anatomist's Garden in Blenheim Street, W1', *London Gardener*, 3 (1997–8), 30–34

——, *West Wycombe Park, Buckinghamshire* (London: National Trust, 2001)

——, 'Another Glimpse of Brookes's Vivarium', *London Gardener*, 10 (2004–5), 107–9

——, 'Sir Francis Dashwood of West Wycombe Park, Buckinghamshire, as a Collector of Ancient and Modern Sculpture', in *Collecting Sculpture in Early Modern Europe*, ed. Nicholas Penny and Eike D. Schmidt (New Haven and London: Yale University Press for the National Gallery of Art, Washington, DC, 2008), 396–419

'Lamport', *Gardeners' Chronicle*, 22 (25 September 1897), 209–10

LAWSON, Charles, *The Private Life of Warren Hastings: First Governor-General of India* (London: Sonnenschein, 1895)

LEWIS, W. S., ed., *Horace Walpole's Correspondence*, 47 vols (New Haven: Yale University Press, 1937–83)

LIEVEN, Princess Dorothea, *The Private Letters of Princess Lieven to Prince Metternich*, ed. Peter Quennell (London: John Murray, 1937)

LLANOVER, Lady [Augusta Hall], *The Autobiography and Correspondence of Mary Granville, Mrs. Delany*, 3 vols (London: Richard Bentley, 1862)

LONGSTAFFE-GOWAN, Todd, 'Stukeley's Travelling Gardens: *Itinerarium Curiosum: Iter Domesticum*; An Account of the Gardens of William Stukeley', *Architectural Review*, 189 (April 1991), 78–84

——, *The Gardens and Parks at Hampton Court Palace* (London: Frances Lincoln, 2005)

LONGVILLE, Tim, 'A Terrier at History's Rabbit Holes – Thomas Bland and his Image Garden', *Cumbria Gardens Trust: Occasional Papers*, 2 (2004), 65–113

LOUDON, Jane, *Ladies' Magazine of Gardening* (London: William Smith, 1842)

LOUDON, John Claudius, *An Encyclopaedia of Gardening* (London: Longman, Hurst, Rees, Orme and Brown, 1822)

——, 'General Results of a Gardening Tour, during July in the Present Year, by a Circuitous Route from Manchester, by Chester and Liverpool, to Dumfries', *Gardener's Magazine*, 7 (1831), 513–57

——, *Arboretum et Fruticetum Britannicum*, 8 vols (London: printed for the author, 1838)

——, 'Hoole House, the Rev. Peploe W. Hamilton; occupied by Lady Broughton', *Gardener's Magazine*, 14 (1838), 353–63, 503, 562

——, *The Suburban Gardener, and Villa Companion* (London: Longman, Orme, Brown, Green and Longmans; Edinburgh: W. Black, 1838)

——, 'Recollections of a Tour chiefly between London and Sheffield, made during the last three Weeks of May, 1839', *Gardener's Magazine*, 15 (1839), 433–63

McCORMICK, Donald, *The Hell-Fire Club: The Story of the Amorous Knights of Wycombe* (London: Jarrolds, 1958)

McGEE, C. E., 'The Presentment of Bushell's Rock: Place, Politics, and Theatrical Self-Promotion', *Medieval & Renaissance Drama in England*, 16 (2003), 39–80

MALLOCK, W. H., *Memoirs of Life and Literature* (London: Chapman & Hall, 1920)

MANNERS, Vicki, '"The Garden of Eden": The Impact of the Panacea Society on Bedford 1919–1949', MA thesis, Open University, 2019

MANNEX, P. J., *History, Topography, and Directory, of Westmoreland* (London: Simpkin, Marshall & Co.; Beverley: printed for the author by W. B. Johnson, 1849)

MANSFIELD, Katherine, 'The Garden Party', in *The Garden Party and Other Stories* (London: Constable, 1922)

MARKHAM, Sarah, *John Loveday of Caversham 1711–1789: The Life and Tours of an Eighteenth-century Onlooker* (Salisbury: Michael Russell, 1984)

MAVOR, W. F., *A New Description of Blenheim* (Oxford: Munday & Slatter, 1817)

'Memoirs of Celebrated Actresses: Maria Foote, Countess of Harrington', *Bow Bells: A Weekly Magazine of General Literature and Art*, 20 (1874), 545–6

'Memoirs of the Life of Warren Hastings, first Governor-General of Bengal. Compiled from Original Papers, by the Rev. G. R. Gleig, M.A.', *Edinburgh Review: Or Critical Journal*, 74 (October 1841–January 1842), 160–255

MENTEATH, James Stuart, 'Some Account of Walton Hall, the Seat of Charles Waterton, Esq.', *Magazine of Natural History and Journal of Zoology, Botany, Mineralogy, Geology, and Meteorology*, 8 (1835), 28–36

MILLER, Wilhelm, 'What England Can Teach Us About Rock Gardening', *Country Life in America*, 16 (August 1909), 391–4

MILTON, John, *Comus and Other Poems by John Milton* (Cambridge: Cambridge University Press, 1906)

MORRELL, Ottoline, *Memoirs of Lady Ottoline Morrell: A Study in Friendship, 1873–1915*, ed. Robert Gathorne-Hardy (New York: Alfred A. Knopf; London: Faber, 1964)

MOULE, Thomas, *The English Counties Delineated*, 2 vols (London: George Virtue, 1837)

'Mr Jamrach's College for Young Beasts', *Leisure Hour*, no. 338 (17 June 1858), 377–80

Museum Brookesianum: A descriptive and historical catalogue of the remainder of the anatomical & zootomical museum, of Joshua Brookes, Esq. FRS FLS FZS &c. (London: Richard Taylor, 1830)

MYLES, Janet, *L. N. Cottingham 1787–1847: Architect of the Gothic Revival* (London: Lund Humphries, 1996)

NEALE, John Preston, *Views of the Seats of Noblemen and Gentlemen, in England, Wales, Scotland and Ireland*, 6 vols (London: Sherwood, Gilbert and Piper, 1824–29)

NETHERCOTE, H. O., *The Pytchley Hunt: Past and Present* (London: S. Low, Marston, Searle & Rivington, 1888)

NEVILL, Dorothy, *Leaves from the Note-Books of Lady Dorothy Nevill* (London: Macmillan, 1907)

——, *Under Five Reigns* (London: Methuen, 1910)

NEVILL, Guy, *The Reminiscences of Lady Dorothy Nevill* (London: Edward Arnold, 1906)

NEVILL, Ralph, *The Life and Letters of Lady Dorothy Nevill* (London: Methuen, 1919)

NEWMAN, John and Nikolaus Pevsner, *The Buildings of England: Shropshire* (New Haven and London: Yale University Press, 2006)

NIGHTINGALE, Revd Joseph, *Shropshire; or Original Delineations, Topographical, Historical, and Descriptive* (London: printed for J. Harris, 1818)

'Obituary: Sir Charles Isham, Bart.', *The Garden*, 63 (18 April 1903), 269–70

OCTAVIA [PSEUD. MABEL BARLTROP], *The Writings of the Holy Ghost*, 16 vols (Bedford: printed for the Panacea Society, 1924)

OSWALD, Arthur, 'The Gardens at Lamport Hall – II: The Northamptonshire Home of Sir Gyles Isham, Bt.', *Country Life*, 128 (17 November 1960), 1164–7

PAGET, Stephen, *John Hunter, Man of Science and Surgeon (1728–93)* (London: T. Fisher Unwin, 1897)

PARDOE, Bill, *Witley Court and Church: Life and Luxury in a Great Country House* (Gloucester: Peter Huxtable Designs, 1986)

PARKER, F.M.H., *The Vale of Lyvennet: Its Picturesque Peeps and Legendary Lore* (Kendal: Titus Walker, 1910)

PARTINGTON, Charles Frederick, *National History and Views of London and its Environs* (London: Allan Bell, 1834)

PEAKE, Richard Brinsley, *Memoirs of the Colman Family*, 2 vols (London: Bentley, 1841)

PERCIVAL, James G., *Elegant Extracts, or Useful and Entertaining Passages*, 6 vols (Boston: Samuel Walker, [1826])

PEVSNER, Nikolaus and John Harris, *The Buildings of England: Lincolnshire* (Harmondsworth: Penguin Books, 1964)

PEVSNER, Nikolaus, John Harris and Nicholas Antrim, *The Buildings of England: Lincolnshire* (New Haven and London: Yale University Press, 2002)

PEVSNER, Nikolaus and Elizabeth Williamson, *The Buildings of England: Buckinghamshire* (New Haven and London: Yale University Press, 2003)

PIGGOTT, Stuart, *William Stukeley: An Eighteenth-Century Antiquary* (Oxford: Clarendon Press, 1950)

——, *Ancient Britons and the Antiquarian Imagination: Ideas from the Renaissance to the Regency* (London: Thames and Hudson, 1989)

PLOT, Robert, *The Natural History of Oxfordshire, Being an Essay toward the Natural History of England* (Oxford: The Theatre; London: S. Miller, 1677)

PLUMB, Christopher, *The Georgian Menagerie: Exotic Animals in Eighteenth-Century London* (London and New York: I. B. Tauris, 2015)

POPE, Alexander, 'An Essay on Verdant Sculpture', *The Guardian*, 173 (29 September 1713), reproduced in Alexander Chalmers, ed., *The Guardian: A new edition, carefully revised* …, 2 vols (London: printed for F. C. and J. Rivington, 1822), 2:422–8

PRATT, Herbert, 'A Wonderful Rock Garden', *Strand Magazine*, 19 (January–June 1900), 225–30

[PÜCKLER-MUSKAU, Prince Hermann von,] *Tour in England, Ireland, and France, in the Years 1826, 1827, 1828, and 1829* (Philadelphia: Carey, Lea & Blanchard, 1833)

PUGIN, Augustus Charles and A.N.W. Pugin, *Examples of Gothic Architecture; Selected from Antient Edifices in England*, 3 vols (London: printed for the author, 1831–8)

RAFFLES, Thomas, *Letters during a tour through some parts of France, Savoy, Switzerland* (Liverpool: Longman, Hurst, 1818)

RAIKES, Thomas, *A Portion of the Journal Kept by Thomas Raikes, Esq.: From 1831 to 1847*, 2 vols (London: Longman, Brown, Green & Longmans, 1856)

[RALPH, James,] *A Critical Review of the Publick Buildings, Statues and Ornaments in, and about, London and Westminster* (London: printed for C. Ackers by J. Wilford and J. Clarke, 1734)

RAZZELL, Peter, ed., *The Journals of Two Travellers in England in Elizabethan and Early Stuart England: Thomas Platter and Horatio Busino* (London: Caliban, 1995)

'Remarks on the Surrey Zoological Garden, established by Mr. Cross', *Horticultural Register, and General Magazine*, 1 (1832), 219–20

REYNOLDS, Samuel, *The Memories of Dean Hole* (London: Edward Arnold, 1893)

RICHARDSON, Tim, *The Arcadian Friends* (London: Bantam, 2007)

ROBINSON, William, 'Garden Memoranda: Dangstein', *Gardeners' Chronicle*, 4 November 1865, 1039

RODENHURST, T. [pseud.], *A Description of Hawkstone*, 2nd edn (London: T. Wood, 1784)

——, *A Description of Hawkstone* (London: printed for John Stockdale, 1807)

——, *A Description of Hawkstone, the Seat of Sir R. Hill, Bart M.P.* (Shrewsbury: printed at the Chronicle Office, 1840)

RUTTER, John, *Delineations of the North Western Division of the County of Somerset and of its Antediluvian Bone Caverns* (London: Longman, Rees and J. & A. Arch, 1829)

SALMON, Joseph Whittingham, *Moral Reflections in Verse, Begun in Hawkstone Park, May 20th and 21st. 1794* (Nantwich and Drayton: E. Snelson, 1796)

SARGENT, H. W., 'Impressions of English Scenery', *Magazine of Horticulture, Botany, and All Useful Discoveries and Improvements in Rural Affairs*, 31 (1865), 325–8

SCURR, Ruth, *John Aubrey: My Own Life* (London: Vintage Digital, 2015)

SHAW, Jane, *Octavia, Daughter of God: The Story of a Female Messiah and her Followers* (London: Jonathan Cape, 2011)

——, 'Englishness, Empire and Nostalgia: A Heterodox Religious Community's Appeal in the Inter-war Years', *Studies in Church History*, 54 (2018), 374–92

SHELLEY, Mary Wollstonecraft, *Frankenstein; or, The Modern Prometheus* (1818), ed. D. L. Macdonald and Kathleen Scherf, facsimile of 3rd edn (Peterborough, Ont., and Buffalo, N.Y.: Broadview Press, 2012)

SHERWOOD, Jennifer and Nikolaus Pevsner, *The Buildings of England: Oxfordshire* (Harmondsworth: Penguin Books, 1975)

SHERWOOD, Philip, *Harlington and Harmondsworth: A History and Guide* (Stroud: Tempus Publishing, 2002)

SIDNEY, Revd Edwin, *The Life of the Rev. Rowland Hill, A.M.* (London: Baldwin & Cradock, 1834)

———, *The Life of Sir Richard Hill, Bart.* (London: Seeley and W. Burnside, 1839)

'Singularities at the late Mr. Tyers's Villa …', *Gentleman's Magazine*, 51 (1781), 123–4

SITWELL, Edith, *English Eccentrics* (Harmondsworth: Penguin Books, 1971)

SMILES, Sam, *The Image of Antiquity: Ancient Britain and the Romantic Imagination* (New Haven and London: Yale University Press for Paul Mellon Centre for Studies in British Art, 1994)

SMITH, James Edward, *A Sketch of a Tour on the Continent, in the Years 1786 and 1787 … in three volumes* (London: Longman, Hurst, Rees and Orme, 1807)

SMITH, John F. H., 'William Stukeley in Stamford: His Houses, Gardens and a Project for a Palladian Triumphal Arch over Barn Hill', *Antiquaries Journal*, 93 (September 2013), 353–400

———, 'William Stukeley in Kentish Town, 1759–65', *London Gardener*, 24 (2020), 11–27

'Some Account of the Parish of Dorking, and its Environs', *Gentleman's Magazine*, 33 (April 1763), 220–23

SOUTH, John Flint, *Memorials of John Flint South: Twice President of the Royal College of Surgeons, and Surgeon to St. Thomas's Hospital … collected by Rev. Charles Fett Feltoe, M.A.* (London: John Murray, 1884)

SPRINGARN, Joel Elias, 'Henry Winthrop Sargent and the Early History of Landscape Gardening and Ornamental Horticulture in Dutchess County, New York', in *Year Book of the Dutchess County Historical Society*, vol. 22 (New York: Dutchess County Historical Society, 1937)

STEELE, Richard and Joseph Addison, *Selections from the Tatler and the Spectator*, ed. Angus Ross (Harmondsworth: Penguin Books, 1988)

STEWART, Susan, *On Longing: Narratives of the Miniature, the Gigantic, the Souvenir, the Collection* (Durham, N.C., and London: Duke University Press, 1993)

STRINGER, Chris, *Homo Britannicus: The Incredible Story of Human Life in Britain* (London: Penguin Books, 2006)

STRONG, Roy, *The Renaissance Garden in England* (London: Thames and Hudson, 1979)

STUKELEY, William, *Itinerarium Curiosum: or, An Account of the Antiquities and Remarkable Curiosities in Nature or Art* [1724], 2 vols (London: printed for Messrs Baker and Leigh, 1776)

SYMES, Michael, 'Flintwork, Freedom and Fantasy: The Landscape at West Wycombe Park, Buckinghamshire', *Garden History*, 33, no. 1 (Summer 2005), 1–30

'Testimony of Sir Charles Isham', *The Spiritualist: A Record of the Progress of the Science and Ethics of Spiritualism*, 3, no. 59 (1 September 1873), 314

'T.G.', *The Flowers of Parnassus: or, the Lady's Miscellany* (London: printed and sold by J. and T. Dormer, 1736)

THACKERAY, William Makepeace, *Vanity Fair*, ed. J.I.M. Stewart (Harmondsworth: Penguin Books, 1968)

THONGER, Charles, *The Book of Rock and Water Gardens* (London and New York: John Lane, 1907)

THORNBURY, Walter, *Old and New London: Westminster and the Western Suburbs* (London: Cassell, 1891)

THORNE, James, *Handbook to the Environs of London; Alphabetically Arranged, Containing an Account of Every Town and Village and of All Places of Interest …*, 2 pts (London: John Murray, 1876)

TIMBS, John, *A Picturesque Promenade round Dorking, in Surrey* (London: J. Warren, 1822)

———, *Curiosities of London* (London: David Bogue, 1855)

TROTTER, W. R., 'The Glasshouses at Dangstein and their Contents', *Garden History*, 16, no. 1 (Spring 1988), 71–89

TROUBRIDGE, Laura, *Memories and Reflections* (London: William Heinemann, 1925)

TURNER, William, *Journal of a Tour in the Levant*, 3 vols (London: John Murray, 1820)

VIATOR [PSEUD.], 'Banwell Cottage, Somersetshire: The Seat of the Bishop of Bath and Wells', *Gentleman's Magazine*, 8, 2nd ser. (1837), 466–72

VIRGIL, *Eclogues. Georgics. Aeneid I–VI*, trans. H. Rushton Fairclough, rev. C. P. Goold, Loeb Classical Library 63 (Cambridge, Mass., and London: Harvard University Press, 1999)

WALPOLE, Horace, *Memoirs of the Reign of King George the Third*, ed. Denis le Marchant, 4 vols (London: Richard Bentley, 1845)

——, *The Letters of Horace Walpole, Earl of Orford*, ed. Peter Cunningham, 9 vols (London: Henry G. Bohn, 1861)

——, *Memoirs of the Reign of George III*, ed. G. F. Russell Baker, 4 vols (London: Lawrence and Bullen; New York: G. P. Putnam's, 1894)

WARNER, Richard, *The Topographical Works of the Rev. Richard Warner* (Bath: R. Crutwell & Son, 1802)

WATERTON, Charles, *Essays on Natural History chiefly Ornithology by Charles Waterton, Esq … with An Autobiography of the Author* (London: Longman, Orme, Brown, Green & Longmans, 1838)

——, 'Flower-Gardens and Song Birds', *Gardener's Magazine*, 18, new series (1842), 252–7

——, *Essays on Natural History, Chiefly Ornithology … with a continuation of the Autobiography of the Author* (London: Longman, Brown, Green & Longmans, 1844)

——, *Essays on Natural History … with a Life of the Author*, ed. Norman Moore (London: Frederick Warne; New York: Scribner, Welford, 1871)

WHELLAN, William, *The History and Topography of the Counties of Cumberland and Westmorland* (Pontefract: W. Whellan and Co., 1860)

WHEREAT, John, *Whereat's Cheddar and Banwell Guide* (Weston-super-Mare: J. Whereat, 1847)

WHITE FRANCIS & CO., *Nottinghamshire: History, Gazetteer, and Directory of the County, and of the Town and County of the Town of Nottingham …* (Sheffield: White Francis & Co., 1864)

WHITE, William, *History, Gazetteer, and Directory of Lincolnshire* (Sheffield: printed for the author by R. Leader, 1856)

'William Barron', *Gardeners' Chronicle*, 25 April 1891, 522–4

WINNICOTT, Donald, *Playing and Reality* (Harmondsworth: Pelican Books, 1974)

WOODFIELD, Paul, 'Early Buildings in Gardens in England', in *Garden Archaeology: Papers Presented to a Conference at Knuston Hall, Northamptonshire, April 1988*, ed. Anthony Ernest Brown, Research report no. 78 (London: Council for British Archaeology, 1991), 123–37

WOOLF, Virginia, *The Essays of Virginia Woolf, Volume I: 1904–1912*, ed. Andrew McNeillie (London: Hogarth Press, 1986)

——, *The Essays of Virginia Woolf, Volume IV: 1925–1928*, ed. Andrew McNeillie (London: Hogarth Press, 1994)

WORDSWORTH, William, *The Prose Works of William Wordsworth*, ed. A. B. Grosart, 3 vols (London: Edward Moxon, 1876)

WRAXALL, N. William, *Historical Memoirs of My Own Time*, 3 vols (London: printed for T. Cadell and W. Davies, 1818)

YOUNG, Arthur, *A Six Weeks Tour through the Southern Counties of England and Wales* (London: printed for Nichol, 1768), 86

ZWERDLING, Alex, *Virginia Woolf and the Real World* (Berkeley, Los Angeles and London: University of California Press, 1986)

[ENGLISH GARDEN ECCENTRICS]

Index

NOTE: Page numbers in italics refer to illustrations and/or information in the associated caption; captions may appear on a facing page. Page numbers followed by *n.* and a number refer to information in a note.

Adam and Eve at Hawkstone 215
Addison, Joseph 69–70, 346*n*.7
Albert, prince consort to Queen Victoria 312
'allotments' at Banwell 198
Alpine gardens
   Friar Park 44–51, *45, 47, 49*
   Hoole House 5–6, 27–8, 31–9, *33, 35*
Alpine models 36–7, *39*, 333
altars 277, 279, 323, 325
'Althalaricus' 112–13, *116*
amateur topiarists 108–9, *108*
Andrews, Malcolm 5
Angell, Samuel 228
animals
   gardens as earthly paradises for 333
   see also birds; menageries; sanctuary for wildlife at Walton Hall; zoological gardens
antiquarianism
   chivalric style for Elvaston interiors 91, 95

classical giants in legend at Hawkstone 224
classical models for buildings and structures 277, 279, 292, 293, 297, 298–9, 300, 301, 308, 313
   and clipped churchyard yews 71, 78
   as influence on Bland 267, 268, 269
   Phené's 'Fête in the Ancient Greek Style' in garden *3*, 313, 333
   Phené's travels and scholarly interests 310, 313
   Stukeley's historical interpretation of place 271, 273, 274, 283
   see also Gothic style in architecture
Appleby, Thomas 96
archaeology
   Bland's interest in 267–8, 363*n*.26
   Phené's interest in and travels 310, 313
architecture: Phené's interest in 310
Arnold, George 78
Arthurian legends: 'Merlin's Cave' 277, *278*, 279
artistry *see* creativity
Ash, Charles: 'The Hermit of Hawkstone' 214
associationist gardening 365*n*.11
asylum inmates at Walton Hall 184, *189*, 333
Aubrey, John 14, 15–16, *17, 18, 19,* 23

autobiography *see* biography and autobiography
automaton hermit at Hawkstone 213, 214
aviaries 112, 118
   Lady Nevill's birds and aviary 140, *141*
   Lady Reade's aviary at Shipton under Wychwood 111–25
   Lamport Hall 56
   see also birds
Aymes-Stokes, Sophie 4–5

Backhouse, James 46, 345*n*.27
Bacon, Sir Francis 15, 20, 23
Baines, Thomas 95
Baird, Thomas *154*
Banks, Sir Joseph 149, 177
Banwell Caves and Pleasure Gardens, Somerset 195–207, 335
   Beard's home at 'Bone Cottage' 198–9, 202
   'Bishop's Chair' *201*, 202
   Bishop's Tower 203, 206
   'Bone Cave' 195, 198, *199*, 201, *201*, 206, 207
   Druidic structures 202–3, 332
   landscaped grounds and gardens 204, 205–6, *205*
   Ornamental Cottage extended as mansion 198, *199*, 202, 203–4, *203*, 205
   Osteoicon 202, 203, 204

remote position as exceptional
destination 207
scientific examination of bones
197, 199
'Stalactite Cave' 195, 198, 201–2,
201
summer-house for refreshments
197, *198*, 203, *204*
tourists and Beard's guided tours
197–202, 206
views and prospects 204, *205*–6
Barltrop, Mabel (née Andrews) 8, 321
Panacea Society and expanding
Garden of Eden 319–30, 337
house in Bedford and Garden
of Eden 320, 322–30, *322*,
333–4
role as 'Octavia' 319–20, 333–4
Barn Hill garden, Stamford 279,
280–81, *282*, 335
barn owls and Waterton's protection
180
Barron, William 86–7, 88, 95
Barry, Mrs (Dashwood's companion
as widower) 303
Bastin, Leonard 106
Beadon, Richard, Bishop of Bath and
Wells 195, 196
Beard, William 198–9, 200, 201–2,
206
Beaver, Alfred 312
Bedfont *see* East Bedfont, Middlesex
Bedford *see* Panacea Society
Bergson, Henri 332
Bernini, Gian Lorenzo, *Neptune and
Triton* 16
Bingley, Robert Benson, 1st Baron
227–8
biography and autobiography
architecture and Phené's ancestry
315
eccentric biography as genre 1–2
gardens as expression of
autobiography 2–3, 4, 6, 9, 334
birds
acquisition of live birds
Brookes's father as trader 146,
150, 152, *152*
Heron's exchanges and
acquisitions 168–9
in Brookes's Vivarium 143, 144–5,
149, 150, *150*, 155

exotic birds 114–15
flower gardens as resource for 182
in Hawkstone Park menagerie
213, 215
Lady Nevill's 'winged orchestra'
135, *137*
on ponds with islands at Stubton
Hall 167–8
Waterton's observation and
protection of 178, *179*, 180–81,
182, 184, 185, 187, 189, 192–3
see also aviaries
black swan at Stubton Hall 167, *168*
Blackburn, Julia 189
Blair, Robert: *The Grave* 246
Bland, John Salkeld 267–8
Bland, Thomas 10–11, 255–69, *256*
sculptures and artworks 7, 256–8,
257, 259–60, *262*, *266*, 338
sketches of gardens and local
scenes 10, 259–60, 263–6
Blenheim Palace, Oxfordshire:
aviary 111
Blundell, William 14
Bobard, Jacob 71, 72
bog gardens 44
bones in gardens 3
'Bone Cave' at Banwell 195, 198,
201, *201*, 206, 207
scientific examination of bones
197, 199
Brookes's jawbone of whale 149,
150, *157*
interest in Rock of Gibraltar
149–50, *151*
skulls and inscriptions at Denbies
247, 250–51
Borch, Ole 13, 14, 25
Boscawen, Miss (neighbour of Lady
Reade) 123
boundaries *see* walls and boundaries
Bowley, W.: Hawkstone views for
Description 216, *218*
Brewer, J. Norris 79
British Empire and Panaceans'
Garden of Eden 326–7
Britton, John: Celtic Cabinet 37, *38*
Brookes, Joshua, junior *147*
career as anatomist and surgeon
146, 158
Museum Brookesianum and
Theatre of Anatomy 146

Vivarium in Blenheim St home
143–58, *156*–7, 337
'Pilgrim's Cell' 149, *150*
Rock of Gibraltar as feature
143, *144*–5, 147–50
sale of museum and vivarium
158, *159*
Brookes, Joshua, senior 146, 150,
152, *152*
Brookes, Paul 150
Brookes, Revd Dr Thomas 111,
116–20, 124–5
Broome, Dr William: 'Ode to
Melancholy' 246
Broughton, Elizabeth, Lady (Dame
Eliza, née Egerton) 27–39, *30*, 336
artistry in creating rock garden
33–4, *36*
will and bequests 36–7
Browne, Henry: cork model of
Stonehenge 37, *38*
Buckland, William 195, 196–7
Buckler, John 198
buildings and structures
classical models for 292, *293*, 297,
298–9, 300, *301*, 308, 313
Stukeley's Roman altar 277, *279*
cottage and summer-house at
Banwell Caves 197, *198*, 199
Druidic structures 202–3, 276,
277, *277*–8, 279, 280–81, *282*, 332
mausoleums 282–3, 297, 298–9,
300, *301*, 338
in menagerie and on islands at
Stubton Hall 167, *168*
Panacea Society's chapel and ritual
structures 322, 323–4, 325
pavilion for antique fête in Dr
Phené's garden 313
see also conservatories and
glasshouses; follies; grottoes;
hermits and hermitages;
rocks and rock gardens; ruins;
temples
Buist, Robert 96
burrowings and excavations 46, 148,
152, 195–6, 213, 230–31, 233–9,
292, 353n.28
Bushell, Thomas 5, 14–25, *15*, 334,
336
Golden Medal 20
Byrne, Julia 188–9

INDEX
– 381 –

Cable, George 334
cacti 28, 46
caprice and whimsicality
　follies and features at Hawkstone 213, 214, 215–17, 217–18, 219, 224–5
　gnomes and figures at Lamport Hall 62
　Lady Nevill's varied interests 141
　views on West Wycombe 293, 296, 303
　see also creativity
Carlyle, Thomas 316–17, 324
carnivorous plants 132, 133–4, 135, 137
Carroll, Victoria 187
Castleside, Bedford 323, 331
Caus, Isaac de 21
Caus, Salomon de: Parnassus fountain 21–3, 22
Cavendish, Henry 146
Cavendish-Bentinck-Scott, William John *see* Portland
caves
　Banwell Caves and Pleasure Gardens 195–207
　caverns and chambers at Friar Park 46, 50, 57, 58, 62
　caverns in Rock of Gibraltar in Brookes's vivarium 149
　Hell-Fire Caves at West Wycombe Park 292–3, 338
　see also grottoes; tunnels and subterranean passages
Celtic Cabinet 37, 38
Chamonix valley, France
　Mer de Glace 34, 35, 36
　models of 37
charitable causes
　'grand fêtes' at Lamport Hall 66
　opening of Banwell Caves 195, 202
　visitors to Walton Hall 182, 184
Charles I, king of England 14, 19
Charlotte, queen of Great Britain 152
Charton, Gratienne Violette ('Hackleplume'): *In My Lady's Garden* anthology 107
Chelsea, London *see* Phené, Dr John Samuel
Chelsea Physic Garden: alpine 'rockwork' 149

Chinese goldfish 165–6, *165*
churchyard topiary in London 69–81, 337
classical models for buildings and structures 277, 279, 292, 293, 297, 298–9, 300, 301, 308, 313
Coleman, George, the Younger 78
collectors
　Beard's bone collection at Bone Cottage 198, 202
　Brookes family and live animals 146, 150, 152, *152*
　eccentricity as feature of gardeners and collectors 3, 141, 317
　Lady Nevill's collection of exotic plants and artefacts 135, 137, 141
　Lady Reade's collection of birds and animals 111–25
　Lord Petersham's trees for topiary 87, 88
　Phené's overwhelming collection 3, *3*, 305, 306–7, 308, 313, 315
　Stukeley's 'curiosities' and gardens 274, 276, 279, 283
　see also aviaries; menageries; museums
Collett, Samuel Russell 161–5, 171, 172–3, 336
Collins, Samuel 292
conifers
　dwarf conifers in Isham's rockery 58
　transplanted trees at Elvaston Castle 88, 89–91
　see also yew trees
conservation: Waterton's sanctuary 178, 179, 180–81, 182, 184, 185, 187, 189, 192–3
conservatories and glasshouses 29, 131, *131*, 132, 166, *166*
Corder, Rosa 78
Correvon, Henry 47, 48, 50, 51
Cottingham, Lewis 91
Cottrell, William 79
creativity
　Bland's sculptures and artworks 256–8, 262
　Crisp's alpine garden at Friar Park 48, 50

death of creator and departure of soul of garden 67, 317, 334
Isham's careful construction of rockery 57–8
Lady Broughton's rock formations 33–4, 36, 39
playfulness
　follies and sham ruins 163, 172–3
　and topiary 108–9
　Waterton's mischievous experiments 193
　and resistance to compliance 9, 10, 332
　see also caprice and whimsicality
Crisp, Frank 41–51, *42*, 336
　rebuilding of house 42, 43
Croker, John Wilson 124
Cromwell, Oliver 13, 23
Cross, Edward 171, 172
cultural appropriation and gardens 332
Curtis, Charles Henry: *The Book of Topiary* 106
Cuvier, Georges 146, 353n.24

Dallimore, William 81
Danby, Earl of 14
Dangstein House, Sussex 129, 130–37, *131*
　museum 135, 141
　sale of house and auction of contents 137
Darwin, Charles 135, 140
　Insectivorous Plants 132, 134
Dashwood, Sir Francis, 2nd baronet, later 11th baron Le Despencer 287–303, *288*, 333, 338
　enthusiasm towards visitors 303
　erotic features in landscape designs 292, 293–4, 295–6
　grand tours and adventures 288–9, 302
　improving impulses 290
Daw, George 137–8
de Crespigny, Mary 123
de Man, Paul 2
death
　and moralising features at Denbies 247–51, 333

ENGLISH GARDEN ECCENTRICS
– 382 –

of owner and departure of soul of garden 67, 317, 334
Denbies, Surrey 241–53, *243*, 335
　Milton and literary extracts 245–7, 251, *252*, 253
　moralising flags and inscriptions and gloomy atmosphere 245–6, 250–51, 253, 333
　Roubiliac's sculptures 246, 251
　Temple of Death 246
　Valley of the Shadow of Death with skulls 247, 250–51
Dibdin, Thomas 187
Dickens, Charles 207
dilettanti *see* Society of Dilettanti
Dodington, George Bubb, 1st baron Melcombe 294, 297, 300
Dombrain, Revd Henry Honywood 130–31, *134*
Donowell, John 292, 297
Downing, Andrew Jackson 39
Drope, John 346n.11
Druce, Thomas Charles: Druce–Portland scandal 238
Druery, Charles T. 46–7
Druidic practices and beliefs
　Druidic structures at Banwell Caves 202–3, 332
　　and religious message of inscriptions 204–5
　Stukeley's Druidic interests and garden features 273, *273*, 276, 282–3
Dudley, Rachel Anne Ward, Countess of (née Gurney) 6, 99–109, *100*, 338
　acquisition of local topiary specimens 106
　'My Lady's Garden' 102, *104–5*, 106–8
　service in World War I 107–8
Dudley, William Humble Ward, 2nd Earl of 99–100
Durrell, Gerald: on Waterton 189
Dutch flower gardens 43, 44
dwarf trees and plants in Isham's rockery 58, 62

Eagle *see* Jungle, The, Eagle, Lincolnshire
eagles 56, 173

East Bedfont, Middlesex: topiary yews in churchyard 69–70, *70*, *71*, 75, 78–9, 81, 337
eccentricity
　as characteristic of gardeners and collectors 3, 141, 317
　compliance and eccentric resistance to 9–10, 332
　cultural appropriation in gardens 332
　Duke of Portland and quest for privacy 232–9
　eccentric biography genre 1–2
　eccentric gardeners as soul of garden 4, 67, 317, 334
　and Englishness 4–5, 326–7
　gardens as space for self-expression 6
　history and studies of 4–5
　picturesque and affinities with 5
　public curiosity
　　in Lady Reade and retinue 120
　　and sale of Dr Phené's effects 3, 305, 307, 308, 315
　twentieth-century turn to affectation 5
　visitors' encounters with garden owners 187, 255, 261–2, 303, 313
　Waterton's singular approach to conservation 189, 192–3
　Waterton's travels and visitor expectations 187–9, *190–91*
Eden *see* Garden of Eden/paradise
Edwardian era as golden age 328–9
Edwards, M. Clarke 42
Edwards, Sarah 328–9
Egerton, Sir Philip de Malpas Grey-, 10th baronet 36–7
Egyptian mummies and sarcophagi 3, 13, 19, 21, 23, 25
electric lighting at Friar Park 46, 50
Elizabethan gardens 43–4
Ellys, Sarah 292
Elton, Mary: on visit to Banwell Caves 205, 206
Elvaston Castle, Derbyshire 83–97, *85*, 335
　'Alhambra Garden' and statues 94, *95*
　'Garden of the Fair Stair' ('Mon Plaisir') 91, *92–3*, 94–5

'Hall of the Fair Stair' 91
　transplanted trees and topiary yew hedges 87, 88–91, *88*, *90*, 92–4, *94–6*, 97
　visiting public after Petersham's death 95, *96*
elves 46
Emes, John: *The Lake at Hawkstone* 217
Emes, William 215
Empire and Panaceans' Garden of Eden 326–7
Enfield, Middlesex: churchyard yew 71, 76, 79, 81
Engelheart, George 78
'English Apennines' 267, 363n.31
Englishness and eccentricity 4–5, 326–7
Enstone, Oxfordshire: Bushell's 'Enston-Rock' 13–25, 334, 336
entertainments
　at Enstone 13, 19
　'Fête in the Ancient Greek Style' in Phené's garden 3, 313, 333
　follies and facilities at Hawkstone 214, 216–17, *217*–18, 219, 224, 225
　garden parties in Garden of Eden in Bedford 326, 327–9, *328*, 330, *331*
　garden's role in social events 329–30
　'grand fêtes' at Lamport Hall 66
　'Grand Jubilee' at West Wycombe Park 300, 302–3
　grotesque and unusual effects at Friar Park 46, 50
　miniature figures in Lamport Hall rockery 58, 59–60, 62, 64–6, *64–5*
　mock battles on lake at West Wycombe 292
　'pic-nic parties' at Walton Hall 182, *183*, 184, 333
　for visiting public at Yew Tree Farm 256–8
　'Grand Fetes' 258, 260–61, 268, 333
erotic features at West Wycombe and Medmenham Abbey 292, 293–4, 295–6
Evelyn, John 25

exotic birds *see* aviaries
exotic plants and hothouses 131, 132–5, 137, 141

fairies *see* gnomes and fairy figures
ferns and ferneries 28, 130, 132, 137, 141
fêtes and garden parties 3, 66, 258, 260–61, 268, 313, 333
    Panacea Society garden parties 326, 327–9, *328*, *330*, *331*
figures *see* gnomes and fairy figures; sculpture and statues
finances *see* wealth
First World War 107–8
Firth, Kate 322–3, 333
Fish, D. T. 102
Fish, Robert 56–7
fish: Chinese goldfish 165–6, *165*
Fitzroy, Lady Charlotte *see* Lichfield, Countess of
Floricultural Cabinet 91, 94–5
flower gardens
    Friar Park 'Dutch' garden 43, *44*
    Hoole House 28, *29*, *31*, 32
    role in supporting birds 182
    'special province of women' 130
follies
    Hawkstone Park 213, 215–17, 219, 224, *225*
    'The Jungle' as sham ruin 161, *163*, 163, 173
Foot, Jesse 152
Foote, Maria (later Maria Stanhope, Countess of Harrington) 83, *84*, 85, 87
Forsyth, William 149
fossils in gardens 3
    see also bones in gardens
fountains
    Enstone 16, *17*, 22–3, *24*–5
    Parnassus fountain at Somerset House 21–2, *22*
    Witley Court 102, *103*
Fox, Rachel 326, 333–4
Francis (Franz) Ferdinand, Archduke of Austria 50
Franklin, Benjamin 287, 293, 333
Frederica Charlotte, Princess 124, *125*
Free, Montague 50

Friar Park, Oxfordshire 41–51
    Alpine Garden 44–51, *45*, *47*, *49*, 336
    miniature Matterhorn 44, *45*, 51, *332*, 333
    negative responses 50–51
    plants and expert planting 46
    praise for ambitious construction 46–7, *47*–8
    Crisp's rebuilding of house in Gothic style 42, *43*
    open to visitors 43, 46, 48, 50
    topiary 44, *44*
    'Wishing Well Cave' 49
Frith, Wendy 296

Gale, Elizabeth 279, 282
Gale, Samuel 276, 279
Garden of Eden/paradise
    evocation in gardens 6, 333, 334
    Hawkstone as earthly paradise 215, 220
    see also Panacea Society and expanding Garden of Eden in Bedford
garden owners
    as guides 220–21, 222, 261, 332
    visitors' encounters with 261–2, 303, 312–13
    owners mistaken for garden workers 187, 255, 262
garden parties *see* fêtes and garden parties
gardeners
    Heron's good treatment of 168
    Waterton sings praises of 181–2
Gardeners' Chronicle 44, 46, 55, 57–8, 128, 168
Gardeners' Magazine 46–7, 108
    Loudon's article on Hoole House 27, 29, 30–34, *32*–3, 35, 36–7
gardens
    ceremonies in 276, 294, 323–4, *325*
    eccentric gardeners as soul of 4, 67, 317, 334
    role in social events 329–30
    transitory nature of 334
    as work in progress 3, 27
Gayton, Edmund 346n.11
Gentleman's Magazine 112–13, 116
    on gardens at Denbies 244, 251

    on 'Grand Jubilee' at West Wycombe 300, 302
    'Viator' on Banwell Caves 203–4, *203*
Geoffrey de Monmouth 279
geographical inspiration for gardens 332
geology 37
    and accounts of the deluge in scripture 196, 205, 207
    Bland's interest in 267–8
    Gibraltar rock 149–50, *151*
    local rocks and fossils in Bland's museums 257
    see also caves; rocks and rock gardens
Germany: gnomes and mountain spirits 64, *65*
giants and Giant's Well at Hawkstone 222, *223*, 224
Gibraltar, Rock of *151*
    in Brookes's Vivarium 143, *144*–5, 147–50
Gillett, Evelyn 326
Girouard, Mark 91
glaciers
    'ice-grotto' at Friar Park 46
    Mer de Glace replica at Hoole House 5–6, 32, 34, *35*, 36, 332
glasshouses *see* conservatories and glasshouses
Glendinning, Robert 85–6, 87, 88
gnomes and fairy figures 46
    at Lamport Hall 58, *59*–60, 62, 64–6, *64*–5, 333
Godwin, Emily 323
goldfish 165–6, *165*
Gosse, Edmund 127, 129, 137
Gothic style in architecture 18, 42, *43*, 91, 149, 246, 282
Grahame, Kenneth: *Wind in the Willows* 238–9, *239*
grand tours 288–9, 309
grasses: 'Garden of all Grasses' at Friar Park 44
Grey-Egerton, Sir Philip de Malpas *see* Egerton
Grindelwald glacier 46
groves 14, 64, 113, 130, 137, 168, 184, *185*, 219, 245, 273, 276, 292, 295, 302, 308
grottoes
    Enstone 13–25, 336

Friar Park 'ice-grotto' 46
Hawkstone 5, 7, 209, 213, 214
    Grotto Rock 210
    Hermit's Lodge and automaton hermit 213, 214, 219
    Stukeley's 'Merlin's Cave' 277, 278, 279
    Walton Hall 182, 183, 184
    see also caves; rocks and rock gardens
guidebooks and plans 43
    Banwell Caves 204, 205
    Description of Hawkstone guide 215, 216–17, *216*, *217*, *218*, 219, 222, 224, 225
    Stowe 219
guides and guided tours
    Beard at Banwell Caves 197–202, 206
    garden owners as guides 220–21, 222, 261, 332
    Hawkstone 219, 222, 224–5
Gurney, Rachel Anne *see* Dudley, Rachel Anne Ward, Countess of

'Hackleplume' *see* Charton, Gratienne Violette
Hammond, Lieutenant 16, 18, 19, 334
Hampton Court Place: topiary in Mount Garden 70
Handel, George Frideric 300
Hannan, William: views of West Wycombe 290, *291*, *293*, *297*
Harcourt, Simon, 1st Earl Harcourt 232
Harcourt House, London 227–39, 337
    garden 232
    glass screens for privacy 233, *234–5*
    stable block as screen 233, *236–7*, *238*
    tunnel and Druce–Portland scandal 238
Hardwick, Philip 310
Harlington, Middlesex: churchyard yews 71, *73*, *74–5*, *76*, *77*, 79–81, *80*, 337
Harpham, T. B. 46

Harrington, Countess of *see* Foote, Maria
Harrington, Leicester Stanhope, 5th Earl of 95
Harrington, 4th Earl of *see* Petersham, Viscount
Harrison, George 336
Harrison, Thomas 360*n*.45
Hastings, Warren 124
Hatchett, John 78
Haven, The, Bedford 322, *323*, *326*, *328*, 331
Hawkstone Park, Shropshire 6, 7, 9, 209–225, *210–11*, 336
    Citadel (dower house) 222
    Description of Hawkstone guide 215, 216–17, *216*, *217*, *218*, 219, 222, 224, 225
    follies and features 213, 214, 215–17, *217–18*, 219, 224–5, 332
    Grotto 5, 7, 209, 213, 214
    Grotto Rock 210
    guided walks 219, 222, 224–5
    Hawk Lake and 'Menagerie Pool' 215–16, *217*
    Hawkstone Hall *212–13*, *212*, *218*
    Hermit's Lodge and automaton hermit 213, 214, 219
    inn for visitors 217, *218*, 219, 225
    landscaping and grounds 215–17, 219
    menagerie 213, 215
    natural beauty and grandeur 209, 212, 219, 224
    Neptune's Whim cottage and statue 216–17, *218*
    Raven's Shelf ('Awful Precipice') 215
    Red Castle and Giant's Well *211*, 213, 222, *223*, 224, 225
    religious dimension to scenery 219–20
    'Stately Lion' 224–5
    visitors to 209, 213, 215, 217, *218*, 219–21, 224–5
Hayman, Francis
    The Bad Man at the Hour of Death 248, *250–51*
    The Good Man at the Hour of Death 249, *250–51*
    'Il Penseroso' 252

Hazlitt, William: 'On the Picturesque and Ideal' 5, 339*n*.7
hedges *see* topiary and clipped trees and hedges; trees and hedges
Hell-Fire Caves at West Wycombe Park 292–3, 338
Hellfire clubs 289, 290
Hemming, John 189
Henrietta Maria, queen consort 14, 19
herbaceous borders 130
Herle, Charles: *Worldly Policy and Moral Prudence* 23, 25
Hermann von Pückler-Muskau, Prince 219
hermits and hermitages 13, 19, 282
    Hermit's Lodge and automaton at Hawkstone 213, 214, 219
    'Pilgrim's Cell' at Brookes's vivarium 149, *150*
    Stukeley's 'hermitages' 277, 278, 279, 280–81, 285, 336
Heron, Sir Robert 163–71, *164*, 338
    collection of Chinese goldfish 165–6
    menagerie and gardens at Stubton Hall 164–71
Hibberd, Shirley 108–9
Hill, Elizabeth: *Hawkstone Park, Shropshire* 210–11, 221
Hill, Miss Jane (d.1794) 6, 9, 10, 209, 220–22, 224, 225, 332, 336
Hill, Jane (niece of Miss Jane Hill): *Some Account of the Antiquities of Hawkstone* 222, *223*
Hill, Sir Richard, 2nd baronet 215, 216–17, *216*, 219, 221, 222, 225, 336
Hill, Revd Rowland 222
Hill, Sir Rowland, 1st baronet 209, 212–13, 220, 221, 222, 225
Hillingdon, Middlesex: churchyard yews 71, 77, *79*, 81, 337
Hoare, Sir Richard Colt 213
Hobson, Richard 183, 184, *185*, *186*, *192*
Hogarth, William 294
    Sir Francis Dashwood at his Devotions *288*
homeopathy 53
Hood, Thomas: *The Two Peacocks of Bedfont* 69

Hooker, Sir Joseph 132, 137
Hoole House, Cheshire 27–39
   Alpine rock garden 27–8, 31–9, 33, 336
      creativity of Lady Broughton 33–4, 36
      Mer de Glace replica 5–6, 32, 34, 35, 36, 332
      possible Alpine models for 36–7, 39, 333
   conservatory 29
   flower garden 28, 29, 31, 32
Horwood's map of London 146–7, 232
hothouses and exotic plants 131, 132–5, 137, 141
Hulbert, Charles 211
Hunter, John 146, 152, 154
   Earl's Court estate and garden 152, 153–5, 154
Hunter, William 146, 149–50
Huysman, J.-K.: *À Rebours* 132, 135

illusions and effects 39, 46, 50, 51
imagination *see* creativity
Impey, Lady (née Reade) 120–21, 121, 124
In My Lady's Garden (poetry anthology) 107
inscriptions and labels
   erotic inscriptions at Medmenham Abbey 295–6
   Hawkstone 211
   moralising flags and inscriptions at Denbies 245–6, 247, 250–51, 333
   placards with verse on fairy tableaux at Lamport Hall 59–60, 62, 66, 333
   religious messages at Banwell Caves 204–5, 332
insectivorous plants 132, 133–4, 135, 137
Isham, Sir Charles Edmund, 10th baronet 3–4, 4, 53–67, 54, 333, 336
   'Notes on Gnomes and Remarks on Rock Gardens: The Lamport Rockery' 62–4, 64
   'Vision of Fairy Blacksmiths at Work' 63, 66

Italian architecture and Phené's house 308–9, 313, 315
Italian gardens and landscape as influence 21, 89
   Italian Garden at Yew Tree Farm 256, 262, 266, 267, 269, 332
   Phené's garden and Isola Bella 308, 332
ivy as shelter for birds 187

Jackson-Stops, Gervase 302
Jamrach, Charles 56, 170
Japanese gardens 43
Jenkins, E. H. 47–8
Johnson, Jessie 320
Johnson, Samuel 5, 209, 212, 215, 220, 224, 241, 332
Johnston, Mark 312
Jolivet, Maurice-Louis 290
Jones, Barbara: 'The Jungle, Lincolnshire' 163
Jones, Captain Edward: sketch of Charles Waterton 189, 190–91
Jungle, The, Eagle, Lincolnshire 161, 162–3, 163, 165, 166, 172–3, 333, 336

kangaroos 165, 170, 171
Kendrick, George 165
Kent, William 277
Kew: aviary in Royal Botanic Gardens 112
Kirby's Wonderful and Eccentric Museum; Or, Magazine of Remarkable Characters 2
Kircher, Athanasius: *Mundus Subterraneus* and *Oedipus Aegyptiacus* 148, 148
Kirkdale Cave 195
Klinkert, John 108
Knights of St Francis of Wycombe 293–4
Knowles, F. 46, 48
Knox, Tim 229, 297, 300

Ladies' Magazine of Gardening 34
'Lamb of God' and Panacea Society rituals 324, 325

Lamport Hall, Northamptonshire 3–4, 4, 53–67, 333, 336
   Box Bowers 54, 55
   Eagle Walk 55, 55–6, 55
   Rockery 4, 56–67, 56, 59–61, 336
      Crystal Cave 58
      gnomes and fairy figures 58, 59–60, 62, 64–6, 64–5, 333
      visitors 66
Law, George Henry, Bishop of Bath and Wells
   and Banwell Caves 196, 197, 198, 199, 204, 205, 206–7, 335
   improvements at Bishop's Palace in Wells 206, 207
Lawson, Sir Charles 124
Le Despencer, Lord *see* Dashwood, Sir Francis
Lichfield, Charlotte Lee, Countess of (née Fitzroy) 23
Lichfield, Edward Henry Lee, 1st Earl of 23
Lindley, John 135
literary extracts and garden at Denbies 245–7, 251, 252, 253
Lockman, John 241, 251
Loft, Major-General John Henry 161, 165, 173, 333
London
   Brookes's museum and vivarium 143–58, 156–7, 337
   churchyard topiary 69–81, 337
   John Hunter's estate and garden 152, 153–5, 154
   Phené and planting of plane trees in streets 312, 316–17
   Stukeley's Kentish Town garden 282–3, 283–5, 337
   Zoological Gardens 171, 172
   see also Harcourt House; Phené, Dr John Samuel; Somerset House; Vauxhall Gardens
Lorton yew tree ('Giant of Lorton') 79
Loudon, Jane 34, 36
Loudon, John Claudius 64, 147, 171, 204
   admiration for ancient yews 79
   dislike of inscriptions 205
   on Lady Broughton's Alpine garden 27, 28, 30–34, 36–7
   on 'rock-works' in gardens 143

on transplanted trees and topiary at Elvaston Castle 87–8, 88–91
Louis XVI, king of France 359n.36
Loveday, John 213
Lovely, Mr (architect) 163
Lyell, Charles 205

Manners, Vicki 320, 322
Mannex, P. J. 258
Mansfield, Katherine: 'The Garden Party' 329–30
Marie Antoinette, queen of France 359n.36
Marlborough, George Spencer, 4th Duke of 111, 123
marsupials 165, 170, 171
Martyn, Thomas 213
Matterhorn, Switzerland 41
  Crisp's bronze model 47, 333
  Crisp's miniature at Friar Park 44, 45, 51, 332
  model at Ice Carnival at Royal Albert Hall (1889) 51
mausoleums 282–3, 297, 298–9, 300, 301, 338
mazes 43
Medmenham Abbey, Buckinghamshire 294
  Dashwood's erotic gardens 293–4, 295–6
Mellet, Laurent 4–5
menageries
  acquisition of live animals 168–9, 170, 171
  Brookes's father as owner of 146, 150, 152, 152
  chained animals in Brookes's Vivarium 144–5, 155, 158
  Collett's 'Jungle' 161
  Hawkstone Park 213, 215
  Heron's menagerie at Stubton Hall 164–71
  John Hunter's estate and garden 152, 153–5, 154
  Lady Impey's menagerie in India 121
  Lady Reade's animals and monkeys 117, 120, 123, 124
  Oatlands, Surrey 124, 169
  private and public zoological gardens 166–73, 172–3, 192–3

travelling menageries 262, 263
see also aviaries; birds; Vivarium of Dr Brookes
mental health see therapeutic value of gardens
Menteath, James Stuart 180, 184, 187, 192, 193
Mer de Glace (glacier): Lady Broughton's replica 5–6, 32, 34, 35, 36, 332
'Merlin's Cave' in Stukeley's garden 277, 278, 279
mesmerism 53
Milner, Henry 43
Milton, John 244, 284
  'Il Penseroso' at Denbies 245, 251, 252, 253
mock battles on lake at West Wycombe 292
models
  Alpine models 36–7, 39, 333
  Browne's cork model of Stonehenge 37, 38
  Matterhorn model in bronze 47, 333
  miniatures and time 39
'Modern Spiritualism' 53
monkeys 117, 120, 123, 124, 215
Monks of Medmenham 293–4
Moore, Norman 184
Morrell, Lady Ottoline 50, 230, 233
mountain landscapes
  as inspiration for Bland's Italian Garden 267, 269
  recreation in gardens
    Friar Park 44–51, 45, 47, 49
    Hoole House 5–6, 27–8, 31–9, 33
  see also Alpine gardens; Matterhorn, Switzerland
mountains
  backgrounds to gardens 10
  the 'English Apennines' 266, 267
  Matterhorn 8, 27, 30, 31, 32, 141, 173, 175
  miniature 5, 27–39, 29, 33, 35, 41–51
  the 'sacro monte' 207
mummies in gardens 3, 13, 19, 23, 25
museums
  Lady Nevill's collections and museum 135, 141

Museum Brookesianum 146
for visiting public at Yew Tree Farm 257

'Natural Religion' 196
Nesfield, William Andrews 101, 108, 109
Neurnayr, J. W. 21–2
Nevill, Lady Dorothy Fanny (née Walpole) 6, 127–41, 128, 139
  collections and museum 135, 141
  departure from Dangstein and move to Stillyans 137–8
Nevill, Ralph 140, 141
Nevill, Reginald Henry 128, 130, 137
Newton, Sir Isaac and 'Newton's rings' 279
Nightingale, Revd Joseph 222
Norse mythology and Yggdrasil tree 324
North, Francis, 1st earl of Guilford 303

optical illusions and effects 39, 46, 50, 51
orchids and orchid houses 46, 130, 132, 135, 136, 137, 140, 141
Owen, Annesley 313
owls 46, 56, 180
owners see garden owners
Oxford Physic Garden (now Botanic Garden) 72
  'Yew-Men of the Guards' 71

Palagonia, Prince: 'Palace of Monsters' 89
palms and palm houses 28, 130, 131, 132
Panacea Society and expanding Garden of Eden in Bedford 9, 319–30, 333–4, 337
  conventional English nature of 322, 322, 324, 327
  expansion beyond garden to 'Royal Domain' 326, 327
  garden parties 326, 327–9, 328, 330, 331
  Yggdrasil tree 8, 324, 325, 326
paradise see Garden of Eden/paradise

INDEX
– 387 –

Parker, F.M.H. 255, 261–2
Partington, C. F. 171
peacock yews in East Bedfont 69–70, 70, 71, 75, 78–9, 81
Pedley, Robert 164
Penrhyn, Anne Susannah Pennant, Lady 123
Petersham, Viscount (Major-General Charles Stanhope, 4th Earl of Harrington) 83–95, 84, 335
Petre, Robert James, 8th Baron Petre 246
petrified objects at Enstone 18
Phelps, William 206
Phené, Dr John Samuel and house in Chelsea 305–317, 308, 337
  decorated facade of house 305, 313, 314, 315, 316
  development of London streets and planting of plane trees 312
  eclectic collection of objects and statuary 3, 305, 306–7, 313, 315
  encounter with trespasser 312–13
  'Fête in the Ancient Greek Style' and pavilion in garden 3, 313, 333
  historical significance of garden 312
  mournful nature of garden 308, 313, 315
  reclusiveness and perceptions of eccentricity 310, 315
  sale of collection on death 3, 305, 306–7, 308, 315
  serpent worship 310, 311
  travels
    additions to collection 305, 307
    grand tour 309
    love of Italy and garden 308–9, 332
    pursuit of scholarly interests 310, 313
Phillibrown, Thomas 292
Phillips, Henry 171, 173, 173
'pic-nic parties' at Walton Hall 182, 183, 184, 333
picturesque 57, 143, 302
  affinities with eccentricity 5
  Banwell bone caves 195, 198, 203
  see also ruins
pigeon-whistles 137
Piggott, Stuart 276–7

Pinetums 44
plane trees in London streets 312, 316–17
plants
  exotic plants and hothouses 131, 132–5, 137, 141
  ivy as shelter for birds 187
  minor role in eccentric gardens 3
  for rockeries and Alpine gardens 28, 34, 46, 50, 57
  Isham's choice of dwarf plants 58, 62
  on Rock of Gibraltar in Brookes's vivarium 149
  and setting for animals in zoological gardens 171
  see also ferns and ferneries; orchids and orchid houses; trees and hedges
Platter, Thomas 70
Plot, Robert: views of 'Enston Waterworks' 22–3, 24–5
poetry
  on Banwell Caves 202
  placards with verse on fairy folk at Lamport Hall 59–60, 62, 66, 333
  on religious inspiration of Hawkstone 220
  on shaped yew trees 69, 73, 74–5, 78
  Stukeley's 'The Druid' 282
  Whitehead on Bland's garden at Reagill 268–9
Pope, Alexander 71
Porch, T. P. 202
Portland, William John Cavendish-Bentinck-Scott, 5th duke of 230, 232–9, 337
  eccentric appearance and habits 232
  obsession with digging and privacy 232–3, 238
  tunnel in garden and Druce–Portland scandal 238
Potter, Richard 345n.27
poultry 123, 150, 152, 215, 308
Pratt, Herbert 65
privacy and seclusion
  Barltrop's faith and limited movements 323, 330
  Harcourt House 227–9, 232–9

Harrington's exclusion of visitors 87–8
Phené's reclusiveness and garden as mournful retreat 308, 310, 315
Portland's quest for privacy 232–9
Walton Hall and Squire Waterton 178–9, 184–5
  see also visitors to gardens
'Psychic Science' 53
Pulham, James 46

Raffles, Revd Thomas 34
Raikes, Thomas 124
Ralph, James 227–8
Randolph, Revd Francis 195
Rasmussen, Peter 323–4, 325
Reade, Harriott, Lady 6, 9, 10, 111–25, 333, 338
  unconventional attentions to animals and birds 116–20, 124–5, 332
  will and bequests 111, 123–4
Reade, Sir John, 5th baronet 112, 117
Reagill *see* Yew Tree Farm, Reagill, Cumbria
reception of gardens and contemporary reactions 9
  Dangstein and Lady Nevill's garden 130–31
  Lady Broughton's rock garden 33–4, 39
  Lamport Hall rockery 56–8
  praise for Friar Park rock garden 46–7, 47–8
  negative reactions 50–51
  on Yew Tree Farm and Bland 256, 257–8, 260–61
  see also Gardeners' Chronicle; Gardeners' Magazine; Gentleman's Magazine
religion
  Catholic overtones of Dashwood's jubilee 302
  Dashwood's unholy activities 293–4
  and Druidic geography of Revd Stukeley 273, 273
  Druidic inscriptions at Banwell Caves 204–5, 332

and experience of Hawkstone's scenery 219–20
geology and accounts of the deluge 196, 205, 207
Hill family's Calvinist faith 215, 222, 224
moralising inscriptions at Denbies 245–6, 247, 250–51, 333
Panacea Society and Garden of Eden 319–30
Phené's beliefs in serpent worship 310, 311
Revett, Nicholas 300
Reynolds, Sir Joshua: portrait of Lady Reade 116
rhododendrons 44, 46
Richmond Nurseries 106, 108
Robinson, William 47, 103, 130
Rochester, John Wilmot, 2nd Earl of 23
rocks and rock gardens 3
 Alpine gardens and plants 28
 Friar Park, Oxfordshire 44–51, 45, 47, 49
 Lady Broughton's garden at Hoole House 5–6, 27–8, 31–9, 33, 35
 'Enston-Rock' 13–25
 islands and mounds in lake at Elvaston Castle 95
 Lamport Hall rockery 4, 56–67, 56, 59–61, 65
 Loudon on decorative 'rock-works' 143
 Rock of Gibraltar in Brookes's Vivarium 143, 144–5, 147–50
 Stukeley's rockwork in gardens 277, 279
 see also caves; geology; grottoes; Hawkstone Park, Shropshire
Rocque, John: Plan of the Cities of London 232
Rodenhurst, T. 219, 222, 224, 225
Roote, Mr (Dr Phené's servant) 315
Roubiliac, Louis-François 251
 monument to Baron Petre 246
Royal Society 196
ruins
 Collett's 'Jungle' as sham ruins 161, 163, 163, 173

Law and Bishop's Palace in Wells 206, 207
Red Castle at Hawkstone 211, 213, 222, 223, 224–5
water gate at Walton Hall 185, 192
 as habitat for birds 180–81, 181
see also Medmenham Abbey, Buckinghamshire
Rutter, John 198

'sacro monte' 207
St James's Chronicle 245–6
Salmon, Joseph Whittingham 219–20
sanctuary for wildlife at Walton Hall 178, 179, 180–81, 182, 184, 185, 187, 189, 192–3
Sannazaro, Jacopo (Sannazarias) 244
Sargent, Henry Winthrop 6, 27–8
Saxy, John 79, 81, 96, 337
 poem on shaped yew tree 73, 74–5
Scharf, George: views of Brookes's vivarium 144–5, 147, 150
Schnebbelie, Robert Blemmell: Mr Brookes's, Blenheim off Oxford St 156–7, 158
sculpture and statues 2, 3
 altars 277, 279, 323, 325
 Bland's classicising statues at Yew Tree Farm 7, 256–8, 257, 259–60, 262, 266, 338
 chivalric statues at Elvaston Castle 94, 95
 Dashwood's erotic figures 292, 295, 296
 decorated facade of Dr Phené's house 305, 313, 314, 315, 316
 in garden of Dr Phené 3, 305, 306–7, 313, 315
 life-size girl in Lamport Hall rockery 61, 62
 Neptune at Hawkstone 216–17
 Neptune carved in wood at Enstone 16, 17, 23
 Roubiliac's work at Denbies 246, 251
 'Stately Lion' at Hawkstone 224–5
 in Stukeley's Temple of Flora 282
 see also fountains; gnomes and fairy figures
seclusion see privacy and seclusion

sense of place
 Banwell Caves and landscape 207
 Stukeley's sensibilities 271, 273, 274
serpent worship: Phené's beliefs 310, 311
Shaw, Jane 319, 320, 323, 326–7, 333
Shelley, Mary: Frankenstein 34, 36
shells: grotto decoration at Hawkstone 213
Shenstone, William 261
Shipton Court, Shipton under Wychwood 113, 338
 Lady Reade's aviary 111–25
Sidney, Edwin 215, 222
signage see inscriptions and labels
silver mines in Wales and Bushell 19
Simpson, Revd James 268
Sitwell, Edith 11, 332
 English Eccentrics 1, 2, 193
Skinner, Revd John 202
Smith, Sir James Edward 37, 39
Smith, John F. H. 273
Smythe, George 128
Soane, Sir John 147–8, 149
social status
 and eccentricity 10–11
 garden owners mistaken for workers 187, 255, 262
 Lady Nevill on upper-class indifference to art and learning 138, 140
 and topiary 71, 108–9, 108
 vegetable patches for labouring poor at Banwell 198
 visitors and social mixing
 'grand fêtes' at Yew Tree Farm 258, 333
 locals at Walton Hall 182, 183, 184, 333
Society of Antiquaries 196
Society of Dilettanti 289
Somerset House, London: Parnassus fountain 21–2, 22
South, John Flint 146
Southcott, Joanna and Southcottians 319, 321
Spenser, Edmund: Faerie Queene 91
spiritualism 53
Squire, Leonard Tucker 323
Stanhope, Major-General Charles see Petersham, Viscount

Stanhope, Leicester, 5th Earl of Harrington 95
Stanhope, Maria *see* Foote, Maria
statues *see* sculpture and statues
Stewart, Susan 39
Stillyans, East Sussex 137–8
Stone, Sarah: A *calcarious Stone full of Bones* 151
Stonehenge, Wiltshire 276, 279
  Browne's cork model 37, 38
Stowe: opening to public 219
Stringer, Chris 207
Strong, Roy 20
Strutt, J. G. 79
Stuart, F. S. 327
Stubton Hall, Lincolnshire 163, 166, 338
  conservatory 166, 166
  Heron's menagerie and gardens 164–71
  pleasure grounds 166–7
  pond with goldfish 165
Stukeley, Revd William 11, 271–85, 272
  collection of 'curiosities' and gardens 274, 276, 279, 283
  Druidic geography and interpretation of place 271, 273, 274
  Itinerarium Curiosum 283
  garden at Grantham
    enjoyment of and beneficial effects 274, 276
    'hermitage vineyard' 276, 277, 279, 336
    'temple of the druids' 276
  garden at Stamford: 'Merlin's Cave'/'hermitage grotto' 277, 278, 279, 336
  later garden in Stamford at Barnhill 279, 280–1, 282, 335
    Gothic rockwork and Temple of Flora 279, 282
    hermitage 279, 280–1
    'spot dyal' 279
  retirement to Kentish Town and Druidic garden 282–3, 283–5, 337
    Eve's Bower 282, 284
    hermitage garden 282, 285
    mausoleum 282–3

Sublime, the 34, 36, 85, 155, 201–12, 267
  'grandeur' and 'majesty' 48, 143, 209, 216, 219, 224
  'horror' and 'terror' 213, 215
  Johnson at Hawkstone 209, 212, 339n.7
  and mountain landscapes 34, 37
Surrey Zoological Gardens 171, 172, 173, 173
Switzerland *see* Matterhorn, Switzerland; Mer de Glace (glacier)
Symes, Michael 365n.11
Symonds, Revd Thomas 111

Tabor, Alan 43
taxidermy
  Lady Reade's 'embalmed' birds 119–20
  Waterton's specimens at Walton Hall 187–8, 188, 190–1
Taylor, Richard 78
temples 246, 276, 279, 282, 308
  West Wycombe 290, 291, 292, 293, 297, 300
Thackeray, William Makepeace: *Vanity Fair* 229
therapeutic value of gardens 66–7, 274, 276
  asylum inmates at Walton Hall 183, 189, 333
Thompson, Captain Edward 294
Thonger, Charles 50
Thornbury, Walter 232
Thorne, James 80
Thrale, Hester (later Piozzi) 209, 220–21, 332
Timbs, John 2, 241
topiary and clipped trees and hedges
  Alpine Garden at Hoole House 28
  Elvaston Castle 87, 88–91, 88, 90, 92–4, 94–6, 97
  Friar Park 44, 44
  as habitat for birds at Walton Hall 181, 187
  Lamport Hall 54–5, 55–6
  London churchyards 69–81, 337
  'modern' topiary at Witley Court 102, 103–5, 106, 108–9

'moveable' and 'bought in' plants 71, 106
  and playfulness 108–9
  and social class 71, 108–9, 108
tourism
  Banwell Caves and picturesque 195, 203
  see also guidebooks and plans; guides and guided tours; visitors to gardens
travel and influence on gardeners 332
  Bland's local travels and excursions 262, 267–8
  Dashwood's grand tours and adventures 288–9, 302
  Hill family at Hawkstone 221
  Isham's gnomes and fairies 65
  Lady Broughton's rock garden 34
  and neglect of Britain 283
  Phené's travels
    love of Italy 308–9, 332
    pursuit of scholarly interests 310, 313
    statues and objects collected on 305, 307
  Swiss Alps as popular destination 41
  Waterton's expeditions 177, 177
  and visitor expectations of eccentricity 187–9, 190–91
trees and hedges
  ancient trees in Dr Phené's garden 312
  Box Bowers at Lamport Hall 54, 55
  Dr Phené and planting of plane trees 312, 316–17
  dwarf trees in Isham's rockery 58, 62
  Heron's tree-planting at Stubton Hall 168
  trade in seeds of American trees 152
  transplanting full-grown trees and hedges 18, 86–7, 86, 88, 89–90
  tropical trees at Dangstein 132, 137
  Waterton's practical involvement 192
  planting as habitat for birds 181, 181, 184, 187

Yggdrasil tree in Bedford 8, 324, 325, 326
see also topiary and clipped trees and hedges
tunnels and subterranean passages 148, 213, 238, 292
  Welbeck Abbey 230–31, 233
  see also caves
Tyers, Jonathan 6, 10, 241–53, 242, 333, 335
  as master of Vauxhall Gardens 241–2, 244

Vair, James 131, 137
Vauxhall Gardens, London 241–2, 243, 244, 245, 251, 253
vegetable patches for labouring poor at Banwell 198
vegetarianism 53
vineyards 213
  Stukeley's hermitage vineyard 276, 277, 279
visitors to gardens 3
  Banwell Caves and Pleasure Gardens 197–207
  Brookes's vivarium 154
  clipped ancient yews as draw for visitors 81
  Dashwood's enthusiasm for 303
  Elvaston Castle 87–8, 95, 96
  encounters with garden owners 187, 255, 261–2, 303, 313
  Friar Park 43, 46, 48, 50
  'Grand Jubilee' at West Wycombe Park 300, 302–3
  Hawkstone Park 209, 213, 215, 217, 218, 219–21, 224–5
  Lady Nevill's museum 135
  Lamport Hall rockery 66
  Phené's 'Fête in the Ancient Greek Style' in garden 3, 313, 333
  'pic-nic parties' for locals at Walton Hall 182, 183, 184, 333
  private and public access at Elvaston Castle 87–8, 95, 96
  Waterton's travels and visitor expectations 187–9, 190–91
  Yew Tree Farm 256
    'Grand Fetes' 258, 260–61, 268, 333

see also entertainments; guidebooks and plans; tourism
Vivarium of Dr Brookes *see* Brookes, Joshua, junior

Walker, Robert 91
walls and boundaries
  privacy at Harcourt House 227–9, 228–9, 232
  erection of glass screens 233, 234–5
  Walton Hall
    moat and access by footbridge 178–9, 178, 181, 185, 185, 192
    wall and hedges 184–5
Walpole, Horace 228, 232, 288–9, 292
Walton Hall, Yorkshire 175–93, 178–9, 186, 190–92, 333, 338
  flower garden 182
  Grotto 182, 183, 184
  moat and access by footbridge 178–9, 178, 181, 185, 185, 192
  'pic-nic parties' for locals 182, 183, 184, 333
  ruined water gate 185, 192
  as habitat for birds 180–81, 181
  sanctuary for wildlife 178, 179, 180–81, 182, 184, 185, 187, 189, 192–3
Warburton, William, Bishop of Gloucester 271
Ward, William Humble *see* Dudley, William Humble Ward, 2nd Earl of
Warner, Revd Richard 219
water features
  and Brookes's Rock of Gibraltar formation 149
  Enstone 13, 14, 16, 17, 18, 19, 21–3, 24–5
  lake and 'Menagerie Pool' at Hawkstone 215–16, 217, 218
  lake at West Wycombe Park and mock battles 290, 291, 292, 293
  moat and access by bridge at Walton Hall 178–9, 178–9, 181, 185, 185, 192
  mountain streams and waterfalls at Friar Park 45, 46, 49

ornamental lake at Elvaston Castle 95
ponds at The Jungle 161, 165
ponds with islands at Stubton Hall 165, 167–8
see also fountains
Waterton, Charles (Squire Waterton) 175–93, 176, 186, 262, 330, 333, 338
  early interest in natural history 175, 177
  exotic travels 177, 177
  Wanderings in South America and visitor expectations 187–9, 188, 190–91
  insularity of family and estate 179
  observation and protection of birds 178, 179, 180–81, 182, 184, 185, 187, 192–3
  mischievous experiments 193
  as precursor to conservation movement 189
  practical involvement with tree care 184, 187
  in praise of gardeners 181–2
  taxidermy specimens and composites 187–8, 188, 190–91
wealth
  ability to indulge eccentricities 10–11, 19, 244, 262, 267
  spending on collections 117, 137, 146, 158
Welbeck Abbey, Nottinghamshire 232–3
  tunnels and underground road 230–31, 233
Wellington, Arthur Wellesley, 1st Duke of 95
Wells, Somerset: Law and Bishop's Palace 206, 207
West Wycombe Park, Buckinghamshire 287–303, 333, 338
  Dashwood's remodelling of house and buildings 296–7, 297
  'Grand Jubilee' 300 302–3
  Hell-Fire Caves 292–3, 338
  lake and mock battles 290, 291, 292, 293
  mausoleum 297, 298–9, 300, 301, 338
  Music Room ceiling 301

INDEX
– 391 –

ornamental buildings and temples 297
Temple of Bacchus 300
Temple of Venus and Venus's Parlour 290, 291, 292, 293
Walton Bridge 290, 291, 293
Westmorland Gazette 256, 257–8, 260–61
Weston, Canon George Frederick 255, 258, 262, 267, 268
whale jawbones 149, 150, 157
Whereat's Cheddar and Banwell Guide 204, 205
White, William 162
Whitehead, Anthony 268–9
Whitehead, Paul 294, 300
Wilkes, John 292, 295–6
Willes, Dame Mary 123
Williamson, Frances 276, 277, 279
Wilmot, John, 2nd Earl of Rochester 23
Winnicott, Donald 9, 109
Witley Court, Worcestershire 101–9, 101, 103, 338
'My Lady's Garden' and topiary 102, 104–5, 106–7, 108–9
Woolf, Virgina: on Lady Nevill 138, 140–41

Wordsworth, William
on Alpine model 37, 39
'Yew Trees' 79
World War I 107–8
Wraxall, Sir Nathaniel 215, 294
Wyatt, James 91
Wyattville, Sir Jeffrey 166

Yew Tree Farm, Reagill, Cumbria 255–69
Bland's statues and artworks 7, 256–8, 257, 259–60, 262, 266, 338
Italian Garden (Image Garden) 256, 262, 266, 267, 269, 332, 338
juxtaposition of local and exotic 269
museums and galleries 257
visitors and 'Grand Fetes' 258, 260–61, 268, 333
yew trees
in Alpine Garden at Hoole House 28
churchyard topiary in London 69–81, 337
transplanted trees and topiary at Elvaston 87, 88–91, 88, 90, 92–4, 94–6, 97

Waterton's planting as habitat for birds 181, 181, 187
Yggdrasil tree in Bedford 8, 324, 325, 326
Young, Arthur 102, 290
Young, Edward: *The Complaint* 246
Young, William 150, 152
Young-Hunter, John: *My Lady's Garden* 106–7, 107

Zain al-Din, Sheikh 121
Sulphur Crested Cockatoo 122
Zoffany, Johann: *Sir Elijah and Lady Impey and their Children* 121
zoological gardens
as setting for animal collections 171–2, 172–3
Waterton's Walton Hall compared to 192–3
Zoological Gardens, Regent's Park, London 171, 172
Zoological Society of London 166, 171
Zouche, Lord (Cecil Bisshopp, 10th baronet of Parham) 130, 133